The

BWD

24/5/18

23 MAY 2019

y

ie

al

nt

RED ANVIL PRESS

Oakland

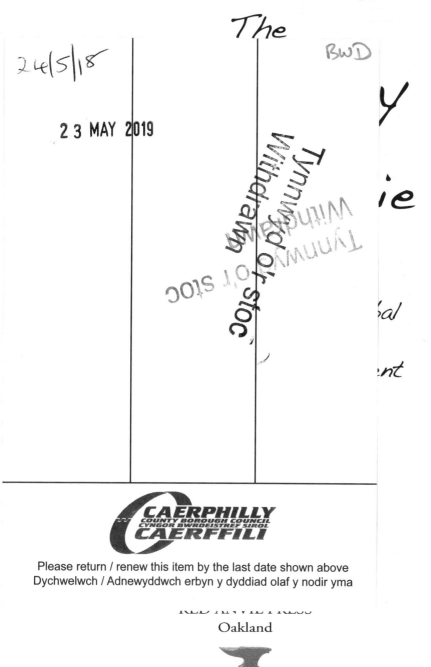

RED ANVIL PRESS is an imprint of
ELDERBERRY PRESS, INC.
1393 Old Homestead Drive
Oakland OR 97462

Publisher's Catalog-in-Publication Data
The Conspiracy That Will Not Die/Robert Gates, Sr.
ISBN-13: 978-1-934956-40-3
ISBN-10: 1-934956-40-6
1. Conspiracy.
2. World Government.
3. Illuminati.
4. Politics
5. CFR.
6. Rockefeller
I. Title
This book was written, printed and bound in the United States of America.

CONTENTS

"I now make it my earnest prayer, that God would have the United States in his holy protection, that he would incline the hearts of the Citizens to cultivate a spirit of subordination and obedience to Government, to entertain a brotherly affection and love for one another, for their fellow Citizens of the United States at large, and particularly for their brethren who have served in the Field, and finally, that he would most graciously be pleased to dispose us all, to do Justice, to love mercy, and to demean ourselves with that Charity, humility, and pacific temper of mind, which were the Characteristics of the Divine Author of our blessed Religion, and without an humble imitation of whose example in these things, we can never hope to be a happy Nation." The above prayer by General Washington was written at Valley Forge during one of the worst winters ever seen by the new settlers.

General Washington's Prayer at Valley Forge.

The story of Valley Forge is a story that should be taught again and again to the children of this country. It will instill in them the true meaning of the words Freedom and Liberty.

Chapter 1

IN THE BEGINNING

At the beginning of the Revolutionary War, the British were contemptuous of the Colonial settlers. A British commander sent home a short report that was read in the House of Commons. The gist of it was: "The Americans will not stand and fight." They were jack-in-the-box guerrillas who would fight like devils for a day and a night and then go home and harvest their crops on the weekend. They would return, not always in any discernible formation, and after a swift onslaught vanish into the country by night, and then again at some unpredictable time come whizzing in like hornets. What baffled and eventually broke the British was what broke the Roman armies in their later campaigns against the barbarians, and for so long frustrated the American army in Vietnam. Edward Gibbon said it in a single passage: "All things became adverse to the Romans ... their armor heavy, the waters deep; nor could they wield, in that uneasy situation, their weighty javelins. The barbarians, on the contrary, were inured to encounters in the bogs." Or as William Pitt sadly commented, looking at his drawn battle-lines on an alien wilderness: "You cannot conquer a map."

The story of General Washington and his men at Valley Forge not only proved the British wrong about their courage but it showed what the colonial men thought about duty and honor. The life of the Father of our country briefly describes the concept of honor and duty. It describes the days when a man's word meant more than a sworn statement on a piece of paper.

Left fatherless at the age of eleven, Washington was shunted between two half- brothers and picked up a little irregular schooling in the intervals of learning how to raise tobacco and stock and manage a plantation. He took to surveying in boyhood and decided that it was to be his profession. One that in those days sent a man roving for weeks on end, improvising his sleeping quarters, shooting wild turkey and chewing it on the bone.

In the French and Indian Wars, he had suffered the horrors of Braddock's rout. He had horses shot from under him and went home to Virginia with a local reputation for being at all times unflappable. Then his health failed him, and he resigned his commission.

At the age of twenty-seven he married a very rich widow and settled on a majestic stretch of land, at Mount Vernon overlooking the Potomac. His wife had brought him a pleasant dowry of some profitable real estate, fifteen thousand acres near Williamsburg— what by today's exchange would be about quarter of a million dollar--and one hundred and fifty slaves, whose condition, he confessed, embarrassed him. But he was an eighteenth-century man, and "emancipation" was a remote and strange doctrine. He assumed he would live out his life as a rich Virginia planter, but then, at the age of forty-three, he received the call.

Most Americans would today be upset by his air of a prosperous idle landowner and real estate operator in the guise of a down-the-nose British colonel. His most ardent biographers have been unable to find much evidence of charm, or even humor, in him. He was massively self-sufficient, and he had decided ideas about the relations of rank and rank, class and class. He did not, for instance, liked to be touched and when he became the first President he laid down a rule that people coming to see him should remain standing in his presence. He arrived for his inauguration with a flourish of grandeur and he shook no hands. Thomas Jefferson was greatly offended by this action at this ceremony and thought it "not at all in character with the simplicity of republican governments, and looking—as if wishfully —to those of European courts." As he took the oath, an official whispered to his neighbor: "I fear we may have exchanged George the Third for George the First."

Yet there were things about him that made him the unquestioned leader of the new nation. A pervasive sense of responsibility, an unflagging impression of shrewd judgment, and total integrity. It can best be summed up in what the drama critics call "presence."

But it was nothing rehearsed. It was the presence of nothing but character.

The war was only eighteen months old when it seemed that all was lost. The British captured Philadelphia, and many of the Congress took to the hills—and with good reason. King George had decree that all rebels would be hung for treason. The rebels were a frightened and divided body of men—divided between genuine revolutionaries and sunshine patriots, between dedicated colonial statesmen and secret Loyalists, and a clutter of money grubbers selling arms or commission or merchants whose anxious interest was to see that Spain got the lands beyond the Appalachians so that trade would not go West. The word got to a delirious London that Washington was trapped in a frigid valley, and that the war was over. The first part was correct—but not the second.

In the bleakest winter, of 1777-1778, Washington was camped in Valley Forge, about twenty miles northwest of Philadelphia. He picked it for obvious military advantages. It lay between a creek and a broad river, and the hills were high enough to survey the main supply routes from the South into New England and the roads from Philadelphia that led to the gunneries and powder mills of the interior. He refused to go inland and leave the fertile Pennsylvania farming country as a granary for the enemy. He refused also to commandeer the villages, which hadn't enough food for the swarms of refugees from Philadelphia. So he chose this bare place, and his eleven thousand men built their cabins with timber from the neighboring woods.

In the beginning life was bearable, even agreeable. The men were snug; Washington moved into a solid farmhouse. Mrs. Washington came to stay, so did some of the officers' wives. There were cheerful dinner parties and no lack of food and wine. But the party was short-lived. The winter snows came early, and by January there were oceans of mud. Congress wouldn't, or couldn't, commission supplies and told Washington to plunder the nearest farmers, which he refused to do. When the main stores ran low, the men started to forage for hickory nuts and the more edible local fauna. By March—when the countryside was blasted by blizzards—a third of them were down with typhus or smallpox and, of course, dysentery.

Medical services barely existed, and the besieged army began to thin out alarmingly, if not from disease and actual starvation, than from desertion. Half of the living had neither shoes nor shirts. In the end, Washington was left with something over three thousand men, technically able-bodied, actually half starving.

To this resolute man the ordeal was grim but quite simple. Being an eighteenth-century gentleman-soldier with a puritan core meant that when all the chips were down, all the agreeable things of life—parties, good food, comfort, professional dignity—were nothing.. The winds blew and the food gave out and the fields stank with death and disease, and Washington's life simplified itself into one hard principle - duty. He had given his word that he would hold on with his army, however sick and bedraggled it might be, and he proceeded to do so. The spring came in and the sickness flourished. But the French formally entered the war and Washington had saved (what was left of it) the Continental Army.

Today, the current curriculum in our schools praise Martin Luther King more than George Washington or Abraham Lincoln. At one time in the past this country celebrated the birthday of Washington and Lincoln on different days in February. Today, we celebrate Presidents Day in February with little or no fan-fare and Martin Luther King Day in January as a holiday with parades and bands. It is called rewriting history. Granted, Martin Luther King Jr. did much for the Negro population but Washington and Lincoln did greater things for the country.

The gripe today of the black community was that George Washington was a slaver. He own slave to take care of his large estate of tobacco, animals, and grain. He never enjoyed it but in those days it was a necessity. It was an era that was referred to as a Slave Economy.

The Slave Economy did not spring up overnight. It occurred in fits and starts. It all started in England where nobody in London wanted to exert itself about governing the colonies, because nobody in London was eager to pay the bill for that. That meant the colonies in North America were on their own. They got freedom, but not freedom in any fashion that anyone had expected. Yet, if the initial experience of colonization was one of disorder and disorientation, rather than some kind of cheerful and optimistic effort to advance into the future, that disorder and disorientation did not last for long.

As they moved into the 1700s, the British colonies began to stabilize, mortality rates began to drop, trading networks were established, and towns and cities sprang up with a life of their own. In Virginia, once Virginia society had stabilized, instead of creating something entirely, completely, and radically original to America, they begin to establish local jurisdictions based on the English county system and, with them, county courts. They divided their counties into parishes just like England, and paid to build and, establish the Church of England as the official church of these Parishes just like England.

None of this development would have been possible without one key factor: cheap labor. In England, wealth and status were based upon land, because England was small and land was expensive; the more you had of this small-held commodity, the more you were guaranteed riches and influence. What was plentiful in England were people. In 1688, one of the pioneers of what we would call social statistics, Gregory King, estimated that there were 2.6 million people in England who could be said to be increasing the wealth of the kingdom by their productivity or the productivity of their land, but there were 2.8 million who were decreasing the wealth of the kingdom through owning no land or having no skilled trade, people who were just plain "surplusage."

The logical solution was to rid the kingdom of as many of these unproductive types as possible, which is one reason why the English government was so happy to see them go to America, but in America the situation was exactly the opposite. There, land could be had in abundance and at a fraction of any European cost, at least once the Indian tribes had been pushed out, or decimated by disease. The difficulty was that labor was extremely expensive simply because the ratio of land to people was so enormous. To manage this, a joint-stock company like the Virginia Company, or the agents of proprietors like William Penn, might pay a nominal sum to the English government, empty out a jail or two of its convicts and put them on a ship to Virginia and Pennsylvania, and sell the remainder of their jail terms to farmers or to merchants as servants.

The problem was that a convict's sentence sooner or later ended, but the farmer's need for servants to work his immense stretches of land did not. The farmer could offer to hire the newly released convict as a free laborer, but it would take a lot of money to persuade the ex-convict to stay on as a laborer when, just over the horizon, he could have undreamed-of amounts of land for a pittance and set up as a farmer himself.

The English government showed little or no interest in sponsoring emigration itself. In the 1600s, that would have cost money. By the 1700s, the crown was starting to notice that all the beggars and convicts and religious icons who had been shipped off to the colonies had turned into happily productive settlers who were starting to out-produce the home islands to the point where, by 1721, England had developed an unfavorable balance of trade with its North American colonies. The English government was not going to permit or promote this, and so waiting for the crown to supply cheap labor to America pretty much meant waiting forever. The English government was not going to assist the colonies in putting it out of its own business.

The alternative to cheap labor, then, was forced labor. Obviously, the convicts and the beggars and the prisoners of war who were shipped to America in the 1600s were examples of forced labor and, depending on how one wants to define "force," so were many other otherwise-free servants the victims of force. The luckless, the unskilled, the social or religious misfits, frequently sold their labor by contract, or indenture, just to get out of England, and while this was technically a "free" transaction and they were "free" laborers, circumstances exerted more than a little force in getting them to sign an indenture. The moment those indentures—like the terms of the convicts and the beggars—expired, there was no legal way that free British subjects could be forced to continue laboring for their masters. Unless their masters were willing to pay wages so ruinous that the masters themselves would end up in prison for debt, those indentured servants and all the others like them would be heading somewhere else at the end of five or seven years (or whenever their indenture expired or their term ran out) to set up for themselves. Of course, when they did, they would start contributing to bidding up the price of labor still further by wanting servants of their own to work their lands. Well, there were ways around this.

In the 1630s, the death rate among new emigrants to Virginia was so steep that few indentured servants lived long enough to survive their indentures and become competitors in the labor market. When the death rate began to fall in the 1660s, landowners found other ways in Virginia to keep their servants enslaved. Terms of service were lengthened, and when the servants responded to this by running away, the county courts, where the judges, of course, were landowners who needed laborers, punished them by doubling their terms of service. Extending terms of service soon became the punishment of the day for a variety of crimes committed by servants, not just running away. Even that, though, kept servants from surviving their indentures and becoming free men only so long. The Virginia House of Burgesses hit upon yet another tactic. Only landowners could vote in elections for the burgesses. That, at least, would keep landless free men from gaining political power.

Then, in 1676, in a suspicious display of benevolence, Governor William Barkley ordered the construction of a series of forts at the heads of the Colony of Virginia's major rivers. Not only would this protect settlers from Indian raids, but it would also keep back rambunctious Virginians from provoking those raids in the first place by trespassing on Indian land. Well, this pleased the planters in the House of Burgesses. Not only would it guarantee peace for them to raise tobacco, but it would deprive the landless free men of new land to settle and so force them to accept whatever work as laborers the planters wanted-and at whatever rates of pay. The result, however, for the planters, was the worst of all possible endings. Enraged and landless, free men made their own wars on the Indians and then, under the leadership of Nathaniel Bacon, a rabble of the basest sort of people, whose condition was such that a change could not invite worse, took over Jamestown. Governor Barkley fled to the eastern shore, while Bacon's rebels proceeded to plan new wars against the Indians and to divide up the estates of Governor Barkley's supporters. Happily for Barkley, Bacon died in October of 1676, and his rebellion fell apart. The lesson the planters learned from this was that indentured servants eventually become rebels. After 1676, Virginia's planters began turning increasingly to a form of forced labor that would never have the chance of turning into Nathaniel Bacon's rabble, and that form of forced labor was slavery.

Virginia had not turned at once to slavery when its labor crunch began, because before the 1680s it simply was not profitable enough. The death rates that killed servants before their indentures ended, also killed the planters, and the cost of a life-long interest in a slave was prohibitive when lives were not likely to be that long. Once the death rates had leveled off, low, and once it became clear that indentured labor was a recipe for political turbulence, planters in Virginia, the Chesapeake, and Carolina found that the cost of slaves was becoming, surprisingly and increasingly, competitive with the costs of servants. To make things easier for them, the Spanish, the Portuguese, and the Dutch had already established a transatlantic trade in African slaves that could be easily diverted to markets in North America.

The problem with enslavement was that it was a violation of everything in the way of freedom that white Europeans hoped for themselves, so slave owners eventually dropped this pragmatic justification for enslaving only blacks and began devising fantasies about racial identity and racial inferiority, which would appear to make black enslavement normal and justified in ways that it would never be if it involved other races. Thus, began the embarrassing American preoccupation with not only race, but racism. All told, something like 11.5 million blacks were ripped away from Africa by the combined efforts of both Europeans and their fellow Africans and Arabs of North Africa, and they became the new labor force of Europe's American colonies. Of these, some 40 percent were swallowed up by Portugal's single great colony of Brazil, while Portuguese slave ships accounted for about three-quarters of the slave-carrying trade throughout the Western Hemisphere.

The other half of the slave population went to the French, English, and Spanish islands of the West Indies to work the vast and lucrative sugar plantations of the Caribbean. Curiously, less than 10 percent were sent to North America. As it was, though, even this comparatively minimal investment in slavery soon became the underpinning of the North American colonies' economy.

Nearly eight percent of the exports of British North America were agricultural goods grown by black slaves, even in colonies where black slave labor was at a minimum in the mid-Atlantic and in New England. Nearly half of the exports from those colonies were dependent on markets in the slave-owning colonies. The few places in British North America that had no links at all to slavery--places like Connecticut--actually wound up becoming the economic backwaters of colonial America. Painful as it frequently is to acknowledge it, black slavery dramatically remade both the economic and social world of Virginia and eventually all the British North American colonies after 1680. Slave labor, by becoming profitable to longer-lived white planters, finally brought the southern colonies a stability that indentured-servant labor had not. Slave labor furnished the wealth the colonies needed to begin transforming themselves into a soothing and believable replica of English society, but it was a stability and a productivity bought at a terrible price- the price of exploitation, dehumanization, and incessant watchfulness and control.

The solution to slavery was a Civil War. It freed the slaves and under President Lincoln's leadership, they were to be sent back to Africa. A colony was established in Africa named Liberia and it was to become the homeland of those freed slaves. Unfortunately, President Lincoln was assassinated and his plan died before it got started. The problem with the free slaves that remained in this country was basic. Their culture was entirely different than the European culture that existed in this country. They did not assimilate into the current society; they did not merge into the melting pot of America. Instead, they changed the melting pot into a salad bowl. Today, we still have the problem of assimilation—only now the blacks want the whites to assimilate with them and not the other way around. Conflict abounds! One of the many problems that occur in a melting-pot society.

During the Pre-Revolutionary days, there was a gentleman who one can say carried the torch and lit the flame that started the fight for freedom. His name was Thomas Paine.

Thomas Paine (1737-1809) wrote of freedom and liberty with thunder and lightning in his words. They were not the conventional words of pleading and humility; they were forthright and uncomfortably bold. He had come to America from England in 1775, armed with a letter from Benjamin Franklin, and was promptly caught up in the tide toward revolution. His historic pamphlet, *Common Sense,* published anonymously, appeared on January 9, 1776. it sold half a million copies and stirred the patriot fervor of every reader. *Common Sense* called for immediate independence from Great Britain. It labeled monarchy a corrupt form of government and insisted that Great Britain was restraining the growth of the American colonies.

Paine joined the Revolutionary Army but continued to write a series of pamphlets under the title *The Crisis.* The opening passage of the first carried the immortal words: "These are the times that try men's souls..." At the request of George Washington, the publication was read to the Colonial troops. By the sheer force of its language and its eloquent patriotism, Paine's words pointed the way for many who were hesitant about the Colonial cause.

In 1776, Paine wrote in his publication *The Crisis,* the following:

"These are the times that try men's souls. The summer soldier and the sunshine patriot will, in this crisis, shrink from the service of their country; but he that stands it now, deserves the love and thanks of man and woman. Tyranny, like hell, is not easily conquered; yet we have this consolation with us, that the harder the conflict, the more glorious the triumph. What we obtain too cheap, we esteem too lightly: it is dearness only that gives every thing its value. Heaven knows how to put a proper price upon its goods; and it would be strange indeed if so celestial an article as FREEDOM should not be highly rated. Britain, with an army to enforce her tyranny, has declared that she has a right (not only to TAX) but "to BIND us in CASES WHATSOEVER," and if being bound in that manner, is not slavery, then there is not such a thing as slavery upon earth. Even the expression is impious; for so unlimited a power can belong only to God...."

Today we have the same specter of tyranny in these United States. Under President Obama leadership the citizens must do as he and his henchmen dictate or else. Take his National Health Plan—each and every person must take out health insurance whether they want it or not. They will be fined and forced to take out insurance by the IRS which in President Obama's thoughts are a duplication of Hitler's German Gestapo when decimating the Jews. This law has established a dictatorship which –whether Democrat, Republican, Independent or other, will be regretted the rest of our lives. It is just a foot in the door to dictate our lives in every aspect of a Communist regime.

More of Paines article in *The Crisis:*

"I have as little superstition in me as any man living, but my secret opinion has ever been, and still is, that God Almighty will not give up a people to military destruction, or leave them unsupported to perish, who have so earnestly and so repeatedly sought to avoid the calamities of war, by every decent method which wisdom could invent. Neither have I so much of the infidel in me, as to suppose that He has relinquished the government of the world, and given us up to the care of devils; and as I do not, I cannot see on what grounds the king of Britain can look up to heaven for help against us: a common murderer, a highwayman, or a housebreaker, has as good a pretence as he."

"'Tis surprising to see how rapidly a panic will sometimes run through a country. All nations and ages have been subject to them. Britain has trembled like an ague at the report of a French fleet of flat bottomed boats; and in the fourteenth century the whole English army, after ravaging the kingdom of France, was driven back like men petrified with fear; and this brave exploit was performed by a few broken forces collected and headed by a woman, Joan of Arc. Would that heaven might inspire some Jersey maid to spirit up her countrymen, and save her fair fellow sufferers from ravage and ravishment! Yet panics, in some cases, have their uses; they produce as much good as hurt. Their duration is always short; the mind soon grows through them, and acquires a firmer habit than before. But their peculiar advantage is, that they are the touchstones of sincerity and hypocrisy, and bring things and men to light which might otherwise have lain forever undiscovered. In fact, they have the same effect on secret traitors, which an imaginary apparition would have upon a private murderer. They sift out the hidden thoughts of man, and hold them up in public to the world. Many a disguised Tory has lately shown his head, that shall penitentially solemnize with curses the day on which Howe arrived upon the Delaware. . . ,"

Where is our Joan of Arc? We need one now. We need a leader that will destroy the evil menace of Communism and reestablish the Constitution that our forefathers gave us. A limited Federal Government that is duty bound to free the people.

More of Paine's article from *The Crisis*:

"I shall conclude this paper with some miscellaneous remarks on the state of our affairs; and shall begin with asking the following question, 'Why is it that the enemy have left the New England provinces, and made these middle ones the seat of war?' The answer is easy: New England is not infested with Tories and we are. I have been tender in raising the cry against these men, and use numberless arguments to show them their danger, but it will not do to sacrifice world either to their folly or their baseness. The period is now arrived, in which either they or we must change our sentiments, or one or both must fall. And what is a Tory? Good God! What is he? I shall not be afraid to go with a hundred Whigs against a thousand Tories, were they to attempt to get into arms. Every Tory is a coward; for servile, slavish, self-interested fear is the foundation of Toryism; and a man under such influence, though he may be cruel, never can be brave."

"But, before the line of irrecoverable separation be drawn between us, let reason the matter together: Your conduct is an invitation to the enemy, yet not one in a thousand of you has heart enough to join him. Howe is as much deceived by you as the American cause is injured by you. He expects you all to take up arms, and flock to his standard, with muskets on your shoulders. Your opinions are of no use to him, unless you support him personally, for it's soldiers, and not Tories that he wants."

Paine's reference concerning Whigs and Tories describe exactly what is happening in this country today. You have true blooded Americans that believe in the Constitution as written by our forefathers and then you have the die-hard Communist that believe that the Constitution is a sheet of toilet paper and needs destroyed. Ever since the Democrats were swept into Office in 2008, they have run rough-shod over this Country in a manner unknown to Americans of the past.

The Liberals who run the government today are the members of the salad bowl. They are the die hard Socialist (Communists, Progressives); they are Organizations, such as the Black Panthers, the Black Caucus, the Farrakhan's Islam Nation organization; the League of Women Voters; the Rainbow Coalition; the Aztlán movement; the ACLU; etc. They are the Moderate Republicans and brainwashed Democrats who believe that survival of mankind can only occur under a New Order, namely, a One-world government. With leaders like these we are certainly doomed.

President Obama, bought and paid for by the Rockefeller/ Rothchild cabal, has set up a semi-dictatorship that is going to be hard to defeat. Why? He has no opposition. The Republican Party is a mixture of tort lawyers and one-worlders that care less about the country than they care about their own pocket books. For example, when the Republicans had control of the House and Senate in 1994 thru 2004 did they try to seriously impeach President Clinton in 1998? No! It was later revealed that if they tried President Clinton on all of the charges that the House Impeachment Committee wanted to bring, than the Senate Democrats would expose the past of many Republican Senators in rebuttal.

Senator Lott and other RINOs turned the rules over to the Democrats which than ensured that President Clinton would not be found guilty as charged. Since the Democrats had forty-five members in the Senate, the only charges brought to the floor of the Senate were perjury charges. It takes 2/3rds of the members of the Senate to find the President guilty and since only the perjury charges were on the calendar, the impeachment proceedings were a farce! The people were never told the truth about all the charges that were pending against President Clinton!

The country needs a few good men to lead us back to the road of Freedom. We need to again light the fire of Independence. The Declaration of Independence (July 4, 1776) was a battle hymn that spurred men to action. So be it again:

*"When in the Course of human events, it becomes necessary for one people to dissolve the political bands which have connected them with another and to assume the Powers of the earth, the separate and equal station to which the Laws of Nature and of Nature's God entitle them, a decent respect to the opinions of mankind requires that they should declare the causes which impel them to the separation." "We hold these truths to be self-evident, that all men are created equal, that they are endowed by their Creator with certain inalienable Rights, that among them these are Life, Liberty, and the pursuit of Happiness. That to secure these rights, Governments are instituted among Men, deriving their just powers from the consent of the governed. That whenever any form of Government becomes destructive to these ends, it is the **Right** of the people to alter or abolish it, and to institute a new Government, laying its foundation on such principles and organizing its power in such form, as to them seem most likely to effect their Happiness..."*

There have been voices in the past who have been shouting 'Wolf' but the liberal press will not warn the people. This is understandable when one realizes that the so called free press is owned, lock, stock and barrel by the Rockefeller/Rothschild cabal.

It has been a known fact that ever since President Roosevelt's era the Communist have infiltrated the government in high places. President Roosevelt's cabinet was rife with them. Since his time they have infiltrated every Department of Government, including Congress. The final act of destruction of our Constitution is at hand. President Obama states he is not a Socialist but his life biographies deny that claim. He is establishing a Communist dictatorship in Washington. This statement is not as hair-brained as some people think when you look at his political upbringing.

Many years ago before Obama was born, his grandparents were active members of the First Unitarian Church of Honolulu. This church was described in an article in the *Honolulu Star Bulletin* as:

"The bumper stickers on cars outside the church gave an insight into its members' beliefs: 'No War.' 'If you want peace, work for justice.' 'An eye for an eye makes the whole world blind.'

"Activism for peace and human rights causes has characterized the congregation of the First Unitarian Church of Honolulu since it was organized 50 years ago. Members were instrumental in founding the League of Women Voters and activating a local branch of the American Civil Liberties Union. It offered sanctuary to servicemen who went AWOL to avoid being sent to Vietnam. It helped launch the Save Our Constitution effort to fight for the constitutional amendment on same-sex marriages. And just recently, the church sponsored a Death with Dignity poll that collected a 72 percent response in favor of end-of-life legislation....

"'Unitarians walk their talk,' said Rosemary Mattson, 85, of Carmel, Calif., one of the charter members. She and Ruth Iams, 90, of Kaneohe, reminisced about the beginnings of the 'Unitarian fellowship of Honolulu' at a Wednesday tea in the church, which occupies a rambling 1910 mansion built by Richard Cooke....

"'What Unitarian Universalists have in common is an attitude toward life, an openness and interest in activities that relate to helping people. You can spot them.'

In a 2006 speech, President Obama explained about his upbringing:

> *"I was not raised in a particularly religious household, as undoubtedly many in the audience were. My father, who returned to Kenya when I was just two, was born Muslim but as an adult became an atheist. My mother, whose parents were non-practicing Baptists and Methodists, was probably one of the most spiritual people and kindest people I've ever known, but grew up with a healthy*

skepticism of organized religion herself. As a consequence, so did I."

But Obama's 2006 speech contradicted his own memoir *Dreams from My Father* (p17) in which he writes of his grandfather:

"In his only skirmish into organized religion, he would enroll the family in the local Unitarian Universalist congregation...."

"After leaving Hawaii to work at the Unitarian seminary in Berkeley, Calif., Mattson and her husband were active in the international peace movement. She escorted more than 25 tours of Americans to the former Soviet Union for people-to-people experience. Still an activist, she took part in the Jan. 17 'No War on Iraq' demonstration in San Francisco.

"A memory that Jim Myers shared at the Wednesday reunion was the brush with history when the church offered 'sanctuary' to infamous atheist Madalyn Murray O'Hair, her mother and son. It was 1966, and 'she was the most hated woman in the United States,' he said. O'Hair was vilified by religious groups after the U.S. Supreme Court upheld her challenge against prayer in public schools. 'We put her upstairs for a while,' Myers said. 'There wasn't really an uproar in Hawaii, probably because of the tolerant situation here.'

"Later in the 1960s, 'we gave sanctuary to Vietnam deserters....'"

Obama hid his Unitarian connections during the campaign.

Stanley and Madelyn Dunham in 1955 picked up and relocated 2,000 miles from Texas to Seattle. The next year they relocated to Mercer Island specifically so their daughter, Obama's future mother, Stanley Ann Dunham could attend Mercer Island High School. Another attraction: The East Shore Unitarian Church, also a hotbed of leftist activism.

The Chicago Tribune mentions a description of the Dunham's chosen church as "The Little Red Church on the Hill". According to its own website, East Shore Unitarian Church got that name because of, "Well-publicized debates and forums on such controversial subjects as the admission of 'Red China' to the United Nations...." Mercer Island's John Stenhouse, according to his 2000 obituary, once served as church president possibly contributing to the 'red' label.

The Dunhams moved to Honolulu in 1960 after Ann graduated and quickly became friends with leftists such as now-Rep. Neil Abercrombie (D-HI) and Communist Party member Frank Marshall Davis. Obama's mother-to-be enrolled at the University of Hawaii and soon met Barack Obama Sr. in a Russian language class. She would remain affiliated with the University for most of her life.

In his books, Obama admits attending 'socialist conferences" and coming into contact with Marxist literature. But he ridicules the charge of being a "hard-core academic Marxist," which was made by his colorful and outspoken 2004 U.S. Senate opponent, Republican Alan Keyes. One must remember that President Obama will say one thing and turn around and do another. He is good at that. He cares less about what the polls say that the people want and he cares less about a second term. He has his ideological plan and he is going to follow it to the end. What is that plan? From what he has done to date, his plan appears to be the destruction of Capitalism and installing a Socialistic (Communistic) style government with a dictatorial leader like Chevez in Venezuela. More about his Communist training follows.

However, through Frank Marshall Davis, Obama had an admitted relationship with someone who was publicly identified as a member of the Communist Party USA (CPUSA). The record shows that Obama was in Hawaii from 1971-1979, where, at some point in time, he developed a close relationship, almost like a son, with Davis, listening to his "poetry" and getting advice on his career path. But Obama, in his book, *Dreams From My Father*, refers to him repeatedly as just 'Frank."

The reason is apparent: Davis was a known communist who belonged to a party subservient to the Soviet Union. In fact, the 1951 report of the Commission on Subversive Activities to the

Legislature of the Territory of Hawaii identified him as a CPUSA member. What's more, anti-communist congressional committees, including the House Un-American Activities Committee (HUAC), accused Davis of involvement in several communist-front organizations.

The communists knew who "Frank was and they know who Obama is. In fact, one academic who travels in communist circles understands the significance of the Davis-Obama relationship.

Professor Gerald Horne, a contributing editor of the Communist Party journal Political Affairs, talked about it during a speech at the reception of the Communist Party USA archives at the Tamiment Library at New York University. The remarks are *posted* online under the headline, "Rethinking the History and Future of the Communist Party."

Horne, a history professor at the University of Houston, noted that Davis, who moved to Honolulu from Kansas in 1948 "at the suggestion of his good friend Paul Robeson," came into contact with Barack Obama and his family and became the young man's mentor, influencing Obama's sense of identity and career moves. Robeson, of course, was the well-known black actor and singer who served as a member of the CPUSA and apologist for the old Soviet Union. Davis had known Robeson from his time in Chicago. As Horne describes it: Davis "befriended" an "Euro-American family" that had "migrated to Honolulu from Kansas and a young woman from this family eventually had a child with a young student from Kenya East Africa who goes by the name of Barack Obama who retracing the steps of Davis eventually decamped to Chicago."

It was in Chicago that Obama became a "community organizer" and came into contact with more far-left political forces, including the Democratic Socialists of America, which maintains close ties to European socialist groups and parties through the Socialist International (SI), and two former members of the Students for a Democratic Society (SDS), William Ayers and Carl Davidson.

The SDS laid siege to college campuses across America in the 1960s, mostly in order to protest the Vietnam War, and spawned the terrorist Weather Underground organization. Ayers was a member of the terrorist group and turned himself in to authorities in 1981. He is now a college professor and served with Obama on the board of the Woods Fund of Chicago.

Davidson is now a figure in the Committees of Correspondence for Democracy and Socialism, an offshoot of the old Moscow-controlled CPUSA, and helped organize the 2002 rally where Obama came out against the Iraq War.

Both communism and socialism trace their roots to Karl Marx, co-author of the Communist Manifesto, who endorsed the first meeting of the Socialist International, then called the "First International." According to Pierre Mauroy, president of the SI from 1992-1996, "It was he [Marx] who formally launched it, gave the inaugural address and devised its structure..."

Dr. Kathryn Takara, a professor of Interdisciplinary Studies at the University of Hawaii at Manoa who also confirms that Davis is the 'Frank' in Obama's book, did her dissertation on Davis and spent much time with him between 1972 until he passed away in 1987. In an *analysis* posted online, she notes that Davis, who was a columnist for the Honolulu Record, brought "an acute sense of race relations and class struggle throughout America and the world' and that he openly discussed subjects such as American imperialism, colonialism and exploitation. She described him as a "socialist realist" who attacked the work of the House Un-American Activities Committee.

Davis, in his own writings. said that Robeson and Harry Bridges. the head of the International Longshore and Warehouse Union (ILWU) and a secret member of the CPUSA, had suggested that he take a job as a columnist with the Honolulu Record and see if I could do something for them." The ILWU was organizing workers there and Robeson's contacts were passed on" to Davis, Takara writes.

Takara says that Davis "espoused freedom, radicalism. solidarity, labor unions, due process, peace, affirmative action, civil rights, Negro History week, and true Democracy to fight imperialism, colonialism, and white supremacy. He urged coalition politics."

Is "coalition politics' at work in Obama's rise to power? Trevor

Loudon, the New Zealand-based blogger who has been analyzing the political forces behind Obama and specializes in studying the impact of Marxist and leftist political organizations, notes that Frank Chapman, a CPUSA supporter, has written a letter to the party newspaper hailing the Illinois senator's victory in the Iowa caucuses. "Obama's victory was more than a progressive move, it was a dialectical leap ushering in a qualitatively new era of struggle." Chapman wrote: "Marx once compared revolutionary struggle with the work of the mole, who sometimes burrows so far beneath the ground that he leaves no trace of his movement on the surface. This is the old revolutionary 'mole,' not only showing his traces on the surface but also breaking through."

WAKE UP AMERICA! Your freedoms are being eroded to the point of nothingness. We are in the Communist fold and it is a hole that will take a lot of sacrifice to get out of. The current Government is controlled by the Democratic Socialist Party and slowly, but surely, turning this country into a United Socialist States of America (USSA) just like Lenin and Stalin turned Russia into a Union of Soviet Socials Republic (USSR). And believe it or not, the KGB is the IRS or under Hitler, in Germany, the Gestapo and SS troops. Remember, under Obama's National Health Plan, it is the IRS who will force you into buying Health Care Insurance or be fined excessively.

This country must find a way to collect reasonable taxes and eliminate the IRS. One way would be to amend the sixteenth Amendment and set tax rate at one-percent of gross Income for all. If the economy is booming, taxes will increase the Governments income, if the economy goes down, taxes will decrease and so will the Governments income. Just like most working-families income. The original concept of the 16th Amendment was sold to the public under the assumption that it would only be a progressive tax of 1% on incomes up to $20,000. This meant that most working citizens would pay little or no taxes. BUT THEY DID NOT PUT THIS INTO THE 16th AMENDMENT ITSELF! That is the way the social Democrats work. They say one thing, but it is all smoke and mirrors. The damage to the American working family is devastating to say the least BUT the law is passed and the taxpayer suffers.

President Wilson raised the income tax rates to pay for WWI and after the war they were returned to their original rates. Along came President Roosevelt who raise the income tax rates astronomically but he promised that they would be reduce at the end of WWII. **THEY WERE NEVER REDUCED.** So much for Democratic promises.

One must wonder 'Where is a good Republican when you need one?' Or better still, 'Where is the so-called Free Press?'

Today we have the economy in a spin fall—a recession that hovers around the seventeen percent underemployment rate. Interest rates are held by the Federal Reserve at less than one percent. Most countries and the American investors no longer invest in Treasury Notes and the country keeps printing more money to pay its bills.

Most investors (American) are reevaluating their retirement Portfolios and investing in the Stock Market and the Commodities Market. The time is ripe for the foreign bankers to pull another shill that will send the World into a double-dip recession which will bring on the greatest depression the world has ever seen. Fantasy—No! They did it in the 1830s, the early 1900s and the collapse of the Stock Market in 1929. They control the money and by withholding it from the public, businesses collapses and unemployment raises until the only thing that remains is despair.

The scenario today, is that low interest rates are pushing investors into other fields of investments like precious metals. Gold and Silver prices are astronomically high and people are placing a large portion of their retirement portfolios into the Gold and Silver commodities. Since the dollar is shrinking and Gold prices are rising it is the logical thing to do.

Unfortunately, people never learn from history. In the 1920s they were investing in Stocks on margin. It was a good deal, BUT when the call came in for the total investment they did not have the money to save their investments and they went BROKE! Today the scenario is similar. What if the international bankers

(Rockefeller/Rothschild cabal) decides to drop the price of Gold back to the Brentwood Treaty value of $35. 00 per ounce. Since they are selling the Gold today at $1200.00 per ounce, they are going to make a killing in profits. The loser will be the investors and the international bankers will buy back all their gold back at the cheap price of $35.00 an ounce and reap an astronomical profit in the transaction.

With this scenario, investors will no longer have the money to invest in the Stock Market and other Institutions which will cause many business to fail, unemployment will hit the ceiling and with the National Debt of at least $20 trillion, this country will go bankrupt. Is this Obama's goal? Your guess is as good as mine.

Chapter 2

Accidental or Conspiracy Theory

"I predict future happiness for Americans if they can prevent the government from wasting the labors of the people under the pretense of taking care of them" Thomas Jefferson

Many Americans are confused, frustrated and downright angry over the direction that this country is taking.. They know that something is drastically wrong, but they cannot phantom what it is. As the saying goes, they feel like mushrooms because the powers that-be and the mass media keep them in the dark and feeds them a lot of misinformation. To be paranoid means to believe in delusions of danger and persecution. If the danger is real, and the evidence credible, then it cannot be delusional. To many, the thought of a world-wide conspiracy is impossible, ignore the facts. Therefore, to disregard the evidence and hope that it cannot be true, is more an evidence of a mental illness that has permeated the Academic community and the media for centuries.

To understand how the most influential people in America came to be members of an organization working purposefully for the overthrow of the Constitution and American sovereignty, we have to go back at least to the early 1900's, though the story begins much earlier (depending on your viewpoint and beliefs). That a ruling power elite does indeed control the U.S. government behind the scenes has been attested to by many Americans in a position to know. Felix Frankfurter, Justice of the Supreme Court (1939-1962), said:

"The real rulers in Washington are invisible and exercise power from behind the scenes."

In a letter to an associate dated November 21, 1933, President

Franklin Roosevelt wrote,

"The real truth of the matter is, as you and I know, that a financial element in the large centers has owned the government ever since the days of Andrew Jackson."

February 23, 1954, Senator William Jenner warned in a speech:

"Outwardly we have a Constitutional government. We have operating within our government and political system, another body representing another form of government, a bureaucratic elite which believes our Constitution is outmoded."

Baron M.A. Rothschild wrote,

"Give me control over a nation's currency and I care not who makes its laws."

All that is needed to effectively control a government is to control it's money: a central bank with a monopoly over the supply of money and credit. This has been done in Western Europe, with the creation of privately owned central banks such as the Bank of England. Before anyone makes up their mind about conspiracy vs. accidental occurrences, remember this:

    a. Politicians are the only people in the world who create problems and then campaign against them.

    b. Have you ever wondered: if both the Democrats and Republicans are against deficits, WHY do we have deficits?

    c. Have you ever wondered: if all politicians are against inflation and high taxes, WHY do we have inflation and high taxes?

    d. The Citizens do not propose the Federal Budget. The President does.

    e. The Citizens do not have the Constitutional authority to vote on appropriations. The House of Representatives does.

    f. The Citizens do not write the Tax Codes, Congress does.

g. The Citizens do not control the money policy. The Federal Reserve does.

h. One Hundred Senators, 435 members of Congress, One president, and nine Supreme Court Justices—545 Americans out of 300 million—are directly, legally, morally, and individually responsible for the domestic problems that plague this country.

i. The Federal Reserve System is a problem created by Congress. In 1913, Congress delegated its Constitutional duty to provide a sound currency to a federally chartered, but *private*, central bank. It was unconstitutional but they did it anyway. How does this abomination work? Well, the Federal Reserve is the banker of the U.S. Every week the Treasury Department places Treasury Bills up for auction. These T– bills supply the Treasure with enough money to keep operational for the next week (to pay its bills). These Treasury Bills are purchased by the Federal Reserve with paper money that is printed by the Government mint. This paper money is printed very cheaply regardless of the denomination of the currency. The Federal Reserve than buys the proffered Treasury Bills with this paper money they purchase from the mint and charge the government a substantial interest rate for the loan—usually 7% or more. The Federal Reserve than put the Treasure Bills on the open market for sale. The Chinese, England, Japan, etc buy up most of the T-bills. The T-bills that are not bought up by foreign countries are then dumped upon the Banks under control of the Federal Reserve. The end result is that the money that the banks usually have for loans, etc. are tied up in T-bills causing a rise in interest rates for public loans. (For example, if the Treasury Department put $1 billion "T" bills up for sale each week and the Federal Reserve picks up these bills and charges the Government 7% interest. They make $70 million out of a paper transaction. Who pays for this? The American taxpayers because it becomes part of the National Debt! Maybe this will explain why the Democrats are always screaming that we are not paying enough taxes. Well think of this: The total interest paid out in interest on the debt in 1990 was $664, 852, 544, 615.90: the interest paid on the debt in 2010 was $395, 768, 649, 928. 52. Averaging roughly over the past decade our Government has given over $3.5 Trillion of taxpayers money to the world financiers. What has Congress done about it? NOTHING! They should all, Republican and Democrat alike, hang their heads in shame and RESIGN! Members of Congress always blame the sitting President for the problems but it is only Congress who can make and approve bills of Appropriation NOT the President. So it is about time that Congress took stock of itself and adopt the biblical saying: "He who has never sin, let him throw the first stone!"

j. In 1974, Congress passed a Budget Act that was signed by President Nixon that was an abomination. It was a law designed to ensure that the government would grow into a bureaucratic monster which it has become today. At the time it was passed a number of Congressmen warn that it could kill this nation. Did Congress ever amend this abomination? NO! They are too busy filling their own wallets to take time to save the country.

k. Special interests and lobbyists can be excluded from being the problem because they have no legal authority. They have no ability to coerce a senator, a congressman, or a President to do one thing for them. Even if they offer a politician $1 million dollars in cash, the politician has the power to accept or reject it. No matter what the lobbyist promises, it is the legislator's responsibility to determine how he votes.

l. Those 545 Americans spend much of their energy

convincing us that what THEY did is not THEIR fault. They cooperate in this common scam regardless of party. What separates a politician from a normal person is an excessive amount of gall. No normal person would have the gall of a Speaker, who stood up and criticized the President for creating deficits. The President can only propose a budget. He cannot force the Congress to accept it.

m. The Constitution, which is the supreme law of the land, gives sole responsibility to the House of Representative for originating and approving appropriations and taxes.

n. Who is the Speaker of the House? Nancy Pelosi. She is the leader of the majority party. She and fellow House Members, not the President, can approve any budget they want. If the President vetoes it, they can pass it over his veto if they so desire.

o. It seems inconceivable that a nation of 300 million cannot replace 545 people who stand convicted—by present facts—of incompetence and irresponsibility. There is not one single domestic problem that is not traceable directly to those 545 people. When you understand that 545 people exercise the power of the federal government, then it must follow that what exists is what they want to exist. For example:

(1) If the tax code is unfair, it's because they want it unfair.

(2) If the budget is in the red, it's because they want it in the red.

(3) If the Military is in Iraq, it's because they want it in Iraq.

p. Don't let these 545 people shift the blame to bureaucrats, whom they hire and whose jobs they can abolish; to lobbyists, whose gifts they can reject; to regulators, to whom they give the power to regulate and from whom they can take the power.

THOSE 545 PEOPLE, AND THEY ALONE, ARE

RESPONSIBLE FOR THIS MESS!

And now the electorate installed a far left ruler, President Obama, to head the Executive Branch of the Government and deserve what they get. Not many knew the current President as others knew him. One who is familiar with the political scene is Dr. Charles Krauthammer who began his writing career 1981, directed psychiatric research for the Carter administration, helped develop the "Reagan Doctrine" in the '80s and appointed to the President Council on Bioethics in 2002, gave a stirring speech at the Center for the American Experiment. A summary of his speech is as follows:

1. Mr. Obama is a very intellectual, charming individual. He is not to be under- estimated. He is a cool customer who doesn't show his emotions. It's very hard to know what's behind the mask. The taking down of the Clinton dynasty was an amazing accomplishment. The Clintons still do not understand what hit them. Obama was in the perfect place and the perfect time.

2. Obama has political skills comparable to Reagan and Clinton. He has a way of making you think he's on your side, agreeing with your position, while doing the opposite. Pay no attention to what he **SAYS,** rather watch what he **DOES!**

3. Obama has a ruthless quest for power. He did not come to Washington to make something out of himself, but rather to change everything, including dismantling capitalism. He can't be straightforward on his ambitions as the public would not go along. He has a heavy hand and wants to level the playing field with income distribution and punishment to the achievers in society. He would like to model the USA to Great Britain or Canada.

4. His three main goals are to control ENERGY, PUBLIC EDU-CATION, and HEALTHCARE by the Federal Government. He doesn't care about the auto or financial service industries, but got them as an early bonus. The Cap and Trade Bill will add costs to everything and stifle growth. Paying for FREE college education is his goal. Most scary is his healthcare program, because if you make it FREE and add 48,000,000

people to a Medicare-type single-payer system, the costs will go through the roof. The only way to control costs is with massive RATIONING of services, like in Canada. God forbid!

5. He has surrounded himself with mostly far-left academic types. No one around him has ever even run a candy store. But they are going to try to run the auto, financial, banking and other industries. This obviously can't work in the long run. Obama is not a socialist, rather he's a far-left secular progressive bent on nothing short of revolution. He ran as a moderate but will govern from the hard left. Again, watch what he does.

Those who voted for this man, have been warned! Understand that there are four political groups in the country:

1. Liberals

2. Conservatives

3. Libertarians

4. Progressives

The only difference between a Progressive and a Communist is the mode of operation. A Communist wishes to change the current Government by revolutionary means while a Progressive wants to change the current Government by destroying the current Constitution——a piece at a time.

When the Socialist Dictatorship is achieved, according to Marx, "the all powerful state will miraculously wither away and state socialism would give way to Communism. Then you would not need any government at all. Everything will be peace, sweetness and light and everybody will live happily ever after." If anyone believes Karl Marx road-to-heaven theory, I have a bridge in Brooklyn that I will gladly sell to them, CHEAPLY.

Georgetown professor Dr. Carroll Quigley (Bill Clinton's mentor while at Georgetown) wrote about the goal of the investment bankers who control central banks: "... nothing less than to create a world system of financial control in private hands able to dominate the political system of each country and the economy of the world as a whole... controlled in a feudalist fashion by the central banks of the world acting in concert, by secret agreements arrived at in frequent private meetings and conferences."

A national income tax was declared unconstitutional in 1895 by the Supreme Court, so a constitutional amendment was proposed in Congress by Senator Nelson Aldrich. As presented to the American people it seemed reasonable enough: income tax on only one percent of income under $20,000, with the ASSURANCE that it would never increase. Since it was graduated, the tax would "soak the rich", ...but the rich had other plans. As described by Gary Allen in his 1976 book; *The Rockefeller File*: "By the time the (16th) Amendment had been approved by the states, the Rockefeller Foundation was in full operation...about the same time that Judge Kenesaw Landis was ordering the breakup of the Standard Oil monopoly...John D...not only avoided taxes by creating four great tax-exempt foundations; he used them as repositories for his 'divested' interests...made his assets non-taxable so that they might be passed down through generations without... estate and gift taxes...Each year the Rockefellers can dump up to half their incomes into their pet foundations and deduct the "donations" from their income tax." (NOTE: The Income Tax remained at one percent until President Roosevelt came into the Presidency. When WW II started, President Roosevelt, with a Democratic Congress, raised the Income Taxes from 1 percent to 20 percent for lower income persons and 70 percent for those in the higher brackets.. He PROMISED that the Income Taxes would be returned to their lower percentages when WW II ended. THEY NEVER WERE REDUCED! So much for socialistic promises.

Exchanging ownership for control of wealth, foundations are also a handy means for promoting interests that benefit the wealthy. Millions of foundation dollars have been donated to causes such as promoting the use of drugs, while degrading preventive medicine. Since many drugs are made from coal tar derivatives, both oil companies and drug manufacturing concerns (many Rockefeller owned or controlled) are the main beneficiaries.

The story of the Rockefellers' power is told in a book by Eustace Mullins entitled:*Murder by Injection (Chapter 10)*. Excerpts from the book follows:

> *"Many American conservatives believe as a matter of faith that the Rockefellers and the Council on Foreign Relations exercise absolute control over the government and the people of United States . This thesis can be accepted as a working formula if one remains conscious of the larger issues . Two writers for whom many writers have great respect, Dr. Emanuel Josephson and Morris Bealle, insisted on focusing on the Rockefellers and excluding all other aspects of the World Order . This severely limited the effect of their otherwise ground breaking work on the Medical Monopoly. (See Bealle's book The Drug Story. Also on the internet see "The Drug Story" by Morris A. Bealle, publisher The Hornet's Nest, 1976 for the entire book about the Rockefeller Drug Cartel. It's about the medical and government agencies pushing useless drugs on an unsuspecting populace.)Another contrary view in "The World Order,' fixing upon the Rothschild monetary power which reached a point of world control by 1885, and its London policy group, the Royal Institute of International Affairs, as the policy makers for what has essentially been since 1900, to re-established colonial government in the United States. The ..... government functions primarily through the Council on Foreign Relations, but only as the subsidiary of RIIA (See Chapter 8 on CFR) and through the Rockefeller Foundation which controls government functions, the educational establishments, the media, the religions and the state legislatures. "*

Although we have presidential elections every four years, the voters can only vote for the candidate that their party leaders select. The Political Parties select a candidate, via convention, and place that person on the ballot. A case in point was the election in 2008. Going into the Democratic convention were two candidates that were head-to-head in the vote— Clinton and Obama. So, prior to the delegates having a chance to select one of them for their presidential candidate, they met in a backroom and made a deal. Obama would run for president and he would name Hillary Clinton as Secretary of State. Controlling the backroom deal was the Rockefeller/Rothchild syndicate because, through their agents, they furnished the money to finance the election. They did not want Hillary because she had botched the Health Care Plan when her husband was in office.

None of our elections are really free. Both parties, Republican and Democrat, are bought and paid for by the Rockefeller Syndicate. Just like the stock market is free for people to invest in whatever stock they wish, the value of the stocks listed on the market are controlled by the Federal Reserve who is controlled by the Bank of England not the government of the United States.

This information comes from Burke's Peerage, which is the Bible of aristocratic genealogy, based in London: Every presidential election in America, since and including George Washington in 1789 to Bill Clinton, has been won by the candidate with the most British and French royal genes. Of the 42 presidents to Clinton, 33 have been related to two people: Alfred the Great, King of England, and Charlemagne, the most famous monarch of France. So it goes on; 19 of them are related to England's Edward III, who has 21st century blood connections to Prince Charles. The same goes with the banking families in America. George Bush and Barbara Bush are from the same bloodline—the Pierce bloodline, which changed its name from Percy, when it crossed the Atlantic. Percy is one of the aristocratic families of Britain, to this day. They were involved in the Gunpowder Plot to blow up Parliament at the time of Guy Fawkes"

The realization that we do indeed live under the dictates of the Rockefeller Syndicate can well be the starting point on the long road back for American independence. In exposing the Rockefellers as agents of a foreign power, which is not merely a foreign power, but a genuine world government, we must realize that this is not merely a group dedicated to making money, but a group which is committed to maintaining the power of a colonial form of government over the American people. The concept of John D. Rockefeller as a man obsessed by greed——a category in which he has plenty of company—— hides the fact that from the day the Rothschilds began to finance his march towards a total oil monopoly in the United States from their money supply at the National City Bank of Cleveland, Rockefeller was never an independent power, nor does any organization of the Rockefeller

Syndicate operate as an independent power. It is known that the Cosa Nostra, or Mafia, which the Syndicate is allegedly allied, has autonomous power in the regions which have been assigned to that particular ``family" by the national directors. So it is between the Rockefellers and the Rothschilds.

The Rockefeller Syndicate operates under the control of the world financial structure, which means that on any given day, all of its assets could be rendered close to worthless by clever financial manipulation. This is the control which ensures that no one can quit the organization. Not only would he be stripped of all assets, but he would be under contract for immediate assassination nor would any member of his immediate family be safe. The Department of Justice is aware that one of the terrorist groups operating in the United States are the agents of the World Order, but they wisely avoid any mention of this fact.

The world financial structure, far from being a hidden organization, is actually well known and well defined. It consists of the major Swiss Banks; the survivors of the old Venetian-Genoese banking axis; the Big Five of the world grain trade; the British combine, centered in the Bank of England and its chartered merchant banks, functioning through the Rothschilds and the Oppenheimers and having absolute control over their Canadian colony through the Royal Bank of Canada and the Bank of Montreal, their Canadian lieutenants being the Bronfmans, Belzbergs, and other financial operators; and the colonial banking structure in the United States, controlled by the Bank of England through the Federal Reserve System; the Boston Brahmin families who made their fortunes in the opium trade, including the Delanos and others and the Rockefeller Syndicate, consisting of the Kissinger network headquartered in the Rockefeller Bank, Chase Manhattan Bank, American Express, the present form of the old Rothschild representatives in the United States, which includes Kuhn, Loeb Company and Lehman Brothers.

The Rockefeller Syndicate is low on the list of the world's financial structure. It is not the crucial factor in financial decision in the Western Hemisphere, it is just the working control mechanism of the American branch of the Bank of England. The Rockefeller family themselves, like the Morgans, Schiffs and Warburgs, have faded into insignificance, but the mechanism created in their name roars along at full steam, still maintaining all of the functions for which it was organized.

Since he help established the Trilateral Commission, David Rockefeller has functioned as an international courier for the World Order, mainly concerned with delivering working instructions to the Communist bloc, either directly in New York or by traveling to the area involved. Laurence Rockefeller is active in the operation of the Medical Monopoly, but his principal interests are in operating various vacation spas in tropical areas. They are the two survivors of the ``Fortunate Five,'' the five sons of John D. Rockefeller, Jr. and Abby Aldrich.

John D. Rockefeller, Jr. died in an institution in Tucson, Arizona and was hastily cremated. John D. Rockefeller III died in a mysterious accident on a New York Parkway near his home. Nelson Rockefeller, named after his grandfather, mysteriously died in the arms of a TV journalist; the death was hushed up for many hours. It is generally believed that he ran afoul of his Colombian drug connection, the disagreement hardly being trivial—it involved several billion dollars in drug profits which had not been properly apportioned. Winthrop Rockefeller died an alcoholic in the arms of his black boy friend. He had been interviewed on television by Harry Reasoner to explain his hasty move from New York to Arkansas. Winthrop said that his black boy friend, an Army sergeant, refused to live in New York. To celebrate this alliance, Winthrop Rockefeller gave magnificently to Negro causes, including the Urban League building on East 48th Street in New York. A plaque on the second floor notes that it was his gift.

This does not imply that the Rockefellers no longer have influence, but that the major policy dictates of the Rockefeller Syndicate are handed down by others, of whom they continue to be a visible force. Through the person of David Rockefeller, the family is sometimes called ``the first family of the Soviet Union.'' ONLY he and Dr. Armand Hammer, the moving force behind USTEC (US—USSR Trade and Economic Council), have permanent permission to land their private planes at the Moscow Airport. Others would suffer the fate of KAL 007.

Both the Rockefeller family fortune and the considerable portion set aside in the foundations of the Rockefeller Syndicate are effectively insulated against any type of government control . *Fortune* magazine noted August 4, 1986, that John D. Rockefeller, Jr. had created trusts in 1934 which now amounted to some $2.3 billion; another $200 million had been set aside for the Abby Rockefeller branch. The five sons had trusts which in 1986 amount to $2.1 billion. These trusts had originally amounted to only $50 million each, showing the increase in their assets as well as inflation during the ensuing half century. *Fortune* estimated the 1986 total Rockefeller wealth as $3.5 billion, of which $900 million was in securities and real estate. They owned 45% of the Time Life Building; Nelson Rockefeller's International Basic Economy Corporation had been sold to a British company in 1980. For years, the Rockefeller family had deliberately kept the rents low in its major holding, the Rockefeller Center, a $1.6 billion investment yielding an annual return of 1%. This was a convenient maneuver, for tax purposes. Rockefeller Center recently went public issuing stock which was sold to public buyers. The Rockefellers are rumored to be liquidating their investments in the New York area, and reinvesting in the West, particularly in the area around Phoenix, Arizona. It is possible that they know something we don't."

The Rockefeller wealth may be attributed to old John D.'s greed and ruthlessness, but its origins are based in his initial financing from the National City Bank of Cleveland, which was identified in Congressional reports as one of the three Rothschild banks in the United States and by his later acceptance of the guidance of Jacob Schiff of Kuhn, Loeb & Company, who had been born in the Rothschild house in Frankfort, Germany and was now the principal Rothschild representative in the United States. With the seed money from the National City Bank of Cleveland, old John D. Rockefeller soon laid claim to the title of 'the most ruthless

American' ".

It is more than likely that it was this quality which persuaded the Rothschilds to back him . Rockefeller realized early in the game that the oil refinery business, which could offer great profits in a short time, also was at the mercy of uncontrolled competition. His solution was a simple one—crush all competition. The famous Rockefeller dedication to total monopoly was simply a business decision. Rockefeller embarked on a campaign of coercing all competing oil refineries out of business. He attacked on a number of fronts, which is also a lesson to all would be entrepreneurs. First, he would send an agent, not known to be working for Rockefeller, with an offer to buy the competing refinery for a low price— but offering cash. If the offer was refused, the competitor would then come under attack from a competing refinery which greatly undercut his price. He might also suffer a sudden strike at his refinery, which would force him to shut down. Control of labor through unions has always been a basic Rockefeller technique. Like the Soviet Union, they seldom have labor trouble. If these techniques failed, Rockefeller would then use violence; beating the rival workers as they went to and from their jobs, or burning or blowing up the competing refinery. These techniques convinced the Rothschilds that they had found their man.

The Rothechilds sent their personal representative, Jacob Schiff, to Cleveland to help Rockefeller plan further expansion. At this time, the Rothschilds controlled 95% of all railroad mileage in the United States, through the J.P. Morgan Company and Kuhn, Loeb & Company according to official *Department of Commerce* figures for the year 1895. J.P. Morgan mentions in his *Who's Who* listing that he controlled 50,000 miles of U.S. railways.

Schiff worked out an elaborate rebate deal for Rockefeller, through a dummy corporation, South Improvement Company. These rebates ensured that no other oil company could survive in competition with the Rockefeller firm. The scheme was later exposed, but by that time Rockefeller had achieved a virtual monopoly of the oil business in the United States. The daughter of one of his victims, Ida Tarbell, whose father was ruined by

Rockefeller's underhanded operations, wrote the first major expose of the Standard Oil Trust. She was promptly denounced as a ``muckraker" by Theodore Roosevelt, who claimed to be a ``trust buster". In fact, he ensured the dominance of the Standard Oil Trust and other giant trusts.

During the next half century, John D. Rockefeller was routinely depicted by socialist propagandists as the archetype of the ruthless capitalist. At the same time, he was the principal financier of the world Communist movement, through a firm called American International Company. Despite the fact that the House of Rothschild had already achieved world control, the sound and fury was directed exclusively against its two principal, representatives, John D. Rockefeller and J.P. Morgan. One of the few revelations of the actual state of affairs appeared in *Truth* magazine, December 16, 1912, which pointed out that ``Mr. Schiff is head of the great private banking house of Kuhn, Loeb & Company, which represents the Rothschild interests on this side of the Atlantic. He is described as a financial strategist and has been for years the financial minister of the great impersonal power known as Standard Oil. Because of these concealed factors, it was a relatively simple matter for the American public to accept the ``fact" that the Rockefellers were the preeminent power in this country. This myth was actually clothed in the apparel of power, the Rockefeller Oil Trust becoming the ``military-industrial complex" which assumed political control of the nation; the Rockefeller Medical Monopoly attained control of the health care of the nation, and the Rockefeller Foundation, a web of affiliated tax exempt creations, effectively controlled the religious and educational life of the nation. The myth succeeded in its goal of camouflaging the hidden rulers, the Rothschilds.

The technique of using the labor unions to control industries is now being used by the Obama Administration to seize control of banks, Corporations, States, etc. The recession was only an excuse to bury the country in a morass of debt and strengthen the power of Unions over businesses. The so called Job Stimulus Bill, for example, has saved or created over 2 million jobs according to the Obama Administration figures, but on closer inspection, one finds this is NOT the case. The concept of 'saving' jobs is now counted as if they were creating new jobs when in reality, those jobs were never in danger of being lost. The way the government passed out $300 billion to the needy States— States that had large budget deficits—was in a lump sum. The States merely paid off their debts or lower them to manageable levels and then reported back to the Government that they had saved so many fireman jobs, police jobs, social service jobs, etc. According to the States, these jobs would have been eliminated if it wasn't for the bailout money. THOSE JOBS WERE NEVER IN DANGER TO BEGIN WITH. But the States couldn't or wouldn't cut their out-of-control spending on frivolous programs like retirement benefits for civil workers, pay raises, etc. They (the States) no longer have to worry about uncontrollable debt. The Federal Government under Obama's Administration are more than willing to tax the rest of the country to bail them out.

Remember that all those jobs that the Obama Administration said they save were UNION jobs. That should teach the non-Union workers of America what the current administration thinks of them.

With the means to loan enormous sums to the government (the Federal Reserve), a method to repay the debt (income tax), and an escape from taxation for the wealthy, (foundations), all that remained was an excuse to borrow money. They found that excuse in starting wars.

We keep electing new Presidents who seemingly promise faithfully to halt this world-wide advance of Communism, to stop extravagant government spending, put a brake on inflation and put the economy on a steady course so that unemployment will be held to a minimum and reverse the secular movement trend that is turning this country into a moral cesspool Yet despite all the promises and shining campaign oratory, these problems still worsen no matter who is in office—be it Democrat or Republican. No wonder the people are confused. It's like those children puzzles of the past—where you would see a picture in a magazine and you are ask to find the Santa Clause, his sleigh, and Rudolph the reindeer. You look and look and cannot find all of them—some couldn't find any of them. You're instructed to turn to another page in the magazine and there the Santa Clause, his sleigh, and Rudolph are heavily outline and you wonder why you couldn't see them in the first place. The reason of course is that the overlaying picture is such that the objects just blend in like a camouflaged army uniform blends into the surrounding terrain. Who draws these pictures to hide the objects? Its members of academia and the mass media. They are good at hiding the real world from the people. Why? Because they are either owned by the One World crowd or are brainwashed into believing that the solution to all the world problems will be solved by a One-World Government controlled by the financiers of the world. Have you noticed that most articles in the current newspapers are listed as coming from the Associated Press, United Press, other News Presses or the east coast Newspapers? All these services are controlled by the One-World financers. Is it any wonder why Newspapers are dying out?

There are two theories concerning major world events and they are the 'conspiracy theory' and the 'accidental theory'. Either things happen by accident—not planned or caused by anybody, or they are planned and somebody causes them to happen. President Roosevelt once said,

> *"In politics, nothing happens by accident. If it happens, you can bet it was planned that way."*

Theodore Roosevelt in 1906 stated,

> *"Behind the ostensible government sits enthroned an invisible government owing allegiance and acknowledging no responsibility to the people. To destroy this invisible government, to befoul the unholy alliance between corrupt business and corrupt politics is the first task of statesmanship of the day."*

There have been other warning from statesmen like Thomas Jefferson, Lord Acton, Fredrich Hayek, Benjamin Franklin, etc. Yet, with all these warnings, practically all members in academia and mass media columnists and commentators reject the cause and effect or conspiratorial theory. The answer is quite simple—most so called scholars follow the crowd in the academic world just like sheep follows the ram—or more realistically—like the European lemmings, they follow even to their own destruction. To buck the tide means social and professional banishment. While Deans and Professors claim to be tolerant and broadminded, in practice, its strictly a one- way street to slavery (socialism).

Why this blind obedience to Socialism? The answer is simple— vanity! The people in academia have over the years acquired a strong vested interest in their own errors. Their intellects and egos are totally committed to the accidental theory of the events in history. Like politicians, they are attracted to the idea that events are driven by some mysterious hand or by accident. By accepting this concept of reasoning, they hope to escape the blame when things go wrong.

With the leaders of the academic and communications world smugly pushing this 'accidental theory' as opposed to a 'conspirator theory' , it is not surprising that millions of well meaning people repeat the misguided information that is given to them. The so-called intellectuals deal with the conspiratorial theory of history simply by ignoring it. For example, the members of academia that see no evil in socialism but embrace it completely, ignore history. They ignore the fact that some of the more advanced nations in the world has fallen to communism. Czechoslovakia was one of the worlds most modern industrial nations and Cuba had the second highest per capita income in Central and South America to indicate a few of the fallen.

It would be remiss to say that all academia believe in the 'accidental theory' because that is not the case. A case in point is Professor Carroll Quigley, former President Clinton's mentor, who reveals in his book '*Tragedy and Hope*' the existence of the conspiratorial network which this book is about. In Professor Quigley's book he states:

> "*The 'network' always prefers big Government, big federal spending and the stability of a planned society rather than the uncertainties of the free market.... I know of the operations of this network because I have studied it for twenty years and was permitted for two years,*

in the early 1960's to examine its papers and secret records. I have NO AVERSION to it or to most of its aims and have, for much of my life, been close to it and many of its instruments. I have objected, both in the past and recently, to a few of its policies..... but in general, my chief difference of opinion, is that it wishes to remain UNKNOWN, and I believe its role in history is significant enough to be known."

The Professor goes on to explain that the network's aim as:

'nothing less than to create a world system of financial control in private hands able to dominate the political system of each country and the economy of the world as a whole. An example of the power of the network is the way it has forced the American tax-payers to spend billions of dollars every year on foreign giveaways every year since World War II. (NOTE: President Oboma's 2010 budget gives the State Department $32 billion dollars in taxpayer's money to spend on foreign aid and the U.S. Government is already in debt to the tune of $14 Trillion!)'

These conspirators want to create a system where they dominate the world. Even more frightening, they want total control over every individual action. As Professor Quigley states:

'(for the individual) freedom and choice will be controlled within very narrow alternatives by the fact that he will be numbered from birth and followed, as a number, through his educational training, his required military or public service, his tax contributions, his health and medical requirements, and his final retirement and death benefits.'

These conspirators want control over all natural resources, business, banking and transportation by controlling governments of the world. In order to accomplish these aims the conspirators have had no qualms about fomenting wars, depressions and hatred. They want a monopoly which would eliminate all competitors and destroy the free enterprise system completely. There are others in academia that recognize a conspiracy does exist but they will not say anything because to challenge the conspirators head-on would destroy their careers. Fear is a great weapon when used by the unscrupulous!

The conspirators needed a vehicle to accomplish their goals –ownership of every thing and enslaving the people. They found their vehicle in a man named Karl Marx. An exile from Germany, Marx spent most of his mature years in London, supported by his friend and collaborator, the German revolutionist Friedrich Engels. The conspirators financed Marx, who had no job and little money, in his quest to liberate the common worker from the chains of slavery. Marx central conflict was between so-called capitalists who owned the means of production—factories and machines— and workers or proletarians who possessed nothing but their bare hands. Exploitation, the heart of Marxist doctrine, is measured by the capacity of capitalists to pay no more than subsistence wages to their employees and extract for themselves as profit (or surplus value) the difference between these wages and the selling price of market commodities. In 1848, Marx (along with Friedrich Engles) published his masterpiece titled "The Communist Manifesto" which laid out the path for all countries to follow. Of course the path to eliminating exploitation by entrepreneurs and landowners required a STRONG central government (preferably dictatorship). To accomplish this totalitarian communists state one had to resort to the meager 10-point program outlined in the 'Communist Manifesto'. The two authors recommended:

1. The abolition of private ownership of land and application of all rents toward public purposes;

2. A progressive income tax;

3. The abolition of the right of inheritance;

4. The confiscation of all property belonging to emigrants and rebels;

5. The centralization of credit in the hands of the state, by means of a national bank with state capital and an exclusive monopoly;

6. The centralization of the means of communication and transportation in the hands of the state;

7. An increase in the number and size of factories and instruments of production owned by the state;

8. Equal liability of all towards labor;

9. The combination of agriculture with industrial production; and, finally,

10. Free education for all children in public (i.e., state) schools, along with the abolition of children's factory labor in its present form and the practice of combining education with industrial production, and other things.

With the above blueprint, the conspirators had the plan for enslaving the world. They realized that Capitalism could not be controlled. On the other hand, Socialism (which is a form of slavery), could be the vehicle to accomplish their goals. They have over the years been working diligently at installing Socialist government all over the world—and they have succeeded. One bastion of Capitalism remained to be subdued—the United States. In later Chapters, I will show how they have done that.

One must remember that the 'Conspirator Theory' is a theory based on cause and effect logic. When something happens (cause) it results in something else happening (effect). Things just don't happen— they are caused. And when something happens it usually has a result which is what the conspirators want. Is there a Conspiracy or not? One has to judge for him/herself. There are those who will admit to it, even those who are a part of it. I have already given a few quotes where the word conspiracy is used. There are many others.

This conspiracy has been going on for centuries and, if one is a student of the true history of the World, one can see time and again the same blunders made by governments which ensure the conspirators will control the earth. For example: 'Taking advantage of Congress' desire to adjourn for Christmas, The Federal Reserve Act was passed on 22 December 1913 by a vote of 298 to 60 in the House and in the Senate by a majority of 43 to 25. There was some opposition to the Act but the opposition went nowhere. Henry Cabot Lodge, Sr. proclaimed with great foresight, 'The Bill as it

stands seems to me to open the way to a vast inflation of currency...
..I do not like to think that any law can be passed which will make
it possible to submerge the gold standard in a flood of irredeemable
paper currency.' Also, Congressman Charles A. Lindbergh, Sr. told
Congress: 'This act establishes the most gigantic trust on earth......
When the President signs this act. the invisible government by the
money powers, proven to exist by the Money Trust investigation,
will be legalized...." (The Reece Committee Hearings exposed
America's Major Tax-Exempt Foundations as moving toward a
One-World State.) In 1953, Carroll Reece, Congressman from
Eastern Tennessee, had his committee begin an investigation
into the American Establishment: the Tax-Exempt Foundations.
(These are sometimes erroneously cited as the Reese Committee
Hearings.) The hearings were held for two weeks. Then, without
warning, the committee stopped them. This was the only period
until 2005 when the Republican Party controlled both houses of
Congress and the Presidency. Yet a Democrat on the committee,
Wayne Hays—whose career ended in a sexual scandal in 1976—
was able to persuade other committee members to pull the plug.
The Committee's findings were summarized by the committee's
counsel, Rene Wormser. His book, *Foundations* (1958), has become
a vital document in understanding the leftward drift of America's
elite. Fortunately, it is still in print.

Mr. Wormser explains how the elite protects their wealth while
controlling education, research and public policy. The success in
creating an *organized* compulsory educational system in this country
has allowed the elite of this country to *prevent* each generation from
truly understanding how this country is actually run, thus keeping
them from doing anything about it. This "dumbing-down" has
enabled the government to more easily assimilate the people of
this country into a population which can be easily deceived and
controlled. (NOTE: Restructuring the Education curriculum is
one of President Oboma's goals.) This is a searching analysis of
some of America's most powerful tax-exempt foundations, their
actions as opposed to their stated purposes, the interlocking groups
of men who run them, their influence on the country at large. It is

a must-read book for all patriotic Americans.

The committee's senior researcher, Norman Dodd, went public about his findings almost immediately after the committee shut down the hearings. He was still trying to get the message out. His interviews are posted all over the Web. (//www.realityzone.com/hiddenagenda2.html)

If one will replace the reference to 'The Federal Reserve Act' and replace it with 'The Health Care Bill' and change the date to 21 December 2009 you have history repeating itself. Another disaster! In both cases, Senators and members of the House were bought off for their vote. The Senate Democratic leadership did not have the sixty votes needed to pass this Ponzie scheme so they inserted exemptions for certain states and thus received the votes needed to pass it. The Senators who received special privileges either for themselves or their states sold out their country for a few pieces of silver. Unfortunately for them, the buy- off was aired in the press and most of the goodies were removed from the bill to save face. History has a way of repeating itself, therefore it can be assumed that the Health Care Bill will end up like the Federal Reserve Act. President Obama has fulfilled two of his obligations that got him elected to the Presidency: he has paid off the Unions with the Stimulus Bill Package and The Rockefeller Drug Cartel with the Health Care Bill. Only a few know what other pay offs are coming. So much for the present day politicians.

Congressman Wright Patman, wrote a number of years ago that ' In the United States today we have in effect, two governments..... We have the duly constituted Government.....Then we have an independent, uncontrolled and uncoordinated government in the Federal Reserve System, operating the money powers which are reserved to Congress by the Constitution' The same thing is going to apply to the Health Care Bill when someone appoints the Health Czar. The bill give this Czar the powers of a dictator over Health Care. Isn't this unconstitutional? It is interesting to note that the national debt has risen from $1 billion when the Federal Reserve was inaugurated to $14 trillion in 2010. Interest payment on the debt is over $383 billion a year. These interest payment are going to the Rockefeller/Rothchild financial cabal. Who is responsible? Congress! Of course Congress blames it on the President, but that is because they couldn't reach a budget agreement for years and the country was run on what they call a 'Continuing Resolution'.

There was much vilification thrown at Congress because of this shortcoming, Congress passed a law which made a department out of the Office for Budget Management (which was under Congressional control) and transferred it to the Executive Branch of Government and made it thereafter the President's Budget. Now they blame the president for any shortcomings. However, when the Democrats controlled both houses of Congress under President Reagan, the House leadership under Representative Tip O'Neal (for two years) and Representative Jim Wright (for 6 years) the true story came out. Representative O'Neal always stated, when the new budget arrived on his desk, that he TRASHED it—'threw it in the waste basket'. Representative Wright coined a new phrase under his leadership saying that the new budget was DOA (DEAD ON ARRIVAL). So if the new budget means nothing to Congress, we are forever going to be in debt. Why? Because the continued resolution is still in effect and that means all departments get the same amount of money as they did last year plus cost of living increases. This is required by The Budget Act of 1974 (passed by a Democratic Congress). If they need more money they only have to request it from Congress and they get it weather they need it or not. That is why they hand out heavy bonus to specific individuals every year within their departments because the Budget Act of 1974 states if they do not spend their last years budget in total, their next years budget is reduced by the amount of the overages. (As an aside, the average working person's salary today is $40,000. while the average government worker's salary is $70,000. Yet Congress feels that they deserve more money therefore, lets raise taxes.) Money? Who cares. The taxpayers will pick up the tab. This Budget Act of 1974 is killing the country and Congress cares less. They would rather hold committee meetings on the rights of terrorists held by the military in Cuba.

Concerning waste in the government has been a subject that Congress refuses to address. To them it is only tax-payers money. For example, it was announced that the FAA (Federal Aviation Authority) is going to give a big Christmas Party for its employees and the cost is $5 million. This money is tax-payers money! Imagine all the other Departments doing the same but not reporting it. How much more tax-payers money is wasted? It is deplorable at a time when the country is in a recession and the underemployment rate stands at 17%. Your Government at work!

Further waste was recently revealed in President Obama's Stimulus Bill. A few incidents:

- $246 million tax break for Hollywood movie producers to buy motion picture film.
- $650 million for the digital television converter box coupon program.
- $88 million for the Coast Guard to design a new polar icebreaker (arctic ship).
- $600 million to buy hybrid vehicles for federal employees.
- $150 million for Smithsonian museum facilities.
- $75 million for "smoking cessation activities."
- $200 million for public computer centers at community colleges.
- $25 million for tribal alcohol and substance abuse reduction.
- $500 million for flood reduction projects on the Mississippi River.
- $10 million to inspect canals in urban areas.
- $6 billion to turn federal buildings into "green" buildings.
- $650 million for wildland fire management on forest service lands.
- $1.2 billion for "youth activities," including youth summer job programs.

There are hundreds of other wasteful projects in this Stimulus Bill, but President Obama and his minions in Congress care less.

Its only taxpayer's money and until they bring down the U.S. Government to third-world status they will not be happy.

Chapter 3

Collectivism vs Liberalism

"To compel a man to subsidize with his taxes the propagation of ideas which he disbelieves and abhors is sinful and tyrannical"
Thomas Jefferson

A reminder concerning the term Liberal or Liberalism. The terms Liberal and Liberalism, are terms that are described below. They do not define current-day neo-Liberals who brag to their constituents and the Press that they are Liberal. In reality, they are Socialist, Communists, Collectivists, Progressives etc. Do they claim Liberiaism because they are ashamed of their true calling? A number of years ago when Socialism was a nasty word, they decided to steal the term liberal and liberalism from the rightful owners. They did this by calling the true Liberal movement 'Conservatives'. Along with that term—Conservative— came various definitions such as 'Old-fashion', Out-dated, archaic, etc. while they referred to themselves as being 'Liberal'. 'Progressive' or 'Moderate'. (In truth, preserving the traditions and values of the past and applying them to the future is the core of the Conservative movement.) The so called free Press, which is owned by the world financers, aided these socialists by referring to them as the true Liberals. These neo-Liberals accused the Conservatives as being the stumbling block to an advanced society. An advanced society where the neo-Liberals are driving all of us down the road that leads to slavery.

Today, correspondents and so called pundits of the press, refer to President Obama's comment about the economy where: 'We are on the right path to recovery from the recession and we must keep to that path.' The problem is that these same correspondents will not tell the people that President Obama's path is the path to socialism. If one recalls Karl Marx statement 'Once Socialism is achieved it will collapse and the Communist will take over. Heaven on earth will then be ours!'

More then 100 years have passed since a few scholars admitted that sociology was not established as a true science and today, nothing has really changed. Today sociology remains more of a roadblock to intelligent human knowledge and behavior than a useful science. And it is a point of view which hates Christianity. Sociology acknowledges groups, but denies the importance of individuals. It sets up systems to control our human environment, behavior, goals, and emotions, but ignores the possibility that most people, if they are properly educated, can develop self control which frees them to set their own goals and enables them to govern their own emotions and behavior in a productive manner.

Current day socialists, like Nancy Pelosi, Senator Reid and President Obama, are continuing to feed lies to the American Public about the "Redistribution of Wealth". Let everyone know that socialism is NOT a share-the-wealth program, but in reality a method to CONSOLIDATE and CONTROL the wealth. Once this is understood the paradox of the superrich men promoting socialism becomes no paradox at all. Instead it becomes the logical, even the perfect tool for power-seeking megalomaniacs. Communism, or more accurately, Socialism is not a movement of the downtrodden masses, but of the economic elite. The plan of the financial elite is to socialize the United States, not to communize it because Communism implies many micro-style communities, whereas Socialism implies slavery of all. Karl Marx stated that when Socialism takes over the World, it will wither away and the only thing left will be Communism. The world will be broken down into small communities that will rule themselves.

An article published by the North American Newspaper Alliance in August of 1967 tells how the Rockefellers paid practically no income taxes despite their vast wealth. The article reveals that one of the Rockefellers paid the grand total of $685 personal income tax during a recent year. The Kennedys have their Chicago Merchandise Mart, their mansions, yachts, planes, etc., all owned by their myriads of family foundations and trusts. Taxes are for the commoners. Yet hypocrites like the Rockefellers, the Fords, and the Kennedys pose as champions of the downtrodden!

A dictatorship was impossible in our Republic because our forefathers wrote a Constitution (plus the Bill of Rights) where power was widely diffused. Today we have a Democratic Socialist style government where all the power is being centralized in the Executive Branch of the government. This concentration of power can only lead to a dictator style of government. The financial elite control the President indirectly and have gained virtual control of the whole country. Check Chapter 8 for a list of Presidents who were members of the CFR which is a branch of The Round Table which, in turn, is controlled by the Rothschild dynasty.

According to the dogmas of universalism, conceptual realism, holism, and collectivism, society is a living entity of its own, independent of and separate from the lives of the different individuals, acting on its own behalf and aiming at its own ends which are different from the ends sought by the individuals. Usually, hostility between the goals of society and those of its members will emerge. In order to safeguard the growth and further development of society it becomes necessary to master the selfishness of the individuals and to compel them to sacrifice their egotistical designs to the benefit of society.

When these conflicts occur, all the socialist doctrines are bound to abandon the secular methods of human science and logical reasoning and change to theological or metaphysical professions of faith. They must assume that Providence, through its prophets, apostles, and charismatic leaders, forces men who are innately wicked, i.e., prone to pursue their own ends, to walk in the ways of righteousness which God or history wants them to walk.

This is the philosophy which has characterized the religions of ancient people. It has been an element in all theological teachings. Man is bound to comply with the law issued by a superhuman power and to obey the authorities which this power has entrusted with the enforcement of the law. The human society created by this law is consequently the work of the Deity and not of man. If the Lord had not interfered and had not given knowledge to erring mankind, society would not have come into existence. Adam and Eve would still be living in Eden by themselves.

It is true that social cooperation is a boon to mankind; it is true that man could work his way up from his primeval stage and the moral and material distress of his primitive state only within the framework of society. However, alone he would never have seen the way to his own salvation. But the needs of social cooperation and subordination to the ideas of the moral law put heavy restraints upon him. From his primitive intellect he would think the loss of some expected advantage an evil and a curtailment of his wants. He would fail to recognize the greater, (but later) advantages which renunciation of present and visible pleasures will procure. But for supernatural revelation he would never have learned what destiny wants him to do for his own good and that of his offspring's.

The scientific theory as developed by the social philosophy of eighteenth-century rationalism and liberalism (liberalism meaning individual freedom from restraint NOT the neo-liberalism that means big government with many restraints) which by modern economics does not resort to any miraculous interference of superhuman powers. Every step by which an individual substitutes concerted action for isolated action results in an immediate and recognizable improvement in his conditions. The advantages derived from peaceful cooperation and division of labor are universal. They immediately benefit every generation and not just later descendants. For what the individual must sacrifice for the sake of society he is compensated by greater advantages. His sacrifice is only apparent and temporary; he foregoes a smaller gain in order to reap a greater one later. *No reasonable being can fail to see this obvious fact. When social cooperation is intensified by enlarging the field in which there is division of labor or when legal protection and the safeguarding of peace are strengthened, the incentive is the desire of all those concerned to improve their own conditions.* In striving after his own interests, the individual works toward an intensification of social cooperation and peaceful relationships. Society is a product of human action, i.e., the human urge to remove uneasiness as far as possible. In order to explain its evolution it is not necessary to have recourse to a doctrine, certainly offensive to a truly religious mind, according to which the original creation was so defective that repeated superhuman intervention is needed to prevent its failure.

The historical role of the theory of the division of labor as developed by British political economy from Hume to Ricardo consisted in the complete destruction of all metaphysical doctrines concerning the origin and the operation of social cooperation. Law and legality, the moral code and social institutions are no longer revered as unfathomable decrees of Heaven. They are of human origin, and the only yardstick that must be applied to them is that of desirability with regard to human welfare.

The utilitarian economist does not ask a man to give up his well-being for the benefit of society. He advises him to recognize what his rightly understood interests are. In his eyes God's magnificence does not manifest itself in busy interference with sundry affairs of princes and politicians, but in endowing his creatures with reason and the urge toward the pursuit of happiness.

The essential problem of all varieties of socialistic philosophy is: 'by what event do I recognize the true law, the authentic apostle of God's word, and the legitimate authority'. For many claim that Providence has sent them, and each of these prophets preaches a different gospel. For the faithful collectivist believer there cannot be any doubt; he is fully confident that he has spoken the only true doctrine. But it is precisely the firmness of such beliefs that renders the antagonisms irreconcilable. Each party is prepared to make its own credos prevail. But as logical reasoning cannot decide between various dissenting creeds, there is no means left for the settlement of such disputes other than armed conflict. The non-rationalist, non-utilitarian, and non-liberal social doctrines must wage wars and civil wars until one of the adversaries is annihilated or subdued. The history of the world's great religions is a record of battles and wars, as is the history of the present-day counterfeit religions, socialism, and nationalism.

Intolerance and propaganda by the executioner's or the soldier's sword are inherent in any system of collectivistic ethics. The laws of God or Destiny claim universal validity, and to the authorities which they declare legitimate all men by rights owe obedience. As long as the prestige of collectivistic codes of morality and of their philosophical inference, conceptual realism, was intact, there could not be any question of tolerance or of lasting peace. When fighting ceased, it was only to gather new strength for further fighting.

The supporters of a collectivistic (Communistic) morality and of the doctrine cannot hope to demonstrate by logic the correctness of their specific variety of ethical principles and the superiority and exclusive legitimacy of their particular socialistic ideal. They are forced to ask people to accept as truth their ideological system and to surrender to the authority they deem to be the right one; they are intent upon silencing dissenters or upon beating them into submission.

Of course, there will always be individuals and/or groups of individuals whose intellect is such that they cannot grasp the benefits which social cooperation brings them. There are others whose moral strength and will power are so weak that they cannot resist the temptation to strive for a temporary advantage by actions detrimental to the smooth functioning of the social system. For the adjustment of the individual to the requirements of social cooperation demands sacrifices. These are only temporary and apparent sacrifices as they are more than compensated for by the greater advantages which living within society provides.

However, in the very act of renouncing an expected pleasure, they are painful, and it is not for everybody to realize their later benefits and to behave accordingly. Socialists believes that education could make all people understand what their own interests require them to do; correctly brain-washed, they would of their own accord, always comply with the rules of conduct required for the preservation of society. The socialists contend that a social order in which nobody enjoys privileges at the expense of his fellow-citizens could exist without any compulsion and coercion for the prevention of action detrimental to society. Such an ideal society could do without state and government, i.e., without a police force, the social apparatus of coercion and compulsion.

The socialists overlook the undeniable fact that some people are either too narrow-minded or too weak to adjust themselves spontaneously to the conditions of social life. Even if we admit that every sane adult is endowed with the faculty of realizing the good of social cooperation and of acting accordingly, there still remains the problem of the infants, the aged, and the insane. Socialists believe that a person who acts antisocially should be considered mentally sick and in need of care. But as long as not all are cured, and as long as there are infants and the senile, some provision must be taken lest they jeopardize society. A Socialistic society would be exposed to the mercy of every individual. Society cannot exist if the majority is not ready to prevent, by the application or threat of violent action, minorities from destroying the social order. This power is vested in the state or government.

State or government is the social apparatus of compulsion and coercion. It has the monopoly of violent action. No individual is free to use violence or the threat of violence if the government has not accorded this right to him. The state is essentially an institution for the preservation of peaceful antihuman relations. However, for the preservation of peace it must be prepared to crush the onslaughts of peace-breakers. In order to do this, the Socialist State must ensure that its citizens are *stripped* of all means of defense. *No guns, clubs, knives, or other implements of defense shall be tolerated.*

Liberal social doctrine, based on the teachings of utilitarian ethics and economics, sees the problem of the relation between the government and those ruled from a different angle than universalism and collectivism. Liberalism (true meaning) realizes that the rulers, who are always a minority, cannot lastingly remain in office if not supported by the consent of the majority of those ruled. Whatever the system of government may be, the foundation upon which it is built and rests is always the opinion of those ruled that to obey and to be loyal to this government better serves their own interests than revolution and the establishment of another regime. The majority has the power to do away with an unpopular government and uses this power whenever it becomes convinced that its own well-being requires it.

Civil war and revolution are the means by which the discontented majorities overthrow rulers and methods of government which do not suit them. For the sake of domestic peace liberalism aims at democratic government. Democracy is therefore not a revolutionary institution. On the contrary, it is the very means of preventing revolutions and civil wars. It provides a method for the peaceful adjustment of government to the will of the majority. *When the men in office and their policies no longer please the majority of the nation, they will—in the next election—be eliminated and replaced by other men espousing different policies.* (This happen during the election in 2010.)

The principle of majority rule or government by the people as recommended by liberalism does not aim at the supremacy of the mean, of the lowbred, of the domestic barbarians. The liberals also believe that a nation should be ruled by those best fitted for this task. But they believe that a man's ability to rule proves itself better by convincing his fellow-citizens than by using force upon them. There is, of course, no guarantee that the voters will entrust office to the most competent candidate. But no other system could offer such a guarantee. *If the majority of the nation is committed to unsound principles and prefers unworthy office-seekers, there is no remedy other than to try to change their mind by expounding more reasonable principles and recommending better men. A minority will never win lasting success by other means.*

Universalism and collectivism cannot accept this democratic solution of the problem of government. In their opinion the individual in complying with the ethical code does not directly further his earthly concerns but foregoes the attainment of his own ends for the benefit of the designs of the Deity or of the collective whole. Moreover reason alone is not capable of conceiving the supremacy of the absolute values and the unconditional validity of the sacred law and of interpreting correctly the canons and commandments. Thus, it is in their eyes a hopeless task to try to convince the majority through persuasion and to lead them to righteousness by peaceful means. Those blessed by heavenly inspiration, to whom their *charisma* has conveyed illumination, have the duty to propagate the gospel to the docile and to resort to violence against the inflexible. The charismatic leader is the Deity's vicar, the director of the collective whole, the tool of history. He is infallible and always right. His orders are the supreme norm.

Universalism and collectivism are by necessity systems of theocratic government. The common characteristic of all their varieties is that they expound the existence of a superhuman entity which the individuals are bound to obey. What differentiates them from one another is only the name they give to this entity and the content of the laws they proclaim in its name. The dictatorial rule of a minority cannot find any legitimacy other than the appeal to an alleged mandate obtained from a superhuman absolute authority. It does not matter whether the autocrat bases his claims on the divine rights of anointed kings or on the historical mission of the vanguard of the proletariat. The terms society and state as they are used by the contemporary advocates of socialism, planning, and social control of all the activities of individuals signify a deity. The priests of this new creed ascribe to their idol all those attributes which the theologians ascribe to God—omnipotence, omniscience, infinite goodness, and so on.

If one assumes that there exists above and beyond the individual's actions an imperishable entity aiming at its own ends, different from those of mortal men, one has already constructed the concept of a superhuman being. Then one cannot evade the question whose ends take precedence whenever an antagonism arises, those of the state or society or those of the individual. The answer to this question is already implied in the very concept of state or society as conceived by collectivism and universalism. If one postulates the existence of an entity which by definition is higher, nobler, and better than the individuals, then there cannot be any doubt that the aims of this eminent being must tower above those of the wretched individuals. If society or state is an entity endowed with determination and intention and all the other qualities attributed to it by the collectivist doctrine, then it is simply nonsensical to set the shabby individual's trivial aims against its lofty designs.

The quasi-theological character of all socialist doctrines

61

becomes appparent in their mutual conflicts. A collectivist doctrine does not assert the superiority of a collective whole; it always proclaims the eminence of a definite collectivist idol, and either flatly denies the existence of other such idols or relegates them to a subordinate and lower position with regard to its own idol. The worshipers of the state proclaim the excellence of a definite state, i.e., their own; the nationalists, the excellence of their own nation. If dissenters challenge their particular program by heralding the superiority of another collectivist idol, they resort to no objection other than to declare again and again: we are right because an inner voice tells us that we are right and you are wrong. The conflicts of antagonistic collectivist creeds and sects cannot be decided by reasoning; they must be decided by arms. The alternatives to the liberal and democratic principle of majority rule are the militarist principles of armed conflict and dictatorial oppression.

All varieties of collectivist creeds are united in their implacable hostility to the fundamental political institutions of the liberal system: majority rule, tolerance of dissenting views, freedom of thought, speech, and the press, equality of all men under the law. This collaboration of collectivist creeds in their attempts to destroy freedom has brought about the mistaken belief that the issue in present-day political antagonisms is individualism versus collectivism. In fact it is a struggle between individualism on the one hand and a multitude of collectivist sects on the other hand whose mutual hatred and hostility is no less ferocious than their abomination of the liberal system.

It is not a uniform Marxian sect that attacks capitalism, but a host of Marxian groups. These groups—for instance, Stalinists, Trotskyists, Mensheviks, supporters of the Second International, and so on—fight one another with the utmost brutality and inhumanity. And then there are again many other non-Marxian sects which apply the same atrocious methods in their mutual struggles. A substitution of collectivism for liberalism would result in endless bloody fighting. A good example is the United States of America. Today, it is blacks against Mexicans; Mexicans against whites; women against men; homosexuals against the church; drug users against anti-drug advocates; etc., etc., etc. The list goes on and on.

The customary terminology misrepresents these things entirely. The philosophy commonly called individualism is a philosophy of social cooperation and the progressive intensification of the social connection. On the other hand the application of the basic ideas of collectivism cannot result in anything but social disintegration and the perpetuation of armed conflict. It is true that every variety of collectivism promises eternal peace—starting with the day of its own decisive victory and the final overthrow and death of all other ideologies and their supporters.

However, the realization of these plans is conditioned upon a radical transformation in mankind. Men must be divided into two classes: the omnipotent godlike dictator on the one hand and the masses which must surrender freedom of choice and reasoning in order to become mere slaves in the plans of the dictator. The masses must be dehumanized in order to make one man their godlike master. Thinking and acting, the foremost characteristics of man as man, would become the privilege of *one* man only. There is no need to point out that such designs are unrealizable. The succession of empires of dictators are doomed to failure; they have never lasted longer than a few years. We have just witnessed the breakdown of several of such "millennial" orders, such as Hitler, Mussolini, etc. Those remaining will hardly fare better.

The modern revival of the idea of socialism, the main cause of all the agonies and disasters of our day, has succeeded so thoroughly that it has shoved into oblivion the essential ideas of liberal social philosophy. Today many of those favoring democratic institutions ignore these ideas. *The arguments they give for the justification of freedom and democracy are tainted with collectivist errors; their doctrines are rather a distortion than an endorsement of true liberalism. In their eyes, majorities are always right simply because they have the power to crush any opposition; majority rule is the dictatorial rule of the most numerous party, and the ruling majority is not bound to restrain itself in the exercise of its power and in the conduct of political affairs.* As soon as a faction has succeeded in winning the support of the majority of citizens and thereby attained control of the government machine, it is free to deny to the minority all those democratic rights by means of which it itself has previously carried on its own struggle for supremacy. A good example today, is President Obama and the Democrats in Congress nationalizing the Health Industry over the objection of the majority of the people.

This neo-liberalism is, of course, the very antithesis of the liberal doctrine. The true liberals do not maintain that majorities are godlike and infallible; they do not contend that the mere fact that a policy is advocated by the many is a proof of its merits for the common good. They do not recommend the dictatorship of the majority and the violent oppression of dissenting minorities. Liberalism aims at a political constitution which safeguards the smooth working of social cooperation and the progressive intensification of mutual social relations. Its main objective is the avoidance of violent conflicts, of wars and revolutions that must disintegrate the social collaboration of men and throw people back into the primitive conditions of barbarism where all tribes and political bodies endlessly fought one another. Because the division of labor requires undisturbed peace, Liberalism aims at the establishment of a system of government that is likely to preserve peace and democracy.

Liberalism, in its nineteenth-century sense, is a political doctrine. It is not a theory, but an application of the theories developed by the study of human action and especially by economics to definite problems of human action within society.

As a political doctrine, Liberalism is not neutral with regard to values and the ultimate ends sought by action. It assumes that all men or at least the majority of people are intent upon attaining certain goals. It gives them information about the means suitable to the realization of their plans. The champions of liberal doctrines are fully aware of the fact that their teachings are valid only for people who are committed to these principles.

While languages, and therefore economics too, use the terms

happiness and removal of uneasiness in a purely formal sense, Liberalism attaches to them a concrete meaning. It presupposes that people prefer life to death, health to sickness, nourishment to starvation, abundance to poverty. It teaches man how to act in accordance with these valuations. It is customary to call these concerns materialistic and to charge Liberalism with an alleged crude materialism and a neglect of the "higher" and "nobler" pursuits of mankind. Man does not live by bread alone, say the critics, and they disparage the meanness and despicable baseness of the utilitarian philosophy. However, these passionate diatribes are wrong because they badly distort the teachings of Liberalism.

Firstly: The Liberals do not assert that men ought to strive after the goals mentioned above. What they maintain is that the immense majority prefer a life of health and abundance to misery, starvation, and death. The correctness of this statement cannot be challenged. It is proved by the fact that all anti-liberal doctrines—the theocratic tenets of the various religious, nationalist, and socialist parties—adopt the same attitude with regard to these issues. They all promise their followers a life of plenty. They have never ventured to tell people that the realization of their program will impair their material wellbeing. They insist—on the contrary—that while the realization of the plans of their rival parties will result in impoverishment for the majority, they themselves want to provide their supporters with abundance. (Take a look at the pay of the average worker compared to the bloated federal workers pay!) The Christian parties are no less eager in promising the masses a higher standard of living than the nationalists and the socialists. Present-day churches often speak more about raising wage rates and farm incomes than about the dogmas of the Christian doctrine.

Secondly: The Liberals do not disdain the intellectual and spiritual aspirations of man. On the contrary, they are prompted by a passionate fervor for intellectual and moral perfection, for wisdom and for aesthetic excellence. But their view of these high and noble things is far from the crude representations of their adversaries. They do not share the naive opinion that any system of social organization can directly succeed in encouraging philosophical or scientific thinking, in producing masterpieces of art and literature and in rendering the masses more enlightened. They realize that all that society can achieve in these fields is to provide an environment which does not put insurmountable obstacles in the way of the genius and makes the common man free enough from material concerns to become interested in things other than mere breadwinning. In their opinion the foremost social means of making man more human is to fight poverty. Wisdom and science and the arts thrive better in a world of affluence than among needy peoples.

It is a distortion of facts to blame the age of Liberalism for an alleged materialism. The nineteenth century was not only a century of unprecedented improvement in technical methods of production and in the material wellbeing of the masses. It did much more than extend the average length of human life. Its scientific and artistic accomplishments are imperishable. It was an age of immortal musicians, writers, poets, painters, and sculptors; it revolutionized philosophy, economics, mathematics, physics, chemistry, and biology. And, for the first time in history, it made the great works and the great thoughts accessible to the common man.

Liberalism is based upon a purely rational and scientific theory of social cooperation. The policies it recommends are the application of a system of knowledge which does not refer in any way to sentiments, intuitive creeds for which no logically sufficient proof can be provided, mystical experiences, and the personal awareness of superhuman phenomena. In this sense the often misunderstood and erroneously interpreted epithets atheistic and agnostic can be attributed to it. It would be a serious mistake to conclude that the sciences of human action and the policy derived from their teachings, Liberalism, are anti-theistic and hostile to religion. They are radically opposed to all systems of theocracy. But they are entirely neutral with regard to religious beliefs which do not pretend to interfere with the conduct of social, political, and economic affairs.

Theocracy is a social system which lays claim to a superhuman title for its legitimacy. The fundamental law of a theocratic regime is an insight not open to examination by reason and to demonstration by logical methods. Its ultimate standard is intuition providing the mind with subjective certainty about things which cannot be conceived by reason and rationalization. If this intuition refers to one of the traditional systems of teaching concerning the existence of a Divine Creator and Ruler of the universe, we call it a religious belief. If it refers to another system we call it a metaphysical belief.

Thus a system of theocratic government need not be founded on one of the great historical religions of the world. It may be the outcome of metaphysical tenets which reject all traditional churches and denominations and take pride in emphasizing their anti-theistic and anti-metaphysical character. Today, the most powerful theocratic parties are opposed to Christianity and to all other religions which evolved from Jewish monotheism. What characterizes them as theocratic is their craving to organize the earthly affairs of mankind according to the contents of a complex of ideas whose validity cannot be demonstrated by reasoning. They pretend that their leaders are blessed by a knowledge inaccessible to the rest of mankind and contrary to the ideas maintained by those to whom the charisma is denied. The charismatic leaders have been entrusted by a mystical higher power with the office of managing the affairs of erring mankind. They alone are enlightened; all other people are either blind and deaf or malefactors.

It is a fact that many varieties of the great historical religions were affected by theocratic tendencies. Their apostles were inspired by a craving for power and the oppression and annihilation of all dissenting groups. However, we must not confuse the two things, religion and theocracy.

William James calls religious "the feelings, acts and experiences of individual men in their solitude, so far as they apprehend themselves to stand in relation to whatever they may consider the divine." He enumerates the following beliefs as the characteristics of the religious life: that the visible world is part of a more spiritual universe from which it draws its chief significance; that union or harmonious relation with that higher universe is our true end;

that prayer or inner communion with the spirit thereof—be that spirit "God" or law"—is a process wherein work is really done, and spiritual energy flows in and produces effects, psychological or material, within the phenomenal world. Religion, James goes on to say, also includes the following psychological characteristics: a zeal which adds itself like a gift to life, and takes the form either of lyrical enchantment or of appeal to earnestness and heroism, and furthermore an assurance of safety and a temper of peace, and, in relation to others, a preponderance of loving affection.

This characterization of mankind's religious experience and feelings does not make any reference to the arrangement of social cooperation. Religion, as James sees it, is a purely personal and individual relation between man and a holy, mysterious, and awe-inspiring divine Reality. It places upon man a certain mode of individual conduct. But it does not assert anything with regard to the problems of social organization. St. Francis d'Assisi, the greatest religious genius of the West, did not concern himself with politics and economics. He wanted to teach his disciples how to live piously; he did not draft a plan for the organization of production and did not urge his followers to resort to violence against dissenters. He is not responsible for the interpretation of his teachings by the order he founded.

Liberalism puts no obstacles in the way of a man eager to adjust his personal conduct and his private affairs according to the mode in which he individually or his church or denomination interprets the teachings of the Gospels. But it is radically opposed to all endeavors to silence the rational discussion of problems of social welfare by an appeal to religious intuition and revelation. It does not enjoin divorce or the practice of birth control upon anybody. But it fights those who want to prevent other people from freely discussing the pros and cons of these matters.

In the Liberal opinion, the aim of the moral law is to impel individuals to adjust their conduct to the requirements of life in society, to abstain from all acts detrimental to the preservation of peaceful social cooperation and to the improvement of human relations. Liberals welcome the support which religious teachings may give to those moral precepts of which they themselves approve, but they are opposed to all those norms which are bound to bring about social disintegration from whatever source they may originate..

It is a distortion of fact to say, as many champions of religious theocracy do, that Liberalism fights religion. Where the principle of church interference with secular issues is in force, the various churches, denominations and sects are fighting one another. By separating church and state, Liberalism establishes peace between the various religious factions and gives to each of them the opportunity to preach its gospel unmolested.

Liberalism is rationalistic. It maintains that it is possible to convince the immense majority that peaceful cooperation within the framework of society better serves their rightly understood interests than mutual battling and social disintegration. It has full confidence in man's reason. It may be that this optimism is unfounded and that the Liberals have erred. But then there is no hope left for mankind's future.

It will take some time and a lot of people to reverse the neo-Liberals damage to the English Language. They—the neo-Liberals— are good at lying and today even they themselves cannot distinguish the truth from the lie.

Today, a new movement is coming to life and growing by leaps and bounds. It is frightening to the neo-Progressives because the goals of the Tea-Party people is conservative in nature. The new Tea-Party members are from the Democratic Party, Republican Party and the Unaffiliated voters. Everything that they stand for: a balanced budget, smaller government, lower taxes, States rights and national security are completely anti-Obama's concepts of big government, big debt, more government interference with the average working man's life and reducing the effectiveness of our military.

Most of the media are spreading false information about the Tea-Party's goals. Instead of reporting about the main body of Tea-Party groups that descend on the Capital to show their concerns about a runaway government. Anti-Tea Party organizations implant some rowdy gangs of hoodlums to try to cause riots or carry signs that are vulgar to give the Tea-Party a bad name. The media only shows these hoodlums and their actions to the American public so that the public will get a bad impression of the Tea-Party as a whole. Typical union action—destroy by character assassination and intimidation. Everyday, more and more people are turning a deaf ear to mass media tirades and going to the few free stations and internet for their news. The so called free press has been bought and paid for by the one-world crowd and therefore, no one will ever hear the truth from them in the future.

Chapter 4

Communism—The Vehicle to One World Government

The idea was that those who direct the overall conspiracy could use the differences in those two so-called ideologies [marxism/fascism/ socialism v. democracy/capitalism] to enable them [the Illuminati] to divide larger and larger portions of the human race into opposing camps so that they could be armed and then brainwashed into fighting and destroying each other."   *Myron Fagan*

The International Bankers endeavor to destroy the U.S. Government established under the U. S. Constitution was of vital necessity for them to rule the World under a One-World Government arrangement. Since they are well versed in establishing governments that enslave the people – people that rely upon the central Government for their livelihood—Communism was their vehicle of choice. They can control the Government through bribes, money, or fear but control of the masses is much more than they can handle. Thus slavery suits their fancy.

Among Communists there is also a view that there is a stage of "socialism" that a society would pass through prior to becoming a communist society. "This transitional stage of socialism, which could perhaps be referred to as Marxist socialism, was an ideology that was developed by Communists as a means to achieve communism. That does not mean that all forms of "socialism" have that objective, in fact only Marxist socialism does, and for the most part Marxists were opposed to all forms of socialism other than their own.

Marxist socialism is, in theory, what was being practiced by all of the countries that we call "Communist". The objective of Marxist socialism is to use the State to prepare society for communism by communalizing all of the productive forces of the society, i.e. by making all of the means of production public property. The policies and procedures of the Soviet Union were not seen as policy of an "end result", but rather as part of a process. The policies of the Soviet Union were seen as steps in a plan to achieve an end result.

The Communist Party evolved out of The International Working Man's Association, which later became the Comintern, or Communist International. The Communist Party was the first truly international major political party. The goal of the Communists was ultimately to put an end to all exploitation, stop imperialism, bring working class people into political power all around the world, stop all war, and create a single unified global community where all people in the world were equal with equal rights in a global democratic society where everyone shared everything. In a nutshell, that's what it was all about."

Thus the selection by the financial cabal of communism as its vehicle to success.

At the start of the twentieth century, we have seen how the Illuminati infiltrated the Government and took over the task of destroying the Constitutions and the Rights given by it to the citizens. The Federal Reserve System, The Income Tax, Formation of the United Nations, etc. were all part of the overall design to set up a socialist style dictatorship to enslave the people. The Illuminati had a built in coconspirator in the Communist Party which they supplied financing and manpower to survive.

The biggest disaster occurred when the President of the United States deliberately destroyed the Constitution by installing 'activist' judges to the Supreme Court. It is a shame—no a crime—that there is no one or even a group of individuals in our current government who will take a stand to defend the one document that stands for freedom throughout the world. The Constitution! Even the press has lost its desire for the truth. Why?

Could it be that those who speak so highly of freedom are really traitors riding in the belly of a Trojan gift horse to get into positions of authority so that they can destroy the one document that was added to our Constitution to ensure freedom for one and all? The Bill of Rights was inserted after the Constitution was signed to insure that ***no federal government*** would have the power to enslave the people. The responsibilities of the Executive Branch, the Legislative Branch, and the Judicial Branch of Government were clearly stated in the Constitution, yet there were those wise men who insisted that man was fallible and could not be trusted to do what was proper when only a hand shake was given. Therefore, they insisted that a Bill of Rights be added so that no despotic branch of Government would disregard the Constitution limitations and enslave the people. The Bill of Rights—the first Amendments to the Constitution—were chiseled in stone (in THEIR minds) so as to prevent the power-hungry politicians and bureaucrats from taking over the lives of the citizenry.

In the 1930 era, when President Roosevelt came into office, he surrounded himself with Communist sympathizers and members of the Council on Foreign Relations. The President's advisors were followers of the Keynes Theory on Economics.

In Keynes's theory, some micro-level actions of individuals and firms can lead to aggregate macroeconomic outcomes in which the economy operates below its potential output and growth. Many classical economists had believed in Say's Law, that supply creates its own demand, so that a "general glut" would therefore be impossible. Keynes contended that aggregate demand for goods might be insufficient during economic downturns, leading to unnecessarily high unemployment and losses of potential output. Keynes argued that government policies could be used to increase aggregate demand, thus increasing economic activity and reducing high unemployment and deflation.

Keynes argued that the solution to depression was to stimulate the economy ("inducement to invest") through some combination of two approaches :

1. A reduction in interest rates.

2. Government investment in infrastructure—the injection of income results in more spending in the general economy, which
in turn stimulates more production and investment involving still more income and spending and so forth. The initial
stimulation starts a cascade of events, whose total increase in
economic activity is a multiple of the original investment.

A central conclusion of Keynesian economics is that in some
situations, no strong automatic mechanism moves output and
employment towards full employment levels. This conclusion
conflicts with economic approaches that assume a general tendency
towards an equilibrium.

Keynes sought to develop a theory that would explain
determinants of saving, consumption, investment and production.
In that theory, the interaction of aggregate demand and aggregate
supply determines the level of output and employment in the
economy. Because of what he considered the failure of the "Classical
Theory" in the 1930s, Keynes firmly objects to its main theory--
adjustments in prices would automatically make demand tend to
the full employment level.

Keynes's theory suggested that active government policy
could be effective in managing the economy. Rather than seeing
unbalanced government budgets as wrong, Keynes advocated
what has been called countercyclical fiscal policies, that is policies
which acted against the tide of the business cycle: deficit spending
when a nation's economy suffers from recession or when recovery
is long-delayed and unemployment is persistently high—and the
suppression of inflation in boom times by either increasing taxes or
cutting back on government outlays. He argued that governments
should solve problems in the short run rather than waiting for
market forces to do it in the long run, because "in the long run, we
are all dead."

There were other areas in Keynes Theory which where
completely anti-capitalistic.Keynesians and redistributionists tend
to associate with each other. Keynes, in the twenties, wrote about
a hydro-electric project. In his opinion it would have been better if
the rewards of the project had gone to the worker-builders rather

than to the investors who had financed the project. Keynesians believe that fiscal policy should be directed towards the lower-income segment of the population, because that segment is more likely to spend the money, contributing to demand, than to save it.

Keynesian ideas were criticized by Austrian economist and philosopher Friedrich Hayek. Hayek's most famous work *The Road to Serfdom,* was written in 1944. Hayek taught at the London School of Economics from 1931 to 1950. Hayek criticized Keynesian economic policies for what he called their fundamentally collectivist approach, arguing that such theories, no matter their presumptively utilitarian intentions, require centralized planning, which Hayek argued leads to totalitarian abuses. Keynes seems to have noted this concern, since, in the foreword to the German version of the 'The General Theory of Employment Interest and Money', he declared that "the theory of aggregated production, which is the point of ['The General Theory of Employment Interest and Money'], nevertheless can be much easier adapted to the conditions of a totalitarian state [eines totalen Staates] than the theory of production and distribution of a given production put forth under conditions of free competition and a large degree of laissez-faire."

Another criticism leveled by Hayek against Keynes was that the study of the economy by the relations between aggregates is fallacious, and that recessions are caused by micro-economic factors. Hayek claimed that what starts as temporary governmental fixes usually become permanent and expanding government programs, which stifle the private sector and civil society. Keynes himself described the critique as "deeply moving", which was quoted on the cover of the Road to Serfdom.

There were numerous criticisms about Keynes Theory. Keynes answered them all but had to admit that his theory would only work in an environment that had a strong dictatorial style government. This admission did not come until after the Roosevelt fiasco. He also did not admit this short-coming to the world. (He did admit to it in an added prefix to the German version of his Theory on Economics.)

Although Roosevelt passed many new laws, referred to as The National Recovery Act, the people reacted adversely to them. For example:

Under the NRA, the federal government set up code authorities (in Fascist Italy they were called corporatives) which made rules and regulations for the governing of each phase of each and every industry. The purpose was to regulate hours, wages, working conditions, trade practices, prices, and everything else that could be thought up by the fertile mind of a government beauracrat. In the code set up for live-poultry business in and around metropolitan New York City one rule provided that diseased and uninspected poultry could not be sold. The NRA cracked down on a certain poultry dealer, A.L.A. Schechter, for violating its rules and convicted him—with a fine and a jail sentence. This incident was matched by many others during those hectic days of the Blue Eagle—the symbol of compliance with NRA directives. One man was arrested, indicted, put in jail for several days, and then required to put up bond for violating a law that didn't exist. A little tailor gained momentary fame when he was sent to jail for pressing a pair of pants for 35 cents—five cents below the code minimum of 40 cents. But the NRA involved a great deal more than price-cutting pants pressers and egg-bound chickens. It was a clumsy attempt to hand over to the federal bureaucrats limitless power over every phase of our economic life.

All nine justices of the Supreme Court joined unanimosely in declaring the NRA unconstitutional. Chief Justice Hughes, speaking for the entire Court, declared: "We think the code-making authority this conferred on the President is an unconstitutional delegation of legislative power." And Justice Cardozo added, "This is delegation running riot."

President Roosevelt was angry. He began to vilify the Court and its members. He spoke sneeringly of them as a "horse-and-buggy court." This vilification—personified in the derisive phrase "the nine old men"—was taken up and expanded in the press, in magazines, and on the radio by the New Deal cohorts and the growing advocates in high places of the socialist revolution. Those advocates saw with clarity that America could never be turned into a centrally dominated collectivist society so long as the Constitution stood as the supreme law of the land and the judges of the Supreme Court interpreted it according to its intended meaning.

Immediately following President Roosevelt's second inauguration, one of his first acts was to launch an all-out attack on the Supreme Court. He demanded of Congress a law by which he might be allowed to appoint a new judge to the Court for every judge then sitting who was 70 years of age or more and thus bring the membership of the Court from nine to 15. This would have allowed Roosevelt to appoint six New Deal justices to nullify the votes on the Court of six sitting judges who were 70 years or older. In this way he could get his unconstitutional New Deal schemes declared valid. This was the famous "court packing" plan. The Congress, although heavily Democratic, would not go along with this scheme.

In the end, Roosevelt won out because he was able to force most of the Supreme Court members to resign. This left him in position to pack the court with his selected henchmen. By the time America entered the Second World War in 1941, there remained on the Supreme Court only two judges who had not been named by President Roosevelt. They were Justices Stone and Roberts—and Justice Stone owed his appointment as Chief Justice to the President. In the pre-war and war years this packed Court proceeded to perform a major operation on the Constitution of the United States by removing many of its vital organs. Succeeding justices named by President Truman, and particularly by President Eisenhower, about completed the job—so much so that we might say that the body of the Constitution remains but only as a mere shell, devoid of arteries, veins, heart and lungs.

You really could not condemn President Truman or President Eisenhower for their selections, because, in their time, the procedure for appointing members of the Court was that the American Bar Association would select the names of three or four Justices and give that list to the President. The President, in turn, would select one of the Judges and submit his name to the Senate for confirmation. In this manner, it was the ABA who loaded the Supreme Court with activist judges. (Remember, it was the English organization of The Round Table that established the ABA in many countries through out the world in their quest for a One-World Government.) Someone later asked Eisenhower if he made any mistakes as President. "Yes two," he replied. "And they are both sitting on the Supreme Court." Eisenhower was referring to Earl Warren and William Brennan, but his biggest mistake in picking Justices came in his fourth nomination. Stanley Reed retired in 1957, opening a seat that could be filled without political considerations. Eisenhower replaced Reed with Charles Whittaker who had practice corporate law in Kansas City for 30 years, and who came to the Court after three years on the federal appellate bench. Whittaker proved absolutely incompetent for his new job. He developed writers block and produce no opinions of any significance. Whittaker retired in 1962 and was rated by scholars as a judicial failure.

There is only one legal way in which the Constitution can be changed—by amendment initiated by the sovereign states or by the Congress and concurred in by three fourths of the states. The nine Supreme Court judges simply usurped and tore to pieces the charter of freedom of the American people. In reality, under the majority rule, it only requires five activist Justices to destroy the Constitution. They did this treasonable work by redefining the meaning of certain word or phrases thus turning the Constitution and previously enacted laws into entirely different meanings. This was MAKING NEW LAWS which they had no authority to do under the original Constitution.

This is treason and they should have been impeached. Impeach in the same fashion as others who were found guilty of treason. They should be stripped of all their possessions and sent to prison for life with no possibility of parole. They should be placed on a ship like another traitor (Philip Nolan—A Man without A Country) of this country and sent out to sea—to never again be able to set foot on the U.S.A. The ship should have a number of cabins because there are more than one Judge who should be impeached. Where is Congress when you need them?

More of President Roosevelt's Court activism:

In farming and agriculture, the Court made possible that myriad of bureaus and bureaucracy which had neatly returned the once free and independent American farmer to European serfdom. The Court has made possible for the central government to take billions upon billions of dollars from the American taxpayers to pay to farmers in order to keep prices of farm products high to those same taxpayers. The government accomplished this by giving bureaucrats the power to fine farmers who produce more than the government say they can produce. In industry, with the blessing of the Court, the federal bureaucrats swarm all over what was known as "free enterprise," telling industries whom, when, where, and how to hire and fire and for what it must sell its products. The bureaucrats do this legally through laws such as The Equal Opportunity Act, The Taft-Hartley Act and so many other laws that it would take a separate tome to list.

One cannot trust judges on what they say because their actions are usually different. Some judges refer to this change of action as the result of time. Things changes. But this is ridiculous. The Constitution does not change (unless it is amended). So how can 'things' change? For example: In the late 1930s, when the vast body of federal law was much smaller and less intrusive, Judge Robert Jackson identified the growing threat to liberty: "With the law books filled with a great assortment of crimes, a prosecutor stands a fair chance of finding at least a technical violation of some act on the part of almost anyone;' However, when the Judge became a member of the Supreme Court he took it upon himself to rewrite the Constitution and thought nothing of it. He did it as follows:

In 1942, the Court used Wickard v. Filburn Case to expand the Interstate Commerce Clause for that very purpose. Roscoe Filburn owned and operated a small dairy farm in Ohio. Every year he would use a section of his land to grow wheat. A portion of the wheat was sold, a portion was fed to livestock (which were also sold), a portion was used to make flour, and the rest was used for seeding the following year. In every respect, Filburn's sale or use of his wheat occurred within the state of Ohio. In 1941, Filburn was assessed a penalty of $117.11 for exceeding the marketing quota established for his farm. It was part of the federal Agricultural Adjustment Act of 1938. Filburn challenged the penalty in court and the case reached the Supreme Court. Incredibly, Justice Robert Jackson, writing for a unanimous Court, ruled that Congress could regulate the amount of wheat that a farmer grew on his farm. The Court reasoned that Filburn's wheat affected interstate commerce-even though none of it ever left the state of Ohio. The Court's rationale was that: (1) Filburn grew excess wheat on his farm, as determined by a marketing quota established by the federal Agricultural Adjustment Act of 1938; (2) Filburn used that excess wheat to feed his livestock; (3) because of the excess wheat, Filburn would not have to purchase wheat on the open market; (4) by not purchasing wheat on the open market, Filburn was affecting interstate commerce. The Court wrote:

It can hardly be denied that a factor of such volume and variability as home-consumed wheat would have a substantial influence on price and market conditions. This may arise because being in marketable condition such wheat overhangs the market and if induced by rising prices tends to flow into the market and check price increases. But if we assume that it is never marketed, it supplies a need of the man who grew it which would otherwise be reflected by purchases in the open market. Home-grown wheat in this sense competes with wheat in commerce. The stimulation of commerce is a use of the regulatory function quite as definitely as prohibitions or restrictions thereon.

As one Professor of Law wrote, "that decision cannot pass even the 'giggle' test under its logic. However it does show the caliber of judges we now have on the Federal benches.

With the appointment of the new judges by President Roosevelt from 1937 on, the socialist revolutionaries in America had what they needed—a Supreme Court which would ignore the rights of the states and set up the central government in Washington as the all-powerful element in American life.

The justices went about their demolition job on the Constitution in the manner characteristic of the past European revolutionaries. They simply changed the meaning of a few words and phrases which had been formerly understood—and interpreted by Supreme Courts for over 150 years. The diabolical cunning involved in this usurpation by the judges of the 'rights of states and citizens' is easily illustrated.

The destruction of the rights of the states was the primary objective because in no other way could a collectivist (progressive) society be imposed on America. In 1942, in the midst of our first year of fighting the Second World War, when nobody was paying much attention to the Supreme Court, Justice Frankfurter struck a major blow for the Constitution wreckers. He, like Justice Jackson, did it by twisting out of all recognition one little phrase in the Constitution which gives the federal government power over "interstate commerce."

The Constitution gave Congress the right to regulate trade which crossed state lines. That trade, and that alone, came within the regulatory power of the federal government, and it had been so held by innumerable Supreme Courts. But this did not suit Justice Frankfurter and his revolutionary cohorts on the court. He cooked up a brand-new decision (A.B. Kirschbaum v. Walling)—with no precedent in law or fact—by which the federal government might intrude into purely state functions. One of the tenants of a loft building in a New Jersey town was a clothing manufacturer who sold most of his products in other states. He was, clearly, in interstate commerce and thus subject to federal regulation.

But Justice Frankfurter DECLARED that the building—inside a town inside the sovereign state of New Jersey—was also engaged in interstate commerce because that one tenant, among many others, was engaged in interstate commerce. And that wasn't all. By means of his judicial "reasoning," Justice Frankfurter went further, saying that, because the building was in interstate commerce, so was the elevator man, who ran the elevator up and down in the building, and the women who washed the windows! By this decision, Justice Frankfurter and his co-conspirators, destroyed the 10th Amendment to the Constitution. To this day there are judges on the Supreme Court that will do all in their power to protect this abominable decision. **President Obama has force his Health Care Plan upon the taxpayers by using this same interpretation of 'Interstate Commerce.'**

Since Roosevelt, the attacks on the individual Amendments of the Bill of Rights and those amendment that followed, have been unrelenting. The socialist judges sitting on their federal benches know full well they have nothing to fear when they make rulings that change the intent of the Constitution. There are enough socialists in Congress to block any impeachment proceedings against them. So whenever the occassion arises they produce new meanings to a word or phrase in the Constitution to further the Socialist agenda of a one world government. It matters not if the Supreme Court rejects their interpretations. They know that sooner or later, the Democrats in the Senate will pack the Supreme Court with Socialists who will back their interpretations.

A simple example of how this scheme (reinterpreting the meaning of words) works can be demonstrated by the following:

> *"In a case of a law that was brought before the Federal Court in California concerning the right of citizens to bear arms under the Second Amendment to the U.S. Constitution. The case was about citizens owning guns for protection in their own homes. The State wanted to eliminate guns in the State of California. The Federal Judge ruled that they could do that because the Second Amendment granted the right to own arms only to the militia, which he defined as "State Police" and "National Guard."*

This decision by the Judge shows either his ignorance or his attempt at destroying the Second Amendment to the Bill of Rights. At the time the Constitution was written there were no "State Police' or 'National Guard". The citizens of every burg, town or colony were the militia. Every one had his rifle for protection against Indian attacks, hoodlum, and yes even other states. It was a way of life. The 'Citizens' are the militia under the Constitution, but there are Judges who by interpretation will change the Bill of Rights. Thus, destroying the Constitution.

During research on these Judges who interpret the law to favor their socialist, one-world agenda, I remember a book that I read few years ago. The book, *Good and Bad English,* by Wilfred Whitten (John O' London) and Frank Whitaker, 1939; London, England was a Guide to Speaking and Writing. It was a very enlightening book that covered such topics as split adverbs, split infinitives, etc. But a lot of time was devoted to words and how, over time, their meanings changed from the original to what they are today. This tactic of changing the meaning of words and thereby changing the meanings of law is a great boon to so-called 'activist' Judges. This method of altering laws and particularly the Constitution is nothing more than treason. Another example follows.

Another word that these same 'activist' Judges use to destroy the Constitution is the word 'welfare'. There are a number of definitions in the new dictionaries but back in the 1750 era there was only one **NOUN** definition of the word welfare.

welfare: (ME. fr. The phrase *wel faren* to fare well) **(n)** 1: the state of doing well esp. in respect to good fortune, happiness , well being, or prosperity.

Another current definition of welfare in the dictionary:

welfare: **(adj)** 1. Of, relating to, or concerned with welfare and esp. with improvement of the welfare of disadvantage social groups. 2: receiving public welfare benefits.

Article I, section 8 of the Constitution states: 'Congress shall have the power To lay and collect Taxes, Duties, Imposts and Excises to pay the Debt and provide for the common Defense and general Welfare of the United States.......' For those Judges who either cannot read or have not read the Constitution, the term 'Welfare' in the Constitution is a **NOUN!**

Judges have completely warp the meaning of the word 'Welfare' to ESTABLISH a Socialistic State and destroy the Constitution—to install a strong dictatorial government that will control every aspect of a persons life. To raise taxes to create a 'Welfare State' and say they are soaking the rich, when in fact they are 'redistributing the wealth'. To the International Communists it is equalizing income. Those who earn more, pay more, to raise the level of income of those who through whatever reason cannot or will not work for their income. It's the communist's selling point "We are going to create a heaven on earth. Everyone will have a tree in his back yard so that any time he wants anything, all he has to do is reach up into the tree and pluck the fruit of his choice!" But on closer inspection one finds that the poor is not elevated out of poverty but it does bring down the so called 'rich' to the poverty level, thereby leveling the playing field. Once this staged is reached, those in power will be able to treat everyone like chattel—slaves.

Following the events of Sept. 11, 2001 Americans have been distracted by the government and the media into formulating a new enemy of our freedom. The corporate controlled news media has been complicit with the federal government in creating an illusion sure to win over most Americans. We are told, for example, that militant Islam has the goal of destroying freedom as we know it and goes by the names, Jihad, Hamas, terrorist, insurgent, Saddam Hussein, Al-Qaeda, bin Laden, al-Zawahiri, etc.

While those may indeed be enemies to our freedom... there is an even more sinister enemy at work within our borders intent on destroying our Constitution and eliminating the civil liberties of Americans and the redefining of justice. It's called: the Progressive Caucus, Homeland Security, multiculturalism, Hillary Clinton's "village", and has names like Ted Kennedy (former Senator), Charles Rangel, Jesse Jackson, Sarah Brady, and Bill Clinton, among others. It is Socialism and it's quickly spreading throughout America.

In this 21st Century new world order, the individual loses all rights and everything is done in the name of the commonwealth (public). You are officially the property of the state and not an individual with wants, desires, and needs. There is only the rich and the commonwealth. If you are not rich, then you are a member of the commonwealth. The needs and wants of the rich come before the needs and wants of the commonwealth. In the commonwealth there are no individuals and no one has any rights whatsoever. All decisions in your behalf are made by the state. Your children are the property of the state and it is decided by the state what they will learn, who will teach them, and what will become of them. As a parent, you have little or no say in what becomes of your children, all decisions are made by the government and you accept or you become an enemy of the state.

In the Progressives' vision for 21st Century America, the government owns and/or controls the basic means of production and distribution of services and goods. We are told that business and other things will be regulated but that we will still be free. Free to do what? They will operate under the illusion of a free enterprise system. All business and land, if not owned by the government or the rich, is controlled and taxed very heavily. What a contradiction of terms. How can anyone have a Socialist form of government with freedom? As stated, in a Socialist form of government the rich rule and have the power, not the people.

It is amazing to a great many of us how Congress ignores the Constitution. For example, the 13th Amendment clearly states: "Neither slavery nor involuntary servitude, except as a punishment for crime whereof the party shall have been duly convicted, shall exist within the United States or any place subject to their jurisdiction." Currently, the average working person pays over forty percent of his earnings to the Government (City, State and National) and IT IS NOT VOLUNTARY! Did the people vote for these taxes? NO! They were imposed by a Communist dominated Congress. Therefore, Congress has declared that each and every wage earner is a SLAVE of the Government and the Government has a right to steal their money. WHY?

Taxes and fees imposed by federal, state or local laws. These taxes were meant to enslaves the people and force them to work for the government with no possibility of any return!

- *Alternative Minimum Tax* (AMT)
- *U.S. capital gains tax*
- *Corporate income tax*
- *U.S. estate tax*
- *U.S. excise tax* (includes taxes on *cigarettes* and *alcoholic beverages*)

- *U.S. federal income tax*
- *Federal unemployment tax* (FUTA)
- *FICA tax* (includes *Social Security tax* and related programs)
- *Gasoline tax*
- *Generation Skipping Tax*
- *Gift tax*
- *IRS penalties*
- *Local income tax*
- *Luxury taxes*
- *Property tax*
- *Real estate tax*
- *Recreational vehicle tax*
- *Rental car tax*
- *Resort tax* (also known as Hotel/Motel tax, occupancy tax)
- *Road usage taxes* (Commercial Vehicle Operators)
- *Sales tax* and equivalent *use tax*
- *School tax*
- *State income tax*
- *State unemployment tax* (SUTA)
- *Tariffs*
- *Telephone federal excise tax*
- *Vehicle sales tax*
- *Workers compensation*

The cruelest tax of all is the U.S. Estate tax. This tax was a favorite of Senator Kennedy. His excuse was that the Government needed the money for their special socialist programs. Since the Kennedy fortune is safe from taxation why not steal from those entrepreneurs that through dint and effort build up a healthy estate? During the debate, the Republicans argued that the Estate (Death) Taxes were unfair. "We charge people income tax when they earn income. With what is left, they make investments, and then as those investments pay dividends or pay income, we tax that. Then we say, 'When you die, we want half of that asset;" Sen. Johnny Isakson, Georgia Republican said. "It is wrong. It is wrong for individuals, it is wrong for family, it is wrong for landowners, and is wrong for America." But according to Representative Pelosi it is only fair that the Government gets its share. Ms Pelosi's idea of fairness is a slap in the face to anyone who dares to think that he/she can earn a fortune through hard work and ingenuity. That path to a fortune is left to the politicians.

There are many hidden taxes which are too numerous to mention or even harder to find. For example, hidden in the Income tax is the tax on Social Security. That is correct! A person works all his life and 13 percent of his wages are sent to the Treasury Department as Social Security Payments required by The Social Security Act of 1935, as amended. The Act was sold to the American people as an Act to ensure that the elderly would be guaranteed an income when they retired. Most Social Security payers realized that the small Social Security payments that were their due when they retired would not be enough to live in decent retirement. So, many of them set up investment plans or investment accounts to supplement their retirement income. Then along came President Clinton, elected in 1992, with a majority of social Democrats in Congress, amended the income tax requirements for people drawing social security payments. Included in the Tax Form 1040 Instructions they inserted a new worksheet titled "Social Security Benefits Worksheet." In this worksheet, a person must compute all his income plus half of his Social Security payment received to determine if he/she must pay taxes on a portion of their Social Security. If you are single, head of a household, etc and your income (plus half you Social Security payments) exceeds $25,000 a year, you must add a certain amount of your Social Security payments to your total Income which is than tax again. This also applies to married couple making over $32,000. Thanks to President Clinton and the social Democrats who pushed this tax through, with little or no fanfare, in 1993, a person now must pay taxes on taxes that he has already paid. Do these taxes affect the President or Congress? Of course not.

Take President Clinton and his retirement, does he pay taxes on his income? Very little if any. How does this work for him? The first thing President Clinton did when he left office in 2001 was to establish a "William Clinton Foundation". This foundation is established to help the Serbs/Albanians in Europe who suffered greatly under Tito or whomever. The Foundation is a charitable organization which under law is a tax-free organization. Since 2001 former President Clinton has given more than 100 speeches (mostly overseas) to organizations that are controlled by the Bilderberg Group (see Chapter 6). He charges a fee of $1 million per speech. Does he pay any taxes on these fees? NO! Because the Bilderberg Group 'donates' the money to the William Clinton Foundation which is a tax free organization. Today, former President Clinton has over $100 million at his disposal all tax free. Now he is one of the rich and not a commoner. This is how the One World elite group reward their fair-hair players. It is rumored that he donates 50% of his Presidential salary retirement to the Foundation, thus he doesn't have to pay income taxes on that amount. Ingenious! Remember, former President Clinton was referred to as "Slick Willy' and you can believe it! He was a Rhodes Scholar, a member of the CFR, a member of the Bilderberg Group, etc.. He is a One-World member that believed the Constitution was just a piece of paper that outlived its usefulness.

It is no pipe dream about former President William Clinton's association with the one-worlders and their Communist connection. The following article was published in the English newspaper *World Net Daily* 4/30/99 by Joel A. Ruth:

".... On December 19, 1969, Bill Clinton had boarded an Aeroflot flight from London for the USSR to Moscow, the center of world atheism and the capital of the Soviet-Marxist state. William Jefferson Clinton's pilgrimage to the Soviet Union was the climax of a busy fall semester as a "Rhodes Scholar" at Oxford. It should perhaps be mentioned to those impressed by such presumed status that Rhodes Scholarships are granted to individuals passing ideological muster whose sentiments during the interview process are reflective of acceptable left-wing views to the selection committees, and not because of good grades..... "

"...While Bill Clinton has never explained who paid for his trip to Moscow, he was accompanied by a friend and fellow Oxford student, Czech Jan Kopold. They were to attend a meeting of the War Moratorium Committee to be held January 2, 1970. Upon arrival, Clinton did not check into a youth hostel, but rather stayed at the Hotel National, the most exclusive and expensive one in Moscow of that time—a ritzy place usually reserved for foreign ambassadors and high-level Communist Party apparatchiks.... Clinton has also never accounted for the 11 days spent in Moscow before the actual meeting of the War Moratorium and has never revealed who paid his expenses or what he did or who he met with during that time....."

"...Even more telling was Clinton's January 4 return trip from Moscow on another Aeroflot jet. The flight terminated in Prague, then the capital of the Czechoslovakian Soviet Socialist Republic (CSSR). There, Clinton was a guest of Jan Kopold's father, Bedrich Kopold and Jan's maternal grandmother Maria Svermova, who was the original founder of the Czech Communist Party in the 1930s...... The entire Kopold clan was a significant part of the ruling Communist party elite and was responsible for those murders and deportations either by the act or as formulators of policy.. ....Years later, when Clinton was President, he again flew to Moscow, this time on Air Force One, to meet Boris Yeltsin. Then, on his return flight he had the plane stop in Prague, where, besides playing the saxophone—important stuff—he went to visit the parents of his Oxford friend Jan Kopold. By then, Maria Svermova had died of old age. As for Jan Kopold, he had been killed earlier in an "accidental fall" in Turkey in 1970, becoming perhaps the first of a long string of former Clinton friends and associates to meet an untimely end. ....."

Apparently, Joel A. Ruth did not know that Bill Clinton's Moscow trip was paid for by the "Vietnam Committee for the Solidarity with the American People". This information can be found in federal district court (Mace vs Blunt, United States District Court, Western District of Missouri, Case #92-4484-CV-C-9. This information states that Clinton's trip to Moscow and his extended stay at the home of roommate from Oxford, Jan Kopold, was paid for by the "Vietnam Committee for Solidarity with the American

People." According to federal documents, the VCSAP was an orgainization established in 1967 by the National Liberation Front and its North Vietnam allies "to collect and organize pacifists and war dissenters to assist their efforts against the U.S. imperialist war of aggression in Vietnam." Chairman of the VCSAP was Hoang Minh Giam, who opened offices in numerous city throughout the world. The North Vietnamese were well bankrolled and established cells across the United States mostly on college campuses where they could fan the flames of protest against the U.S.

Certainly, the bulk of Americans who voted for Clinton/Gore never envisioned the global socialist state that they and those who dictate policy to them would institute and are now continuing to build. But, then again, those same voters have proven they don't care anymore. The price we paid was that now America had an administration with an openly socialist agenda. They did not see what was going on because everything was smoke and mirrors.

Behind Bill Clinton was an economic adviser, Derek Shearer, though appointed to no official post, helped form his economic strategy. Mr. Shearer was a longtime associate fellow at the Institute for Policy Studies (CFR), "which is committed to socialism in America and sides with the Soviet Union on almost every important foreign policy issue," according to a 1988 article in Policy Review (CFR monthly publication). Shearer favors socialism, but don't look for the words communist or socialism to show up any time in Clinton's speeches.

In the book *Economic Democracy*, written with Martin Cornoy, Shearer says corporations are too "impersonal and powerful" and that a strategy to achieve economic democracy "must start by dismantling, or at least restricting, the power of these corporations." Shearer and Carnoy call for a "democratically" planned economy— one planned by government bureaucrats. They also call for nothing less than complete government control of capital markets. "A strategy of reform," they write, "must transfer capital from the corporations to the public.... The logical vehicle for that process should be the government." The objective, according to the book, is to provide a vehicle for governmental takeovers of entire industries "without the immediate financial and ideological burdens that large-scale nationalization efforts would entail." This has been and continues to be attempted with the Clinton Health Care plans and recent government intervention into the tobacco industry. Today, President Obama is following this plan down the road to destruction of the U. S. Federal Government and a capitalistic economy. Destroy the Capitalist system through Labor Unions which are, in the most part, Communist controlled.

In 1994 the Republican Party members were elected in enough numbers to control both houses of Congress. President Clinton stated that he wasn't concern, because he was going to run the Government by Presidential Proclamations. In other words, he was going to assume the role of a dictatorship. No wonder he considers the Constitution as a radical piece of paper! It was no mistake saying that William Clinton thinks that the Constitution was a radical piece of paper because he called it that in an interview on MTV's "Enough is Enough", March 22, 1994. He said:

"When we got organized as a country and we wrote a fairly *radical Constitution* with a *radical Bill of Rights*, giving a *radical amount of individual freedom* to Americans... And so a lot of people say there's *too much personal freedom*. When personal freedom's being abused, *you have to move to limit it.* That's what we did in the announcement I made last weekend on the public housing projects, about how we're going to have weapon sweeps and more things like that to try to make people safer in their communities."

The following was taken from the internet DSAUS.com. It needs repeating. The American public has a right to know how these One-World conspirators are destroying this great nation (divide and conquer):

"THE DESTRUCTION FROM WITHIN. Socialism has been a mass movement in America without much organization. Its control of the Democratic platform has been through single-issue organizations and the recruitment of millions of single-issue Americans. In taking over the Democratic Party, the *Democratic Socialists of America* has installed its platform which is clearly stated in its paper on "Where We Stand." The paper states:

"In the United States, we must fight for a humane public policies that will provide quality health care, education, and job training and that redirect public investment from the military to much neglected urban housing and infrastructure. Such policies require the support of a majoritarian coalition of trade unionists, people of color, feminists, gays and lesbians and all other peoples committed to democratic change. Our greatest contribution as American socialists to global social justice is to build that coalition, which is key to transforming the power relations of global capitalism."

The paper further states:

*"A democratic socialist politics for the 21st century must promote an **international solidarity dedicated to raising living standards across the globe, rather than "leveling down" in the name of maximizing profits and economic efficiency. Equality, solidarity, and democracy can only be achieved through international political and social cooperation aimed at ensuring the economic institutions benefit all people.** (100% Illuminati propaganda)" Democratic socialists are dedicated to building truly inter- national social movements—of unionists, environmentalists, feminists, and people of minority organizations."*

The DSA (which by its own words have taken over the Democratic Party) is listed as a 'Full Member Party" of the Socialist International organization. In their brochure, the Socialist International have in a sense corrupted the term "democratic" For example their discussion of shaping the Twenty-first century they state:

"59. Democratic socialism today is based on the same values on which it was founded. But they must be formulated critically, both assimilating past experience and looking ahead to the future. For instances, experience has shown that while nationalization in some circumstances may be necessary, it is not by itself a sovereign remedy for social ills. Likewise, economic growth can often be destructive and divisive, especially where private interests evade their social and ecological responsibility. Neither private nor State ownership

by themselves guarantee either economic efficiency or social justice.

60. The democratic socialist movement continues to advocate both socialization and public property within the framework of a mixed economy. It is clear that the internationalization of the economy and the global technological revolution make democratic control more important than ever. But social control of the economy is a goal that can be achieved through a wide range of economic means according to time and place"""

64. A democratic society must compensate for the defects of even the most responsible market systems. Government must not function simply as the repair shop for the damage brought about by market inadequacies or the uncontrolled application of new technologies. Rather the State must regulate the market in the interest of the people and obtain all workers the benefits of technology, both in work experience and through the growth of leisure time and meaningful possibilities for individual development." (NOTE: This is the exact excuse being used by the President Obama today to take government control of large Corporations, Banks, Automotive, Education etc . by using tax-payers money to save union jobs. In bragging about saving jobs, only Union members need apply.)

If one reads carefully the above objectives, the term democratic is nothing but propaganda. The point being that they are trying to sugar coat the term socialism which, after all of its failures over the last two centuries, has left a bad taste in millions and millions of peoples' mouths. The concept of a democratic country as opposed to a federalist style of government is the concept of the poor, the fringe elements of society, etc. who will have the power to tell all others what they must do. Thus the term 'Democratic' meaning 'one man- one vote'. Since the sick, lame, and lazy will always be with us, the Socialist state will win the elections by promising 'heaven on earth' to all. States with small populations will be dominated by the larger populated states and will no longer have any say in laws enacted by the socialist. One-World dictatorship will result..

There are a number of writers today that warn of Democratic Party's socialist agenda is undistinguishable today from the European socialist model. They base their claims on such events that occurred in the middle of June 2003. More than 1000 progressives -representing labor unions, feminists, environmentalists, etc -convened in Washington, D.C. according to Campaign for America's Future, the socialist advocacy group that organized the event.

The conference was called to motivate those forces necessary for the 2004 election. After three days of speeches and strategy sessions, they left the event determined to steer the Democratic Party even further to the left.

The list of speakers was a roster of the liberal wing, including former Labor Secretary Robert Reich, AFL President John Sweeney, PBS commentator Bill Moyer, Ralph Neas of People For the American Way, and nearly a dozen liberal College professors.

Most speeches were of the typical liberal tirade on anti-Capitalism, anti-Business, anti-Profits, and anti-Military. "We believe in the politics where people come ahead of profits," said an AFL-CIO official.

Socialist of the world have always regarded the United States as their mortal enemy for the simple reason that every time they tried to take over the world, America's commitment to freedom stood in their way. Knowing that freedom and socialism were mutually exclusive, most Americans looked upon socialism with disdain.

World socialists have had over two hundred years of failure to know how to infiltrate and then destroy. For example, the fierce patriotism of Americans were undermined during the Vietnam War. The socialists took to the streets, burning the American flag, denigrating those in the military, and causing anarchy in many cities throughout the United States. Today they still attack those who are patriotic.

The new socialists in America no longer refer to themselves as socialists. They know that most older American have learned that being a socialist means an anti-freedom, pro-slavery agenda. Today, with the help of the socialist press, they proudly refer to themselves as being left or liberals or progressives. The connotation being that Left is OK therefore being Right is bad:. It is strange how these two terms came into being when originally both terms referred to socialism.

Nancy Pelosi, Speaker Of the House, is a socialist that believes in stealing from the wealthy and giving to the poor—called ***income redistribution***- in the case of the government forcefully – and she is also an advocate (remember she is from California) to give amnesty to 12 million lawbreakers (illegal immigrants).. Pelosi and the Democrats have been rolling back the Bush tax cuts – and you can be sure this axe job will happen within two years after President Obama takes office..

Here are some facts about Pelosi:

President Bush:

When we lowered the taxes for families with children, she voted against it. And when we put the death tax on the road to extinction, she voted against it. ...

And yet, Nancy Pelosi said of the Republicans and Bush:

They'll take food out of the mouths of children in order to give tax cuts to the wealthiest.

And, yet, there are blogs out there who are repeating these words as if they were true. .

As far as Pelosi's voting record:

- Voted NO on retaining reduced taxes on capital gains & dividends.

- Voted NO on providing tax relief and simplification as prescribed by the Working Families Tax Relief Act of 2004.

- Voted NO on making permanent an increase in the child tax credit.

- Voted NO on making the Bush tax relief permanent that are to expire in 2010.

- Voted NO on $99 economic stimulus: capital gains & income tax cuts in 2002.

- Voted NO on eliminating the Estate Tax ("death tax") – so, Bush was right to make that comment above.

- Voted NO on $46 billion in tax cuts for small business – 2000.

Nancy Pelosi says and does real things that is detrimental to America and its people – no one need to make up stories, such as the one about the super Jet she requires to fly back and forth from California to Washington D.C., because the truth is damning as it is. The lesson to remember from Mrs. Pelosi (a former member of the Progressive Caucus) is that she is a Socialist and is out to destroy this country economically, thus fulfilling Karl Marx Plan laid out in his book "The Communist Manifesto". Mrs. Pelosi is controlled by members of the Democratic Socialist of America, which is an arm of the Socialist International whose headquarters was in London, England and seat of the Communist International. Mrs. Pelosi is not alone in Congress as I stated above. There are many more like her in Congress and their one goal is to destroy the Constitution of the United States and thus change this country from a Federal Government to a Socialist Government. And what is sad about this situation is that they are ELECTED into office. The Democrats in their district either are brain washed or they want to destroy this country. One must make their own conclusion.

The Congressional Progressive Caucus (CPC) was established in 1991 by five members of the United States House of Representatives: Representatives Ron Dellums (D-CA), Lane Evans (D-IL), Peter DeFazio (D-OR), Maxine Waters (D-CA), and Bernie Sanders (I-VT). Then-Representative Bernie Sanders was the convener and first. The founding members were concerned about the economic hardship imposed by the deepening recession, and the growing inequality brought about by the timidity of the Democratic Party response at the time.

The CPC's founding statement of purpose states that it was "organized around the principles of social and economic justice, a non-discriminatory society, and national priorities which represent the interests of all people, not just the wealthy and powerful". The founding members underscored that the Cold War was over, and that the nation's budget and overall priorities should reflect that. They called for cuts in outdated and unnecessary military spending, a more progressive tax system in which wealthy taxpayers and corporations contribute their fair share, a substantial increase in federal funding for social programs designed to meet the needs of low and middle-income American families, and trade policies that increase the exports of more American products and encourage the creation of well-paying jobs and sound investment in America. They also expressed their belief that those policy goals could be achieved in concert with a commitment to long-term fiscal responsibility.

In addition, an array of national liberal organizations work to support the efforts of the Progressive Caucus, including the Institute for Policy Studies, *The Nation* magazine, MoveOn. org, National Priorities Project, Jobs with Justice, Peace Action, Americans for Democratic Action, and Progressive Democrats of America. Also co-sponsoring the kickoff event were the NAACP, ACLU, Progressive Majority, League of United Latin American Citizens, Rainbow/PUSH Coalition, National Council of La Raza, Hip Hop Caucus, Human Rights Campaign, Association of Farmworker Opportunity Programs, and the National Hip Hop Political Convention. See Appendix B for a membership list of the Progressive Caucus and the States they represent.

Chapter 5

FREEMASONRY AND THE ILLUMINATI

"The tree of liberty must be refreshed from time to time with the blood of patriots and tyrants." Thomas Jefferson

INTRODUCTION

It's the nightmare that's still there after we wake up. It reads like a horror movie script. The most trusted and richest society leaders have secretly organized into a satanic cult and are conspiring to turn humanity into their mind-controlled slaves. The process is designed to appear natural: "making the world a better place." All wars are hoaxes designed to consolidate their power.

In the past, writers have ascribed humanity's woes to a conspiracy of inbred British aristocrats', their American toadies, Zionists and central bankers. So far many have overlooked the most important ingredient, the "Freemasons" the world's largest secret society with five million members (including three million Americans.) Only their inner circles are aware that the "Craft" is in fact devoted to Satanism.

The conspirators all belong to it. George W. Bush was a member. As a student at Yale, Bush joined its "Skull and Bones" chapter and referred to it in August 2000 in these terms: "My heritage is part of who I am."

Dick Cheney and Colin Powell are also high level Freemasons. So is Al Gore and Ariel Sharon. Past Presidents FDR, Harry Truman, Ronald Reagan and Lyndon Johnson were also members. So are Henry Kissinger, Allen Greenspan and World Bank President James Wolfensohn. In fact devil worship seems to be a prerequisite for power and success today.

Freemasonry has been blamed for many cases of child sexual abuse and ritual murder. There are at least three books out about people who claim to have been brainwashed and sexually exploited as children by certain members of our power elite. "The Franklin Cover-Up" (get the 2nd. Edition, 1996) by John W. DeCamp describes a homosexual and satanic child sex ring based in Omaha, which serviced members of the Reagan administration. In "Transformation of America," (1995) Cathy O'Brien describes her experiences as a mind-controlled sex slave with members of the current and past administrations.

It gets more bizarre. In addition to oil, the war against Iraq is part of a long-term plan to establish the rule of Satan on earth. The New World Order is Masonic in character. Sadaam Hussein (and Islam in general) represent an obstacle to the Masonic plan to rebuild Solomon's Temple on the Temple Mount in Jerusalem. This will be the seat of a new world religion subtly devoted to Lucifer.

The war is the latest in a step-by-step plan to enslave humanity. For example, the United Nations' true character is revealed by the fact that the only religious chapel at its headquarters is run by a satanic cult, the "Lucis Trust." The name was changed from Lucifer Trust to make the nature of the organization less conspicuous. For more background, see an online article entitled "The Real History of Satanism."

The Satanists disguise their agenda in warm and fuzzy buzzwords like "economic justice" and "international peace." They are drafting a new world constitution called the "Earth Charter" which will have the authority of holy writ. Eventually the Earth Charter will be presented to the United Nations in a pantheistic 21st Century replica of the Ark of the Covenant. Stephen Rockefeller and the Rockefeller Brothers Fund is behind this initiative. According to Joseph Farah, "these are dangerous and diabolical folks making long-term plans to seize even more power and destroy any vestige of freedom left in the world. ("World Net Daily, Sept.")

On September the 9th, 2001 a celebration of the Earth Charter was held at Shelburne Farms, Vermont for the unveiling of the

Earth Charter's final resting place. This "Ark of Hope" was to be presented to the United Nations along with its contents in June of 2002. It is hoped that the United Nations will endorse the Earth Charter document on this occasion; the tenth anniversary of the UNCED Earth Summit in Rio.

Placed within the Ark, along with the Earth Charter, were various items called "Temenos Books" and "Temenos Earth Masks." Temenos is a concept adopted by Carl Jung to denote a magic circle, a sacred space where special rules and energies apply. Some of the Temenos Books were created within this magic circle by children, who filled them with visual affirmations for Mother Earth. Fashioned with the "earth elements", the Temenos Earth Masks were also worn and created by children.

In 1992 Maurice Strong was the Secretary General of the historic United Nations (UNCED) Earth conference in Rio. This gathering featured an international cast of powerful figures in the environmental movement, government, business, and entertainment. Maurice Strong's wife Hannah, was involved in the NGO alternative meeting at the Summit called Global Forum '92. The Dalai Lama opened the meeting and, according to author Gary Kah, to ensure the success of the forum, Hannah Strong held a three-week vigil with Wisdomkeepers, a group of "global transformationalists." Through round-the-clock sacred fire, drumbeat, and meditation, the group helped hold the "energy pattern" for the duration of the summit.

It was hoped that an Earth Charter would be the result of this event. This was not the case; however an international agreement was adopted – Agenda 21 – which laid down the international "sustainable development" necessary to form a future Earth Charter agreement.

Maurice Strong hinted at the overtly pagan agenda proposed for a future Earth Charter, when in his opening address to the Rio Conference delegates he said, *"It is the responsibility of each human being today to choose between the force of darkness and the force of light."* [note: Alice Bailey, and Blavatsky before her, used these terms often.] Their writings state that the 'force of darkness' are those who adhere to the 'out-dated' Judeo-Christian faith; those who continue along their 'separative' paths of the one true God. The 'force of light' (Lucifer), in their view, is the inclusive new age doctrine of a pagan deistic New World Religion. In the New Age of Aquarius there will be no room for the 'force of darkness' and 'separativeness'. *"We must therefore transform our attitudes and adopt a renewed respect for the SUPERIOR LAWS OF DIVINE NATURE,"* Strong finished with unanimous applause from the crowd.

Humanity has a terminal disease and is in a collective state of denial.

FREEMASONRY

"Architects of Deception", a 600-page history of Freemasonry by Estonian writer Jüri Lina, offers profound insight into the true character of modern history.

Essentially, a dominant segment of Western society has joined the Jewish financial elite in embracing Freemasonry, a satanic philosophy that represents a death wish for civilization. They imagine somehow they will profit from the carnage and suffering by the "New World Order."

Incredible, bizarre and depressing as it sounds, Lina writes that 300 mainly Jewish banking families have used Freemasonry as an instrument of subversion, control and degrade the Western world.

This view is consistent with the 1938 NKVD interrogation of an illuminati member who names many of these banking families and confirms that Freemasons are expendable tools. (See Henry Makow's "Rothschild Conducts Red Symphony")

Based on the archives of the powerful French Grand Orient Lodge, captured in June 1940 and later made public by the Russians, Lina details how Freemasonry has conspired for world domination and orchestrated all major revolutions and wars in the modern era. (Lina, Page 332..)

Masons, often Jewish, are responsible for communism,

Zionism, socialism, liberalism (and feminism.) They love big government because it is the ultimate monopoly. "World government" (dictatorship) is the final trophy. This is the vision behind 9-11 and the "War on Terror."

These "world revolutionary" "progressive" movements all mirror Lucifer's rebellion against the laws of God and nature which is at the heart of Freemasonry. They ensnare millions of gullible idealists by promising a utopia based on materialism and "reason" and dedicated to "liberty, equality and fraternity," "public ownership" or some other idealistic sounding nonsense. It's called bait-and-switch.

According to Lina: "The primary aim of modern freemasonry is to build the New World Order, a spiritual Temple of Solomon, where non-members are nothing but slaves and ...where human beings would be sacrificed to Yahweh." (page 52)

Lina cites numerous Jewish sources that claim Freemasonry is based on Judaism and is "the executive political organ of the Jewish financial elite." (pages 81-83).

The common goal of these Masonic inspired movements is to undermine race, religion, nation and family ("all collective forces except our own") by promoting social division, self indulgence and "tolerance" i.e. mixture of races, atheism, nihilism, global-ism, sexual "liberation" and homosexuality thereby reducing humanity to a uniform dysfunctional and malleable mush.

Lina and others who attempt to alert humanity to its real condition are routinely slandered as anti-Semitic, fascist, and right wing "haters" by people indirectly employed by the bankers. This tactic shields the conspirators from scrutiny and makes discussion of our grim predicament impossible.

Henry Makow in his writings using Lina's reference made it known that although he is a Jew he was not part of this banking monopoly, nor is the majority of Jews. By way of analogy, he stated that the mafia are mostly Italian but most Italians do not belong to the mafia.

Italians don't viciously attack opponents of organized crime and call them "racists" and "hate mongers". That would look awfully suspicious. Jews compromise themselves by their defence of the Masonic bankers and their perverse vision for humanity.

Makow stated that four of his grandparents perished in the Jewish holocaust. He demand to know the real reason they were murdered. London-based Masonic bankers and their cronies brought Hitler to power in order to provoke war, control Stalin, and justify the creation of Israel. They betrayed non-Zionist Jews and let them perish. They are using the Jewish people in the same way they use the Masons.

We cannot understand the modern world unless we appreciate that it is the result of the Masonic conspiracy. People scoff yet the evidence stares them in the face every day. The Great Seal of the United States on every dollar bill is a Masonic symbol. There are 33 steps on the side of the pyramid representing the 33 degrees of Freemasonry. The Masons established the United States as a base to advance their goal of world supremacy. Similarly, the emblem of the United Nations is also a Masonic symbol. The world is caught in a grid consisting of 33 spaces surrounded by acacia leaves, which signifies intense activity in masonry.

Three-quarters of US presidents in the Twentieth Century were high-level Masons. Both Bush and Kerry are Masons (Skull and Bones.) FDR, Churchill, Lenin, Trotsky and Stalin were masons. Most Zionist leaders were and are Masons. Gerhard Schroeder, Jacques Chirac and Tony Blair are Freemasons. So was Sadaam Hussein, which suggests the Iraq war could be a sadistic charade.

There are over six million Masons in 32,000 lodges around the world including 2.5 million in the US. In 1929, 67% of Members of Congress were Masons. There are 360,000 Masons in England. More than five per cent of British judges are Masons. Lina believes, "Freemasonry plays the same role in Western society as the Communist Party did in the Soviet Union. Without belonging to the freemasonry there is no chance of a fast career, regardless of how talented one is."

Keep in mind that Communism was a Masonic enterprise and the puzzle starts to take shape.

Lina says Freemasons not only control politics but also virtually every sector of Western society, including science and culture. "The present cultural life has become virtually unconscious," he writes. "We have witnessed the beginning of cultural senility." (page 333)

In his pamphlet "The Open Conspiracy: Blueprint for a World Revolution" (1929) the Freemason H.G. Wells describes an "open secret society" consisting of society's leading men operating as a hidden force to secure world resources, reduce population through war and replace the nation state with world dictatorship. (Lina page 340)

Human beings are naturally attracted to good and repulsed by evil. Thus evil always represents itself as good. To the public, and its own lower ranks, Freemasonry pretends to be dedicated to "making good men better", humanism, tolerance, Christianity and you-name-it.

If this were true, would they have to extract vows of secrecy from members on pain of slitting their throat? Would they have been condemned by many Popes and banned from numerous countries? (page 84)

No one is impugning the many good and decent men in the lower "Blue Degrees" who are unaware of Freemasonry's true function and character. But there is abundant evidence and testimony that Freemasonry is a satanic cult dedicated to the worship of death. (Lina—134-138)

For example, when the Italian Grand Orient Lodge was evicted from the Pazzio Bourghese in Rome in 1893, the owner found a shrine dedicated to Satan. The Italian freemasons published a newspaper in the 1880's where they admitted time and again, "Our leader is Satan!" (page 135)

The Masons also admit to having a revolutionary political agenda. Typical of statements Lina cites from Masonic publications is the following from a German magazine in 1910: "The driving thought is at all times focused on destruction and annihilation, because the power of this great secret society can only rise from the ruins of the existing order of society." (page 272)

The Illuminist Conspiracy is the brake responsible for humanity's arrested development. Mankind resembles a person suffering from a serious disease and sinking into a coma.

Jüri Lina has written a courageous book to revive us. He says we face "the largest spiritual crisis in the history of mankind ... They have taken our history, our dignity, our wisdom and our honor, sense of responsibility, spiritual insights and our traditions."

We are partly to blame, he says: "We have failed to act against the Masonic madness due to our enormous gullibility. We have been totally fooled and ignored the warning signals." (Lina—274)

He ends on a hopeful note, saying evil is dysfunctional and inevitably destroys itself. "Freemasonry carries within it the seeds of its own destruction." (Lina—563)

Wars, revolutions and depressions are all part of a "revolutionary" process designed to march humanity to "world government" under the ritual of Freemasonry which may be a surrogate for an alliance of occult Jewish and gentile financial elites. Their "self-destruction" seems to be our best hope since the public is too ineffective and weak to resist.

As a side note, everyone should read Lina's book "Architect of Deception." It contains many gossipy nuggets such as Hitler had a son; Lenin was a homosexual; Castro is Jewish and a multimillionaire; and Henry Kissinger was/is a Soviet agent! He says the Mormons, Jehovah Witnesses, Rotary and Lions Clubs were founded by Masons.

ILLUMINATI

Every facet of Western society has been subverted. This includes business, education, military, mass media, government and all religions.

The Illuminati literature control current events and determine human history according to their "Plan.". What we call "secular humanism" is nothing but a facade for Luciferianism. Modernism is the substitution of their occult interests disguised as "reason" for Moral Order and Objective Truth i.e. God. Our modern world is a fraud dedicated to enthroning Satan worshipers as rulers of this planet. (http://www.savethemales.ca/001155.html)

The word "Illuminati" sounds incredible but unfortunately it's very real. It's plans and correspondence were seized in 1784. The "Plan' for conquering the world, as written by General Pike, was adopted by the Rothschilds and incorporated into the Round Table Groups as their mode of operation.

The relationship of Zionists to the Illuminati mirrors that of Freemasonry, which the Illuminati also tried to control. Most are pawns and dupes. "The Lodge shall be our nursery garden," Illuminati founder Adam Weishaupt wrote. "All those who are not suited to the work shall remain in the Masonic Lodge and advance in that without knowing anything of the further system."

It can be confusing, but that is what the conspirators want—confusion! The Illuminati that we are discussing in this book is NOT a benevolent secret society who wants to bring about peace and harmony to this world by helping to bring back freedom to the people. The Illuminati Plan we are exposing is the Plan that the super-rich are using to create a slave society!

In an internet article (*Global Research, Dec 02, 2006)* Adrian Salbuchi said "As we now have it, globalization can be defined as an ideology that identifies the Sovereign Nation-State as its key enemy, basically because the State's main function is (or should be) to prioritize the interests of the Many—i.e., "the People"—over the interests of the few. Accordingly, the forces of globalization seek to weaken, dissolve and eventually destroy the very foundations of the Nation-State as a basic social institution, in order to replace it with new supra-national worldwide political, economic, financial and military management structure."

A more correct term for this super-rich group would be "The Power Elite". A power elite, in political and sociological theory, is a small group of people who control a disproportionate amount of wealth, privilege, and access to decision-making of global consequence. The term was coined by Charles Wright Mills in his 1956 book, *The Power Elite*, which describes the relationship between individuals at the pinnacles of political, military, and economic institutions, noting that these people share a common world view. The power elite is described as consisting of members of the corporate community, academia, politicians, media editors, military service personnel, and high-profile journalists. Individuals identified as belonging to the power elite include David Rockefeller, Averell Harriman and Robert McNamara.

Socially, the power elite are the leadership of the upper class, able to shape the economy through their simultaneous access to both state and corporate power. Unlike the ruling class, a social formation based on heritage and social ties, the power elite is characterized by the organizational structure through which its wealth is acquired. According to Mills, the power elite is "the managerial reorganization of the propertied classes into the more or less unified stratum of the corporate rich. Domhoff further clarified the differences in the two terms: "The upper class as a whole does not do the ruling. Instead, class rule is manifested through the activities of a wide variety of organizations and institutions... Leaders within the upper class join with high-level employees in the organizations they control to make up what will be called the power elite."

The current Power Elite on this Earth have its Headquarters in Great Britain and in Rome, with Queen Elizabeth II as a major player, but there are bloodlines more important to them above hers that we know nothing about. Even the Presidents of the United States have royal blood, although not as thick as the Queen and the pure royalty. But they are all branching out from the same tree and they stick together on their sacred mission. You have to have royal blood to even become the President of the United States.

Another term frequently used is "New World Order". After George H.W Bush rang in the New World Order in the early 1990s, this term has been used by all researchers of the Power Elite. To make things even more confusing, Bush and other powerful people before and after him used this term for a reason. The Power Elite wants to accomplish two main things:

1. They want to maintain their power and expand it to include the whole world.

2. To safeguard their control and power, in constant fear that the masses will overthrow them like they did in the French Revolution, they want to expand their power by centralizing it as much as they can. Therefore they either create catastrophic world events, or let these events happen without intervening, so they can restructure and centralize as a result of the catastrophe.

Henry Kissinger mentioned this when asked about the Financial Meltdown. He said that from each catastrophe [referring mainly to the financial crisis] there is a new opportunity, and this is what he wanted to focus on. Understanding whom Kissinger works for, we know what opportunities he is talking about. History proves that this crisis has happened before, most notably in 1907-1908 and 1929. What Kissinger meant by a new opportunity was that failed business could be gobbled up by the rich for pennies on the dollar, thus weakening the economy of the country more—giving more power to the bankers and increasing their wealth.

Government mind control overlaps with many other things—it overlaps with a higher government and a secret world government called the Intelligence Sector. They hide behind the veil of National Security. They use our patriotism against us and make us think that for our own interest, for our own security of our own nations that we have to subject ourselves to all the secrecy that they impose upon us.

As we now have it, globalization can be defined as an ideology that identifies the Sovereign Nation-State as its key enemy, basically because the State's main function is (or should be) to prioritize the interests of the many—i.e., "the People"—over the interests of the few. Accordingly, the forces of globalization seek to weaken, dissolve and eventually destroy the very foundations of the Nation-State as a basic social institution, in order to replace it with new supranational worldwide social, political, economic, financial and military management structures.

This centralization of power within business and politics

(Globalization) and by using sophisticated mind control and surveillance techniques, they think they will eventually keep the masses obedient enough so they won't ever have to fear that we will rebel against them again. To be able to maintain the control and fear/negativity they feed on, they need to keep us in a spiritual trap, in which we certainly are. Although, we must remember that ultimately we put ourselves in this trap by letting us be ruled by these people in the first place and by looking the other way when truth is knocking on the door.

Whenever conspiracy theory is expounded, the mysterious "Illuminati" along with the Bilderbergs, The Trilateral Commission, The Council of Foreign Relations, and a bushel of other organizations are most often named as being responsible. However, while many people can name those other organizations, the Illuminati is always left hanging as some secret, shadowy entity which no one can quiet describe. If the Illuminati still exists as a secret society, one has to give them credit because after nearly 250 years no one has seemed to have left their organization to reveal its secrets. (See Appendix B for 'Illuminati and CFR Exposé,)

Because of Freemasonry's inadvertent involvement and the misuse of Freemasonry by the Illuminati's founder who had become a Mason, the legends of its continued existence (and influence) persist into the twenty-first century tying the organizations somehow together. In fact, Weishaupt founded the organization and then tried to get the Freemasons involved. He achieved a very limited success in a couple of lodges but was soon seen as a 'user' and his group removed—not unlike the 'fake Masonry' of today!

A huge amount of interest in the Illuminati stems, for those today, from Robert Anton Wilson (1932-2007). A self-described agnostic mystic, he was also an author, philosopher and, some would say, a comedian. Many endow Wilson with all-seeing power while others read his works as poking fun at society and those who would blindly read his writings as fact.

In 1977, Wilson published "Cosmic Trigger I : Final Secret of the Illuminati " in which he wrote on pages 3-4:

"Briefly, the background of the Bavarian Illuminati puzzle is this. On May 1, 1776, in Bavaria, Dr. Adam Weishaupt, a professor of Canon Law at Ingolstadt University and a former Jesuit, formed a secret society called the Order of the Illuminati within the existing Masonic lodges of Germany. Since Masonry is itself a secret society, the Illuminati was a secret society within a secret society, a mystery inside a mystery, so to say. In 1785 the Illuminati were suppressed by the Bavarian government for allegedly plotting to overthrow all the kings in Europe and the Pope to boot. This much is generally agreed upon by all historians. Everything else is a matter of heated, and sometimes fetid, controversy.

It has been claimed that Dr. Weishaupt was an atheist, a Cabalistic magician, a rationalist, a mystic; a democrat, a socialist, an anarchist, a fascist; a Machiavellian amoralist, an alchemist, a totalitarian and an "enthusiastic philanthropist." (The last was the verdict of Thomas Jefferson, by the way.) The Illuminati have also been credited with managing the French and American revolutions behind the scenes, taking over the world, being the brains behind Communism, continuing underground up to the 1970s, secretly worshipping the Devil, and mopery with intent to gawk. Some claim that Weishaupt didn't even invent the Illuminati, but only revived it. The Order of Illuminati has been traced back to the Knights Templar, to the Greek and Gnostic initiatory cults, to Egypt, even to Atlantis. The operational plan was devised from the tactics developed by the Muslim Assassins and Indian Thug gees organizations. The one safe generalization that can make is that Weishaupt's intent to maintain secrecy has worked; no two students of Illuminology have ever agreed totally about what the "inner secret" or purpose of the Order actually was (or is . . .). There is endless room for spooky speculation, and for pedantic paranoia, once one really gets into the literature of the subject; and there has been a wave of sensational "exposes" of the Illuminati every generation since 1776. If you were to believe all this sensational literature, the damned Bavarian conspirators were responsible for everything wrong with the world, including the energy crises and the fact that you can't even get a plumber on weekends."

No matter how little we may know about the "Illuminati", we know from literature that has been published over the centuries by leaders of the "Illuminati" society some of the schemes and plots that they did concoct and pull off. It is quite possible but not proven that the financial cabal has hired former Bavarian Illuminatis and they also adopted many or their plans to arrive at a point were a 'One World Government' will be formed but the old Bavarian Illuminati does not exist today.—but the cabal adopted its name (Illuminati) to hide behind. For this book, we will look at the conspiracy that has unfolded in the United States and how it came about. One can only judge for himself where the blame should fall.

ALBERT PIKE (1809-1901)

Albert Pike also of Newbury Port moved to Arkansas where he became a prominent member of the secessionist movement. He was chosen by Mazzini to head the Illuminati operations in America and moved to Charleston, South Carolina, in 1852. During the war he was made a brigadier general and placed in charge of raising an army of Indians. Pike's reign of terror was so despicable that foreign governments intervened to put an end to his savagery. Mazzini was not only the head of the Illuminati, he was the leading revolutionist in Europe. He was determined to establish a New World Order on the rubble of the old order and created a plan to accomplish his goal. He detailed his plan for world domination in a letter to Pike on January 22, 1870: "We must allow all the federations to continue just as they are, with their systems, their central authorities and their diverse modes of correspondence between high grades of the same rite, organized as they are at the present, but we must create a super rite, which will remain unknown, to which we will call those Masons of high degree whom we shall select. With regard to our brothers in Masonry, these men must be pledges to the strictest secrecy. Through Octhis supreme rite, we will govern all Freemasonry which will become the one international center, the more powerful because its direction will be unknown. (Lady Queensborough, *Occult Theocracy*, pp. 208-

209.)

This secret rite is called "The New and Reformed Palladian Rite." It has headquarters in Charleston, S.C., Rome, Italy and Berlin, Germany. Pike headed this rite in the Western Hemisphere while Mazzini headed it in the East. Pike wrote about his beliefs and goals in 1871 in "Morals and Dogma of the Ancient and Accepted Scottish Rite of Freemasonry." In this massive volume he explained that the "blind Force of the people is a Force that must be economized, and also managed. . . it must be regulated by intellect. "To attack the citadels (Institutions) built up on all sides against the human race by superstitions (religion), despotisms, and prejudices, the force must have a brain and a law (the Illuminati's). Then its (Force) deeds of daring produce permanent results, and there is real progress. Then there are sublime conquests. . . When all forces combined, and guided by the Intellect (Illuminati), and regulated by the Rule of Right, and Justice, and of combined and systematic movement and effort, the great revolution prepared for the ages will begin to march. . . It is because Force is ill regulated that revolutions prove failures" Albert Pike, *Morals and Dogma of the Ancient and Accepted Scottish Rite of Freemasonry, 1-2 (second Ed. 1950)*.

The secret rite, "The New and Reformed Palladian Rite", is why very few members of the Illuminati talk about it's inner workings. The select who join this secret society are sworn to secrecy under penalty of death. Not only their own death but those in their family as well. To prove a case in point the following documented event occurred overtly:

'In 1828, a Captain William Morgan decided it was his duty to inform all Masons and the general public what the full proof was regarding the Illuminati, their secret plans, intended objectives and to reveal the identities of the masterminds of the conspiracy. The Illuminati promptly tried Morgan in absentia and convicted him of treason. They ordered Richard Howard, and English Illuminist, to carry out their sentence of execution as a traitor. Morgan tried to escape to Canada, but Howard caught up with him near the border, near the Niagara Gorge, where he murdered him. This was verified in a sworn statement made in New York by one Avery Allen to the effect that he heard Howard render his report of the execution to a meeting of "Knights Templars", in St. John's Hall in New York. He also told how arrangements had been made to ship Howard back to England. That affidavit is on record in New York City Archives.'

Even though Pike was a confederate general who committed the most heinous atrocities of the war his tomb is located just 13 blocks from the Capitol Building. He was a high ranking member of the Illuminati who is still revered by the New World Order Organization.. The god of the Illuminati and the New World Order Group is Lucifer. "The Masonic religion should be, by all of us initiates of the high degrees, maintained in the purity of the Luciferian doctrine. . . Yes, Lucifer is God, and unfortunately Adonay (Jesus) is also God. For the eternal law is that there is no light without shade, no beauty without ugliness, no white without black, for the absolute can only exist as two Gods: darkness being necessary to light to serve as its foil as the pedestal is necessary to the statue, and the brake to the locomotive. . ."The doctrine of Satanism is a heresy; and the true and pure philosophic religion is the belief in Lucifer, the equal of Adonay (Jesus); but Lucifer, God of Light and God of Good, is struggling for humanity against Adonay, the God of darkness and evil." A.C. De La Rive, La Femme et l'enfant dans la Franc-Maconnerie Universelle, p. 588; Lady Queenborough, *Occult Theocracy pp. 220-221.*

Pike designed a plan for world conquest and wrote of it in a letter to Mazzini dated August 15, 1871. He said three future world wars would prepare the world for the New World Order.

Albert Pike's plan for the Illuminati was as simple as it has proved effective. He required that Communism, Nazism (National Socialism), Political Zionism, and other International movements be organized and used to foment the three global wars and three major revolutions. The First World War was to be fought so as to enable the Illuminati to overthrow the powers of the Tsars in Russia and turn that country into the stronghold of Atheistic-Communism. The differences stirred up by agents of the Illuminati between the British and German Empires were to be used to foment this war. After the war ended, Communism was to be built up and used to destroy other governments and religions.

World War Two, was to be fomented by using the differences between Fascists and Political Zionists. This war was to be fought so that Nazism would be destroyed and the power of Political Zionism increased so that the sovereign state of Israel could be established in Palestine. During World War Two International Communism was to be built up until it equaled in strength that of united Christendom. At this point it was to be contained and kept in check until required for the final social cataclysm. Can any person deny that Roosevelt and his staff at the Yalta Conference did put this plan into effect?

World War Three is to be fomented by using the differences the agents of the Illuminati stir up between Political Zionists and the leaders of the Moslem world. The war is to be directed in such a manner that Islam (the Arab World including Mohammedanism) and Political Zionism (including the State of Israel) will destroy themselves while at the same time the remaining nations, once more divided against each other on this issue, will be forced to fight themselves into a state of complete exhaustion physically, mentally, spiritually and economically. Can any unbiased and reasoning person deny that the intrigue now going on in the Near, Middle, and Far East is designed to accomplish this purpose? After World War Three is ended, those who aspire to undisputed world domination will provoke the greatest social cataclysm the world has ever known.

The quote below is Pike's own written words taken from the letter catalogued in the British Museum Library, London England:

"We shall unleash the Nihilists and Atheists, and we shall provoke a formidable social cataclysm which in all its horror will show clearly to the nations the effect of absolute atheism, origin of savagery and of the most bloody turmoil. Then everywhere, the citizens, obliged to defend themselves against the world minority of revolutionaries, will exterminate those destroyers of civilization, and the multitude, disillusioned with Christianity, whose deistic spirits will be from that moment without compass (direction), anxious for an ideal, but without knowing where to render its adoration, will receive the true light through the universal manifestation of the pure doctrine of Lucifer, brought finally out in the public view, a manifestation which will result from the general reactionary movement which will follow the destruction of Christianity and atheism, both conquered and exterminated at the same time" (William Guy Carr, Pawns in the Game. This strategy is corroborated by Dr. Dennis L. Cuddy PhD. in *The Power Elite's use of Wars and Crises. pike.htm*)

Pike explanations:

Who are the Illuminati?

"The Illuminati are the movers and shakers of the world. They are an elite group of bloodlines. There are 13 major bloodlines. They are what are called "generational satanists". That means that they have practiced their secret witchcraft for many centuries and they have passed their religion down from one generation to the next. They lead double lives. They have one life that the world sees and then they have a hidden life that the world doesn't see. There have been very few people that have been able to break through the secrecy."

"The top 13 bloodlines are the Astor, Bundy, Collins, Dupont, Freeman, Kennedy, Li, Onassis, Rockefellers, Rothschild, Reynolds, Krupp, Russell ... then there is a 13th bloodline which is the Merovingian bloodline. It is simply called the 13th and then there is the Van Duyn Illuminati bloodline. The 13th bloodline, the Merovingian, is extremely important. It includes the royal families of Europe."

What is their goal?

"Ultimately [their goal is] to bring in what people have termed the New World Order with a man who will hold the world's attention and carry the title 'The Antichrist.' That's the ultimate goal. When you get into deprogramming people you will see that a lot of the things they have been programmed to do tie in with a very sophisticated plan to unify the world under the reign of the Antichrist."

"[Princeton historian] James Billington (/*Fire in the Minds of Men/*) traces how all the revolutions were started by this occult elite. The term revolution came from the occult idea that we were going to revolve ourselves back to the Golden Age. There is this great quest for the Golden Age, this millenialism. That's what communism is about. If you look at the early founders of communism—they were trying to revolve us back through revolution to the Golden Age that had been lost. ...it's always for a socialistic, communistic type utopia.

Why do they use trauma-based mind control on their own family members?

"It's really essential. If you are going to participate in the Illuminati secret life, being a programmed multiple [personality] is basic. There are a few in the Illuminati who aren't programmed multiples, but considering what one has to participate in. You've got a number of standard rituals involved—St. Weinbald, St. Agnes, Grand Climax, Walpurgis, Beltane, all your solstices and equinoxes, Lamas, All Hallow's Eve, High Grand Climax—all of these standard rituals. These rituals are very horrific. They involved human sacrifice. Sacrifices of babies on the High Grand Climax. On various Sabbats you've got a young female or a male being sacrificed.

This is not something that the normal mind is going to be able to handle. The mind control and the creation of multiple personalities where you get a Dr. Jekyll and Mr. Hyde effect—is very crucial to this thing continuing from generation to generation. They will be trained in alchemy, in Indian sorcery, Druidism, Enochian magik, Gnosticism, Hermetic magik, cabbalism, Plato, Sufism—they will know all the different branches of occult systems."

What is the function of trauma?

"The Illuminati take a small child about two years old, and they begin traumatizing it with the worst traumas that are imaginable so that they can create these amnesia walls. They find these dissociated pieces of the mind that are just like ...floppy disks, then they put in their programming to the dissociated parts of the mind as to what they want that part to become... (Elsewhere he says mind control was behind Josef Mengele's experiments; that Mengele was Illuminati and continued his work in the US after the war.)

The Illuminati can take a particular child and manipulate things from behind the scenes and open all the right doors for this person, and they can get them the grants and the schooling and everything they need and adding impetus to this person's career is the mind control that is steering them in that direction too. The end product is you end up with somebody who is an engineer or a lawyer or a politician who is very highly qualified for what they are doing. (Can anyone think of a recent president who fits this 'political' category?)

A very conservative estimate of 2 million Americans have been programmed with trauma based total mind control."

The Ultimate Goal?

"The whole long-range end-goal of this is to eventually create an entire planet of mind controlled slaves that can be controlled by one super computer. They are manipulating our thoughts and our attitudes, and steering us, herding us (they consider us animals— the Illuminati consider themselves god, god men and us to be the animals) they are herding us in the direction they want us to go."

In an interviewed by Wayne Morris, Jan 04, 1998, Fritz Springmeier said:

"Government mind control overlaps with many other things— it overlaps with a higher government and a secret world government called the Illuminati. As I investigated the Illuminati I had to also learn about their front that they operate. They hide behind the veil of National Security. They use our patriotism against us and make us think that for our own interest, for our own security of our own nations, that we have to subject ourselves to all the secrecy that they impose upon us."

Samples of how the Ruling Elite Illuminati have celebrated "anniversaries" of some Key Events through "History": (Ref: "Occult Numerology In Timing Events Of Terrorism" an essay by Eric Rainbolt.)

Could "history" possibly not be 'accidental' but rather 'concocted'? Is the world seeming crazy enough yet for you to seek answers other than what the television will tell you? Could a cabal of Luciferian Freemasons in power over the major governments of the world be setting the 'timing' of terror events? Could a small group of hidden financeers be playing all of humanity like a deck of cards? All the evidence points unmistakably to 'yes'. That is what this frightening report will summarize for everyone.

Freemasonry is the world's largest semi-secret society with millions in its membership roles. However, there is a hierarchy resembling a pyramid within the world-wide organization.

There are two sects of Freemasonry known as the York Rite (that has "9" degrees of secrecy) and the Scottish Rite (which has "33" public degrees of secrecy).

Masons are very prideful. Any of them will tell you that most presidents have been either 32 or 33 degree Freemasons. Bush I and II and their COO, VP Cheney, are all 33rd degree Freemasons. The UK's Tony Blair is a 33rd degree Freemason, as is Vladimir Putin, Mikhail Gorbechev, Ariel Sharon, and the list goes on and on...

Even NY Mayor Rudy Giuliani was knighted into the Masonic order by the Queen of England on Feb "13"th, 2002 for his role in 9-11.

The origin of Freemasonry goes back to "1111"AD where "9" European separatists declared themselves the "Knights Templar". This is why the numbers in the date "9"-"11", are so important to the powers that be. For instance, they celebrated the groundbreaking of the Pentagon on "September 11th", 1941. (9th month, 11th dat.)

On the anniversary of that 60 years later elite Freemasons architected the events of 9-11-2001 so they could operate a war between the East and West, between the Christian world and the Muslim world for world domination. It turns out the "Holy Roman Empire" never fell; they are still at it. The "Fourth Reich" as it is seen has been assuming power on a global scale.

They like to celebrate anniversaries of their control over 'history'. For instance, Bush's dad gave a speech on September 11th, 1990 when he was president in front of the congress. He stated "Out of these troubled times, our 5th objective, a New World Order, can emerge." "11" years to the morning from that date 9-11-2001 occurred with the first airliner, Flight "11", hitting the North Tower at 11 minutes to 9am.

They are particularly fond of the number "11". They use that most often. They think by using the number 11 that it gives them more power over humankind. They are that freakish.

Bush I delivered a speech in front of the United Nations on 2/1/1992 where he stated: "Americans will soon pledge their allegiance to the sacred principles enshrined in the United Nation's charter." On the morning of the "11"th anniversary of that speech, they celebrated their control over world events by sacrificing the Columbia STS 107 Space Shuttle over Dallas, which is on the "33rd" parallel. Dick Cheney was conveniently in Dallas that morning to see the comet come in. It was an intentional ritual sacrifice of the shuttle. These are the unmistakable facts of 'history'.

Freemasons are very prideful architects. They are a very influential group in modern day building architecture. They like to use certain mathematical principles, such as Euclid's "47th" proposition. They also stick to using their sacred number set wherever they can (3,7,"11",13 (and multiples of those),19,47,93, and 111). They use those numbers in architecting Masonic lodges, corporate buildings, and "history".

This control over 'history' is real high level stuff of course. For instance the popular president JFK, not a Freemason but from the billionaire Kennedy family,

didn't even seem to be aware of this type of power and

manipulation while he was President.

For instance, the hidden money power of the world wished to create a lot of fear in the world. For "13" days, they made it seem like Russia and the US were going to bomb each other with nuclear weapons; known as the "13 Days of October" or the "Cuban Missile Crisis." In the middle of that staged conflict, on 10/"22"/1962(2x11=22) they put JFK on world TV to deliver a speech. Soon after that, the illuminati had the Russian government remove the nuclear missile sites from Cuba. The "Cold War" continued; trillions of taxpayer's money was spent on militaries and bombs over the next decades—on both sides of the world.

However, since JFK was going against the grain of the illuminati bankers (he set up new currency and by-passed the Federal Reserve) , they set up his assassination exactly "13" months later from his world televised speech. He was taken out in Dallas on the "33"rd parallel on "11"/"22"/1963. ("22" is a multiple of "11", as is "33"—the highest degree in Scottish Rite Freemasonry.) Simply stated, this was a Freemasonic ritual assassination.

The "Architects of History" are not public figures. The American government is just a bunch of puppets of the London financiers, who call themselves the 'illuminati'. They finance the 'establishment' with paper money they assume the rights to print out-of-thin-air. They put in puppet governments, such as the Bush regime, to do their dirty work and deliver their propaganda to the public for them. The international banking elite have simply taken the American flag over time and used it as their gang symbol. The US government is a branch of the Freemason steeped London monarchy as much as Tony Blair's puppet government in the UK. The London banks have always secretly controlled America, even since 1776, the year of so called American "independence"; also the year Adam Weishaupt's secretive Order of the 'Illuminati' formed in opposition in Europe.

This is strange to find out because they have never wanted to reveal how the world is really operated to masses of the American people, especially since their banking organization hijacked America's currency in 1913 with the corrupt Federal Reserve Act.

In 19"33" the masons controlling the US government put their symbolism all over the back of the US $1 note. They control the monopoly board by issuing their paper monopoly money. It costs them as much to print a $20 US note as a $1 US note, a few copper cents. "The Fed" bank prints up as much as they secretly decide on. They lend it back to the US so Americans can have money to pass around in order to have commerce. They draw 'interest' of all the money they print and loan out. That's why it is called a Federal Reserve "Note". It is not money backed by Reserves—it is simply a loan, a paper "IOU", based only on the credit of the US government! (which is not credit-worthy by the way.)

Their puppet the head of the Federal Reserve announces if it is going to cost more or less to borrow money from the Fed Reserve Bank. It's just a giant privately run scam. Economists have been writing books exposing the monstrous fraud for decades. People still seem not to care. They must think the billionaire Freemasons and the trillionaire illuminati devil worshipping international bankers running the world's finances are going to take care of them and their children and so forth. They must think they will one day stop terrorizing ordinary people, creating wars, and not crash the economies of the world to cash in like they did during the "Great Depression", or try to put the military on the streets of America under "Martial Law".

However, they are currently setting it all up. 9-11 created a world again at war and more centralized federal power over all the American people. "3/11"/2004 in Madrid they killed (1)9(1) more people to set up more police power over the people in Spain. (3x11="33"—the Freemasons are so prideful they have to 'sign' all their bombings.) Also, "3/11"/1985 was the "19th" anniversary of the inauguration of "33"rd degree Freemason Mikhail Gorbachev. 5 months after he oversaw the Berlin Wall fall on "11"-"9"-1989, he publicly stated: "We are only beginning to shape the New World Order."

The London 7/7 bombings (7x11) {Like flight "77" or 9-11)

gave the Crown more police power over the people of Europe. They next bombed Egyptians on 7/"22" killing 88(8x"11") Amazingly they signaled the timing of the that event by jamming/slowing the London Big Ben clock on 5/27/2005 for the "13" minutes between "22:07" and 22:20. Europeans write the date for July 22nd, 2005 as "22/7".

Could the timing of all these major terror events just be "33" coincidences? Obviously not. It would be against billion to 1 odds or greater. Also that would be excluding all the other evidence that is out there explaining that this is happening.

The ebook Revelation 9-11 {Now renamed "The Architecture of History"} available at *http://www.threeworldwars.com/occult. htm* contains hundreds of more examples of freemasonic control and intrigue throughout 'history'. The past should really be called "their story". What are we going to call the future once it has also past?

If you are still not convinced: on the 1st anniversary of 9-11 they made the NY city lottery balls come up "911" and the Chicago S&P futures exchange index come up "911.00".

That's impossible to both happen on the 1st anniversary of 9-11, but they were happily boasting "We did it!", "We have this much power and control over all of you." "We control not only the TV and Hollywood, but lotteries, and stock exchange indexes too!" That's how they have dropped their hints apparently to help shed their guilt amongst themselves.

On the 6th month anniversary of 9-11, they put "88"(8x11) flood-lamps where the buildings used to be. They made a giant "11" again from March "11th" to April "13th", 2002 for "33" nights. They turned the lights off each night at "11 pm".

The Freemasonic illuminists were only showing off; certainly not mourning with the rest of the world who naturally perceived the situation differently.

All these are the facts of 'history'. George Orwell who wrote "1984" stated "Who controls the past controls the present. Who controls the present controls the future." The Democratic and Republican parties are all just used-car salesmen to the American people, selling lemon after lemon—while keeping quiet about the intentions of their dark overlords, People need to understand a $1 US Federal Reserve (actually not Federal) Note is just like a stock certificate. It only has "perceived" value and the value of it may go up & down. They issue more notes or 'currency stock' at any time. The more money they print up, the more the value of every dollar goes down as it filters about. They plan on soon crashing the US note, and replacing it with the "Amero", like the Euro, when they financially rig all the American countries from Canada to Chile, under one illuminati privately run central bank. They plan to send more non-thinking American soldiers to war with dissenting countries like Venezuela.

Once we reach the threshold of debt (around $22 Trillion) The finance cabal will call in all their notes and the Capitalistic System in the United States will vanish along with all the peoples savings, properties, currencies and dreams. That is what the current Obama administration is doing today. It is death to freedom and the rise of International Socialism. Wake up America!

Chapter 6

THE BILDERBERG /ONE-WORLD GROUPS

"When we get piled upon one another in large cities, as in Europe, weshall become as corrupt as Europe."   *Thomas Jefferson*

Since the late 1950s, the Bilderberg Group has been the subject of a variety of conspiracy theories. For the most part, conspiracy theories emanate from political extremist organizations, Right and Left. The "Radical Right" view Bilderberg as an integral part of the 'international Zionist-communist conspiracy'. At the other end of the political spectrum, the "Radical Left" perceive Bilderberg as a branch of the "Rockefeller/Rothschild grand design to rule the world". For many, it is less frightening to believe in hostile conspirators than it is to face the fact that no one is in control. After all, isn't conspiracy the normal continuation of normal politics by normal means?

Conspiracy or not, the Bilderberg Group is an example of behind-the-scenes influence-peddling in action. Bilderbergers represent the elite and wealthy establishment of every Western nation. They include bankers, industrialists, politicians and leaders of giant multinational corporations. Their annual meetings, which take place at different locations each year, go unannounced, their debates unreported, their decisions unknown.

The original Bilderberg conference was held at the Hotel de Bilderberg, near Arnhem in The Netherlands, from 29 May to 31 May 1954. It was initiated by several people, including Denis Healey and Józef Retinger, who were concerned about the growth of anti-Americanism in Western Europe. They proposed an international conference at which leaders from European countries and the United States would be brought together with the stated aim of promoting understanding between the cultures of the United States and Western Europe. In reality, it was for the purpose of bringing the United States, as a colony, into a universal form of government with the U. S. paying most of the bills.

Retinger contacted Prince Bernhard of the Netherlands, who agreed to promote the idea, together with Belgian Prime Minister Paul Van Zeeland, and the head of *UNILEVER* at that time, the Dutchman Paul Rijkens. Bernhard, in turn, contacted Walter Bedell Smith, then head of the CIA, who asked Eisenhower adviser, Charles Douglas Jackson, to deal with the suggestion. The guest list was to be drawn up by inviting two attendees from each nation, one of each to represent conservative and liberal points of view. Fifty delegates from 11 countries in Western Europe attended the first conference along with 11 Americans.

The success of the meeting led the organizers to arrange an annual conference. A permanent Steering Committee was established, with Retinger appointed as permanent secretary. Besides organizing the conference, the steering committee also maintained a register of attendee names and contact details, with the aim of creating an informal network of individuals who could call upon one another in a private capacity. Conferences were held in France, Germany, and Denmark over the following three years. In 1957, the first US conference was held in St. Simons, Georgia, with $30,000 from the Ford Foundation. The foundation supplied further funding for the 1959 and 1963 conferences.

Because of its secrecy and refusal to issue news releases, the group is frequently accused of secretive and dire world plots. Critics include the John Birch Society, the Canadian writer Daniel Estulin, British writer David Icke, American writer Jim Tucker and radio host Alex Jones.

Bilderberg founding member and, for 30 years, a steering committee member, Denis Healey has said:

" To say we were striving for a one-world government is exaggerated, but not wholly unfair. Those of us in Bilderberg felt we couldn't go on forever fighting one another for nothing and killing people and rendering millions homeless. So we felt that a single community throughout the world would be a good thing."

This secrecy, and lack of reporters in attendance was also noted by *Guardian* writer Charlie Skelton in his reports on the 2009 conference held in Athens, Greece. Skelton himself was detained by police on three occasions for taking photographs in the vicinity of the conference resort. According to the investigative journalist Chip Berlet, the origins of Bilderberg conspiracy theories can be traced to activist Phyllis Schlafly. In Berlet's 1994 report *Right Woos Left*, published by *Political Research Associates*, he writes:

" The views on intractable godless communism expressed by Schwarz were central themes in three other best-selling books which were used to mobilize support for the 1964 Barry Goldwater campaign. The best known was Phyllis Schlafly's *A Choice, Not an Echo*, which suggested a conspiracy theory in which the Republican Party was secretly controlled by elitist intellectuals dominated by members of the Bilderberg group, whose policies would pave the way for global communist conquest."

According to the *American Friends of Bilderberg*, the 2008 agenda dealt mainly with a nuclear free world, cyber terrorism, Africa, Russia, finance, protectionism, US-EU relations, Afghanistan and Pakistan, Islam and Iran.

The Bilderberg Secretariat proclaims the conferences to be '... private in order to encourage frank and open discussion'. Frank and open discussion are a good thing in any forum but when those doing the discussing are some of the very most powerful financiers and media tycoons in the world it causes suspicion: "If what they discuss is for the good of ordinary people why not publicize it!" Isn't it a corrupted use of the word 'open' when no one can find out what they're saying? Is Bilderberg a secret society? Judge for yourself from the following:

When such rich and powerful people meet up in secret, with military intelligence managing their security, with hardly a whisper escaping of what goes on inside, people have a right to be suspicious. No, it's not a 'conspiracy'. The world's leading financiers and foreign policy strategists don't get together at Bilderberg to draw up their 'secret plans for the future'. It's subtler than that. These meetings create an artificial 'consensus' in an attempt to spellbind visiting politicians and other men of influence. It's about reinforcing the illusion that Globalization is 'good', 'popular' and that it's inevitable. When looking at one of the (partially reliable) participant lists it should be remembered that quite a number of participants are invited in an attempt to get them on-board the globalization project. These are carefully selected people of influence, who have been openly critical of globalization. Examples are Jonathan Porritt (Bilderberg 1999) and Will Hutton (Bilderberg 1997) but there are many others. Most of these participants are happy to speak about the conference afterwards, and may even be critical.

Bilderberg is an extremely influential lobbying group. That's not to say that the organizers don't have a hidden agenda; they do, namely accumulation of wealth and power into their own hands while explaining to the participants that globalization is for the good of all. It is also a very good forum for 'interviewing' potential future political figures such as Clinton (1991) and Blair (1993).

The ideology put forward at the Bilderberg conferences is that what's good for banking and big business is good for the mere mortals of the world. Silently banished are the critical voices, those that might point out that debt is spiraling out of control, that wealth is being sucked away from ordinary people and into the hands of the faceless corporate institutions, that millions are dying as a direct result of the global heavyweight Rockefeller/Rothschild economic strategies.

See Appendix A for Bilderberg membership and Organizational Structure (2002).

Bilderberg organizers are accepted, by those 'in the know', as the prophets of Capitalism. Will Hutton, deputy Editor of The Observer newspaper in London and left-leaning *Economist,* described private clubs of the elite as masterminded by "The High Priests of Globalization". The ecclesiastical allusion is not accidental. The Bilderberg high-priests are a force against good, out to wipe morality from the earth. For the organizers of Bilderberg Conferences are an annual ideological assault by the world's most power-hungry people. Not content with owning unimaginable amounts of money and property they want to use that wealth to acquire even more power for themselves. Power is the most dangerous and addictive drugs known to man. Will the craving be satisfied when a handful of men own and control everything on earth?

And just like the Nazi party in the 1930's, the global Capitalist Elite are rising in power by peaceful means. There are some very uncomfortable and unexplained connections between Bilderberg and the Nazis through the Conference's founder Prince Bernhard.

These crown princes of capital use violence when necessary for the destruction of dissent; for the repossession of homes that men and women have worked a lifetime for; needless deaths from starvation and geopolitical machinations—this violence is notable by their absence from the annual meetings.

One can't help but wonder, when the Bilderberg organizers, Rothschild, Rockefeller, Kissinger and the rest have completed their project of enclosing all global goods and services into their own hands, enclosing too the media, to stop people freely discussing what they are up to. What then? What happens when the men who would be gods turn out to be global devils?

Who is behind Bilderberg? Bilderberg is run by a Steering Group—if you're wondering who's responsible for so much of the capital-friendly and dissent-crushing law-making, poverty and general misery in the world this may be the place to look. Up-to-date lists are available from the Bilderberg Secretariat. This is the closest approximation to a shadow, transatlantic government that can be seen. And this is another hidden agenda at Bilderberg. There may be other groups pulling the strings behind even the Steering Group possibly even high degree occult groups such as The Masons or Illuminati—but that is 'conspiracy theory',.

There must certainly be some sociopathic minds behind Bilderberg since they go to so much trouble to promote policies that lead to exploitation, inequality and despair. These individuals seem oddly switched off from the suffering they are clearly causing. Surely only deranged people would want to control the ideology of the world's mainstream press, and undermine natural political discourse. *Public opinion* and *democratic institutions* are a threat when you want to own the world.

The perverse objective of the Bilderberg Steering Group is to dress totalitarian ideology up to appear rational and push it out for mass consumption under Chatham House rules. Meanwhile, outside the Bilderberg-bubble, 'god-is-money' globalization is the new religion. The greedy are given a pat on the back as they plunder both the earth and do their best to destroy the human spirit.

How the financiers work in secrecy can be told by the story of C. Gordon Tether. Since the financiers own or control the media, they can remove any writer from publishing his manuscripts or cut off his voice so that the public will be the loser. The story about C. Gordon Tether was told by a pamphlet that was published , titled: *The Banned Articles of C. Gordon Tether* by GOODHEAD NEWS PRESS—Bicester—1977. Extracts of the story follows:

"C. Gordon Tether entered economic journalism at the height of the 1930's slump. War service in the R.A.F. apart, he spent the whole of his working life first with the Financial News and then with the Financial Times when the two papers merged after World War II. He took over the banking and finance column under the pen name 'Lombard' in the mid 1950's and built it into one of the papers' leading features.

His views came to be widely quoted abroad, while in England, Sir Harold Wilson paid tribute to him on more than one occasion as one of Britain's most distinguished independent journalists. His column eventually achieved such longevity that it earned an entry in the Guinness book of Records as the longest running feature in the British press.

Believing the meaningful freedom of the press provides the best safeguard of the democratic way of life, Mr. Tether has always attached the greatest importance to the preservation of his independence. This brought him into serious conflict with the Financial Times after the appointment of a new editor in 1973, attempts being made to establish closer control over the contents of his daily columns and his choice of subject. Although the result was the increasingly frequent suppression of his work, he refused to abandon his stand.

A disputes committee set up by the National Union of Journalists and the Newspaper Publishers Association eventually found that the Financial Times had sought to change Mr. Tether's conditions of working and that the change was concerned with eroding the independence of his work. It also, however, declared itself unable to resolve the dispute and shortly after it had reported the Financial Times took Mr. Tether's column away from him and handed it over to a team of writers.

Mr. Tether was a professional and decided to do something about his abrupt dismissal. He searched for other publishers but most did not want to become involved because of the money involved. He finally found a publisher that would publish his banned articles and wrote as an introduction the following:

"The attack on my independence had taken several forms, of which the most conspicuous was the total suppression of columns on an ever-increasing scale. In all nearly fifty articles suffered this fate, about half of this number during the six months before I was finally exiled on 20th July 1976.

All these banned articles are now being published for two reasons. In the first place, many of those who were not acquainted with the background may have been puzzled by the Financial Times' treatment of my column, or may have gained a false impression of what was involved. They will now be able to see for themselves what they were being denied the opportunity of reading. Secondly, their publication can make a useful contribution to the important debate on Press freedom now taking place with special regard to the writer's duty—as expressed in the NUJ's code of conduct— 'to defend the principle of freedom of the Press in relation to the collection of information and the expression of comment and criticism".

A pamphlet published by an organization calling itself the 'American Friends of Bilderberg' noted that the Bilderberg group owed its origin to the fact that, in the early 1950's a number of people on both sides of the Atlantic were seeking a means of bringing together leading citizens—in and out of government—for informal discussions on problems facing the Atlantic community. 'It was felt' the pamphlet continues, 'that such meetings would create a better understanding of the forces and trends affecting Western nations, and, in particular, would help to clear up differences and misunderstandings that might weaken the West.' Nothing much wrong with that, you might say. Are there not, indeed, many other organizations that concern themselves with the same good cause? And this being so, why should the activities of the Bilderberg group be singled out for special attention—and largely hostile attention at that?

"One of the reasons why the Bilderberg set-up has come to be a favorite target for the finger of suspicion is to be found in the nature of its 'invitational-list'. There are no members of Bilderberg as such. Each year an invitation list is compiled by Prince Bernhard in consultation with an informal international steering committee. This list invariably includes 80 to 100 participants who are representatives of many of the world's largest capitalist empires—men wielding immense power in the fields of economics and business. And many of these attend all the meetings , along with a number of 'regulars' operating in other parts of the corridors of power—one of them being Mr. Healy, the Chancellor of the Exchequer.

"The Elite people who control our lives from behind the scene are so hidden that the average person doesn't realize that he is being manipulated. C. Wright Mills' classic 1950's book titled "What Is The Power Elite", describes fully what they are. Excerpts from the book are as follows:

'The power elite is composed of men whose positions enable them to transcend the ordinary environments of ordinary men and women; they are in positions to make decisions having major consequences. Whether they do or do not make such decisions is less important than the fact that they do occupy such pivotal positions: their failure to act, their failure to make decisions, is in itself an act that is often of greater consequence than the decisions they do make.

For they are in command of the major hierarchies and organizations of modern society. They rule the big corporations. They run the machinery of the state and claim its prerogatives. They direct the military establishment......."

'The power elite are not solitary rulers. Advisers and consultants, spokesmen and opinion-makers are often the captains of their higher thought and decision. Immediately below the elite are the professional politicians of the middle levels of power, in the Congress and in the pressure groups, as well as the new and old upper classes of town and city and region.

Mingling with them, in curious ways ....., are those professional celebrities who live by being continually displayed but are never, so long as they remain celebrities, displayed enough........They do have the power to distract the attention of the public or afford sensations to the masses, or, more directly, to gain the ear of those who do occupy positions of direct power."

The alignment of the most powerful banking, media, and political forces at unaccountable forums must be taken seriously. Will Hutton calls them 'The High Priests of Globalization'. Vandana Shiva, at last years People's Summit in Birmingham, called Globalization: 'The New Totalitarianism'. We would hardly expect Bilderberg—which was started by Prince Bernhard of the Netherlands – card-carrying member of the SS at the beginning of World War II [www.bilderberg.org/bernhard.htm]—to be open about their activities or averse to a bit of disinformation.

Globalization of their ownership power is the goal. 'Public opinion' and 'democracy' are competition that must be taken out of the picture. The annual Bilderberg meetings attempt to persuade powerful people who are critical of Globalization to 'join up'. This leaves the prime movers behind the pseudo-philosophy of Globalization as a rich and powerful clutch of unaccountable 'High Priests': David Rockefeller, Evelyn De Rothschild, Henry Kissinger etc.. The Blairs and the Clintons of this world are merely their 'followers'.

We are entering a very precarious time in history with the prospect of Global Corporate Rule moving ever nearer. These corporations and their top-down structures are totalitarian and apparently immortal. It is important that people are informed as to the dangers but they stand little chance of that with the media becoming ideologically narrower and every day being consolidated into fewer hands. As one pundit stated: "It is worth remembering that the solution to the cloud of darkness these great de-humanized profit machines cast across our world may well be spiritual rather than political."

The One-World instigators are rich and usually get what they want by bribes, payoffs, or threats. Many of the innocents are fooled by their propaganda, but worldly people who back the elite are not fooled – they follow and spread the propaganda that there is only one possible way to live and that is under one sovereign Government. To prove a point, former President William Clinton who has been to the Bilderberg meeting said the following in a speech at the Seventh Annual Awards Dinner of the *National Albanian American Council*, June 19, 2003 in New York:

"It's just human nature people defining themselves as 'us' and 'them'. But we live in a global society, and cannot escape the each other. Albania and Southeast Europe – all the Balkans – have enormous strategic importance.

Consider this, there is no way in the right world we can build the 21st century of peace and prosperity and freedom unless Europe is prosperous, and peaceful and united. We can't do it. So, the next big project is to get Kosovo and Albania and everybody else together and be a real part of Europe, to bring Southeast Europe into Europe."

Former President Clinton, CFR members, and others in this country believe in the concept of one-world government. They also understand that One-world government means all countries must give up their sovereignty and live under the yoke of slavery and be governed by the Elite. Remember what Baron M. A. Rothschild said: "Give me control over a nation's currency and I care not who makes its laws."

To understand how the power in the World Elite operate, one has to follow the history of the Rockefeller family in America.. Years ago a myth was started in American conservative circles, effectively spread by active double agents. This myth found a host of eager believers, because it indicated a growing crack in the monolithic power which had been oppressing the peoples of the world. This new ``revelation" was that a struggle to the death for world power had developed between the Rockefellers and the Rothschilds. According to this startling development, one faction or the other, depending on which agent you were listening to, had gained control of the Soviet Union and would use its power as the basis for achieving the overthrow of the other faction. The sudden death of several members of the Rockefeller family was cited as ``proof" that such a struggle was taking place, although no Rothschild is known to have succumbed during this `war'. This ignored the general understanding that Nelson Rockefeller had been ``eliminated" as the result of losing deposit slips for several billion dollars of drugs from the Colombian cartel, or that the other Rockefeller deaths showed no trace of a ``Rothschild connection".

A number of knowledgeable people could not believe anyone could be so misinformed as to think that ``the Rockefellers" were now trying to seize power from the Rothschilds, at a time when the influence of members of the Rockefeller family was already in great decline, their family finances being handled by J. Richardson Dilworth, their legal affairs being handled by John J. McCloy, and other faithful retainers; none of these retainers would have been willing to engage in a genuine power struggle, as they were faceless managers who lived only for their weekly paycheck. They had no ambitions of their own. Nevertheless, many hopeful Americans grasped the will-o-the-wisp idea that the Rockefellers were now ``good Americans" who were willing to risk all to overthrow the Rothschilds. Amazingly, this noxious story persisted for almost a decade before being consigned to the curiosities of history.

Like J.P. Morgan, who had begun his commercial career selling the U.S. Army some defective guns, the famous fall carbine affair,

John D. Rockefeller also was a war profiteer during the Civil War; he sold unstamped Harkness liquor to Federal troops at a high profit, gaining the initial capital to embark on his drive for monopoly. His interest in the oil business was a natural one; his father, William Rockefeller had been ``in oil" for years. William Rockefeller had become an oil entrepreneur after salt wells at Tarentum, near Pittsburgh, were discovered in 1842 to be flowing with oil. The owners of the wells, Samuel L. Kier, began to bottle the oil and sell it for medicinal purposes. One of his earliest wholesalers was William Rockefeller. The ``medicine" was originally labeled ``Kier's Magic Oil". Rockefeller printed his own labels, using ``Rock Oil" or ``Seneca Oil," Seneca being the name of a well-known Indian tribe. Rockefeller achieved his greatest notoriety and his greatest profits by advertising himself as ``William Rockefeller, the Celebrated Cancer Specialist". It is understandable that his grandsons would become the controlling power behind the scenes of the world's most famous cancer treatment center and would direct government funds and charitable contributions to those areas which only benefit the Medical Monopoly.

William Rockefeller spared no claim in his flamboyant career. He guaranteed ``All Cases of Cancer Cured Unless They Are Too Far Gone." Such were the healing powers that he attributed to his magic cancer cure that he was able to retail it for $25 a bottle, a sum then equivalent to two months' wages. The ``cure" consisted of a few well known diuretics, which had been diluted by water. This carnival medicine show barker could hardly have envisioned that his descendants would control the greatest and the most profitable Medical Monopoly in recorded history.

As an itinerant, traveling carnival peddler, William Rockefeller had chosen a career that interfered with developing a stable family life. His son John rarely saw him, a circumstance which has inspired some psychological analysts a conjecture that the absence of a father figure or parental love may have contributed to John D. Rockefeller's subsequent development as a money mad tyrant who plotted to maim, poison and kill millions of his fellow American during almost century of his monopolistic operations and whose influence, reaching up from the grave, remains the most dire and malignant presence in American life. This may have been a contributing factor—however, it is also possible that he was totally evil.

It has long been a truism that you can find a horse thief or two in any prominent American family. In the Rockefeller family it was more than a truism. William seems to have faithfully followed the precepts of the 'Will of Canaan' throughout his career, ``love robbery, love lechery." He fled from a number of indictments for horse stealing, finally disappearing altogether as William Rockefeller and re-emerging as Dr. William Levingston of Philadelphia, a name which he retained for the rest of his life. An investigative reporter at Joseph Pulitzer's *New York World* received a tip that was followed up. The *World* then disclosed that William Avery Rockefeller had died May 11, 1906 in Freeport, Illinois, where he was interred in an unmarked grave as Dr. William Levingston.

William Rockefeller's vocation as a medicine man greatly facilitated his preferred profession of horse thief. As one who planned to be in the next county by morning, it was a simple matter to tie a handsome stallion to the back of his wagon and head for the open road. It also played a large part in his vocation as a woman-chaser; he was described as being ``woman-mad". He not only concluded several bigamous marriages, but he seems to have had uncontrolled passions. On June 28, 1849, he was indicted for raping a hired girl in Cayuga, New York; he later was found to be residing in Oswego, New York and was forced once again to decamp for parts unknown. He had no difficulty in financing his woman-chasing interests from the sale of his miraculous cancer cure and from another product, his ``Wonder Working Liniment," which he offered at only two dollars a bottle. It consisted of crude petroleum from which the lighter oils had been boiled away, leaving a heavy solution of paraffin, lube oil and tar, which comprised the ``liniment." William Rockefeller's original miracle oil survived until quite recently as a concoction called *Nujol,* consisting principally of petroleum and peddled as a laxative. It was well known that *Nujol* was merely an advertising sobriquet meaning ``new oil," as opposed, apparently, to ``old oil".

Sold as an antidote to constipation, it robbed the body of fat-soluble vitamins, it being a well-established medical fact that mineral oil coated the intestine and prevented the absorption of many needed vitamins and other nutritional needs. Its makers added carotene as a sop to the health-conscious, but it was hardly worth the bother. *Nujol* was manufactured by a subsidiary of *Standard Oil of New Jersey*, called *Stanco,* whose only other product, manufactured on the same premises, was the famous insecticide, *Flit.*

Nujol was hawked from the Senate Office Building in Washington for years during a more liberal interpretation of ``conflict of interest." In this case, it was hardly a conflict of interest, because the peddler, Senator Royal S. Copeland, never had any interests other than serving the Rockefellers. He was a physician whom Rockefeller had appointed as head of the *New York State Department of Health* and later financed his campaign for the Senate. Copeland's frank display of commercialism amazed even the most blasé Washington reporters. He devoted his Senate career to a daily program advertising *Nujol.* A microphone was set up in his Senate office each morning, the first order of business being the *Nujol* program, for which he was paid $75,000 a year, an enormous salary in the 1930s and more than the salary of the President of the United States. Senator Copeland's exploits earned him a number of nicknames on Capitol Hill. He was often called the "Senator from the American Medical Association," because of his enthusiastic backing for any program launched by the AMA and Morris Fishbein. More realistically, he was usually referred to as ``the Senator from Standard Oil". He could be counted on to promote any legislation devised for the greater profit of the Rockefeller monopoly. During congressional debate on the Food and Drug Act in 1938, he came under criticism from Congresswoman Leonor Sullivan, who charged that Senator Copeland, a physician who handled the bill on the Senate floor, frankly acknowledged during the debate that soap was exempted from the law, because the soap manufacturers, who were the nation's largest advertisers, would otherwise join with other big industries to fight the bill. Congresswoman Sullivan complained : ``Soap was officially declared in the law not to be a cosmetic . .. The hair dye manufacturers were given license to market known dangerous products, just so long as they placed a special warning on the label—but what woman in a beauty parlor ever sees the label on the bulk container in which hair dye is shipped ?"

Just as the elder Rockefeller had spent his life in the pursuit of his personal obsession, women, so his son John was equally obsessed, being money-mad instead of women-mad, totally committed to the pursuit of ever-increasing wealth and power. However, the principal accomplishments of the Rockefeller drive for power, the rebate scheme for monopoly, the chartering of the foundations to gain power over American citizens, the creation of the central bank, the Federal Reserve System, the backing of the World Communist revolution and the creation of the Medical Monopoly, all came from the Rothschilds or from their European employees. There cannot be found in the records of John D. Rockefeller that he originated any one of these programs. The concept of the tax exempt charitable foundation originated with the Rothschild agent, George Peabody, in 1865. The Peabody Educational Foundation later became the Rockefeller Foundation. It is unlikely that even the diabolical mind of John D. Rockefeller could have conceived of this devious twist. A social historian has described the major development of the late nineteenth century, when charitable foundations and world Communism became important movements, as one of the more interesting facets of history, perhaps equivalent to the discovery of the wheel. This new discovery was the concept developed by the rats, who after all have rather highly developed intelligences, that they could trap people by baiting traps with little bits of cheese. The history of mankind since then has been the rats catching humans in their traps. Socialism—indeed any government program—is simply the rat baiting the trap with a smidgen of cheese and catching himself a human. Congressman Wright Putman, chairman of the House Banking and Currency Committee, noted from the floor of Congress that the establishment of the Rockefeller Foundation effectively insulated Standard Oil from competition.

The controlling stock had been removed from market manipulation or possible buy-outs by competitors. It also relieved Standard Oil from most taxation, which then placed a tremendous added burden on individual American taxpayers. Although a Rockefeller relative by marriage, Senator Nelson Aldrich, Republican majority leader in the Senate, had pushed the General Education Board charter through Congress, the Rockefeller Foundation charter proved to be more difficult. Widespread criticism of Rockefeller's monopolistic practices was heard, and his effort to insulate his profits from taxation or takeover was seen for what it was. The charter was finally pushed through in 1913 (1913 was also the year the progressive income tax and of the enactment of the Federal Reserve Act). Senator Robert F. Wagner of New York, another senator from Standard Oil (there were quite a few), ramrodded the Congressional approval of the charter. The charter was then signed by John D. Rockefeller, John D. Rockefeller, Jr., Henry Pratt Judson, president of the Rockefeller established University of Chicago, Simon Flexner, director of the Rockefeller Institute, Starr Jameson, described in *Who's Who* as ``personal counsel to John D. Rockefeller in his benevolences," and Charles W. Eliot, president of Harvard University.

The Rockefeller Oil Monopoly is now 125 years old, yet in 1911, the Supreme Court, bowing to public outrage, had ruled that it had to be broken up. The resulting companies proved to be no problem for the Rockefeller interests.

The family retained a two per cent holding in each of the ``new" companies, while the Rockefeller foundations took a three per cent stock holding in each company. This gave them a five per cent stock interest in each company ; a one per cent holding in a corporation is usually sufficient to maintain working control.

The involvement of the Rockefellers in promoting the world Communist Revolution also developed from their business interests. There was never any commitment to the Marxist ideology; like anything else, it was there to be used. At the turn of the century Standard Oil was competing fiercely with Royal Dutch Shell for control of the lucrative European market. Congressional testimony revealed that Rockefeller had sent large sums to Lenin and Trotsky to instigate the Communist Revolution of 1905. His banker, Jacob Schiff, had previously financed the Japanese in their war against Russia and had sent a personal emissary, George Kennan to Russia to spend some twenty years in promoting revolutionary activity against the Czar. When the Czar abdicated, Trotsky was placed on a ship with three hundred Communist revolutionaries from the Lower East Side of New York. Rockefeller obtained a special passport for Trotsky from Woodrow Wilson and sent Lincoln Steffens with him to make sure he was returned safely to Russia. For traveling expenses, Rockefeller placed a purse containing $10,000 in Trotsky's pocket.

On April 13, 1917, when the ship stopped in Halifax, Canadian Secret Service officers immediately arrested Trotsky and interned him in Nova Scotia. The case became an international cause celebre, as leading government officials from several nations frantically demanded Trotsky's release. The Secret Service had been tipped off that Trotsky was on his way to take Russia out of the war, freeing more German armies to attack Canadian troops on the Western Front. Prime Minister Lloyd George hurriedly cabled orders from London to the Canadian Secret Service to free Trotsky at once--they ignored him. Trotsky was finally freed by the intervention of one of Rockefeller's most faithful stooges, Canadian Minister Mackenzie King, who had long been a ``labor specialist" for the Rockefellers. King personally obtained Trotsky's release and sent him on his way as the emissary of the Rockefellers, commissioned to win the Bolshevik Revolution. Thus Dr. Armand Hammer, who loudly proclaims his influence in Russia as the friend of Lenin, has an insignificant claim compared to the role of the Rockefellers in backing world Communism. Although Communism, like other isms, had originated with Marx's association with the House of Rothschild, it enlisted the reverent support of John D. Rockefeller because he saw Communism for what it is, the ultimate monopoly, not only controlling the government, the monetary system and all property, but also a monopoly which, like the corporations it emulates, is self-perpetuating and eternal. It was the logical progression from his Standard Oil monopoly.

An important step on the road to world monopoly was the far-reaching corporation invented by the Rothschilds. This was the international drug and chemical cartel, I.G. Farben. Called ``a state within a state," it was created in 1925 as Interessen Gemeinschaft Farbenindustrie Aktien gesellschaft, usually known as I.G. Farben, which simply meant ``The Cartel". It had originated in 1904, when the six major chemical companies in Germany began negotiations to form the ultimate cartel, merging Badische Anilin, Bayer, Agfa, Hoechst, Weiler-ter-Meer, and Greisheim-Electron. The guiding spirit, as well as the financing, came from the Rothschilds, who were represented by their German banker, Max Warburg, of M.M. Warburg Company, Hamburg. He later headed the German Secret Service during World War I and was personal financial adviser to the Kaiser. When the Kaiser was overthrown, after losing the war, Max Warburg was not exiled with him to Holland, instead he became the financial adviser to the new government.

Monarchs may come and go, but the real power remains with the bankers. While representing Germany at the Paris Peace Conference, Max Warburg spent pleasant hours renewing family ties with his brother, Paul Warburg, who, after drafting the Federal Reserve Act at Jekyl Island, had headed the U.S. banking system during the war. He was in Paris as Woodrow Wilson's financial advisor.

I.G. Farben soon had a net worth of six billion marks, controlling some five hundred firms. Its first president was Professor Carl Bosch. During the period of the Weimar Republic, I.G. officials, seeing the handwriting on the wall, began a close association with Adolf Hitler, supplying much needed funds and political influence. The success of the I.G. Farben cartel had aroused the interest of other industrialists. Henry Ford was favorably impressed and set up a German branch of Ford Motor Company. Forty per cent of the stock was purchased by I.G. Farben. I.G. Farben then established an American subsidiary, called American I.G., in cooperation with Standard Oil of New Jersey . Its directors included Walter

Teagle, president of Standard Oil, Paul Warburg of Kuhn Loeb & Company and Edsel Ford, representing the Ford interests. John Foster Dulles, for the law firm, Sullivan and Cromwell, became the attorney for I.G., frequently traveling between New York and Berlin on cartel business. His law partner, Arthur Dean, is now director of the $40 million Teagle Foundation which was set up before Teagle's death. Like other fortunes it had become part of the network. Like John Foster Dulles, Arthur Dean has been a director of *American Banknote* for many years; this is the firm which supplies the paper for our dollar bills. Dean also has been an active behind the scenes government negotiator, serving as arms negotiator at disarmament conferences. Dean was also a director of Rockefeller's American Ag & Chem Company. He was a director of American Solvay, American Metal and other firms. As attorney for the wealthy Hochschild family, who owned Climax Molybdenum and American Metal, Dean became director of their family foundation, the Hochschild Foundation. Dean is director emeritus of the Council on Foreign Relations, the Asia Foundation, International House, Carnegie Foundation Foundation, and the Sloan Kettering Cancer Center.

In 1930, Standard Oil announced that it had purchased an alcohol monopoly in Germany, a deal which had been set up by I.G. Farben. After Hitler came to power, John D. Rockefeller assigned his personal press agent, Ivy Lee, to Hitler to serve as a full-time adviser on the rearmament of Germany, a necessary step for setting up World War II. Standard Oil then built large refineries in Germany for the Nazis and continued to supply them with oil during World War II. In the 1930s Standard Oil was receiving in payment from Germany large shipments of musical instruments and ships which had been built in German yards.

The dreaded Gestapo, the Nazi police force, was actually built from the worldwide intelligence network which I.G. Farben had maintained since its inception. Herman Schmitz, who had succeeded Carl Bosch as head of I.G., has been personal advisor to chancellor Brüning; when Hitler took over, Schmitz then became his most trusted secret counselor. So well concealed was the association that the press had orders never to photograph them together. Schmitz was named an honorary member of the Reichstag, while his assistant, Carl Krauch, became Göring's principal advisor in carrying out the Nazis' Four Year Plan. A business associate, Richard Krebs, later testified before the House Un-American Activities Committee, ``The I.G. Farbenindustrie was already, in 1934, completely in the hands of the Gestapo." This was a misstatement; the I.G. Farben had merely allied itself with the Gestapo.

In 1924 Krupp Industries was in serious financial difficulty; the firm was saved by a $10 million cash loan from Hallgarten & Company and Goldman Sachs, two of Wall Street's best known firms. The planned re-armament of Germany was able to proceed only after Dillon Read floated $100 million of German bonds on Wall Street for that purpose. It was hardly surprising that at the conclusion of the Second World War, General William Draper was appointed Economic Czar of Germany, being named head of the Economic Division of the Allied Military Government. He was a partner of Dillon Read.

In 1939 Frank Howard, a vice-president of Standard Oil visited Germany. He later testified "We did our best to work out complete plans for a modus vivendi which would operate throughout the term of the war, whether we came in or not." At this time American I.G. had on its board of directors Charles Mitchell, president of the National City Bank, the Rockefeller bank, Carl Bosch, Paul Warburg, Herman Schmitz and Schmitz' nephew, Max Ilgner. Although his name is hardly known, Frank Howard was for many years a key figure in Standard Oil operations as director of its research and its international agreements. He also was chairman of the research committee at Sloan Kettering Institute during the 1930s; his appointee at Sloan Kettering, Dusty Rhoads, headed the experimentation in the development of chemotherapy. During the Second World War Rhoads headed the Chemical Warfare Service in Washington at U.S. Army Headquarters. It was Frank Howard who had persuaded both Alfred Sloan and Charles Kettering of General Motors in 1939 to give their fortunes to the Cancer

Center, which then took on their names.

A member of the wealthy Atherton family, Frank Howard (1891-1964) had married a second time, his second wife being a leading member of the British aristocracy, the Duchess of Leeds. The first Duke of Leeds was titled in 1694, Sir Thomas Osborne, who was one of the key conspirators in the overthrow of King James II and the seizure of the throne of England by William III in 1688. Osborne had made peace with Holland during the reign of King Charles II, and single-handedly promoted the marriage of Mary, daughter of the Duke of York, to William of Orange in 1677. The *Dictionary of National Biography* notes that Osborne ``for five years managed the House of Commons by corruption and enriched himself." He was impeached by King Charles II for treasonous negotiations with King Louis XIV and imprisoned in the Tower of London from 1678 to 1684. After his release, he again became active in the conspiracy to bring in William of Orange as King of England and secured the crucial province of York for him. William then created him Duke of Leeds. The placing of William on the throne of England made it possible for the conspirators to implement the crucial step in their plans, setting up the Bank of England in 1694. This enabled the Amsterdam bankers to gain control of the wealth of the British Empire. Osborne's biography also notes that he was later accused of Jacobite intrigues and was impeached for receiving a large bribe to procure the charter for the East India Company in 1695, but ``the proceedings were not concluded". It was further noted that he ``left a large fortune". The 11th Duke of Leeds was Minister to Washington from 1931 to 1935, Minister to the Holy See from 1936 to 1947, that is, throughout the Second World War. One branch of the family married into the Delano family, becoming relatives of Franklin Delano Roosevelt . A cousin, Viscount Chandos, was a prominent British official, serving in the War Cabinet under Churchill from 1942 to 1945, later becoming a director of the Rothschild firm, Alliance Assurance, and Imperial Chemical Industries.

Frank Howard was the key official in maintaining relations

between Standard Oil and I.G. Farben. He led in the development of synthetic rubber, which was crucial to Germany in the Second World War; he later wrote a book, ``Buna Rubber''. He also was the consultant to the drug firm, Rohm and Haas, representing the Rockefeller connection with that firm. In his later years, he resided in Paris, but continued to maintain his office at 30 Rockefeller Center, New York.

Walter Teagle, the president of Standard Oil, owned 500,000 shares of American I.G., these shares later becoming the basis of the Teagle Foundation. Herman Metz, who was also a director of American I.G., was president of H.A. Metz Company, New York, a drug firm wholly owned by I.G. Farben of Germany. Francis Garvan, who had served as Alien Property Custodian during the First World War, knew many secrets of I.G. Farben's operations. He was prosecuted in 1929 to force him to remain silent. The action was brought by the Department of Justice through Attorney General Merton Lewis, the former counsel for Bosch Company. John Krim, former counsel for the German Embassy in the United States, testified that Senator John King had been on the payroll of the Hamburg American Line for three years at a salary of fifteen thousand dollars a year; he appointed Otto Kahn as treasurer of his election fund. Homer Cummings, who had been Attorney General for six years, then became counsel for General Aniline and Film at a salary of $100,000 a year. During the Second World War, GAF was supposedly owned by a Swiss firm; it came under considerable suspicion as an ``enemy'' concern and was finally taken over by the United States government. John Foster Dulles had been director of GAF from 1927 to 1934; he was also a director of International Nickel, which was part of the network of I.G. Farben firms. Dulles was related to the Rockefeller family through the Avery connection. He was attorney for the organization of a new investment firm, set up by Avery Rockefeller, in 1936 which was called Schröder-Rockefeller Company. It combined operations of the Schröder Bank, Hitler's personal bank and the Rockefeller interests. Baron Kurt von Schröder was one of Hitler's closest confidantes, and a leading officer of the SS. He was head of the Keppler Associates, which funneled money to the SS for leading German Corporations. Keppler was the official in charge of Industrial Fats during Göring's Four Year Plan, which was launched in 1936.

American I.G. changed its name to General Aniline and Film during the Second World War, but it was still wholly owned by I.G. Chemie of Switzerland, a subsidiary of I.G. Farben of Germany. It was headed by Gadow, brother-in-law of Herman Schmitz. I.G. Farben's international agreements directly affected the U.S. war effort, because they set limits on U.S. supplies of magnesium, synthetic rubber and, crucial medical supplies. The director of I.G. Farben's dyestuffs division, Baron George von Schnitzler, was related to the powerful von Rath family, the J.H. Stein Bankhaus which held Hitler's account and the von Mallinckrodt family, the founders of the drug firm in the United States. Like other I.G. officials, he had become an enthusiastic supporter of the Hitler regime. I.G. Farben gave four and a half million Reich marks to the Nazi Party in 1933; by 1945, I.G. had given the Party 40 million Reich marks, a sum which equaled all contributions by I.G. to all other recipients during that period. One scholar of the Nazi era, Anthony Sutton, has focused heavily on German supporters of Hitler, while ignoring the crucial role played by the Bank of England and its Governor, Sir Montague Norman, in financing the Nazi regime. Sutton's position on this problem may have been influenced by the fact that he is British. In view of the outspoken statements from Adolf Hitler about Jewish influence in Germany, it would be difficult to explain the role of I.G. Farben in the Nazi era. Peter Hayes' definitive study of I.G. Farben shows that in 1933 it had ten Jews on its governing boards. We have previously pointed out that I.G., from its inception was a Rothschild concern, formulated by the House of Rothschild and implemented through its agents, Max Warburg in Germany and Standard Oil in the US.

Prince Bernhard of the Netherlands joined the SS during the early 1930s. He then joined the board of an I.G. subsidiary, Farben Bilder, from which he took the name of his postwar supersecret policy making group, the Bilderbergers. Farben executives played an important role in organizing the Circle of Friends for Heinrich

Himmler, although it was initially known as Keppler's Circle of Friends, Keppler being the chairman of an I.G. subsidiary. His nephew, Fritz J. Kranefuss, was the personal assistant to Heinrich Himmler. Of the forty members of the Circle of Friends, which provided ample funds for Himmler, eight were executives of I.G. Farben or of its subsidiaries.

Despite the incredible devastation of most German cities from World War II air bombings, the I.G. Farben building in Frankfort, one of the largest buildings there, miraculously survived intact. A large Rockefeller mansion in Frankfort also was left untouched by the war, despite the saturation bombing. Frankfort was the birthplace of the Rothschild family. It was hardly coincidental that the postwar government of Germany, Allied Military Government, should set up its offices in the magnificent I.G. Farben building. This government was headed by General Lucius Clay, who later became a partner of Lehman Brothers bankers in New York. The Political Division was headed by Robert Murphy, who would preside at the Nüremberg Trials, where he was successful in glossing over the implication of I.G. Farben officials and Baron Kurt von Schröder. Schröder was held a short time in a detention camp and then set free to return to his banking business. The Economic Division was headed by Lewis Douglas, son of the founder of Memorial Cancer center in New York, president of Mutual Life and director of General Motors. Douglas was slated to become U.S. High Commissioner for Germany, but he agreed to step aside in favor of his brother-in-law, John J. McCloy. By an interesting circumstance, Douglas, McCloy and Chancellor Konrad Adenauer of Germany had all married sisters, the daughters of John Zinsser, a partner of J.P. Morgan Company.

As the world's pre-eminent cartel, I.G. Farben and the drug companies which it controlled in the United States through the Rockefeller interests were responsible for many inexplicable developments in the production and distribution of drugs. From 1908 to 1936 I.G. held back its discovery of sulfanilamide, which would become a potent weapon in the medical arsenal.

In 1920, I.G. had signed working agreements with the

important drug firms of Switzerland, Sandoz and Ciba-Geigy. In 1926, I.G. merged with Dynamit-Nobel, the German branch of the dynamite firm, while an English firm took over the English division. I.G. officials then began to negotiate with Standard Oil officials about the prospective manufacture of synthetic coal, which would present a serious threat to Standard Oil's monopoly. A compromise was reached with the establishment of American I.G., in which both firms would play an active role and share in the profits.

Charles Higham's book, ``Trading with the Enemy," offers ample documentation of the Rockefeller activities during the Second World War. While Hitler's bombers were dropping tons of explosives on London, the Germans were paying royalties on every gallon of gasoline they burned to Standard Oil, under existing patent agreements. After World War II, when Queen Elizabeth visited the United States, she stayed in only one private home during her visit, the Kentucky estate of William Irish, of Standard Oil.

Nelson Rockefeller moved to Washington after our involvement in World War II, where Roosevelt named him Coordinator of Inter-American Affairs. Apparently his principal task was to coordinate the refueling of German ships in South America from Standard Oil tanks. He also used this office to obtain important South American concessions for his private firm, International Basic Economy Corporation, including a corner on the Colombian coffee market. He promptly upped the price, a move which enabled him to buy seven billion dollars worth of real estate in South America and also gave rise to the stereotype of the ``Yanqui imperialismo". The attack on Vice President Nixon's automobile when he visited South America was explained by American officials as a direct result of the depredations of the Rockefellers, which caused widespread agitation against Americans in Latin America.

After World War II, twenty-four German executives were prosecuted by the victors, all of them connected with I.G. Farben, including eleven officers of I.G. Eight were acquitted, including Max Ilgner, nephew of Herman Schmitz. Schmitz received the most severe sentence, eight years. Ilgner actually received three years, but the time was credited against his time in jail waiting for trial, and he was immediately released. The Judge was C.G. Shake and the prosecuting attorney was Al Minskoff.

The survival of I.G. Farben was headlined by the Wall Street Journal on May 3, 1988—GERMANY BEATS WORLD IN CHEMICAL SALES. Reporter Thomas F. O'Boyle listed the world's top five chemical companies in 1987 as

1. BASF $25.8 billion dollars.

2. Bayer $23.6 billion dollars.

3. Hoechst $23.5 billion dollars.

4. ICI $20 billion dollars.

5. DuPont $17 billion dollars in chemical sales only.

The first three companies are the firms resulting from the "dismantling" of I.G. Farben from 1945 to 1952 by the Allied Military Government, in a process suspiciously similar to the ``dismantling'' of the Standard Oil empire by court edict in 1911. The total sales computed in dollars of the three spin-offs of I.G. Farben, some $72 billion, dwarfs its nearest rivals, ICI and DuPont, who together amount to about half of the Farben empire's dollar sales in 1987. Hoechst bought Celanese Corp. in 1987 for $2.72 billion. O'Boyle notes that ``The Big Three (Farben spin-offs) still behave like a cartel. Each dominates specific areas; head to head competition is limited. Critics suspect collusion. At the least, there's a cosiness that doesn't exist in the U.S. chemical industry.''

After the war, Americans were told they must support an ``altruistic'' plan to rebuild devastated Europe, to be called the Marshall Plan, after Chief of Staff George Marshall, who had been labeled on the floor of the Senate by Senator Joseph McCarthy as ``a living lie''. The Marshall Plan proved to be merely another Rockefeller Plan to loot the American taxpayer. On December 13, 1948, Col. Robert McCormick, editor of the Chicago Tribune, personally denounced Esso's looting of the Marshall Plan in a signed editorial. The Marshall Plan had been rushed through Congress by a powerful and vocal group, headed by Winthrop

Aldrich, president of the Chase Manhattan Bank and Nelson Rockefeller's brother-in-law, ably seconded by Nelson Rockefeller and William Clayton, the head of Anderson, Clayton Company. The Marshall Plan proved to be but one of a number of lucrative postwar swindles, which included the Bretton Woods Agreement, United Nations Relief and Rehabilitation and others.

After World War II, the Rockefellers used their war profits to buy a large share of Union Miniere du Haut Katanga, an African copper lode owned by Belgian interest, including the Societe Generale, a Jesuit controlled bank.

Soon after their investment, the Rockefellers launched a bold attempt to seize total control of the mines through sponsoring a local revolution, using as their agent the Grangesberg operation. This enterprise had originally been developed by Sir Ernest Cassel, financial advisor to King Edward VII—Cassel's daughter later married Lord Mountbatten, a member of the British royal family, who was also related to the Rothschilds.

Grangesberg was now headed by Bo Hammarskjold, whose brother, Dag Hammarskjold was then Secretary General of the United Nations—Bo Hammarskjold became a casualty of the Rockefeller revolution when his plane was shot down during hostilities in the Congo. Various stories have since circulated about who killed him and why he was killed. The Rockefeller intervention in the Congo was carried out by their able lieutenants, Dean Rusk and George Ball of the State Department and by Fowler Hamilton.

In the United States, the Rockefeller interests continue to play the major political role. Old John D. Rockefeller's treasurer at Standard Oil, Charles Pratt, bequeathed his New York mansion to the Council on Foreign Relations as its world headquarters. His grandson, George Pratt Shultz, became Secretary of State. The Rockefellers also wielded a crucial role through their financing of the Trotskyite Communist group in the United States, the League for Industrial Democracy, whose directors include such staunch ``anti-communists'' as Jeane Kirkpatrick and Sidney Hook. The Rockefellers were also active on the "right-wing" front through their sponsorship of the John Birch Society. To enable Robert Welch, a

32nd degree Mason, to devote all of his time to the John Birch Society, Nelson Rockefeller purchased his family firm, the Welch Candy Company, from him at a handsome price. Welch chose the principal officers of the John Birch Society from his acquaintances at the Council On Foreign Relations. For years afterwards, American patriots were puzzled by the consistent inability of the John Birch Society to move forward on any of its well-advertised ``anti-Communist'' goals. The fact that the society had been set up at the behest of the backers of the world Communist revolution may have played some role in this development. Other patriots wondered why most American conservative writers were steadily blacklisted by the John Birch Society for some thirty years.

In a desperate effort to restore its image, William Buckley, the CIA propagandist, launched a ``fierce'' attack against the John Birch Society in the pages of his magazine, the National Review. This free publicity campaign also did little to revive the moribund organization.

The Rockefeller monopoly influence has had its effect on some of New York's largest and wealthiest churches. Trinity Church on Wall Street, whose financial resources had been directed by none other than J.P. Morgan, owns some forty commercial properties in Manhattan and has a stock portfolio of $50 million, which, due to informed investment, actually yields a return of $25 million a year! Only $2.6 million of this income is spent for charitable work. The rector, who receives a salary of $100,000 a year, lives on the fashionable Upper East Side. Trinity's mausoleum sells its spaces at fees starting at $1250 and rising to $20,000 . St. Bartholomew, on Fifth Avenue, has an annual budget of $3.2 million a year of which only $100,000 is spent on charity. Its rector resides in a thirteen room apartment on Park Avenue.

In medicine, the Rockefeller influence remains entrenched in its Medical Monopoly. Its control of the cancer industry through the Sloan Kettering Cancer Center. We have listed the directors of the major drug firms, each with its director from Chase Manhattan Bank, the Standard Oil Company or other Rockefeller firms. The American College of Surgeons maintains a monopolistic control of hospitals through the powerful Hospital Survey Committee, with members Winthrop Aldrich and David McAlpine Pyle representing the Rockefeller control.

A medical fraternity known as the ``rich man's club,'' the New York Academy of Medicine, was offered grants for a new building by the Rockefeller Foundation and the Carnegie Foundation, its subsidiary group. This ``seed money'' was then used to finance a public campaign which brought in funds to erect a new building. For Director of the new facility, the Rockefellers chose Dr. Lindsly Williams, son-in-law of the managing partner of Kidder, Peabody, a firm strongly affiliated with the J.P. Morgan interests (the J.P. Morgan Company had originally been called the Peabody Company). Williams was married to Grace Kidder Ford. Although Dr. Williams was widely known to be an incompetent physician, his family connections were impeccable. He became a factor in Franklin D. Roosevelt's election campaign when he publicly certified that Roosevelt, a cripple in a wheelchair who suffered from a number of oppressive ailments, was both physically and mentally fit to be the President of United States. Dr. Williams' opinion, published in an article in the widely circulated Collier's Magazine, allayed public doubts about Roosevelt's condition. As a result, Williams was to be offered a newly created post in Roosevelt's cabinet, Secretary of Health. However, it was another thirty years before Health became a cabinet post, due to the politicking of Oscar Ewing.

The Rockefellers had greatly extended their business interests in the impoverished Southern states by establishing the Rockefeller Sanitary Commission. It was headed by Dr. Wickliffe Rose, a longtime Rockefeller henchman whose name appears on the original charter of the Rockefeller Foundation. Despite its philanthropic goals, the Rockefeller Sanitary Commission required financial contributions from each of the eleven Southern states in which it operated, resulting in the creation of State Departments of Health in those states and opening up important new spheres of influence for their Drug Trust. In Tennessee, the Rockefeller representative was a Dr. Olin West, who moved on to Chicago to become the power behind the scenes at the American Medical Association for forty years, as secretary and general manager. The Rockefeller Institute for Medical Research finally dropped the ``Medical Research" part of its title; its president, Dr. Detlev Bronk, resided in a $600,000 mansion furnished by this charitable operation.

Rockefeller's general Education Board has spent more than $100 million to gain control of the nation's medical schools and turn our physicians to physicians of the allopathic school, dedicated to surgery and the heavy use of drugs. The Board, which had developed from the original Peabody Foundation, also spent some $66 million for Negro education.

One of the most far-reaching consequences of the General Education Board's political philosophy was achieved with a mere six million dollar grant to Columbia University in 1917 to set up the ``progressive" Lincoln School.

From this school descended the national network of progressive educators and social scientists, whose pernicious influence closely paralleled the goals of the Communist Party, another favorite recipient of the Rockefeller millions . From its outset, the **Lincoln School** was described frankly as a revolutionary school for the primary and secondary schools of the entire United States. It immediately discarded all theories of education which were based on formal and well-established disciplines, that is, the McGuffey Reader type of education which worked by teaching such subjects as Latin and algebra, thus teaching children to think logically about problems. Rockefeller biographer Jules Abel hails the Lincoln School as ``a beacon light in *progressive education* ".

Rockefeller Institute financial fellowships produced many prominent workers in our atomic programs, such as J. Robert Oppenheimer, who was later removed from government laboratories as a suspected Soviet agent. Although most of his friends and associates were known Soviet agents, this was called ``guilt by association." The Rockefeller Foundation created a number of spin-off groups, which now plague the nation with a host of ills, one of them being the **Social Science Research Council**, which single-handedly spawned the nationwide ``poverty industry," a business which expends some $130 billion a year of taxpayer funds while grossing some $6 billion income for its practitioners. The money, which would amply feed and house all of the nation's ``poor,'' is dissipated through a vast administrative network which awards generous concessions to a host of parasitic ``consultants''.

Despite years of research, writers has been able to merely scratch the surface of the Rockefeller influences listed above. For instance, the huge Burroughs Wellcome drug firm is wholly owned by the ``charitable'' Wellcome Trust. This trust is directed by Lord Oliver Franks, a key member of the London Connection which maintains the United States is a British Colony. Franks was Ambassador to the United States from 1948 to 1952. He is now a director of the Rockefeller Foundation, as its principal representative in England. He also is a director of the Schröder Bank, which handled Hitler's personal bank account, director of the Rhodes Trust in charge of approving Rhodes scholarships, visiting professor at the University of Chicago and chairman of Lloyd's Bank, one of England's Big Five.

Other Rockefeller Foundation spin-offs include the influential Washington think-tank, the **Brookings Institution**, the **National Bureau of Economic Research**, whose findings play a critical role in manipulating the stock market; the **Public Administration Clearing House,** which indoctrinates the nation's municipal employees ; the **Council of State Governments**, which controls the nation's state legislatures; and the **Institute of Pacific Relations**, the most notorious Communist front in the United States. The Rockefellers appeared as directors of this group, funneling money to it through their financial advisor, Lewis Lichtenstein Strauss, of Kuhn, Loeb Company.

The Rockefellers have maintained their controlling interest in the Chase Manhattan Bank, owning five per cent of the stock. Through this one asset they control $42.5 billion worth of assets. Chase Manhattan interlocks closely with the Big Four insurance companies, of which three, Metropolitan, Equitable and New York Life had $113 billion in assets in 1969.

With the advent of the Reagan Administration in 1980, the Rockefeller interests sought to obscure their longtime support of world Communism by bringing to Washington a vocally "anti-Communist" administration. The Reagan campaign had been managed by two officials of Bechtel Corporation, its president, George Pratt Schultz, a Standard Oil heir, and his counsel, Casper Weinberger. Shultz was named Secretary of State, Weinberger, Secretary of Defense, Bechtel had been financed by the Schröder-Rockefeller Company, the 1936 alliance between the Schröder Bank and the Rockefeller heirs.

The Rockefeller influence also remains preeminent in the monetary field. Since November, 1910, when Senator Nelson Aldrich chaired the secret conference at Jekyl Island which gave us the Federal Reserve Act, the Rockefellers have kept us within the sphere of the London Connection.

During the Carter Administration, David Rockefeller generously sent his personal assistant, Paul Volcker, to Washington to head the Federal Reserve Board . Reagan finally replaced him in 1987 with Alan Greenspan, a partner of J.P. Morgan Company. Their influence on our banking system has remained constant through many financial coups on their part, one of the most profitable being the confiscation of privately owned gold from American citizens by Roosevelt's edict. Our citizens had to turn over their gold to the privately owned Federal Reserve System. The Constitution permits confiscation for purposes of eminent domain, but prohibits confiscation for private gain. The gold's new owners then had the gold revalued from $20 an ounce to $35, giving them an enormous profit.

In reviewing the all-pervasive influence of the Rockefellers and their foreign controllers, the Rothschilds, in every aspect of American life, the citizen must ask himself, "What can be done?" Right can prevail only when the citizen actively seeks justice . Justice can prevail only when each citizen realizes that it is his God-given duty to mete out justice. History has documented all of the crimes of the usurpers of our Constitution. Many have learned the painful lesson that the Rockefeller monopolists exercise their evil power almost solely through federal and state agents. We should follow former Congressman Ron Paul who ran for the Presidency of the

United States on an eminently sensible and practical campaign—abolish the Federal Reserve System—abolish the FBI—abolish the Internal Revenue Service—and abolish the CIA. It has been known for years that 90% of the Federal Bureau of Investigation, ostensibly set up to ``fight crime" has been to harass and isolate political dissidents.

The criminal syndicates are now looting the American nation of one trillion dollars each year, of which about one-third, more than three hundred billion dollars per year, represents the profitable depredations of the Drug Trust and its medical subsidiaries . Before a sustained effort to combat these depredations can be mounted, Americans must make every effort to regain their health. As Ezra Pound demanded in one of his famous radio broadcasts, ``Health, dammit !" America became the greatest and most productive nation in the world because we had the healthiest citizens in the world. When the Rockefeller Syndicate began its takeover of our medical profession in 1910, our citizens went into a sharp decline. Today, we suffer from a host of debilitating ailments, both mental and physical, nearly all of which can be traced directly to the operations of the chemical and drug monopoly and which pose the greatest threat to our continued existence as a nation. Unite now to restore our national health—the result will be the restoration of our national pride, the resumption of our role as the inventors and producers of the modern world, and the custodian of the world's hopes and dreams of liberty and freedom.

In order to teach the drug and serum ideology it is necessary to teach that God didn't know what he was doing when he made the human body. Statistics issued by the Children's Bureau of the Federal Security Agency do not bear out this ideology. They show that since the all-out drive of the drug trust for drugging, vaccinating and serumizing the human system, the health of our nation has declined enormously, especially among children

Children are now given "shots" for this and "shots" for that, when the only immunity known to science is a healthy human body and a pure blood stream. Ponder these government findings:

a. Nearly hall a million children are affected by rheumatic fever.

b. Ten million boys and girls under 21 have defective vision.

c. A half million have orthopedic or spastic conditions.

d. Two million have impaired hearing.

e. Seventeen thousand are deaf.

g, Four hundred thousand have tuberculosis.

h. Seventy-five percent have dental defects.

i. Three out of every 100 draft registrants (18 and 19 years old) had heart trouble.

j. Three out of every hundred had a mental disease.

k. Two out of every 100 had a neurological difficulty.

l. Ten out of every 100 had defective vision.

m. One out of 40 had defective hearing.

These conditions didn't exist in the youth of today's middle aged and old people. Vaccination was the only unnatural practice then and most of us had enough vitality eventually to throw off the effects of this blood pollution. But if we had quadrupled or decupled this dose, as is being done to children today, our present middle aged people probably would be old and our present old people dead.

(The above Rockefeller information can be found at: http://www.goldismoney.info/forums/ showthread.php?t= 4298& goto= nextoldest)

Although the history of the Rockefeller depicts one member of the Bilderberg Group there are others. The origin of the Bilderberg Group is well known but as a secret organization what was its goals? Nowhere is it ever written about goals of these secret organizations. That is left up to the reader. One goal that we know of now has been the dream of European Socialists for years—maybe even centuries. This goal was European Unification. It is now a fact. How it came about and how the Bilderberg Group fits in is as follows.

"The present article is concerned with one specific facet

of American power-structure research which has important implications for the study of power in the UK. This is the subject of power-elite networks and forums, conceptualized as arenas for the conduct of intra-capitalist and inter-corporate strategic debates and long-range social planning, from which wider 'democratic' interference is carefully excluded.

The so-called 'Bilderberg Group', which is an interesting example of this kind of power-elite forum. It is one among a number of little-publicized institutions which have played an important role providing a means for debates and discussions to take place amongst different capitalist groups and different national governments over long-term planning issues and, especially, in coordinating strategic policy at an international level. Other such bodies on this trans-national scale include the Council on Foreign Relations (CFR) in the USA, with its UK sister organization, the Royal Institute of International Affairs (otherwise known simply as Chatham House) and the Trilateral Commission (which itself grew out of Bilderberg meetings and has been essentially a more global version of the latter, since it incorporates Japanese representatives).

One of the 'functions' such institutions appear to serve is that of 'mediating' between the economic interests of private capital and the requirement of a general interest on the part of the capitalist class as a whole. Much of the theorizing about the 'state' in the tradition of structural Marxism since the 1970s has confused this relation between capital and national governments, owing to the tendency to identify the abstraction called 'the state' and presume it as enjoying a virtual autonomy vis-à-vis capital; whereas the empirical evidence lends more support to the rather hastily dismissed model called 'instrumentalism'.

One of the key assumptions often made by structural Marxists, namely that the capitalist class is always divided into competing factions which have no mechanisms for co-ordination other than the state, is not empirically sustainable. Part of this misconception derives from an over-literal understanding of the concept of the 'market' as constituting the only social relation amongst different fractions of capital. At least as far as the very large international corporations are concerned, this is definitely not the case: very sophisticated organs do exist whereby these capitalist interests can and do hammer out common lines of strategy. Bilderberg is one of these mechanisms.

As the second world war drew to a close, the capitalist class in Western Europe was under severe threat from an upsurge of working class radicalism, the management of which required a strategy more sophisticated than conventional repression, and the first steps were taken, by political parties of both left and right, to develop 'corporatist' programs based on a kind of national protectionism. By contrast, in the USA, the war had brought to dominance an internationally-oriented capitalist class who saw very clearly that their interests lay in a thorough 'liberalization' of the world market, abolition of tariffs etc.. Only the false wisdom of hindsight could make the eventual Atlantic Alliance system that emerged by 1950 seem preordained by 'objective' historical forces. Indeed, so used have we become to hearing phrases like 'American imperialism' and witnessing US interventions throughout the world that we can forget just how difficult it was for this internationally oriented fraction of the American capitalist class to impose its agenda upon the US state: the deep-rooted tendency of American political culture has always been what Europeans call Isolationist' and it took extensive political work to drag the Americans into these foreign entanglements.

The Marshall Plan is named after the speech on June 5 1947 by US Secretary of State Marshall, which invited European countries to join in a co-operative plan for economic reconstruction, with explicit requirements for trade liberalization and increases in productivity. Over the next ten months there emerged the Foreign Assistance Act of 1948, which set up the Economic Co-operation Agency (ECA) to administer the European Recovery Program (ERP)—the so-called 'Marshall Aid'—which gave $13 billion in aid to 16 western European states. In four years, the ECA was superseded by the Mutual Security Agency (MSA) in 1951 which in turn was transformed into the Foreign Operations Agency (FOA) in 1954, later the International Co-operation Agency (ICA) in 1955 and finally the Agency for International Development (AID) in 1961 . It is generally recognized that this aid had a decidedly militaristic purpose, being essentially a prerequisite for the development of NATO.

It is less generally acknowledged, however, that this unprecedented exercise of international generosity (dubbed by Churchill the 'most unsordid act in history') served direct economic purposes for the internationally oriented US corporations which promoted it. William Clayton, for example, the Under-secretary for Economic Affairs, whose tour of Europe and letters sent back to Washington played a key role in preparing the plan, and who pushed it through Congress, personally profited to the tune of $700,000 a year; and his own company, Anderson, Clayton & Co. secured $10 million of Marshall, Plan orders up to the summer of 1949. General Motors similarly got $5.5 million worth of orders between July 1950 and 1951 (14.7% of the total) and the Ford Motor Company got $1 million (4.2% of the total).

The origin of the Marshall Plan are in fact to be found in the 'War and Peace Study Groups' instituted by the Council on Foreign Relations (CFR) in 1939. On December 6, 1939 the Rockefeller Foundation granted the Council nearly $50,000 to finance the first year of the project. Well over 120 influential individuals (academics and business leaders), at least 5 cabinet levels departments and 12 separate government agencies, bureaus or offices were involved in this. There were altogether 362 meetings and no less than 682 separate documents produced. Its astonishing that virtually none of the British academic scholarship on this period even acknowledges the existence of the CFR, let alone the War and Peace Study Groups.

The plan which Marshall presented in his speech had already been outlined in the proposals of a CFR study group of 1946 headed by the lawyer Charles M. Spofford and David Rockefeller, entitled 'Reconstruction in Western Europe'; and the specific proposal for unifying the Western European coal and steel basin as a bulwark against the USSR was made by John Foster Dulles in January 1947.

To trace the origin of the movement for European unification, however, requires that we go back to May 8 1946 and an address given at Chatham House by a Pole named Joseph Retinger. In this talk he outlined a plan for a federal Europe in which the states would relinquish part of their sovereignty. At the time, Retinger was secretary general of the Independent League for European Co-operation (ILEC), run by the Belgian Prime Minister Paul van Zeeland. During the war Retinger worked closely with van Zeeland and other exile leaders who would become prominent in the Bilderberg network (including Paul Rijkens). Out of these connections was born in 1942-3 the Benelux customs union, a kind of prototype of the Common Market.

The ideas outlined by Retinger were not new: there is a whole history of such projects for European unification and for even larger global schemes. One might just note here the assumption of the need for a 'great power' status as well as the almost taken-for-granted racism which drove Retinger's thinking: 'The end of the period during which the white man spread his activities over the whole globe saw the Continent itself undergoing a process of internal disruption........ there are no big powers left in continental Europe....... whose inhabitants after all, represent the most valuable human element in the world.'

Thus was formed the European Movement (whose first congress at the Hague in 1948 is the origin of the Council of Europe), which received substantial contributions from US government secret funds as well as private sources via the American Committee for a United Europe (ACUE). The names mentioned above are significant in the present context: Leffingwell preceded John McCloy and David Rockefeller as CFR chair, 1946-53, and had been a CFR director since 1927, while Franklin was executive director of the CFR 1953-7 and was later a Trilateral Commission Coordinator: also, incidentally an in-law of the Rockefellers.

US funding for the European Movement extended beyond 1952, most of it going to the European Youth Campaign, initiated by John McCloy, whose own career virtually personifies the Atlantic ruling class as a whole: a corporate lawyer of relatively humble origins, he became, through his contacts at Harvard, assistant Secretary of War 1941-45 and first President of the World Bank (IBRD), which he revamped to suit the interests of Wall Street; and then US High Commissioner for Germany 1949-52 (where, among other things, he enabled Krupp to regain control of his steel companies, advising on the establishment of the Krupp-Stiftung, modeled on the Ford Foundation—he was connected to Adenauer through his German wife, whose sister married Lewis Douglas, J. P. Morgan financier and later US ambassador to Britain), after which he became a director of both the Chase Manhattan Bank and the Ford Foundation in 1953. He was also an active member of the Bilderberg Group, becoming chair of the Council on Foreign Relations itself.

The Treaty of Rome [1957], which brought the Common Market into being, was nurtured at Bilderberg meetings."

As one can see, there is no conspiracy—it is the powerful Rich elite just doing their thing through bribery, wars and intimidations. Until the people take back their government, the above listed controls will remain in effect at taxpayers expense. Between 1980 and 1994, the U.S. taxpayers have invested the following Foreign Aid in:

Europe: $1.73 trillion

France: $126 million

Germany: $184 million

Britain: $461 million

Latin America: $115 million

Yet the progressive Democrats and President Obama say that the citizens of United States aren't paying enough taxes! THIS COUNTRY IS $14 TRILLION IN DEBT and the latest Congressional Budget Office estimate is that at our current spending forecast to support all of President Obama programs, the national debt, by 2020, will be $20 Trillion. SHOULDN'T WE BE GIVING OURSELVES THIS MONEY TO PAY THE DEBT? Instead of leaving this debt for our children and their children to pay?

President Obama's stimulus package which he touted as get the country out of a deep recession was just another 'smoke and mirror' scheme to put this country deeper in debt. Where did all of the money go? It went to Democrat contributors, organizations (ACORN), and unions—including billions of dollars to save or create jobs of government employees across the country. It went to save GM and Chrysler so that their employees could keep paying union dues. It went to AIG so that Goldman Sachs could be bailed out (after giving Obama almost $1 million in contributions). A staggering $125 billion went to teachers (thereby protecting their union dues). All those public employees will vote loyally Democrat to protect their bloated salaries and pensions that are bankrupting America. The country goes broke and generations of Americans face a bleak future.

Apparently, President Oboma role in the power elite plan is to bankrupt America. At least, on the surface that is the goal. Once this country is bankrupt we will become another Sudan. Sudan is a divided country in Africa, controlled by the northern half which is Communists and the southern section that can only be described as Christian. Under this status, we no longer will have to worry about our children paying off some insurmountable debt. They will be slaves of the power elite who will control their livelihood and their lives!

Chapter 7

CECIL RHODES
And
THE ROUND TABLE

The trouble with this country is that there are too many politicians who believe, with a conviction based on experience, that you can fool all the people all the time!   Franklin Pierce Adams

Cecil Rhodes had a dream and his dream drove him to his grave. He was not a conspirator but a dreamer. His story has been told many times but many readers only have heard his name but know nothing about his life or ambitions.

At the end of the 19th century the British Empire was the largest the world had ever seen, covering some 19 million square kilometers of territory and nearly a quarter of the world's population. Britain was also the pre-eminent global power, possessing the strongest navy in the world, the largest merchant fleet and dominating the global economy as the biggest investor, banker, insurer and commodity dealer. According to Niall Ferguson, author of *Empire: How Britain Made the Modern World (2003),* this Pax Britannica was not only a force for good, but also the "nearest thing there has ever been to a world government". Perhaps it was, though for the millions of indigenous peoples who had been colonized, often with great brutality, and whose lands and natural resources were now being plundered by the British while they were relegated to the status of second-class subjects, the benefits of being part of the British Empire were somewhat elusive.

Despite all these strengths, Britain was no longer at the peak of its power, a point it reached in the 1870s. Indeed, the start of the 20th century marked the final phases of its inevitable decline.

The erosion of British power was occurring on two fronts: first, through the imperial expansion of the other European powers, which encroached on its military dominance; and second, by the gradual loss of its industrial and commercial supremacy, upon which its military might had rested. The British Establishment was already reading these omens of imperial decay. The First Lord of the Admiralty, for example, had warned in 1900 that in coming years Britain,

"...by itself will not be strong enough to hold its proper place alongside of the US or Russia and probably not Germany. We shall be thrust aside by sheer weight."

It was in the midst of this pervading sense of gloom that, in 1909, a movement emerged which sought to preserve British power by converting its Empire into an "*Imperial Federation*" or "*Imperial Union*" This movement was known as the Round Table. David Icke, for example, writes that the Round Table "spawned a network of interconnecting groups in many countries working toward a common aim... *world government*".

The Round Table Group had as its purpose to instill its members into high places in governments and private-industry news sources, in different nations thus controlling the government and news in their individual countries. In order to do this, The Round Table Group formed the following branches around the world:

United States Council On Foreign Relations

Britain's Royal Institute of International Affairs

The Canadian Institute of International Affairs

The New Zealand Institute of International Affairs

The Australian Institute of International Affairs

The South African Institute of International Affairs

The Indian Institute of International Affairs

The Netherlands Institute of International Affairs

The Japanese Institute of Pacific Relations

The Chinese Institute of Pacific Relations

The Russian Institute of Pacific Relations

To this day, the above organizations are actively doing their nefarious work.

The three men who formed the original Round Table group were already well known in England. The leader was Cecil Rhodes, fabulously wealthy empire builder, and the most important person in South Africa. The second was William T. Stead, the famous, and probably also the most sensational, journalist of the day. The third was Reginald Baliol Brett, later known as Lord Esher, and confidant of Queen Victoria, and later to be the most influential advisor of King Edward VII, and King George V.

The three men drew up a plan for organization for their secret society, and a list of original members. The plan for organization provided for an inner circle, to be know as "The Society of the Elect", and an outer circle, to be known as "The Association of Helpers". Within The Society of the Elect, the real power was to be exercised by the leader, and a "Junta of Three". The leader was to be Rhodes, and the Junta was to be Stead, Brett, and Alfred Milner. In accordance with this decision, Milner was added to the society by Stead shortly after the meeting.

Of the Secret Societies goals, and methods of operation Professor Quigley writes, "The goals which Rhodes, and Milner sought, and the methods by which they hoped to achieve them were so similar by 1902 that the two were almost indistinguishable. Both sought to unite the world, and above all the English-speaking world, in a federal structure around Britain. Both felt that this goal could best be achieved by a secret band of men united to one another by devotion to the common cause, and by personal loyalty to one another. Both felt that this band should pursue its goal by secret political and economic influence behind the scenes, and by the control of journalistic, educational, and propaganda agencies...." This plan formed what was known as the Round Table Groups. (See above listing.)

The Round Table occupies a special place in most populist accounts of the New World Order, the group given a pivotal role in the World Government conspiracy. The reason for this focus on the Round Table is the rather sensational analysis of the group provided by Carroll Quigley (1910-1977) in his 1966 book, 'Tragedy and Hope: A History of the World in Our Time'. A professor of history and international relations at Georgetown University, Quigley discussed the Round Table movement in some detail, claiming it formed the hub of an "international Anglophile network" which had exercised disproportionate influence over the American and British governments for much of the 20th century Moreover, despite its apparent wealth and political connections and an ambitious propaganda program, the Round Table conspicuously failed to achieve its goal of imperial federation. It also fell short in its attempts to remold the League of Nations concept into a form that would support the Round Table's imperialist ambitions. The movement would also be beset by divisions between those who viewed the federation of the British Empire as an end in itself, and those who believed imperial federation should be a stepping-stone to world government.

Nevertheless, the movement's vision of a world ruled by an Anglo-American federation represented one of the first attempts in the 20th century by a power-elite clique to bypass democracy in order to achieve its goal of overriding national sovereignty and establishing a supranational form of governance. Yet the Round Table movement's legacy was not one of success but of failure. Its members' efforts to arrest Britain's decline by unifying the Empire soon proved futile, and their dream of ruling the world slipped from their grasp.

The Round Table was the product of two people: Cecil Rhodes (1853-1902) and Lord Alfred Milner (1854-1925). This was not to be a living partnership, given Rhodes's untimely death well before the Round Table was founded and their limited contacts while he was alive, but more of a posthumous association in which Milner sought to realize Rhodes's dream of a unified British Empire. As prominent Round Table member Leopold Amery (1873-1955) later observed,

"If the vision was Rhodes', it was Milner who over some twenty years laid securely the foundations of a system whose power...

throughout the English-speaking world...would be difficult to exaggerate"

While his claims of the Round Table's power can be forgiven as wishful thinking, Amery by no means overstates the importance of Rhodes and Milner.

Cecil Rhodes is better known as the founder and primary owner of the famous diamond company, De Beers; as creator of the colonies of Northern and Southern Rhodesia (now Zambia and Zimbabwe); and as Prime Minister of the Cape Colony from 1890 to 1896. Compelled by a life-threatening heart condition to leave Britain, Rhodes had traveled in the 1870s to southern Africa where he made his fortune in the diamond-mining boom in the Kimberley region. It was there that Rhodes first demonstrated his desire for centralized control.

Rhodes believed the intense competition between the hundreds of small mining companies was damaging the viability of the diamond industry. His solution was to establish a company with monopoly control over the supply of diamonds, thus making it more profitable in the long term. In 1888 Rhodes realized his vision, collaborating with share dealer Alfred Beit and the London bankers Nathaniel M. Rothschild and Sons to buy out rival mining companies throughout the Kimberley region. The product of this collusion was a single diamond mining company, De Beers Consolidated Mines. This bold move gave Rhodes and his backers "control of the commanding heights of the Cape economy" (Thomas) and made him, "almost overnight, the most powerful man in Africa" (Rotberg).

As Prime Minister of the Cape Colony, Chairman of De Beers and one of the richest and most aggressive imperialists in southern Africa, Rhodes commanded considerable power and his exploits earned him the admiring accolade of "the Colossus of Africa". Driven by an imperialist fervor, Rhodes embarked on a number of bold schemes devoted to the expansion and consolidation of British rule in Africa. Some of these plans were partially successful, such as the annexation of Matabeleland and Mashonaland in support of the British South Africa Company's goal of controlling all the land in the interior of Africa between the Limpopo and the Nile. Other schemes, such as his attempt to overthrow the Boer government in the Orange Free State through the Jameson Raid and his plans for a trans-African railway stretching from the Cape to Cairo, were for him personally costly and conspicuous failures.

Yet, in pursuing these various projects, Rhodes was not enacting his own ideas but using the plans of others to fulfill his broader vision. As one historian observed:

"Rhodes was not a thinker; he was doer. He appropriated the ideas of others rather than conceiving ideas himself.

Significantly, the only exception to this rule was his most ambitious grand design of all: imperial federation.

One key influence in Rhodes life was William Winwood Reade's book, The Martyrdom of Man (1872), a neo-Darwinian book which presents a universal history of humanity supporting the argument that suffering is necessary to the achievement of progress. Rhodes had read Martyrdom, describing it as a "creepy book", but he also said, somewhat ominously, that it had "made me what I am".

He also found inspiration in the imperialist fervor generated by Prime Minister Benjamin Disraeli's expansion of the British Empire in the 1870s. Disraeli himself was an advocate of imperial federation.

Rhodes first put his vision of imperial unity to paper on 2 June 1877 in his handwritten testimony, the so-called "Confession of Faith". In the Confession, Rhodes stated he had concluded that his chosen calling in life was not marriage, travel or the accumulation of wealth, but to make himself useful to his country. Expressing his belief in the inherent racial and cultural superiority of Anglo-Saxons, Rhodes argued that only the British should rule the world:

"I contend that we are the finest race in the world and the more of the world we inhabit the better it is for the human race. Just fancy

those parts that are at present inhabited by the most despicable of human beings; what an alteration there would be in them if they were brought under Anglo-Saxon influence... Added to which the absorption of the greater portion of the world under our rule simply means the end of all wars."

To this end, Rhodes put forward his own vision of an expanded British Empire that would be achieved by the formation of a secret society:

"Why should we not form a secret society with but one object: the furtherance of the British Empire and the bringing of the whole uncivilized world under British rule for the recovery of the United States for making the Anglo-Saxon race but one Empire. What a dream, and yet it is probable, it is possible."

Rhodes took his own first steps towards imperial federation on 5 February 1891 when he and Stead agreed on the structure of the secret society, or "Society of the Elect", that he had sought since 1877. Like Weishaupt's Illuminati (see Chapter 5), this proposed secret society had an elaborate hierarchical structure, based on that of the Jesuits, which comprised: at the top, the position of "General of the Society"—a position modeled on the General of the Jesuits—to be occupied by Rhodes, with Stead and Lord Rothschild as his designated successors; an executive committee called the "Junta of Three", comprising Stead, Milner and Reginald Baliol Brett (Lord Esher); then a "Circle of Initiates", consisting of a number of notables including Cardinal Manning, Lord Arthur Balfour, Lord Albert Grey and Sir Harry Johnston; and outside of this was the "Association of Helpers", the broad mass of the Society.

One of the puzzles surrounding this meeting is whether the "Society of the Elect" actually came into being. Quigley claims in Tragedy and Hope (1966) that Rhodes's "Society of the Elect" was not only "formally established" in 1891, but also that its "outer circle known as the 'Association of Helpers'" was "later organized by Milner as the Round Table".

Milner had access to Professor Weishaupt's Illuminati organizational plans and use these plans to organize the different groups within the Round Table's organization.

This secret society (Round Table Groups) would have "its members in every part of the British Empire", including in the schools and universities to select new members and in the Colonial legislatures, where they would "advocate the closer union of England and colonies, to crush all disloyalty and every movement for the severance of our Empire". He also envisaged this secret society owning "portions of the press, for the press rules the mind of the people". In addition, the use of the Jesuit's membership oath dictated secrecy. The oaths of the Knights of Columbus, Knights of Malta and Rhodes Scholars are similar to that of the Jesuits.

Rhodes's motivation for creating his own secret society stemmed from his disappointment and contempt for Freemasonry, which he had recently joined. His disdain for the Craft had been almost immediate, demonstrated at his induction banquet in June 1877 where, as a new life member for the Apollo Chapter of the Masonic Order, Rhodes scandalized his brethren by casually revealing the mystic cult secrets of the 33rd Degree Rite. In his Confession, Rhodes denigrated the Freemasons as an essentially pointless organization whose members "devote themselves to what at times appear the most ridiculous and absurd rites without an object and without an end". However, this was not a blanket rejection of *secret societies*, as he expressed his admiration for the Jesuits whom he believed had achieved much despite their "bad cause" and "bad leaders".

Elements of Rhodes's Confession were incorporated into his wills, of which eight were produced over the years as his fortune and ambitions increased but his cardiovascular problems worsened, reminding the Colossus that his time in this world was short. His second will of 19 September 1877, for example, was produced following a "heart attack" he had suffered in August of that year. Although it had only two executors, that document clarified Rhodes's essential vision of establishing a "Secret Society" devoted to "the extension of British rule throughout the world", including the "ultimate recovery of the United States as an integral part of the

British Empire". This would culminate in:

> *"...consolidation of the whole Empire, the inauguration of a system of Colonial Representation in the Imperial Parliament which may tend to weld together the disjointed members of the Empire, and finally the foundation of so great a power as to hereafter render wars impossible and promote the best interests of humanity."*

All that remained was to bring about this desired state of affairs, and in successive wills Rhodes continuously refined his envisaged secret society. In a letter accompanying his fourth will, written in June 1888, Rhodes instructed Lord Nathaniel M. Rothschild (1840-1915)—his collaborator and financier at De Beers and to whom he originally left most of his fortune—to obtain the Constitution of the Jesuits and "insert English Empire for Roman Catholic Religion" so the secret society could use the document as its charter.

But Lord Rothschild, although a supporter of imperial expansion, soon proved unworthy of this task. For one, Rothschild failed to meet Rhodes's immediate demands for assistance in achieving his various schemes in Africa. This frustrated the Colossus of Africa, who had apparently believed in the great power of the Rothschild name to work the all-too-numerous miracles he required.

Lord Rothschild also seemed unable to absorb Rhodes's ultimate imperial vision. The disappointment was obvious. Rhodes was to confide to his friend Lord Esher in 1891 that Lord Rothschild,

> *"...is absolutely incapable of understanding my ideas. I have endeavored to explain them to him, but I could see from the look on his face that it made no impression... and that I was simply wasting my time."*

The fate of Britain's richest banker was to be removed from Rhodes's subsequent wills and replaced with an anonymous trustee. Rhodes was to find a more understanding audience through his friendship with William T. Stead (1849-1912), editor of the Pall Mall Gazette and founder of the periodical, Review of Reviews. Stead was an ardent supporter of imperialism, conceiving it in Ruskinian terms of Britain's moral duty to the rest of the world, which he defined as the "imperialism of responsibility". He was a supporter of imperial federation, evident in the avowed purpose of Review of Reviews of "promoting the re-union of the English-speaking race".

However, Stead had also been a member of the South Africa Committee, which was opposed to Rhodes's brutal methods of expanding British rule in southern Africa. Nevertheless, it was an article by Stead in the Pall Mall Gazette, endorsing an "Anglo-American re-union", that had prompted Rhodes to seek him out during his visit to England in April 1889. Their subsequent meeting was to have a profound effect on Stead, who was to put aside his previous reservations and write excitedly of his newfound admiration for Rhodes, proclaiming that he had never before "met a man who, upon broad Imperial matters, was so entirely of my way of thinking". Stead was especially impressed with Rhodes's "gorgeous" ideas for the "federation, expansion and consolidation of the Empire".

The impact appears to have been mutual, with Rhodes giving Stead a gift of £2,000 to settle an adverse libel judgment and promising £20,000 to promote their ideas of imperial federation through the British media. In time, Rhodes was to show his confidence in Stead by naming him a trustee in one his wills. Stead was also to have an impact on the Anglo-American component of Rhodes's imperial vision. It is noted by Quigley that Rhodes accepted Stead's proposal to modify his vision of imperial federation to make "Washington the capital of the whole organization or allow parts of the empire to become states of the American Union". According to Stead's own account (and Quigley's most likely source), it was during Rhodes's visit to England in February 1891 that the diamond magnate had finally:

> *"...expressed his readiness to adopt the course from which he had at first recoiled... that of securing the unity of the English-speaking race*

by consenting to the absorption of the British Empire in the American Union if it could not be secured any other way... He expressed his deliberate conviction that English-speaking re-union was so great an end in itself as to justify even the sacrifice of the distinctive features and independent existence of the British Empire."

This Anglo-American arrangement thus became one of the central components of his envisaged supranational enterprise, if not an obsession. Rhodes often blamed King George III for the loss of the American colonies and once lamented to Stead that "if we had not lost America... the peace of the world [would have been] secured for all Eternity!" The postscript to his will of September 1893, for example, expressed his belief that the merger of Britain and the United States would "take the government of the whole world", leading to the "cessation of all wars and one language throughout the world".

Elsewhere, Rhodes envisaged joining the British House of Commons to the United States Congress, establishing an "Imperial Parliament" that would sit for five-year periods, alternating between London and Washington.

Rhodes's vision can appear quite idealistic, even naïve, in its motivations. Quigley contends that Rhodes's utopian scheme for a world-dominating Anglo-American Federation was driven not by greed or other materialist wants but by a sincere belief in Britain's mission to spread its culture and values worldwide for the common good. However, Rhodes also made some quite rational calculations about British power, particularly its declining economic fortunes. He recognized that British trade was suffering due to "hostile tariffs" imposed by America and Europe. As he was to tell Prime Minister Gladstone, the only logical solution was the "further acquisition of territory", giving Britain a domain large enough to maintain tariffs against the rest of the world. "Great Britain's position depends on her trade," Rhodes argued, saying that if Britain did not "take and open up the dependencies of the world which are at present devoted to barbarism, we shall shut out the world's trade".

Quite simply, Rhodes did not believe that free trade in itself would benefit Britain unless there were some political action to support it, preferably in the form of imperial expansion and consolidation. "Being a Free Trader," he was to write to Stead, "I believe that until the world comes to its senses you should declare war with those who are trying to boycott your manufactures." He had been particularly taken by South African politician Jan Hendrik Hofmeyr's proposal, first raised at the 1887 Colonial Conference, of an Empire-wide two-per-cent tariff against foreign goods. "The politics of the next hundred years are going to be tariffs and nothing else," Rhodes proclaimed while Prime Minister of the Cape Colony. In his letter to Stead, Rhodes identified the only possible solution:

> "You might finish the [tariff] war by union with America and universal peace, I mean after a hundred years and a secret society organized like [St Ignatius] Loyola's [founder of the Jesuits]."

In pursuing this course, Rhodes was in many respects one of the first true modern heirs to Adam Weishaupt, founder of the Bavarian Illuminati (see Chapter 5). A Professor of Law at the University of Ingolstadt and a former a Jesuit priest, Weishaupt created the Illuminati in 1776 to achieve his radical, utopian goal of transforming society. He envisaged a world devoid of "princes and nations", in which the human race would "become one family".

Rhodes's similarities with Weishaupt are threefold:

first, he came to the same conclusion as Weishaupt that creating his own **secret society** for the purposes of changing elite opinion was the only means to ensure that his goals could be achieved

second, he was similarly unimpressed by the Freemasons and the Jesuits, yet he copied their methods

finally, his ultimate goal was essentially the same as Weishaupt, in that he sought to create a world order in which peace would prevail as divisions would be overcome by a global civilization, albeit an

Anglo-Saxon one

There were a number of important differences, however, with Rhodes being influenced by Classical philosophers rather than by the Enlightenment theorists whom Weishaupt admired; this had made him into an ardent imperialist rather than the cosmopolitan idealist that Weishaupt clearly was. Unlike Weishaupt, a radical thinker who aspired to overthrow the existing political and religious order, Rhodes sought only to expand and preserve what he regarded as the absolute pinnacle of human civilization: the British Empire.

Furthermore, Weishaupt was an academic of limited means, whose only hope of realizing his vision was to use the Illuminati to try to infiltrate existing centers of power and sway elite opinion. His ambitious endeavor met with some success, but ultimately ran afoul of the Bavarian authorities, culminating in his exile and the banning of the Illuminati.

Rhodes, in contrast, with a controlling stake in southern Africa's diamond monopoly, two terms as Prime Minister of the Cape Colony and feted by Britain's Establishment, had at his disposal enormous financial and political resources-and, as such, ample opportunity to act on his ideas without fear of persecution by the state because, especially in southern Africa, *he was the state*.

Having such considerable political and economic power at his disposal, Cecil Rhodes had the luxury of being able to delegate responsibility for realizing his vision to other figures within the British Establishment; of these, Alfred Milner was to become his principal representative.

Of English and German parentage, Milner spent his early years in Germany before moving to England in 1869. He attended Oxford as an undergraduate from 1872 to 1876, becoming one of its more distinguished students. He was president of the Oxford Union in 1875 and later achieved first-class honors. Although at Oxford at the same time as Rhodes, and even in the same clubs, remarkably there is no evidence that they actually knew each other at that time.

His post-Oxford career also followed a somewhat different path to that of Rhodes. In 1881 Milner became a journalist for the Pall Mall Gazette, working with William Stead and eventually rising to the position of assistant editor. In the mid-1880s he dabbled in politics, making an unsuccessful run for Parliament in 1885. Milner then moved into the public service, attaining a number of senior positions befitting an Oxford-educated man, including: private secretary to George Goschen, Chancellor of the Exchequer; Undersecretary to the Egyptian Ministry of Finance from 1889 to 1892; and, on his return to England, Chairman of the Internal Revenue Board. In February 1897 he was appointed High Commissioner for South Africa and Governor of the Cape Colony, a dual appointment that was to prove to be one of the highlights of his Government career.

Milner's definitive personal statement of his support for imperial federation is his so-called "Credo", a document written late in his life and not published until after his death in 1925 by the Times—then under the editorship of fellow Round Table member Geoffrey Dawson. The Credo expressed Milner's thoughts about the British Empire that he had held since Oxford. It was also an affirmation of Milner's belief in the inherent superiority of the British people as a race and culture. The Credo was also Milner's way of definitively identifying himself as British, effectively repudiating his German parentage. In the Credo, Milner declared himself a "British Race Patriot" and "a Nationalist and not a cosmopolitan". Milner, however, recognized that Britain was "no longer a power in the world which it once was" and he expressed the hope that the Dominions could be "kept as an entity". He redefined the British state from a purely geographical unit to one based on race: wherever British people were in appreciable numbers should be considered part of Britain.

For Milner, imperial federation was but an end in itself—one that would preserve and perpetuate British power in the guise of a supranational state encompassing the United Kingdom and all its Dominions. He had made this sentiment quite clear as early as 1885 in a speech he delivered while campaigning for Parliament. Milner's speech not only expressed views that he would retain for the rest of his life—as revealed in his Credo—but also exposed his apparent conviction that imperial federation would hasten world peace.

> *"...I am no cosmopolitan... I think we can foresee a time when the great Anglo-Saxon Confederation throughout the world, with its members self-governing in their domestic concerns, but firmly united for the purposes of mutual protection, will not only be the most splendid political union that the world has ever known, but also the best security for universal peace."*

However, unlike Rhodes and Stead, Milner was skeptical that an Anglo-American re-union was possible. In fact, he was wary of American intentions and did not believe the division caused by the American Revolution could be so easily reversed.

> *"No doubt a great many Americans are thoroughly friendly to us,"* Milner was to write to a colleague in 1909, *"but a great number are hostile. The best thing we can hope for is to keep on good terms with them. I neither anticipate nor desire anything more."*

For Milner, preserving the British Empire in some new form was the highest priority; the goal of recovering the US he regarded as an unrealistic distraction.

More importantly, Milner did not share Rhodes's obvious enthusiasm for enlarging the British Empire. In 1884, for example, Milner explained to the Secretary of the Oxford Liberal Association his conviction:

> *"I am not anxious to extend the bounds of an Empire already vast or to increase responsibilities already onerous. But if I desire to limit the sphere of our actions abroad, it is in order that within this limited sphere we may be more and not less vigorous, resolute & courageous."*

Milner was also a socialist, though some observers suggest he adopted more of a Germanic or "Bismarckian state socialism" that favored the application of political will or state planning rather than natural forces to achieve desired outcomes. According to Stokes, Milner sought to fit people into a "pre-arranged scheme of society"; the people were not to be involved in its creation. Milner's enthusiasm for this state-socialist model stemmed from his "early faith in a planned society conceived and ordered by the scientific intelligence". Influenced by Otto von Bismarck's methods of uniting the Germanic people under one state, Milner had as his goal the consolidation of all the British people through an act of political will rather than through popular consent.

Chapter 8

COUNCIL ON FOREIGN RELATIONS

"The democracy will cease to exist when you take away from those who are willing to work and give to those who would not."

Thomas Jefferson

"The true equation is 'democracy' = government by world financiers... The main mark of modern governments is that we do not know who governs, de facto any more than de jure. We see the politician and not his backer; still less the backer of the backer; or what is most important of all, the banker of the backer. Enthroned above all, in a manner without parallel in all past, is the veiled prophet of finance, swaying all men living by a sort of magic, and delivering oracles in a language not understood [sic] of the people."

J.R.R. Tolkien, *Candour Magazine*, 13 July 1956.

"Since its founding... the CFR has been the preeminent intermediary between the world of high finance, big oil, corporate elitism, and the U.S. government. Its members slide smoothly into cabinet-level jobs in Republican and Democratic administrations. The policies promulgated in its quarterly journal, *Foreign Affairs*, become U.S. government policy."—Jonathan Vankin

Thomas Jefferson wrote: "The Central Bank is an institution of the most deadly hostility existing against the principles and form of our Constitution...if the American people allow private banks to control the issuance of their currency, first by inflation and then by deflation, the banks and corporations that will grow up around them will deprive the people of all their property until their children will wake up homeless on the continent their fathers conquered."

Does that not describe the situation in America today?

The shadowy political and even "foreign" beginnings of the Council on Foreign Relations have long been intentionally obscured. For more than nine decades the CFR received no notice by authors, the general public or serious researchers. When mentioned, it is almost always in articles detailing how many of the appointees of a given administration have a "CFR connection".

Santa Barbara sociologist G. William Domhoff wrote in 1978 that the CFR had been the subject of only two "academic studies." This, he said, provided "an impressive commentary in itself on how little social scientists know about policy-making in the United States." A lack of academic commentary has also been paralleled by little coverage in the media or press. It was not until some 37 years after the creation of the CFR that a mainstream magazine article was published in Harper's by Joseph Kraft in July 1958 entitled: "School for Statesmen."

The Council on Foreign Relations is an organization whose mission is to redefine American policy and push this republic into a one-world government – a NIGHTMARE beyond what most Americans can imagine. Rear Adm. Chester Ward was a member of the CFR for 16 years and later warned the American people as to the true intentions of this treasonous operation:

> *The most powerful clique in these elitist groups have one objective in common – they want to bring about the surrender of the sovereignty of the national independence of the United States. A second clique of international members in the CFR comprises the Wall Street international bankers and their key agents. Primarily, they want the world-banking monopoly from whatever power ends up in the control of global government.*

Former Congressman John R. Rarick warned:

> *The CFR, dedicated to one-world government, financed by a number of the largest tax-exempt foundations, and wielding such power and influence over our lives in the areas of finance, business, labor, military, education and mass communication media, should be familiar to every American concerned with good government and*

with preserving and defending the U.S. Constitution and our free-enterprise system. Yet, the nation's right to know machinery – the news media – usually so aggressive in exposures to inform our people, remain conspicuously silent when it comes to the CFR, its members and their activities.

The CFR is the establishment. Not only does it have influence and power in key decision-making positions at the highest levels of government to apply pressure from above, but it also finances and uses individuals and groups to bring pressure from below, to justify the high-level decisions for converting the United States from a sovereign constitutional republic into a servile member of a one-world dictatorship.

Professor Dr. Carroll Quigley, President Clinton's Law School mentor at Georgetown University, described the Council on Foreign Relations as one of several "front" organizations set up by the "network" for the purpose of advancing its internationalist schemes. He boasted:

"I know of the operations of this network because I have studied it for 20 years and was permitted for two years, in the early 1960s, to examine its papers and secret records."

A major clue was given by Professor Quigley in an interview. Professor Quigley dismissed the Radical-Right interpretation as 'garbage'. But he then added: 'To be perfectly blunt, you could find yourself in trouble dealing with this subject." He explained that his career as a lecturer in the government institution circuit was all but ruined because of the twenty or so pages he had written about the existence of Round Table Groups. As we will see, the CFR was, indeed, a British Round Table creation. This is one of the most important hidden secrets of the NYC-based CFR.

The story of the British connection to the Council on Foreign Relations may be traced back to George Peabody, J.P. Morgan, Andrew Carnegie, Nicholas M. Butler and Col. Edward House— all who may be described as British loyalists. A Secret Society was established by Cecil Rhodes in connection with Rothschild,

Morgan, Carnegie, and Rockefeller. A small highly secret group called the Round Table directed operations.

The story begins when George Peabody moved to London and took up English residence in 1837—the same year Queen Victoria ascended the throne. He joined with other merchant bankers who traded in dry goods in "high finance." This consisted of exclusive service to "governments, large companies and rich individuals." Soon after his arrival in London, Peabody was summoned by Baron Nathan Mayer Rothschild. Rothschild offered to pay all his entertainment bills. Hence, the famous Peabody July 4th dinners were bought and paid for by funds from the Rothschilds. In 1837, Peabody was warned, in advance, by his British friends of their decision "to withdraw credits from the worldwide markets and thereby depress commercial values; so he was fully liquid and ready to pounce on the American properties rendered bargains by the British move. In the crash of 1837 Peabody made a fortune purchasing depressed property in America. In 1854 the American Ambassador to London, James Buchanan, stormed out of the room when George Peabody toasted Queen Victoria before President Pierce. Peabody "was the founder of the Morgan financial empire." In 1859 Junius Morgan assumed control of George Peabody and Company. He traded Union bonds. The Civil War was "a bonanza for German-Jewish bankers on Wall Street, who raised loans from the numerous Union sympathizers in Germany." Peabody's American agent was the Boston firm of Beebe, Morgan and Company—headed by Junius Morgan. When J. Pierpont Morgan was in Vienna, his father wrote that Alexander Duncan had an opening in Duncan, Sherman & Company—a bank affiliated with George Peabody in London. Pierpont "soon was acting as George Peabody & Company's American representative.

Andrew Carnegie (1835-1919), in 1872, was paid a $150,000 commission for placing $6 million of bonds of a Pennsylvania branch road in Europe. He made another $75,000 on a second trip. While in England in 1873, on one of his frequent trips to Great Britain, he met Henry Bessemer and saw the Bessemer process of making steel. He then organized Carnegie, McCandless

& Company with a capital of $700,000 and built a new steel plant named the Edgar Thompson Steel Works (to flatter the president of the Pennsylvania Railroad to get generous rebates).

In the original edition of Andrew Carnegie's 1893 book, *Triumphant Democracy*, he stated: "Time may dispel many pleasing illusions and destroy many noble dreams but it will never shake my belief that the wound caused by the wholly unlooked for and undesired separation of the Mother from her child is not to bleed forever. Let men say what they will, therefore I say, that surely as the sun in the heavens once shone upon Britain and America united, so surely is it one morning to rise, shine upon, and greet again the United States, the British American Union." In 1948 a bio of Carnegie ended: "There is bound to be universal peace, through the final interlocking of the national interests of the U.S. and Britain. Andrew Carnegie, J.P. Morgan and Otto Kahn backed a 1915 Anglo-French loan which was said by Morgan to be made for "trade" purposes, however it was to aid the allies in WW1.

The League of Free Nations was created in early 1918 (in 1920 it became the Foreign Policy Association). The Foreign Policy Association "grew out of a meeting of nineteen writers, editors, educators, and such with a view to selling Wilsonian policies and the League of Nations to the public." The Foreign Policy Association, however, soon began to play "second fiddle" to the CFR.

In June 1918, a "more discrete" club of New York "financiers and international lawyers" was formed headed by Elihu Root (an Andrew Carnegie lawyer). The 108 members of the original Council on Foreign Relations were described by Whitney Shepardson as "high-ranking officers of banking, manufacturing, trading and finance companies, together with many lawyers." ***International Bankers provided the money***: In Britain the organization was (initially) called the Institute for International Affairs (IIA) while in New York it operated as the Council for Foreign Relations (CFR). The CFR was founded by East Coast bankers, lawyers and academicians. By April 1919, however, the CFR "went dormant.

Woodrow Wilson was elected President in 1913, beating incumbent William Howard Taft, who had vowed to veto legislation establishing a central bank. To divide the Republican vote and elect the relatively unknown Wilson, J.P. Morgan and Co. poured money into the candidacy of Teddy Roosevelt and his Progressive Party. According to an eyewitness, Wilson was brought to Democratic Party headquarters in 1912 by Bernard Baruch, a wealthy banker. He received an "indoctrination course" from those he met, and in return agreed, if elected: to support the projected Federal Reserve and the income tax, and "listen" to advice in case of war in Europe and on the composition of his cabinet.

Wilson's top advisor during his two terms was a man named Colonel Edward M. House. House's biographer, Charles Seymour, called him the "unseen guardian angel" of the Federal Reserve Act, helping to guide it through Congress. Another biographer wrote that House believed: "...the Constitution, product of eighteenth-century minds...was thoroughly outdated; that the country would be better off if the Constitution could be scrapped and rewritten..." House wrote a book entitled "Philip Dru: Administrator," published anonymously in 1912. The hero, Philip Dru, rules America and introduces radical changes, such as a graduated income tax, a central bank, and a "league of nations."

World War I produced both a large national debt, and huge profits for those who had backed Wilson. Baruch was appointed head of the War Industries Board, where he exercised dictatorial power over the national economy. He and the Rockefellers were reported to have earned over $200 million during the war. Wilson backer Cleveland Dodge sold munitions to the allies, while J.P. Morgan loaned them hundreds of millions, with the protection of U.S. entry into the war.

While profit was certainly a motive, the war was also useful to justify the notion of world government. William Hoar reveals in "Architects of Conspiracy" that during the 1950s, government investigators examining the records of the Carnegie Endowment for International Peace, a long- time promoter of globalism, found that several years before the outbreak of World War I, the Carnegie trustees were planning to involve the U.S. in a general war, to set the stage for world government.

The biggest drawback was that Americans did not want any involvement in European wars. Some kind of incident, such as the explosion of the battleship Main, which provoked the Spanish—American war, would have to be provided as provocation. This occurred when the Lusitania, carrying 128 Americans on board, was sunk by a German submarine, and anti-German sentiment was aroused. When war was declared, U.S. press portrayed all Germans as Huns and fanged serpents, and all Americans opposing the war as traitors.

What was not revealed at the time, however, was that the Lusitania was transporting six million pounds of war munitions to England, making it a legitimate target for the Germans. Almost two years before the Lusitania was sunk, the *New York Tribune* (June 19, 1913) carried a story which stated: "Cunard officials acknowledged to the *Tribune* correspondent today that the greyhound (Lusitania) was being equipped with high powered naval rifles..." In fact the Lusitania was registered in the British Navy as an auxiliary cruiser. Even so, the Germans had taken out large ads in the New York papers, warning Americans *not* take passage on the ship because it was carrying munitions and therefore a legitimate target of war. The evidence seems to point to a deliberate plan to have the ship sunk by the Germans. Colin Simpson, author of "The Lusitania," wrote that Winston Churchill, head of the British Admiralty during the war, had ordered a report to predict the political impact if a passenger ship carrying Americans was sunk. German naval codes had been broken by the British, who knew approximately where all U-boats near the British Isles were located.

According to Simpson, Commander Joseph Kenworthy, of British Naval Intelligence, stated: "The Lusitania was deliberately sent at considerably reduced speed into an area where a U-boat was known to be waiting...escorts withdrawn." Thus, even though Wilson had been reelected in 1916 with the slogan "He kept us out of war," America soon found itself fighting a European war. Actually, Colonel House had already negotiated a secret agreement with England, committing the U.S. to the conflict. It seems the American public had little say in the matter. But the biggest crime was that although President Wilson and Colonel House knew of the plan to sacrifice the Lusitania. (it was actually illegal for American passengers to be aboard a ship carrying munitions to belligerents), they DID NOT NOTIFY OR PREVENT Americans from sailing to Europe on it. This arrangement between Winston Churchill, President Wilson and Colonel House was treasonous to say the least. But to knowingly sacrifice American lives is murder. (The same thing happen just prior to WW II, President Roosevelt and his staff knew that the Japanese were going to attack Pearl Harbor four days before the event occurred, but didn't notify anybody until after it occurred. They stated the delay in notifying Pearl Harbor personnel about the attack was caused by radio interference and sent the message by other means. Thousands of Americans lost their lives at Pearl Harbor also.)

With the end of the war and the Versailles Treaty, which required severe war reparations from Germany, the way was paved for a leader in Germany such as Hitler. Wilson brought to the Paris Peace Conference his famous "fourteen points," with point fourteen being a proposal for a "general association of nations," which was to be the first step towards the goal of One World Government- the League of Nations. Even as the treaty was being written the fourteen points were whittled down in the peace negotiations because the victorious nations would not agree to Wilson's demands for: "freedom of the seas", an end to all trade barriers, and the self-determination of colonial states. Ray Stannard Baker, revealed that the League was not Wilson's idea. "...not a single idea--in the Covenant of the League was original with the President." Colonel House was the author of the Covenant, and Wilson had merely rewritten it to conform to his own phraseology.

The League of Nations was established, but it, and the plan for world government eventually failed because the U.S. Senate would not ratify the Versailles Treaty. Americans had tried the life of the international policeman and found that they preferred to leave such business to others. By the 1930's, a poll showed that more than 70% concurred that it was "a mistake for the United States to have entered World War I. Pat Robertson, in "The

New World Order," states that Colonel House, along with other internationalists, realized that America would not join any scheme for world government without a change in public opinion.

After a series of meetings, it was decided that an "Institute of International Affairs", with two branches, one in the United States and one in England, would be formed. The British branch became known as the Royal Institute of International Affairs, with leadership provided by members of the Round Table. Begun in the late 1800's by Cecil Rhodes, the Round Table aimed to federate the English speaking peoples of the world, and bring it under their rule.

The Council on Foreign Relations that was dormant was incorporated as the American branch in New York on July 29, 1921. Founding members included Colonel House, and "... such potentates of international banking as J.P. Morgan, John D. Rockefeller, Paul Warburg, Otto Kahn, and Jacob Schiff...the same clique which had engineered the establishment of the Federal Reserve System," according to Gary Allen in the October 1972 issue of "AMERICAN OPINION."

The founding president of the CFR was John W. Davis, J.P. Morgan's personal attorney, while the vice-president was Paul Cravath, also representing the Morgan interests. Professor Carroll Quigley characterized the CFR as "...a front group for J.P. Morgan and Company in association with the very small American Round Table Group." Over time Morgan influence was lost to the Rockefellers, who found that one world government fit their philosophy of business well. As John D. Rockefeller, Sr. had said: "Competition is a sin," and global monopoly fit their needs as they grew internationally.

Antony Sutton, a research fellow for the Hoover Institution for War, Revolution, and Peace at Stanford University, wrote of this philosophy: "While monopoly control of industries was once the objective of J.P. Morgan and J.D. Rockefeller, by the late nineteenth century the inner sanctums of Wall Street understood the most efficient way to gain an unchallenged monopoly was to 'go political' and make society go to work for the monopolists--

under the name of the public good and the public interest."

Frederick C. Howe revealed the strategy of using government in a 1906 book, "Confessions of a Monopolist": "These are the rules of big business...Get a monopoly; let society work for it. As corporations went international, national monopolies could no longer protect their interests. What was needed was a one world system of government controlled from behind the scenes. This had been the plan since the time of Colonel House, and to implement it, it was necessary to weaken the U.S. politically and economically.

During the 1920's, America enjoyed a decade of prosperity, fueled by the easy availability of credit. Between 1923 and 1929 the Federal Reserve expanded the money supply by sixty-two percent. When the stock market crashed, many small investors were ruined, but not "insiders." In March of 1929 Paul Warburg issued a tip that the 'Crash' was coming (just like the rich being warned in 1837), and the largest investors got out of the market, according to Allen and Abraham in "None Dare Call it Conspiracy."

With their fortunes intact, they were able to buy companies for a fraction of their worth. Shares that had sold for a dollar might now cost a nickel, and the buying power, and wealth, of the rich increased enormously. The small investors were left to commit suicide!

Louis McFadden, Chairman of the House Banking Committee declared: "It was not accidental. It was a carefully contrived occurrence...The international bankers sought to bring about a condition of despair here so that they might emerge as rulers of us all."

Curtis Dall, son-in-law of FDR and a syndicate manager for Lehman Brothers, an investment firm, was on the N.Y. Stock Exchange floor the day of the crash. In "FDR: My Exploited Father-In-Law," he states: "...it was the calculated 'shearing' of the public by the World-Money powers triggered by the planned sudden shortage of call money in the New York Market."

The 'Crash' paved the way for the man Wall Street had groomed for the presidency, FDR. Portrayed as a "man of the little people", the reality was that Roosevelt's family had been involved in New

York banking since the eighteenth century. Frederic Delano, FDR's uncle, served on the original Federal Reserve Board. FDR attended Groton and Harvard, and in the 1920's worked on Wall Street, sitting on the board of directors of eleven different corporations.

Dall wrote of his father-in-law: "...Most of his thoughts, his political 'ammunition,'...were carefully manufactured for him in advance by the CFR-One World Money group. Brilliantly... he exploded that prepared 'ammunition' in the middle of an unsuspecting target, the American people--and thus paid off and retained his internationalist political support."

Taking America off the gold standard in 1934, FDR opened the way to unrestrained money supply expansion, decades of inflation--and credit revenues for banks. Raising gold prices from $20 an ounce to $35, FDR and Treasury Secretary Henry Morgenthau, Jr. (son of a founding CFR member), gave international bankers huge profits.

FDR's most remembered program, the New Deal, could only be financed through heavy borrowing. In effect, those who had caused the Depression loaned America the money to recover from it. Then, through the National Recovery Administration, proposed by Bernard Baruch in 1930, they were put in charge of regulating the economy. FDR appointed Baruch disciple Hugh Johnson to run the National Recovery Act (NRA), assisted by CFR member Gerard Swope. With broad powers to regulate wages, prices, and working conditions, it was, as Herbert Hoover wrote in his memoirs: "...pure fascism;...merely a remaking of Mussolini's 'corporate state'..." The Supreme Court eventually ruled the NRA unconstitutional.

During the FDR years, the Council on Foreign Relations captured the political life of the U.S. Besides Treasury Secretary Morgenthau, other CFR members included Secretary of State Edward Stettinus, War Secretary Henry Stimson, and Assistant Secretary of State Sumner Welles.

Since 1934 almost every United States Secretary of State has been a CFR member; and ALL Secretaries of War or Defense, from Henry L. Stimson through Richard Cheney.

The CIA has been under CFR control almost continuously since its creation, starting with Allen Dulles, founding member of the CFR and brother of Secretary of State under President Eisenhower, John Foster Dulles. Allen Dulles had been at the Paris Peace Conference, joined the CFR in 1926, and later became its president.

John Foster Dulles had been one of Woodrow Wilson's young protégés at the Paris Peace Conference. A founding member of the CFR...he was an in-law of the Rockefellers, Chairman of the Board of the Rockefeller Foundation, and Board Chairman of the Carnegie Endowment for International Peace.

In 1940 FDR defeated internationalist Wendell Willkie, who wrote a book entitled "One World," and later became a CFR member. Congressman Usher Burdick protested at the time on the floor of the House that Willkie was being financed by J.P. Morgan and the New York utility bankers. Polls showed few Republicans favored him, yet the media portrayed him as THE Republican candidate.

Since that time nearly ALL presidential candidates have been CFR members. President Truman, who was not a member, was advised by a group of "wise men," all six of whom were CFR members, according to Gary Allen. In 1952 and 1956, CFR Adlai Stevenson challenged CFR Eisenhower.

In 1960, CFR Kennedy (who was probably killed because he had the courage NOT to go along with all their plans) CFR Nixon. In 1964 the GOP stunned the Establishment by nominating its candidate over Nelson Rockefeller.

Rockefeller and the CFR wing proceeded to picture Barry Goldwater as a dangerous radical. In 1968 CFR Nixon ran against CFR Humphrey. The 1972 "contest" featured CFR Nixon vs. CFR McGovern.

CFR candidates for president include George McGovern, Walter Mondale, Edmund Muskie, John Anderson, and Lloyd Bentsen. In 1976 we had Jimmy Carter, who is a member of the Trilateral Commission, created by David Rockefeller and CFR member Zbigniew Brzezinski with the goal of economic linkage between Japan, Europe, and the United States, and: "...managing the world economy...a smooth and peaceful evolution of the global system." We have also had (though his name strangely disappears from the membership list in 1979) CFR director (1977-79) George Bush, and last but not least, CFR member Bill Clinton.

They have all promoted the "New World Order," controlled by the United Nations. The problem is that "...the present United Nations organization is actually the creation of the CFR and is housed on land in Manhattan donated to it by the family of current CFR chairman David Rockefeller," as Pat Robertson describes it.

The original concept for the UN was the outcome of the Informal Agenda Group, formed in 1943 by Secretary of State Cordell Hull. All except Hull were CFR members, and Isaiah Bowman, a founding member of the CFR, originated the idea. The American delegation to the San Francisco meeting that drafted the charter of the United Nations in 1949 included CFR members Nelson Rockefeller, John Foster Dulles, John McCloy, and CFR members who were communist agents--Harry Dexter White, Owen Lattimore, and the Secretary-General of the conference, Alger Hiss. In all, the Council sent forty-seven of its members in the United States delegation, effectively controlling the outcome.

Since that time the CFR and its friends in the mass media (largely controlled by CFR members such as Katherine Graham of the "Washington Post" and Henry Luce of" Time, Life"), foundations, and political groups have lobbied consistently to grant the United Nations more authority and power. Bush and the Gulf War were but one of the latest calls for a "New World Order."

Admiral Chester Ward, a member of the CFR for over a decade, became one of its harshest critics, revealing its inner workings in a 1975 book, "Kissinger ON THE COUCH." In it he states "The most powerful cliques in these elitist groups have one objective in common: they want to bring about the surrender of the sovereignty and national independence of the United States."

Most CFR members are one-world-government ideologists whose long- term goals were officially summed up in September 1961 State Department Document 7277, adopted by the Nixon

Administration: "...elimination of all armed forces and armaments except those needed to maintain *INTERNAL* order within states and to furnish the United Nations with peace forces...by the time it (UN global government) would be so strong no nation could challenge it."

Within the CFR there exists a "much smaller group but more powerful...made up of Wall Street international bankers and their key agents. Primarily, they want the world banking monopoly from whatever power ends up in control of the global government ...This CFR faction is headed by the Rockefeller brothers," according to Ward. What must be remembered is that this is not some lunatic-fringe group...these are members of one of the most powerful private organizations in the world: the people who determine and control American economic, social, political, and military policy. Members' influence and control extends to "leaders in academia, public service, business, and the media," according to the CFR 1993 "Annual Report."

Their founding they describe as: "American Participants in the Paris Peace Conference decided that it was time for more private Americans to become familiar with the increasing responsibilities and obligations of the United States...there was a need for an organization able to provide for the continuous study of U.S. foreign policy for the BENEFIT OF ITS MEMBERS (emphasis mine) and a wider audience of interested Americans."

They sponsor hundreds of programs, where members "exchange views with American and foreign officials and policy experts... discuss foreign policy issues...consider international issues of concern to the business community" (Corporate business), and "...affiliated groups of community leaders throughout the United states...meet with decision makers."

The CFR states that it is "host to many views, advocate of none," and it "has no affiliation with the U.S. government." No, no affiliation at all, if you don't count: "A Council member was elected president of the United States...Dozens of other Council colleagues were called to serve in cabinet and sub-cabinet positions," as they describe it in "Foreign Affairs," along with many members of Congress, the Supreme Court, the Joint Chiefs, the Federal Reserve, and many other Federal bureaucrats. They are not AFFILIATED with government, they ARE the government, in effect. (See Appendix C for a list of infiltrators.)

One re-occurring view was stated in the 50th anniversary issue of "Foreign Affairs," the official publication of the CFR. In an article by Kingman Brewster, Jr. entitled "Reflections on Our National Purpose." Our purpose should be, according to him, to do away with our nationality, to "take some risks in order to invite others to pool their sovereignty with ours..."

These "risks" include disarming to the point where we would be helpless against the "peace-keeping" forces of a global UN government. We should happily surrender our sovereignty to the world government in the interests of the "world community."

In the past, we had the spectacle of Spc. 4 Michael New, a U.S. soldier in Germany who refuses to wear the uniform of the UN, facing an "administrative discharge." He states rightly that he swore an oath to defend the U.S. Constitution, not the United Nations. Many other Americans have taken that same oath, such as myself, and believe it is our sworn duty still to defend the Constitution, since an oath sworn before God must be fulfilled. (Why else do we swear to tell the truth in our courts, or when taking public office?) Is it a crime these days to actually BELIEVE in God and the oath that was taken?

Meanwhile, others who attempt to destroy the Constitution and our sovereignty are given honors and position...At least they are not hypocrites...only supremely arrogant.

"In short, the 'house of world order' will have to be built from the bottom up rather than from the top down...An end run around national sovereignty, eroding it piece by piece, will accomplish much more than the old fashioned assault..." in the opinion of Richard N. Gardner, former deputy assistant Secretary of State in "Foreign Affairs," April 1974.

James Warburg, son of CFR founder Paul Warburg, and a member of FDR's "brain trust," testified before the Senate Foreign Relations Committee on February 17, 1950, "We shall have world government whether or not you like it--by conquest or consent."

Is this an AMERICAN speaking, or a dangerous lunatic? Who is this "We" who threatens to CONQUER us? They are a group that actually has the power to do it, and is doing it every day, bit by bit.

CFR Members in the mass media, education, and entertainment push their propaganda of "humanism" and world brotherhood. We should all live in peace under a world government, and forget about such selfish things as nationalities and patriotism. We can solve our own problems. We don't need God, or morals, or values: it's all relative, anyway, right?...Because if we actually had some moral character and values, we might be able to discern that these people are actually EVIL.

These people are evil because they love money and power, and greed drives them to do anything to achieve their goals. They have lost all morality and conscience, and believe such concepts, as well as our Constitution, "outdated".

THAT is insanity--to have more wealth than can be spent, and still it is never enough. They have to control governments, start wars, conspire to rule the world; least the "common people" wake up to how they have gained their wealth, take it away from them, and demand that they pay the price for their crimes. That is why they constantly pit us one against the other, with "Diversity," Affirmative Action, and other programs,...black against white, men against women, rural against urban, ranchers against environmentalists, and on and on...least we look in their direction. The cruelest crime of all is our schools teaching our young children from kindergarten through Universities that we are a diverse country. WE ARE NOT A DIVERSE COUNTRY! Yes, we have a diverse population but we are—or we all should be—AMERICANS. This is not being taught in our schools. Divide and conquer is the theme of a Socialist Government. As long as they can divide the populace into little pockets of ethnic background, the populace will never be able to united and throw the scoundrels out of office.

We The People are held to a much higher standard. If we threaten the President or a public official, we are charged with a crime...yet the One-World-Gang can threaten the Constitution and the liberties of We The People, the sovereign rulers of this nation, and nothing is said or done. Perhaps they do not fear what man can do to them... they believe they have arranged everything, and their power and wealth will prevail in this world. However, those among them who have sworn an oath before God to uphold and defend the Constitution: the President, Federal Judges, members of Congress, and the military; may find one day that they do indeed have something to fear.

However, they really don't have any fear of the Government. Former President Clinton can prove that! The House and Senate were controlled by the Republican Party and the House voted to bring impeachment proceeding against than President Clinton on a number of counts.

All Democratic Senators were against the impeachment and a number of Republicans Senators (RINOs) went along with them- especially, Senator Collins and Senator Snow of Maine. Three Republicans and three Democrats established the rules and what charges could be presented to the Senate. The Senators set up a group of rules that the House members had to follow. These rules were roadblocks to a fair trail. In my opinion, what Senator Stevens and the other members of the Senate panel did was unconstitutional! The Constitution is quite clear on how an impeachment proceeding is to be handled. The HOUSE is the PROSECUTOR, The SENATE is the JURY and the SUPREME COURT JUSTICE is the PRESIDING JUDGE. WHERE IN JUDICIAL PRUDENCE DOES A JURY HAVE THE RIGHT TO TELL THE PROSECUTOR WHAT HE CAN PRESENT OR NOT PRESENT? It happened because Senator Lott who was leader of the Senate at the time, told the House Republicans' prosecuting staff that if they did not follow the rules required by the Senate, he would not schedule a date for the impeachment proceedings thus killing the trial.

Talking about justice, let's take a closer look at the Council on Foreign Relations. The CFR is a branch of a foreign entity called "The Round Table" which makes it a foreign entity. Have the CFR and all of its members registered as foreign agents? They should be or they should be taken to Court and prosecuted for breaking the law. The Foreign Agents Registration Act of 1938:

The act requires people and organizations who are under foreign control ("agents of a foreign principal") to register with the Department of Justice when acting on behalf of foreign interests. This law defines the agent of a foreign principal as someone who:

1. Engages in political activities for or in the interests of a foreign principal;

2. Acts in a public relations capacity for a foreign principal;

3. Solicits or dispenses anything of value within the United States for a foreign principal;

4. Represents the interests of a foreign principal before any agency or official of the U.S. government.

The Department of Justice has found that most violations of this law are unintentional and is attempting to work out problems without legal action. This is called *selective justice.* What the Justice Department cannot explain is where in the Law does it give them the authority to define who is guilty or not. A common citizen, for example, who is speeding down the highway at 70 mph and the speed limit is 60 mph and is stopped by a Patrol Officer and given a ticket for speeding. Should the Officer tear up the ticket because the driver was speeding UNINTENTIONALLY? Of course not—that is up to the Court to decide.

Colonel House, the fallen angel, still has relatives controlling the CFR. Karen Elliot House is Chairman of the Membership Committee, and a member of the Nominating Committee, along with Jeane Kirkpatrick. David Rockefeller is now "Honorary Chairman of the Board", after serving as Chairman 1970-1985; and "Director Emeritus," after serving as a Director 1949-1985. Peter G. Peterson is Chairman, Admiral B. R. Inman is Vice Chairman, while Thomas Foley and Jeane Kirkpatrick are Directors serving on the Executive Committee.

These "private citizens" have access to government officials and policy makers as often as they wish, yet the results of their meetings can only be given to other government officials, corporate officers, or law partners. Participants are forbidden to transmit an attributed statement to any public medium, such as newspapers or TV, where there is "risk that it will promptly be widely circulated or published," as the CFR "Annual Report" puts it.

Should not OUR public officials be forbidden to meet in secret with private groups? Public officials should only be allowed to discuss public business and policy in a public forum. The Public... remember us? There is much more to say about this group and their plans for America. Gary Allen, in "The Rockefeller File," states that they are behind the many regional government plans, which would abolish city, county, and state lines, leaving us at the mercy of federal bureaucrats; and behind the push for "land use" controls. They want "federal control of everything since they intend to control the federal government..."

There are also the many allegations of involvement (especially the CIA) in gun running, drug smuggling, prostitution and sex slaves; and the many mysterious assassinations and "suicides" of witnesses and others who get too close to the truth...but that is another story.

The Secretary of the Treasury is the public official responsible for keeping an eye on domestic and international monetary and financial policy. The following Secretaries of the Treasury *are members of the Council on Foreign Relations*:

- Robert B. Anderson (Eisenhower)

- Douglas C. Dillion (Kennedy/Johnson)

- Henry Hamill Fowler (Johnson)

- David M. Kennedy (Nixon)

- William Edward Simon (Nixon/Ford)

- W. Michael Blumenthal (Carter)

- G. William Miller (Carter)

- James A. Baker 3rd (Reagan)

- Nicholas F. Brady (Reagan/Bush)

The National Security Council provides intelligence support to the Secretary of the Treasury. The nature of the support, is classified. The support insures the Department of the Treasury acts in accord with recommended national security policy and makes its full contribution to the attainment of national security objectives and to the particular climate of opinion the United States is seeking to achieve in the world.

The Joint Chiefs of Staff DoD Publication 1 (1987) Glossary of Department of Defense Military Associated Terms defines:

"COVERT OPERATIONS: (DoD, Interpol, Inter-American Defense Board) Operations which are so planned and executed as to conceal the identity of or permit plausible denial by the sponsor. They differ from clandestine operations in that emphasis is placed on concealment of identity of sponsor rather than on concealment of the operation."

The Council on Foreign Relations has used covert operations to conceal their identity while methodically taking control of the Department of State, Central Intelligence Agency, and the Executive, Legislative, and Judicial branches of the Government.

As mentioned previously, President Truman was not a member of the Council of Foreign Relations but his Advisory Staff was made up of six members who where. It is almost certain that President Truman did not on his own draft the following directive. The directive was certainly written by his staff and he was hoodwinked into signing it.

On 20 June 1951, Harry S. Truman signed a directive establishing the Psychological Strategy Board. The directive read:

"Directive to:

The Secretary of State

The Secretary of Defense

The Director of Central Intelligence

It is the purpose of this directive to authorize and provide for the more effective planning, coordination and conduct, within the framework of approved national policies, of psychological operations. There is hereby established a Psychological Strategy

Board responsible, within the purposes and terms of this directive, for the formation and promulgation, as guidance to the departments and agencies responsible for psychological operations, of over-all national psychological objectives, policies and programs, and for the coordination and evaluation of the national psycho-logical effort. The Board will report to the National Security Council on the Board's activities and on its evaluation of the national psychological operations, including implementation of approved objectives, policies and programs by the departments and agencies concerned. Board shall be composed of:

> a. The undersecretary of State, the Deputy Secretary of Defense, and the Director of Central Intelligence, or in their absence, their appropriate designees

> b. An appropriate representative of the head of each other department or agency of the Government as may, from time to time, be determined by the Board.

The Board shall designate one of its members as Chairman. A representative of the Joint Chiefs of Staff shall sit with the Board as its principal military adviser in order that the Board may ensure that its objectives, policies and programs shall be related to approved plans for military operations..."

The Directorate Board Members:

The Psychological Strategy Board was Gordon Gray

Henry Kissinger was Gray's Consultant

Kissinger was also the paid political consultant to Rockefeller family.

Gray, Kissinger, and Rockefeller were members of the Council On Foreign Relations.

Gray served in the administration of Truman, Eisenhower, Kennedy, Johnson, Nixon and Ford.

Gordon Gray was heir to the R. J. Reynolds tobacco fortune and

President of the University of North Carolina.

Gray was a broadcast and publication media specialist.

Gray was instrumental in keeping the electorate uninformed when Eisenhower signed Presidential Executive Order 10483 replacing the Psychological Strategy Board with the Operations Coordinating Board.

The Operations Coordinating Board was composed of,

(1) The Under Secretary of State, who shall represent the Secretary of State and shall be the chairman of the Board.

(2) The Deputy Secretary of Defense, shall represent the Secretary of Defense.

(3) The Director of the Foreign Operations Administration

(4) The Director of Central Intelligence

(5) A representative of the President to be designated by the President.

(6) The Undersecretary or corresponding official of any Presidential agency that has been assigned responsibilities for the implementation of national security policy.

(7) The Special Assistant to the President for National Security Affairs.

(8) The Director of the United States Information Agency.

On 19 February 1961, President John F. Kennedy issued a Statement abolishing the Operations Coordinating Board.

No President ever wrote or signed an Executive Order establishing the Special Group. No President had a way of abolishing the Special Group. The Special Group was not established by Executive Order, it established itself. This was no accident. This was illegal. When Kennedy killed the Operations Coordinating Board, the Special Group operated as normal without the designated Presidential representative.

The Special Group is alive and well today. It consists of:

The Secretary of State

The Secretary of Defense

The Director of the CIA

none of which are elected officials.

The only way to abolish this ad hoc committee is to abolish:

The Department of Defense

The Central Intelligence Agency

The Department of State.

President Clinton, Secretary of State Warren Christopher, and Director of the CIA, John Deutch, and his predecessor James Woolsely belong to the Council on Foreign Relations. Les Aspin, Secretary of Defense

William Perry's predecessor also belonged to the Council on Foreign Relations.

The Joint Chiefs of Staff have defined psychological operations (PSYOPS) as those that:

"include psychological warfare and, in addition, encompass those political, military, economic and ideological actions planned and conducted to create in neutral or friendly foreign groups the emotions, attitudes, or behavior to support achievement of national objectives."

Another proposal "develops the concept of 'strategic psychological operations' as aimed at influencing and shaping decision-makers' power to govern or control their followers."

Council on Foreign Relations members in:

the State Department

the National Security Council

the Central Intelligence Agency

the Department of Defense

continue to control the lives of American people through well planned psycho-political operations. These psychological operations rob American citizens of the present, by creating false reality worlds. These false reality worlds are created to trick the American people into acting not in their own best interest but in the best interest of a group of subtle socialists intent on creating one world order under their control.

The Council on Foreign Relations is well known but its inner operations and how they control governments and the press is somewhat of a mystery. The following information was taken from *The Roundtable* website recovered through *WayBackMachine* website.

Monday, March 15, 1999, an AP article titled "Trilateral Commission reaches out to others," was published on the Tampa Bay Tribune website. The article is about the Council on Foreign Relations—the real story is hidden between the lines.

The Trilateral Commission *is a Council on Foreign Relations front organization*, established to influence American foreign policy, and facilitate Council on Foreign Relations expansion into Europe, Canada and Japan. The Council on Foreign Relations uses front organizations to protect it from connection to illegalities that could lead to a Congressional investigation.

Recent economic upheavals in the Far East and Russia have made them ripe for Council on Foreign Relations expansion. Chinese, Korean, Russian, and Ukrainian movers and shakers were invited to the Trilateral Commission meeting to participate in "discussion-groups." The material generated will be used to prepare propaganda designed to influence United States national policy makers to support foreign policy favorable to Council on Foreign Relations controlled corporate expansion into those nations, and manipulate United States public opinion to favor those policies.

The Trilateral Commission was not the first front organization used to cover-up Council on Foreign Relations manipulation of U.S. foreign policy concerning Russia and the Far East. In 1951 a Senate Judiciary Subcommittee on Internal Security, known as the

McCarren Committee, investigated another Council on Foreign Relations front organization, the American Institute of Pacific Relations, for its role in controlling and coordinating actions favorable to the Soviet Union, the expansion of international communism, and the loss of China to the Communists.

The Council on Foreign Relations established the American Institute of Pacific Relations in 1925. Morgan and Rockefeller controlled Wall Street interests, foundations , and corporations closely allied to them (including Standard Oil, International Telephone and Telegraph, and Chase National Bank) provided the funding. The Institute influenced United States policy towards Russia, China, and Japan, and helped establish Council on Foreign Relations controlled corporations in these areas.

The McCarren Committee never investigated the Council on Foreign Relations. The investigation created a battle between the "Left" and the "Right" over communism, that still serves to confuse Americans to this day, and divert attention from the organization responsible for the problems-- the Council on Foreign Relations.

The article quotes Paul Volcker. The article tells us the Trilateral Commission was founded by David Rockefeller. The article doesn't mention Volcker and Rockefeller are Council on Foreign Relations members. Or, that Council on Foreign Relations members Zbigniew Brzezinski, and Jimmy Carter helped Rockefeller found the Trilateral Commission.

The article tells us,

"The commission, founded 26 years ago by banker David Rockefeller, includes at least 300 private citizens from the United States, Canada, Europe and Japan." The article warps the truth by failing to mention that over 90% of the members are American citizens that belong to the Council on Foreign Relations.

Council membership is by invitation only, and

restricted to American citizens. The Trilateral Commission is an inner circle of Council on Foreign Relations members. The *RoundTable* website contains a 1992 list of Trilateral Commission members. It contains 337 names, 316 are found on various Council on Foreign Relations (1992, 1990, 1988, 1987, 1985, and 1984) membership lists. The other 21 people are either Americans not found on these Council on Foreign Relations rosters, or are *European and Japanese members.*

The Council on Foreign Relations *operates by influencing public opinion.* Well planned psycho-political operations are focused at influential decision makers. The operations manipulate decision makers to influence national policy to maximize Council member controlled industry profits. Council member controlled medicine, munitions, media, banking, energy, and food industries profit most during periods of unrest and war.

The current plan (1999) to bomb Serbia, is the latest example of this sort of Council on Foreign Relations psycho-political operation. On March 18th, Council on Foreign Relations member Madeleine Albright announced,

"..if Belgrade doesn't reverse course the Serbs alone will be responsible for the consequences and I would like to remind President Milosevic that NATO stands ready to take whatever measures are necessary."

As we all know, in Council on Foreign Relations members Albright and Clinton's book that means bombing the Serbs. Increasingly, it appears, key members of Congress are beginning to suspect that they have been lied to by the Clinton White House and are showing signs of real concern that the entire nation is about to become perpetrators of an attack upon a sovereign nation that could involve not peacekeeping but guerrilla warfare. Council on Foreign Relation member Clinton's Whitehouse contains 300 or more Council on Foreign Relations members he appointed to the CIA, NSC, State Department, and other agencies. Whose orchestrating the lying, Albright, Clinton, the Clinton Whitehouse, or the Council on Foreign Relations?

The Council on Foreign Relations member controlled media industry broadcasts the propaganda. "Discussion-group" sessions are closed to news coverage, but are attended by Council on Foreign Relations members who are prominent news and media figures. Security is usually tight, keeping the general public and news media out of the discussion, and identifying, photographing, adding as many "outsiders" as possible who do show up, to a list of potential "security" threats.

Any connections to the Council on Foreign Relations are edited out of the "news." Council on Foreign Relations success is largely due to keeping its identity a secret. Adopting an organization of overlapping circles helps them do this. The Trilateral Commission *is one inner circle of Council on Foreign Relations* members used to extend its influence abroad and to act as a cover to protect it from the scrutiny of a congressional investigation.

Fact: The Council on Foreign Relations evolved from the Institute of International Affairs. British and American branches of the Institute of International Affairs were established on May 30, 1919, at a meeting in the Hotel Majestic in Paris, by American and British Paris Peace Conference delegates who belonged to the American and British branches of a secret-organization founded by Cecil Rhodes.

Fact: "Discussion-groups" were a Rhodes' Secret-Society instrument developed and used to influence public opinion. The Institutes of International Affairs adopted their use. "Study-Groups" are formalized "discussion-groups" used by the Council on Foreign Relations and its branch organizations in other nations; Council controlled think tanks such as,

- Rand

- Brookings

- Council for Strategic International Studies

- John Hopkins Nitze School of Advanced International Studies

And, Council controlled governmental agencies like,
- the Central Intelligence Agency

- the State Department

Fact: The meetings are limited to a small group experts. Tight security is provided. Discussions and material generated are often classified. The material is used to produce classified reports and digests meant to influence select groups of high-ranking public officials, as well as articles, essays and stories meant to influence the public to accept the proposed national policy decisions.

By 1936 Institutes of International Affairs were established in,
- Australia

- Canada

- New Zealand

- South Africa

- India

- Newfoundland

Fact: Each Institute, under the *guise of world peace*, concentrated on influencing national-policy to achieve unity of all nations under one world government. By controlling public opinion tension is created between nations wary of losing their national identity, mores, and cultures, resulting in a state of perpetual warfare used to justify peace-time National Security Emergency measures and large military budgets. The groups goal was to maximize Institute member industry profits by selling both guns and butter. Could the reason famous economist John Kenneth Galbraith has never written a book exposing the Council on Foreign Relations effect on the economy because Galbraith *is a Council on Foreign Relations member?*

Fact: In 1918 a group of international lawyers and high-ranking officers of banking, manufacturing, trading and financing companies, headed by Theodore Roosevelt's Secretary of State Elihu

Root, founded the Council on Foreign Relations. Its purpose was to promote commerce through contact with distinguished foreign visitors.

Fact: After returning from the Paris Peace conference the American Institute of International Affairs approached the Council on Foreign Relations and proposed a merger. On July 29, 1921, the American Institute of International Affairs *merged with the Council on Foreign Relations* adopting their name. The new Council on Foreign Relations adopted the American Institute of International Affairs policy—unity of all nations under one world government.

Fact: In 1925 ten independent national councils holding territory in the Pacific Area were created to extend the influence of the Royal Institute of International Affairs and Council on Foreign Relations into Russia and the Far East. Institutes of Pacific Relations were established in an interlocking fashion with four existing Institutes of International Affairs (Britain, Canada, Australia, New Zealand) and the Council on Foreign Relations in the United States.

Fact: Institutes of Pacific Relations were established in five additional countries:

- 1. China
- 2. Japan
- 3. France
- 4. the Netherlands
- 5. the Soviet Union

Fact: By 1939 the Institutes of Pacific Relations in the four British areas had merged with the local Institutes of International affairs. The *American Institute of Pacific Relations remained a* Council on Foreign Relations front organization until it was eventually dissolved after the McCarren Committee investigation in 1951. The Institutes of Pacific Relations held joint meetings every two years.

Fact: The Pacific Council was a seven member Institute of Pacific Relations inner circle set up in 1927. Members of the four Commonwealth Institutes of Pacific Relations (Britain, Canada, Australia, New Zealand) also belonged to the Institute of International Affairs. The other three members belonged to the Chinese, Japanese, and American Institutes of Pacific Relations. Greene had attended the Paris Peace Conference, and after the conference was one of the early figures in the establishment of the Council on Foreign Relations. The Pacific Council planned and coordinated psycho-political operations designed to achieve the unity of all nations under one world government. One operation focused on extending the organizations influence and control throughout the League of Nations.

Fact: The annual Trilateral Commission meeting in Washington DC, *is nothing more than a Council on Foreign Relations discussion group*. Influential European, Canadian, and Japanese citizens were invited to join the Trilateral Commission so that they could help shape United States Foreign policy and participate in the profits of Council on Foreign Relations controlled Companies in their nations. Now, the Trilateral Commission is inviting Chinese, Korean, Russian, and Ukrainian movers and shakers to join in discussions that will be used to create psycho-political operations to influence United States Foreign policy allowing the Council on Foreign Relations to establish and control corporations is their countries.

SHOULD NOT MEMBERS OF CFR BE REQUIRED TO REGISTER AS FOREIGN AGENTS?

If any wrong-doings resulting from the psycho-political operations are discovered Congress will focus their investigation on the Trilateral Commission *and not the Council on Foreign Relations*. If such an investigation does take place, you will find, as in past congressional investigations, such as the Rockefeller Commission , the Church Committee, the Warren Commission, and the Tower Commission, that many of the Congressional investigators are members of the Council on Foreign Relations. (See the printer-friendly translation of Myron C. Fagan's recording *Illuminati and CFR Exposé* on the internet. It is easily assessable. Just Google Myron C. Fagan and when the list of articles appear select 'The Illuminati and CFR Expose'. Mr. Fagan tried to get his article published, but the so-called free press would not touch it. Mr. Fagan is not a fly-by-night writer but a well known producer and director of Drama, Comedies, Melodramas etc. He wrote and produced twelve plays. In his *Illuminati and CFR Exposé* he tells the true story of the Illuminati and the Council on Foreign Relations. He recorded it and it was later translated and put on the internet. It is a must reading of all American's who are fed up with a corrupt government.)

When the investigators, and those investigated, are closely connected, and the investigators don't disqualify themselves because of prejudice or personal interest, hasn't a crime called conspiracy to obstruct justice been committed? If the investigators are high-ranking public officials aren't the crimes high crimes, that call for impeachment and trial before Congress? Have you requested your elected representatives to call for a Congressional investigation of the Council on Foreign Relations?

FYI: Can any of you speak Greek? A friend sent a link to a website about Athanasios Strigas. The website seems to be a work in progress. The website says,

> "Athanasios Strigas is an agent of NATO and the Trilateral Commission and has written more than 8 big books about the Trilateral Commission and the politics in general...His books are written in Greek and are related mainly to the connection and the involvement of the Bilderberg Club in the Greek politics and political events (Turkish invasion in Cyprus, Military junta etc.). Nevertheless they give very much information on the Trilateral Commission, Bilderberg Club, NSA, NATO and the secret agencies."

Could this be why the Greek Government is bankrupt?

Chapter 9

The Church Commission Investigation

Politics is supposed to be the second oldest profession. I have come to realize that it bears a very close resemblance to the first. President Ronald Reagan

How the Council on Foreign Relations ensures that its organization remains in the background and is never in the news can be illustrated by reviewing the reports from the various committees and commissions that the Government establishes to investigate certain crimes and misdemeanors that occur in all facets of government. The Church Commission Investigation is a good example of what occurs. A review of this Commission follows. It was presented in an article "A Nation Deceived: Council on Foreign Relations Sponsorship of Covert Activities at Home and Abroad." from the *TheRoundTable* website.

In 1994, CFR member William Clinton's Council on Foreign Relations run administration began using the terrorist threat as an excuse to keep America in a state of perpetual National Security. The Council on Foreign Relations is the same group that planned and directed a psycho-political operation (psyop) called **Mutually Assured Destruction (MAD).** Latest warnings include the scenario of some rogue nation terrorizing the United States with a thermonuclear device or biological weapons.

On September 21, 1994, Reuter's reporter Steve Holland, wrote,

"UNITED NATIONS (Reuters)—As his grand jury testimony drowned out his message Monday, President Clinton soldiered on with a U.N. speech urging a united international effort against terrorism, which he called a "threat to all humankind."

Looking haggard and tired, Clinton received sustained applause from standing world leaders and other delegates to the packed U.N. General Assembly as he walked out."

Clinton's UN terrorism message got out loud and clear. Clinton, a *Council on Foreign Relations* member, is bearing false witness to his audience. Clinton's terrorism speech is another lie that enhances terrorism. The speech conceals the group sponsoring the terrorism—the Council on Foreign Relations. By concealing the sponsor, the terrorism becomes impossible to stop. By making it impossible to stop the terrorism, the terrorists targets are made to feel helpless, increasing their fear.

Steven Emerson who was part of the Council on Foreign Relations secret team was playing a role in the CFR's terrorist psyop. The Council on Foreign Relations works by targeting different groups and creating tension and hate between them. The Council on Foreign Relations works by creating an enemy the American people will hate, loath, fear, and be willing to fight.

Emerson's job was to *create hate between Muslims and Christians*. His job was to keep the Council on Foreign Relations sponsorship of this hate a secret. The terrorist psycho-political operation is particularly nasty because target groups are being worked up to murder innocent civilians. The CFR was creating a situation that would bring an enemy to American soil to kill innocent men, women, and children. If something was not done to stop the CFR, it is only a matter of time, until some Americans are injured or killed by an act of terrorism resulting from the CFR covert psycho-political operation.

In 1978 CFR member *Emerson* served on the staff of Frank Church's Senate subcommittee investigating *Aramco* and Saudi oil production. Subpoena power persuaded *SoCal* and *Exxon*, to produce some information. The investigation failed to uncover the links between Aramco, Saudi oil production and the Council on Foreign Relations. This was not the first Church run Senate committee investigation, staffed by Council on Foreign Relations members that failed to link the Council on Foreign Relations to wrong-doings. This was not the first Senate Committee that was mislead and lied to by Council on Foreign Relations members.

In 1975 during its first session the 94th Congress passed *Senate Resolution 21*. The resolution created a Senate Committee, chaired by Senator Frank Church, tasked with investigating intelligence activities of the CIA, FBI, and NSA. The Senate Committee's charter was to find out who was responsible for numerous civil liberty violations.

The committee established that the civil liberties of American citizens were violated. The committee discovered that a group called the "40 committee played a key role in coordinating the wrong-doings abroad." What the committee did not discover was that the "40 committee" evolved from the *Council on Foreign Relations* designed Psychological Strategy Board; was staffed and run by Council on Foreign Relations members; and coordinated psycho-political covert operations focused at American citizens violating their civil rights.

The civil liberty violations that existed in 1975 exist today. The following information provides evidence that Council on Foreign Relations members on the committee and who testified before the committee worked together to obstruct justice and keep CFR sponsorship of the psycho-political operations a secret. The sources of information are in the public domain and can be found by visiting your Federal Depository and Public Libraries.

The Church Committee's real name was the US Senate Select Committee To Study Governmental Operations With Respect to Intelligence Activities. On Tuesday, September 23, 1975 Senator Frank Church of Idaho called the committee to order. Senator Church said:

"The end of our involvement in Vietnam brought to a close a

tragic and turbulent chapter in American history. In Southeast Asia, well over 50,000 American soldiers lost their lives.

Here at home, massive antiwar demonstrations filled the streets. At Kent State and Jackson State, college students were shot down as they protested the policies of their Government.

Just as the country was obsessed by Vietnam, so too the White House became transfixed by the wave of domestic protest that swept the country. On June 5, 1970, President Nixon called in J. Edgar Hoover of the FBI, Richard Helms of the CIA, and others from military intelligence agencies. He charged them with getting better information on domestic dissenters, and directed them to determine whether they were subject to foreign influence.

After a series of meetings throughout June 1970, a special report was prepared for the President. It set forth several options which ranged from the innocuous to the extreme, from doing nothing to violating the civil liberties of American citizens. In a memorandum, White House aide Tom Charles Huston recommended the extreme options to the President. These recommendations have become known as the Huston plan. The President approved the plan, and it was sent to the FBI, CIA, and the military intelligence agencies for implementation.

Some provisions of the plan were clearly unconstitutional; others violated Federal statutes. As the distinguished American journalist Theodore White has observed, the Huston plan would have permitted Federal authorities to reach "all the way to every mailbox, every college campus, every telephone, every home."

Five days after the President approved the plan, he revoked it at the insistence of the FBI Director and Attorney General—to the dismay of those CIA, NSA, and FBI representatives who helped Huston develop it.

All this is a part of the public record, thanks to Senator Sam Ervin's hearings on Watergate. Yet, the matter does not rest here. Our investigations have revealed that the Huston plan itself was only an episode in the lawlessness which preceded and followed its brief existence.

First we have discovered that unlawful mail openings were being conducted long before the President was asked to authorize them in June 1970. The President and Mr. Huston, it appears, were deceived by the intelligence officials.

Second, even though the President revoked his approval of the Huston plan, the intelligence agencies paid no heed to the revocation. Instead, they continued the very practices for which they had sought presidential authority, expanding some of them and reinstating others which had been abolished years before. As in the case of the shellfish toxin, the decision of the President seemed to matter little.

Finally, the Huston plan, as we know now, must be viewed as but one episode in a continuous effort by the intelligence agencies to secure the sanction of higher authority for expanded surveillance at home and abroad.

As these hearings will reveal, the leaders of the CIA and individuals within the FBI continued to seek official blessing for the very wrongs envisaged in the Huston plan.

We open this public inquiry to reveal these dangers, and to begin the task of countering the erosion of our freedoms as American citizens."

While the hearings successfully pointed out many wrong-doings, they didn't identify the true sponsor of the wrong-doings— the Council on Foreign Relations. It was The Council on Foreign Relations not the US Government who was responsible for the 50,000 American soldiers lost in Vietnam, and the policies protested against by the students at Kent State and Jackson State. It was the *Council on Foreign Relations* who sponsored the reports, plans, and legislation that encouraged government agencies to violate the civil liberties of American citizens. Since CFR sponsorship was not disclosed, the Council on Foreign Relations continues the erosion of our freedoms as America citizens to this day.

The *Senate Select Committee members* were:
- Frank Church, Idaho, Chairman
- John G. Tower, Texas, Vice Chairman
- Philip A. Hart, Michigan
- Council on Foreign Relations member Walter Mondale, Minnesota
- Walter D. Huddleston, Kentucky
- Robert Morgan, North Carolina
- Gary Hart, Colorado
- Council on Foreign Relations member Howard H. Baker, Jr., Tennessee
- Barry Goldwater, Arizona
- Council on Foreign Relations member Charles McC. Mathais, Jr. Maryland
- Richard Schweiker, Pennsylvania
- Council on Foreign Relations member William G. Miller, Staff Director
- Council on Foreign Relations member Frederick A. O. Schwarz, Jr. Chief Counsel

- Curtis R. Smothers, Counsel to the Minority
- Audrey Hatry, Clerk of the Committee

Church Committee Staff members included:
- Council on Foreign Relations member Karl Inderfurth, Council on Foreign Relations member Zbigniew Brzezinski special assistant
- Council on Foreign Relations member David L. Aaron, deputy to Council on Foreign Relations member Zbigniew Brzezinski, and CFR member Walter Mondale's personal designee to the Church committee.
- Council on Foreign Relations member Gregory Treverton, a staff specialist on Western Europe.
- Council on Foreign Relations member Richard K. Betts, NSC consultant.
- Council on Foreign Relations member Lynn Etheridge Davis, who authored the initial draft of the Church Committee's report dealing with the National Security Council.
- Council on Foreign Relations member William B. Bader, professional staff member.

All of the *Church Committee Council on Foreign Relations Staff* members would be chosen to work in Council on Foreign Relations member Jimmy Carter's presidential administration. At least two, Karl Inderfurth and Lynn Etheridge Davis work in Council on Foreign Relations member Bill Clinton's administration.

Senate Resolution 21 resulted in seven hearings before the Church Committee. The subjects of the Hearings included:

Hearing 1

September 16, 17, and 18 1975—Unauthorized Storage of Toxic Agents. The CIA's Involvement in the development of bacteriological warfare materials.

Hearing 2

September 23, 24 and 25 1975—The Huston Plan. A plan to

permit Federal Authorities, including the FBI, CIA, NSA, and military intelligence agencies to use unconstitutional methods of gathering information about people labeled as domestic dissenters.

Hearing 3

October 2, 1975—The Internal Revenue Service. The FBI's use of IRS tax information to disrupt political activists and to harass citizens for political reasons.

Hearing 4

October 21, 22, and 24, 1975—Mail Opening. Why the Federal Government had been opening the mail of American citizens for over two decades.

Hearing 5

October 29 and November 6, 1975—The National Security Agency and Fourth Amendment Rights. The fourth amendment is,

"The right of the people to be secure in their persons, houses, papers, and effects, against unreasonable searches and seizures, shall not be tolerated, and no Warrants shall be issued, but upon probable cause, supported by Oath or affirmation, and particularly describing the place to be searched, and the persons or things to be seized."

The committee investigated the NSA's capacity to monitor the private communications of American citizens by using technology for intercepting international communications signals sent through the air to monitor domestic communications. Like the CIA, and IRS the NSA had a "watch list" containing the names of US citizens. The dominate concern of the committee was the intrusion by the Federal Government into the inalienable rights guaranteed Americans by the Constitution. The hearing revealed the *NSA* did not escape the temptation to have its operations expanded into provinces protected by the law.

Hearing 6

November 18, 19, December 2,3,9, 10, and 11, 1975—
The Federal Bureau of Investigation. The investigation of
the domestic intelligence activities of the FBI, concentrating
on domestic surveillance programs, and an inquiry into FBI
intelligence activities relating to foreign espionage and national
defense.

Hearing 7

December 4, and 5 1975- Covert Action. The committee
investigated the involvement of the United States in covert
activities in Chile from 1963 through 1973.

.

The Council on Foreign Relations Forty-Committee

In his opening remarks at the Church Committee's 7th hearing,
on December 4, Senator Frank Church said,

"The nature and extent of the American role in the overthrow
of a democratically-elected Chilean Government are matters
for deep and continuing public concern. While much of this
sad story had been revealed already, the public record remains
a jumble of allegations, distortions, and half-truths. This record
must be set straight. "

[CFR member]" President Ford has defended covert US activities
in Chile during 1970-73 as "in the best interest of the Chilean
people and certainly in our best interest." Why is that so? What
was there about the situation in Chile and the threat it posed
to our national security which made covert intervention into
political affairs of another democratic country either good for
Chile or necessary for the United States? These questions must
be answered. The committee's purpose is less to pass judgment
on what has been done than to understand, so that it may frame
appropriate legislation and recommendations to govern what
will be done in the future. "

"Given the President's statement, it is particularly unfortunate in my opinion that the administration has refused to testify and has planned to boycott the committee's hearings. The American people deserve to know the reason why the United States first undertook extensive, if not massive, covert operations within a democratic state in this hemisphere. They deserve to know why their Government sought, in 1970, to overthrow a popularly elected government."

"The administrations [there were over 100 CFR members in Nixon's administration] prohibition on testifying in a public forum on this subject has extended to the point of preventing CIA employees, both past and present, from coming before this committee. I find this particularly ironic since I spent the whole morning at the Pacxem in Terris [Peace on Earth] conference at the Sheraton Park Hotel here in Washington, publicly debating with [CFR member] Mr. Colby the covert operations that occurred in Chile during the period under investigation. And so it is not denied to him to discuss such matters publicly and before the assembled press at the Sheraton Park Hotel. It is denied him that he should come and testify here at the Capitol before this committee."

"I believe the position of the [Council on Foreign Relations run] administration is completely unjustified. [CFR member] Secretary Kissinger has argued that it would be inappropriate to appear before Congress and the American people to discuss covert action operations in which he was involved, yet only last week he gave a speech defending covert action. If the Secretary can give speeches on covert action, I believe he should be prepared to answer questions before Congress and the people of the country..."

The Church Committee would never learn "the reason why the United States first undertook extensive, if not massive, covert operations within a democratic state in this hemisphere, [or] why their Government sought, in 1970, to overthrow a popularly elected government." The reason was that a small group of selfish greedy men who belonged to the Council on Foreign Relations, had taken control of the United States government, and used massive covert operations to create tension and hate between different groups of people throughout the world. By creating tension and hate the Council on Foreign Relations kept the world in a state of perpetual warfare. While countless millions of people suffered from this condition Council on Foreign Relations medicine, munitions, media, food and energy industries at home and abroad reaped obscene profits. Today CFR members control more than 3/4ths of our nations wealth.

President Ford, *CIA* director William Colby and Secretary of State Henry Kissinger were all Council on Foreign Relations members. Over 100 CFR members served in the administration that refused to testify. At the hearing, Council on Foreign Relations member Karl F. Inderfurth, Professional Staff Member of the Senate Select Committee stated,

> "The United States was involved in the 1964 election on a massive scale. The Special Group, which was the predecessor of today's 40 Committee, authorized over $3 million between 1962 and 1964 to prevent the election of a Socialist or Communist candidate. In all, a total of nearly $4 million was spent by the CIA on some 15 covert action projects. These projects ranged from organizing slum dwellers to passing funds to political parties."

CFR member *Karl F. Inderfurth* is misinforming and deceiving the Church committee by understating the power of the "Special-Group," failing to trace the history of the "Special Group," back through the Operations Coordinating Board, to the Psychological Strategy board; and failing to inform the committee that all these groups were designed and staffed by members of the Council on Foreign Relations. It was Council on Foreign Relations members that planned and coordinated the Chile psycho-political operation.

CFR member Inderfurth served in several government positions. From 1975—1976 he was a Professional Staff Member of the Senate Intelligence Committee. From 1977 to 1979 he served on the staff of the National Security Council at the White House, as Special Assistant to CFR member Zbigniew Brzezinski, CFR member President Carter's National Security Adviser. And from 1979 to 1981, Mr. Inderfurth was the Deputy Staff Director for the Senate Foreign Relations Committee. Following the Senate Foreign Relations Committee, Inderfurth joined ABC News, first as a National Security Correspondent with a special focus on arms control.

Inderfurth was Moscow Correspondent for ABC News from February, 1989 to August 1991. In this capacity he reported on the historic transformation of the Soviet Union. During his two and a half year assignment, Mr. Inderfurth traveled to 12 of the then 15 Soviet republics and broadcast more than 400 reports for ABC News. Was Inderfurth an intelligence operative doubling as a news correspondent?

Between 1963 and 1974 thirteen million dollars were spent on covert operations in Chile. Congress received some kind of briefing (sometimes before, sometimes after the fact) on projects totaling about 7.1 million dollars. The **Church Committee** Staff report on covert action in Chile contains a section on the 40 committee (see following). The section leaves out key facts that connect the Council on Foreign Relations to the 40 committee. The number of Council on Foreign Relations members on the Church Committee and Church Committee staff provide compelling evidence that this information is missing by design. Conspicuously absent from the section is the mention of the Psychological Strategy Board; the Operations Coordinating board; the CFR's role in establishing these groups; and CFR 40 committee membership.

The section follows:

"1. 40 Committee Functions and Procedures

Throughout its history, the 40 Committee and its direct predecessors the 303 Committee and the Special Group—have had one overriding purpose to exercise political control over covert operations abroad. The 40 Committee is charged with considering the objectives of any proposed activity, whether or not it would accomplish these aims, and in general whether or not it would be "proper" and in the American interest. Minutes and summaries of 40 Committee meetings on Chile indicate that, by and large, these considerations were discussed and occasionally debated by 40 Committee members.

In addition to exercising political control, the 40 Committee has been responsible for framing covert operations in such a way that they could later be "disavowed" or "plausibly denied" by the United States government—or at least by the President. In the case of Chile, of course, this proved to be an impossible task. Not only was CIA involvement in Chile "blown," but in September 1974, [CFR member] President Ford publicly acknowledged at a press conference U.S. covert involvement in Chile.

Before covert action proposals are presented to the Director for submission to the 40 Committee, an internal CIA instruction states that they should be coordinated with the Department of State and that, ordinarily, concurrence by the ambassador to the country concerned is required. "Should," and "ordinarily" were underscored for an important reason--major covert action proposals are not always coordinated among the various agencies. Nor, for that matter, are they always discussed and/or approved by the 40 Committee. The Chile case, demonstrates that in at least one instance, the so-called Track II activity, the President instructed the CIA not to inform nor coordinate this activity with the Departments of State or Defense or the ambassador in the field. Nor was the 40 Committee ever informed.

Not all covert activities are approved by the 40 Committee. Projects not deemed politically risky or involving large sums of money can be approved within the CIA. By CIA statistics, only about one-fourth of all covert action projects are considered by the 40 Committee. The Committee has not been able to determine what percentage of covert action projects conducted by the CIA in Chile were approved within the CIA or required 40 Committee authorization.

Despite this fact, the Committee had found evidence of projects not considered by the 40 Committee, thus conforming to this general authorization rule. This is not to imply that the CIA undertook activities in Chile behind the back of the 40 Committee or without its approval. The Agency was simply following the authorization procedures for covert projects that then existed. These same procedures exist today.

There have been numerous criticisms of the 40 Committee procedures, some of which follow:

The criteria by which covert operation are brought before the 40 Committee appear to be fuzzy. The real degree of accountability for covert actions remains to be determined.

There is a basic conflict between sufficient consultation to insure accountability and sound decision on the one hand, and secure operations on the other. The risk of inadequate consultation may be aggravated by the more informal procedure of telephone clearances which has been used by the 40 Committee for several years.

The review of covert actions by the 40 Committee does not appear to be searching or thorough. There still appear to be serious risk that operations will end only when they come to grief."

The Joint Chiefs of Staff DoD Publication 1 (1987) Glossary of Department of Defense Military Associated Terms defines:

"COVERT OPERATIONS: (DoD, Interpol, Inter-American Defense Board) Operations which are so planned and executed as to conceal the identity of or permit plausible denial by the sponsor. They differ from clandestine operations in that emphasis is placed on concealment of identity of sponsor rather than on concealment of the operation."

The Senate Committee Report section on the 40 Committee is misleading. The statement holds the CIA accountable for sponsorship of the covert operations. The Council on Foreign Relations, not the CIA was the party responsible for planning and coordinating the covert operations under investigation. The Director of the CIA, usually a Council on Foreign Relations member, was also a member of the 40 Committee. Other 40 Committee members included the Secretary of State, the Secretary of Defense, who were also Council on Foreign Relations members. Many Department of State Ambassadors are also CFR members. The members of the 40 committee are much closer than the Senate committee report indicates. These men planed covert operations that would benefit the members of the Council on Foreign Relations and members of CFR branch organizations in other nations.

The 40 Committee was not only responsible for covert actions abroad but for covert actions focused at the American people. **The CFR sponsored covert actions included fixing American presidential elections.** The elections were rigged in such a way as to insure an administration, whether Democrat or Republican, packed with 100 or more Council on Foreign Relations members in key administrative positions. In at least five instances the President was a Council on Foreign Relations member (Eisenhower, Ford, Carter, Bush, Clinton). (See Appendix C for a partial list of CFR members in Government.)

The CFR members on the Church committee's failure to link the Council on Foreign Relations to the matters under investigation were playing a part in a covert operation. CFR member testimony before the committee and CFR members on the committee's reaction to the testimony concealed Council on Foreign Relations sponsorship to the wrong-doings being investigated by design.

The accountability for the *covert actions* lies with the Council on Foreign Relations and their counterparts in other nations such as Britain's Royal Institute of International Affairs. Besides membership in the Council on Foreign Relations, President Ford was a member of the Council on Foreign Relations international organization the Bilderbergers. *The foreign nationals in the Bilderberger group have more influence on America then the American people's Congressional representatives. President Clinton, and Britain's Prime Minister Tony Blair are also Bilderberger members*

The connection: CFR Coordination of Psycho-political Operations—The Psychological Strategy Board aka The Operations Coordinating Board aka The Special Group aka The Forty Committee

The Council on Foreign Relations propaganda machine manipulates American Citizens to accept the particular climate of opinion the Council on Foreign Relations seeks to achieve in the world. Council on Foreign Relations members working in an ad hoc committee called the "Special Group" and through a vast intra-governmental undercover infrastructure called the "Secret Team" formulate this opinion in the US. The Council on Foreign Relations, has methodically taken over the Department of State, The Federal Reserve, and the CIA.

The dominant Council on Foreign Relations members belong to an inner circle that plan and co-ordinate the psycho-political operations used to manipulate the American public. These are the Council on Foreign Relations members in the "Special Group."

The rest of the Council on Foreign Relations members, past and present, inside and outside of the government, are part of a "Secret Team" that play key parts in carrying out the psycho-political operations. The "Secret Team" is set up as circles within circles. Not every Council member knows exactly what psycho-political operations are being planned or what their exact role in the operation is. This allows them to deny responsibility and deny Council sponsorship of the operation.

Secret Team circles include Council on Foreign Relations members in top positions in:

- the legislative, executive, and judicial branches of government
- who control television, radio, and newspaper corporations
- who head the largest law firms
- who run the largest and most prestigious universities
- who direct the largest private foundations
- who direct the largest public corporations
- who direct and staff the major think tanks and University Institutes
- who hold top commands in the military

Up to 1961 every Secretary of State except *Cordell Hull*, and *James Byrnes*, were members of the Council on Foreign Relations. The undersecretaries, almost to a man, were also Council on Foreign Relations members. Secretaries of state have frequently been foundation officers. CFR member Dean Rusk went from the State Department after the war, to the presidency of the Rockefeller Foundation from 1952-60, and then back to State for eight years as secretary. CFR member John Foster Dulles was a trustee at Rockefeller while chairman at Carnegie. Other secretaries of state from the foundations included Edward R. Stettinius, Jr., Henry L. Stimson, Frank B. Kellogg, and Charles Evans Hughes.

In the 1950's Psychological operations, were coordinated by a Governmental agency called the Psychological Strategy Board. The architect of the Psychological Strategy Board was Gordon Gray. Gray had a consultant named Henry Kissinger. Kissinger was the paid political consultant to the Rockefeller family. Gordon Gray, Henry Kissinger, and many members of the Rockefeller family belonged to the Council on Foreign Relations. On Thursday 26 July 1951, President Truman would tell the press that the Psychological Strategy board was a part of the Central Intelligence Agency.

As head of the Office of Policy Coordination Council on Foreign Relations member, OSS veteran Frank Wisner ran most of the early peacetime covert operations. The Office of Policy Coordination was funded by the CIA and integrated into the CIA's Directorate of Plans in 1952, under Council on Foreign Relations member Allen Dulles. Both Wisner and Dulles were enthusiastic about covert operations. By mid-1953 the department was operating with 7,200 personnel and 74 percent of the CIA's total budget.

In the book 1984 Big Brother controlled the people by invading their privacy and using psychological manipulation to control and change reality through conscious deception, deliberate lying, and an official ideology that abounded in contradictions. The *Council on Foreign Relations* and its British counterpart the Royal Institute of International Affairs employ the same techniques to control people—including their fellow countrymen.

Hadley Cantril and Lloyd Free were Princeton University Social Psychologists; researchers; and members of the intelligence community. Council on Foreign Relations Member Nelson Rockefeller funded them to develop psycho-political policy strategies and techniques. Council on Foreign Relations Member Edward R. Murrow, would, with Rockefeller Foundation Funding conduct a research project to perform a systematic analysis of Nazi radio propaganda techniques and the political use of radio. This study would result in a world wide monitoring and broadcasting Government agency called the Foreign Broadcast Intelligence Service (FBIS).

The FBIS would become the United States Information Agency (USIA). The USIA was established to achieve US foreign policy by influencing public attitude at home and abroad using psycho-political policy strategies. The USIA Office of Research and reference service prepares data on psychological factors and propaganda problems considered by the Policy Planning Board in formulating psycho-political information policies for the National Security Council.

The Psychological Strategy Board became the renamed super-powered Operations Coordinating Board (OCB). The OCB had a vague ambiguous name that didn't provoke curiosity. It had more members than the Psychological Strategy board. It had the same mission, to use psychological strategy, propaganda, and mass media, to manipulate huge groups of individuals. It had a psychological warfare machine—the United States Information Agency at its disposal. The USIA would be responsible for foreign policy propaganda for the NSC.

The National Security Council (NSC) is responsible for recommending national security policy. The President for having the policy approved. The Operations Coordinating Board for coordinating interdepartmental aspects of operational policy plans to insure their timely and coordinated execution.

The National Security Council's recommended national security policy is the de- facto foreign policy of the United States. The Department of State's Policy Planning Board scripted the policy for the NSC. The USIA Office of Research and Reference service prepared data on psychological factors and propaganda problems. The Policy Planning Board used the data in formulating psycho-political information policies for the NSC. In 1955 the Director of the USIA became a voting member of the Operations Coordinating board; USIA representatives were invited to attend meetings of the NSC Planning Board; and the USIA Director was invited to Cabinet meetings.

From 1950-1953 CFR member Paul Nitze directed the Department of State Policy Planning Board. Nitze and crew scripted psycho-political operations for the National Security Council. The Paul H. Nitze School of Advanced International Studies (SAIS),

Johns Hopkins University, is the nation's second oldest graduate school of international relations. It was founded by Council on Foreign Relations members Paul Nitze and Christian Herter in 1943. SAIS Resident Faculty includes 36 professors. At least 20 are CFR members, two are CFR fellows.

SAIS Chairman and Dean CFR member Paul Wolfowitz, also directed the Department of State Policy Planning Board. Wolfowitz was undersecretary of defense during CFR member George Bush's administration and served as assistant secretary of state for East Asian and Pacific affairs. He authored PRESERVING PEACE IN THE NUCLEAR AGE (1983) and numerous articles on political science, economics and defense issues. Are the books, documentaries, and articles produced by SAIS faculty and alumni Department of State propaganda meant to trick, manipulate, and brainwash Americans into accepting Council on Foreign Relations doctrine?

On 19 February 1961, President John F. Kennedy issued a Statement abolishing the Operations Coordinating Board:

"I am today issuing an Executive Order abolishing the Operations Coordinating Board. This Board was used in the last Administration for work which we now plan to do in other ways. This action is part of our program for strengthening the responsibility of the individual departments.

First, we will center responsibility for much of the Board's work in the Secretary of State. He expects to rely particularly on the Assistant Secretaries in charge of regional bureaus, and they in turn will consult closely with other departments and agencies. This will be our ordinary rule of continuing coordination of our work in relation to a country or area.

Second, insofar as the Operations Coordinating

Board—as a descendent of the old Psychological Strategy Board—was concerned with the impact of our actions on foreign opinion—our "image" abroad—we expect its work to be done in a number of ways; in my own office, in the State Department, under Mr. Murrow of USIA, and by all who are concerned with the spirit and meaning of our actions in foreign policy. We believe that appropriate coordination can be assured here without extensive formal machinery.

Third, insofar as the *Operations Coordinating Board* served as an instrument for ensuring action at the President's direction, we plan to continue its work by maintaining direct communication with the responsible agencies, so that everyone will know what I have decided, while I, in turn, keep fully informed of the actions taken to carry out decisions. We of course expect that the policy of the White House will be the policy of the Executive Branch as a whole, and we shall take such steps as are needed to ensure this result.

I expect the senior officials who served as formal members of the Operations Coordinating Board will still keep in close and informal touch with each other on problems of common interest. Mr. Bromley Smith, who has been the Executive Officer of the Operations Coordinating Board, will continue to work with my Special Assistant, Mr. McGeorge Bundy [Bundy was a member of the Council on Foreign Relations], in following up on White House decisions in the area of national security. In these varied ways we intend that the net result shall be a strengthening of the process by which our policies are effectively coordinated and carried out, throughout the Executive Branch."

Kennedy's executive order didn't dissolve the Operations Coordinating Board, it made it invisible. The OCB became an ad hoc committee called the "Special Group." In *The CIA File*, author David Wise writes,

"In "The Invisible Government", published in 1964, Thomas B. Ross and I disclosed for the first time the existence of the "Special Group," the interagency government committee customarily cited by intelligence officials as the principal mechanism for control of covert operations.

The special Group was also known during the Eisenhower years as the *54/12 Group* and has been periodically renamed as the 303 committee—after a room number in the Executive Office Buildings—and during the Nixon administration, it acquired the name "Forty Committee. "...

It was this committee to which [CFR member] *Allen Dulles* was referring when he wrote in a now famous statement, 'The facts are that the CIA has never carried out any action of a political nature, given any support of any nature to any persons, potentates or movements, political or otherwise, without appropriate approval at high political level in our government outside the CIA. '"

Wise fails to connect the *"Special Group"* to the *Operations Coordinating Board*, or the *Psychological Strategy Board*, or the *Council on Foreign Relations*.

In 1975, Philip Agee, in the CIA DIARY, links the "Special Group" to the Operations Coordinating Board. A box on an organization chart writes,

"Operations Co-ordination Board (OCB) (later renamed the 54-12 Group, The Special Group, the 303 group and the 40 Committee) Director of Central Intelligence, Under Secretary of State, Deputy Secretary of Defense are ad hoc members. "

Agee fails to connect the Operations Coordinating board to the Psychological Strategy Board, or the Council on Foreign Relations.

Air Force Intelligence Officer L. Fletcher Prouty writes,

"During the Eisenhower years the NSC, which at times was a large and unwieldy body, was reduced for special functions and responsibilities to smaller staffs. For purposes of administering the CIA among others, the NSC Planning Board was established. The men who actually sat as working members of this smaller group were not the Secretaries themselves. These men are heads of vast organizations and have many demands upon their time. This means that even if they could attend most meetings, the essential criteria for leadership and continuity of the decision making-process simply could not be guaranteed.

Thus the sub-committee or special group idea was born, and these groups were made up of men especially designated for the task. In the case of the Special Group, called by many codes during the years, such as "Special Group 5412/2," it consists of a designated representative of the President, of the Secretary of State, of the Secretary of Defense, and the Director of The Central Intelligence Agency in person. This dilution of the level of responsibility made it possible for the CIA to assume more and more power as the years went by, as new administrations established their own operating procedures, and the control intended by the law became changed."

Prouty is understating what "this dilution did"—it made it impossible to dissolve the Special Group. Prouty fails to connect the "Special Group" to the Psychological Strategy board, the Operations Coordinating Board or the Council on Foreign Relations.

In an article titled *Journalism and the CIA: The Mighty Wurlitzer*, published on the Public Information Research (PIR—http://www. pir.org/) website NameBase NewsLine, No. 17, April-June 1997 the following was noted:

"The final months of 1977 produced three significant pieces of journalism on the CIA and the media, just before the issue was abandoned altogether. The first, by Joe Trento and Dave Roman, reported the connections between Copley Press and the CIA. Owner James S. Copley cooperated with the CIA for three decades. A subsidiary, Copley News Service, was used as a CIA front in Latin America, while reporters at the Copley-owned San Diego Union and Evening News were instructed to spy on antiwar protesters for the FBI. No less than 23 news service employees were simultaneously working for the CIA. James Copley, who died in 1973, was also a leading figure behind the CIA-funded Inter-American Press Association.

The next article was by Carl Bernstein of Watergate fame. In a long piece in *Rolling Stone*, he came up with the figure of 400 American journalists over the past 25 years, based primarily on interviews with Church committee staffers. This figure included stringers and freelancers who had an understanding that they were expected to help the CIA, as well as a small number of full-time CIA employees using journalism as a cover. It did not include foreigners, nor did it include numerous Americans who traded favors with the CIA in the normal give-and-take between a journalist and his sources. In addition to some of the names already mentioned above, Bernstein supplied details on Stewart and Joseph Alsop, Henry Luce, Barry Bingham Sr. of the Louisville Courier-Journal, Hal Hendrix of the Miami News, columnist C.L. Sulzberger, Richard Salant of CBS, and Philip Graham and John Hayes of the Washington Post.

Bernstein concentrated more on the owners, executives, and editors of news organizations than on individual reporters. "Lets's not pick on some poor reporters, for God's sake," William Colby said at one point to the Church committee's investigators. "Let's go to the management. They were witting (cognizant)."

Bernstein noted that Colby had specific definitions for words such as "contract employee," "agent," "asset," "accredited correspondent," "editorial employee," "freelance," "stringer," and even "reporter," and through careful use of these words, the CIA,

> "managed to obscure the most elemental fact about the relationships detailed in its files: i.e., that there was recognition by all parties involved that the cooperating journalists were working for the CIA—whether or not they were paid or had signed employment contracts."

The reaction to Bernstein's piece among mainstream media was to ignore it, or to suggest that it was sloppy and exaggerated. Then two months later, the New York Times published the results of their "three-month inquiry by a team of Times reporters and researchers." This three-part series not only confirmed Bernstein, but added a wealth of far-ranging details and contained twice as many names. Now almost everyone pretended not to notice.

The Times reported that over the last twenty years, the CIA owned or subsidized *more than fifty newspapers, news services, radio stations, periodicals and other communications facilities*, most of them overseas. These were used for propaganda efforts, or even as cover for operations. Another dozen foreign news organizations were infiltrated by paid CIA agents. At least 22 American news organizations had employed American journalists who were also working for the CIA, and nearly a dozen American publishing houses printed some of the more than 1,000 books that had been produced or subsidized by the CIA. When asked in a 1976 interview whether the CIA had ever told its media agents what to write, William Colby replied, "Oh, sure, all the time."

Since domestic propaganda was a violation of the their charter, the CIA defined the predictable effects of their foreign publications as "blowback" or "domestic fallout," which they considered to be "inevitable and consequently permissible." But former CIA employees told the Times that apart from this unintended blowback, "some CIA propaganda efforts, especially during the Vietnam War, had been carried out with a view toward their eventual impact in the United States." The Times series concluded that at its peak, the CIA's network "embraced more than 800 news and public information organizations and individuals."

Conspicuously absent from the CIA and the media articles are links to the Council on Foreign Relations. How many of the journalists, owners, executives and editors that the reporters concentrated on were also members of the Council on Foreign Relations. Are Joe Trento, Dave Roman, Carl Bernstein and the New York Times reporters near-sighted, poorly informed investigative journalists, or , CFR insiders or CIA operatives participating in keeping CFR sponsorship of covert operations a secret? Why haven't they connected "The Special Group" (aka the 40-Committee, aka the Operations Coordinating Board, aka the

Psychological Strategy Board) to the Council on Foreign Relations? Was deep throat the Council on
Foreign Relations "Special Group?"

The House Committee Fails To Uncover (Council on Foreign Relations Sponsorship of Covert Activities)

In 1975 the House also established a committee to look into constitutional violations committed by various intelligence agencies. The House committee was chaired by Otis Pike. Under pressure from the executive branch, which contained over 100 Council on Foreign Relations members, the House voted not to release its report. The report was leaked to the Village Voice. The Voice printed the report. Arron Latham wrote an introduction summarizing the second section, "The Select Committee's Investigative Record."

Latham's introduction talks about the 40-committee. Like the Senate, the House concluded the 40-committee coordinated covert operations focused at various nations including our own. In his introduction Latham writes,

> "One of the most important conclusions reached by the Pike committee's report is that the CIA is not a "rogue elephant"—as Senator *Church*. the chairman of the Senate select committee on intelligence, once called it. The Pike report says" All evidence in hand suggests that the CIA, far from being out of control. has been utterly responsive to the instructions of the president and the the Assistant to the President for National Security Affairs."

The committee came to this conclusion after an unprecedented study of all operations approved by the Forty-Committee over the past ten years. The Forty-Committee, which is chaired by the president's foreign policy adviser, is supposed to pass on all sensitive covert activities undertaken by the CIA. *The Pike committee* categorized different types of covert operations and looked for patterns.

It may surprise some to discover that the largest single category of covert activity concerned tampering with free elections around the world. These election operations make up a full 32 per-cent of the covert action projects approved by the Forty-Committee since 1961. The report says the operations usually mean "providing some form of financial election support to foreign parties and individuals. Such support could be negative as well as positive." Most of the money has gone to developing countries and generally "to incumbent moderate party leaders and heads of state." One "Third World leader" received $960,000 over a 14-year period.

The second largest covert action category is "media and propaganda." The committee found that 29 percent of the covert projects approved by the Forty-Committee fell under this heading. The report says:

"Activities have included support of friendly media, major propaganda efforts, insertion of articles into the local press, and distribution of books and leaflets. By far the largest single recipient has been a European publishing house funded since 1951. About 25 percent of the program has been directed at the Soviet Bloc, in the publication and clandestine import and export of Western and Soviet dissident literature."

The third largest category is "Paramilitary/Arms Transfers." These make up 23 percent of the total Forty-Committee approved covert action projects. Although these rank third in total numbers. They rank first in expense. The committee report states:

"By far the most interesting, and important fact to emerge was the recognition that the great majority of these covert action projects were proposed by parties outside CIA. Many of these programs were summarily ordered over CIA objections. CIA misgivings, however, were at times weakly expressed, as the CIA is afflicted with a 'can do' attitude."

Latham writes,

"As a part of its investigation of covert action, the Pike committee examined three recent operations: our funding of pro-U.S. elements during the 1972 Italian election; our funding of the Kurdish rebellion in Iraq; and our assistance to one of the contending factions in Angola.

The committee report says that we spent $10 million in the 1972 Italian general election "perhaps needlessly." The election produced not only a bitter struggle between Italy's Christian Democratic party—it also produced an even more bitter struggle between our CIA station chief in Rome and our ambassador in Rome."

If the Pike Committee had been more thorough they would have discovered that the first fully sanctioned and funded CIA covert operation resulted in the outcome of the Italian election of 1948, and that the Council on Foreign Relations played a significant part in carrying out the covert operation. In "How Nations See Each Other." (1953) Hadley Cantril writes about a tool, developed prior to 1939, to investigate people's perception of their nationality and other nationalities. The tool became known as the Buchanan-Cantril "Adjective Check List."

The "Adjective Check List", contained twelve adjectives: Hard-working; Intelligent; Practical; Generous; Brave; Progressive; Self-Controlled; Peace-Loving; Conceited; Cruel; Domineering; Backward. It was based on the observation people tend to ascribe to their group a set of characteristics different from the character traits ascribed to other groups. The resulting self-image is predominantly flattering, while their picture of "others" is strongly influenced by how much they perceive those others to be like themselves. The relative "similarity" or dissimilarity" between group stereotypes is a useful indicator of the degree of like or dislike between groups or nations.

The adjective check-list is used to help script and test the effectiveness of psycho-political operations focused at entire nations. Groups are tested to determine the degree of like/dislike between them. The Information is used to script the PSYOP. The PSYOP is carried out without the groups knowledge. The groups are tested again. The increase or decrease of like/dislike indicates the PSYOP's effectiveness.

The adjective check list was used to gather information that Council on Foreign Relations George Kennan used to script the 1948 Italian Election *PSYOP*. Lloyd Free broadcasted the script over the radio. Hadley Cantril evaluated the effectiveness of the broadcasts in influencing public opinion. The Italian public was manipulated into electing CFR insider Luigi Einaudi the President of Italy.

In 1948 Einaudi's son Mario, was a professor at Cornell University. Among other projects Mario was a contributor to a book titled *Foreign Government—The Dynamics of Politics Abroad.* Mario's bio reads,

"Mairo Einaudi, a research fellow of the Rockefeller Foundation 1927-29, professor of government at Cornell University. He has been a faculty member of the University of Messina (Italy), Harvard University, and Fordham University. His principal fields of teaching are comparative government and political theory. His books include a study of the political thought of Edmund Burke (1930) and Pysiocratic Doctrine of Judicial Control (1938). He is a frequent contributor to such journals as Foreign Affairs, Review of Politics, Social Research, and American Political Science Review. He has recently returned from an extended field investigation of Western Europe."

Foreign Affairs magazine is published by the CFR. Today, *Mario Einaudi* and his son *Luigi Einaudi* (President Einaudi's grandson) are both CFR members.

At the end of his introduction, Latham writes,

"in many ways the moral of the Pike papers seems to be: controlling the intelligence community must begin with controlling Henry Kissinger."

Controlling the intelligence community must begin with controlling the Council on Foreign Relations. Both the *Church Committee*, and the *Pike Committee* investigated the 40-committee, finding it responsible for covert operations, and constitutional violations at home and abroad. Neither Committee tied the Council on Foreign Relations to the 40-committee nor even mentioned the organization in their report. The 40-committee evolved from *The Psychological Strategy Board*. The Psychological Strategy board was designed by Council on Foreign Relations members Gordon Gray and Henry Kissinger, and created by an Executive Order written by Harry Truman.

At the fifth hearing about the National Security Agency, Senator Church commented that,

"Actually the [National Security] Agency name is unknown to most Americans, either by its acronym or its full name. In contrast to the CIA, one has to search far and wide to find someone who has ever heard of the NSA. This is peculiar, because the National Security Agency is an immense installing..."

If most Americans were unfamiliar with the NSA even more Americans, then and now are unfamiliar with the "Special Group" and the "Council on Foreign Relations."

When CFR member Inderfurth testified, before the Church Committee about the 40-committee and special group he was misinforming the Senate Select committee. The 40 committee, can be traced to the Special Group, which can be traced to the Operation's Coordinating Board which can be traced to the Psychological Strategy Board. All these groups were established and run by members of the Council on Foreign Relations.

Isn't it illegal to misinform a Senate Committee? If any of the Council on Foreign Relations members sitting on the committee were not willing participants in a conspiracy to hide the Council on Foreign Relations sponsorship of covert activities, why didn't any of them point out the links to the Council on Foreign Relations? Were Council on Foreign Relations members on the Committee and who testified before the committee participating in a covert operation designed to cover up links of Governmental wrong doings, illegalities and abuse? Isn't that treason?

The *Pike Committee*, discovered that America was mislead in such a way as to bring our country to the brink of war. In the *Village Voice* article, Latham wrote,

> "Moving to the Holy Land, the committee reported, "The Mid-East war gave the intelligence community a real test of how it can perform when all its best technology and human skills are focused on a known world 'hot spot.' It failed."

The failure of our intelligence before the Arab assault has been generally recognized for some time, but the Pike Papers maintain that there may have been an even more serious intelligence failure after the attack. Since we had not anticipated trouble in the Middle East. our spy satellites were caught out of position. We were therefore unable to monitor adequately the progress of the fighting and wound up relying "almost unquestioningly" on Israeli battle-field reports. We therefore believed the Israelis when they said they had not violated the cease-fire.

The Pike committee concluded:

> "Thus misled. the U.S. clashed with the better-informed Soviets on the latter's strong reaction to Israeli cease-fire violations. Soviet threats to intervene militarily were met with worldwide U.S. troop alert. Poor intelligence had brought America to the brink of war."

Moving on to Portugal. the committee asked:

> "Do our intelligence services know what-is going on beneath the surface in allied nations that are not making headlines."

The answer on April 25, 1974, turned out to be no.

We failed equally to predict the first nuclear test in the Third World. It happened in India on May 18, 1974. A Defense Intelligence Analysis report issued shortly before the test carried this title:

> "India: A nuclear weapons program will not likely be pursued in

the near term."

A CIA post-mortem report said of our intelligence blind spot:

"This failure denied the U.S. Government the option of considering diplomatic or other initiative to try to prevent this significant step in nuclear proliferation."

Our nation is still being deceived. On June 11, 1997, CFR member President Clinton nominated CFR member Inderfurth to serve as the Assistant Secretary of State for South Asian Affairs . He was confirmed by the Senate on July 31 and took office on August 4. Inderfurth has responsibility for the countries of India, Pakistan, Afghanistan, Nepal, Bhutan, Bangladesh, Sri Lanka, and Maldives. In addition to being a member of the Council on Foreign Relations in New York, *Inderfurth* is also a member of the International Institute for Strategic Studies in London.

With the help of CFR member Ambassador Inderfurth and his fellow CFR members, the world was recently brought to the brink of Nuclear War between India and Pakistan. Like 1974, the CIA was blamed for failing to anticipate nuclear tests in India. The tests were conducted on May 11, and 13th, 1998. On September 14, CNN news reported a subcommittee of the Senate Foreign Relations committee held the first of several expected Congressional hearings on the issue of the testing. "I am astonished that the Indian government was able to catch the U.S. intelligence capability so sound asleep at the switch," said Committee Chairman Jesse Helms, R-North Carolina.

On May 13th, the day of the second test, Dorian Benkoil, ABCNEWS.com, reported, "India's first nuclear blasts caught President Clinton by surprise. "Before this round of tests started, I did not know it was going to start," Clinton said today. The president said he has ordered CIA Director George Tenet to launch a "thorough review" of U.S. intelligence in the matter.

Tenet appointed retired Adm. David Jeremiah to lead a review team that was to report in 10 days...Today's tests on May 13th, apparently, were less of a surprise. A White House official told

ABCNEWS' Ann Compton that Undersecretary of State Thomas Pickering was not given assurances he sought after Monday's explosions that no more tests would be conducted." Thomas Pickering and Bill Clinton are Council on Foreign Relations members.

On May 17th in,

"India nuke test fiasco leaves U.S. seeking answers," John Diamond, Associated Press reported, "U.S. intelligence officials, lawmakers who oversee the CIA and outside experts point to a wide range of flaws—technical, organizational and human—that contributed to what Senate Intelligence Committee Chairman Richard Shelby, R-Ala., called a "colossal failure" by the CIA."

Tuesday, August 18, the British Broadcasting Company (BBC) reported,

"The CIA did not spot Indian nuclear test preparations. With the failure of US intelligence to detect both the East Africa bombings and India's recent nuclear tests, Defense Correspondent Jonathan Marcus investigates whether the CIA is losing its edge. The bombings in Nairobi and Dar es Salaam came from out of the blue. America's huge and sophisticated intelligence gathering machine seemingly provided no warnings of the attack....

Gone is the existential Soviet threat—replaced by a world more like the 1920s, where future threats are harder to define. New issues are forcing themselves onto the security agenda. Earlier this year, for instance, the CIA established an Environment Centre.

The CIA must also learn to work more closely with US law enforcement agencies like the FBI. The investigation of the bomb attacks against the US embassies in Tanzania and Kenya will provide an important test of this new inter-agency cooperation."

What neither the Pike or Church committees discovered was that it was the Council on Foreign Relations, not the CIA, that was responsible for deceiving the country. While the CIA may have planned and conducted some covert operations without the express approval of the CFR run "Special Group [aka 40-Committee]", Council on Foreign Relations members in the CIA and State Department made sure the "Special Group" was aware of all covert operations run by the CIA. If a covert operation would adversely effect a CFR plan, that covert operation would be sabotaged. If the covert operation would help achieve CFR goals, the operation would be allowed to go forward, as if the "Special Group" had no knowledge of the operation. The "Special Group" has, and is using the CIA, to distract the Countries attention from the group that is responsible for the sponsorship and coordination of covert operations at home and abroad—The Council on Foreign Relations.

Shouldn't the Church and Pike Committee Committee hearings be reopened, and revisited? Shouldn't those Council on Foreign Relations members under investigation, who testified before the committees, and who served on the Committees be called before Congress and made to explain their actions? Shouldn't the Council on Foreign Relations members in the "Special Group" [aka *Psychological Strategy Board*] and The Secret Team, who served during the Nixon Administration and participated in the Covert actions against Chile be indicted?

Shouldn't Council on Foreign Relations links to the transfer of sensitive military technology to China be investigated? Council on Foreign Relations member Presidents Ford, Carter, Bush, and Clinton; the Council on Foreign Relations members who served in their administrations; and the Council on Foreign Relations members who served in non-CFR member Presidential administrations; should be called before Congress and made to acknowledge and explain the Council on Foreign Relations role in designing and coordinating covert operations at home and abroad.

The British Parliament should do the same with *Bilderberger* Prime Minister Tony Blair, and any other Prime Minister, and member of Parliament linked to Britain's *Royal Institute of*

International Affairs. The Canadian Parliament should do the same with any Canadian Prime Minister, or Canadian member of Parliament linked to the Canadian Institute of International Affairs.

Title-50 War and National Defense § 783 states—

> "It shall be unlawful for any person knowingly to combine, conspire, or agree with any other person to perform any act which would substantially contribute to the establishment within the United States of a totalitarian dictatorship, the direction and control of which is to be vested in, or exercised by or under the domination of control of, any foreign government."

The Council on Foreign Relations are in violation of *Title-50 War and National Defense § 783.* The Council on Foreign Relations has unlawfully and knowingly combined, conspired, and agreed to substantially contribute to the establishment of one world order under the totalitarian dictatorship, the direction and the control of members of Council on Foreign Relations, the Royal Institute of International Affairs, and members of their branch organizations in various nations throughout the world. That is totalitarianism on a global scale.

Chapter 10

Crimes amd Misdemeanors by The U. S. Government

"The strongest reason for the people to retain the right to keep and bear arms is, as a last resort, to protect themselves against tyranny in government"   Thomas Jefferson

Although the Federal Government has been known to make mistakes, most of which where errors of omission, they seem to become more intrusive into and harmful to the citizens of these United States. The Government, through mind-control psychological propaganda uses lies to impose what appears to be a Gestapo-style approach to controlling the inhabitants. There are many —but a few of the most egregious examples follow:

The Ruby Ridge Massacre

The following article does not tell the full story of what happened at Ruby Ridge, but it does give a synopsis of the killing of innocent citizens for apparently no reason. The article states:

"FBI ASSASSIN LON HOUIUCHI SHOT WEAVERS WIFE WHILE SHE WAS HOLDING A BABY. If you look at what has happened since the August 1992 outrage at Ruby Ridge, you can see why this event was the turning point for America. Shortly afterwards you had the election of Bill Clinton, possible the most corrupt individual to ever ....into the White House. That was followed by the atrocities at Waco, the OKC bombing, school and office massacres on scales unseen before, and then came September 11, 2001, and the police state, wars, and chaos that followed. God has been lifting his blessing off this nation in more noticeable ways than ever, and many people believe it all began right around the time of Ruby Ridge. The United States government was created to serve its citizen, not to entrap them, not to defame them, and not to falsify evidence against them, something we have forgotten in this post 9-11 age of Homeland Security. What can be done about the deaths of Vicki Weaver, a mother who was killed with a baby in her arms, and Sammy Weaver, a 14-year old boy who was shot in the back, both innocent victims of their own government? The killers, of course, got off the hook."

A favorite activity of our government today is spying on its own citizens. They do not care for being hindered by such things as the Bill of Rights, and the FBI has been censured by Congress several times for illegal investigations. The BATF (Bureau of Alcohol, Tobacco and Firearms) sent informant Kenneth Fadeley to pose as a gun dealer to spy on groups that opposed oppressive government in Idaho. The BATF targeted Randy Weaver to be duped into breaking the law. Fadeley approached Weaver and pressured him to sell him sawed-off shotguns. Weaver at first refused., but Fadeley persisted and finally bought two shotguns, thereby violating federal law. They set the trail date but Weaver did not show up. BATF agents lied to the U.S. attorney's office, claiming Weaver had a criminal record and that he was a suspect in several bank robberies. Both charges were fabrications according to BATF Director John Magaw who admitted the accusations were "inexcusable" in testimony before Congress.

After Weaver missed his court appearance, Federal agents launched an elaborate 18-month surveillance of Mr. Weaver's cabin and land. The U.S. marshals called in military aerial reconnaissance and had photos studied by the Defense Mapping Agency. They had psychological profiles and installed $130,000 worth of solar-powered long-range spy cameras. They intercepted the Weaver's mail. They even knew the menstrual cycle of Weaver's teenage daughter, and planned an arrest scenario around it.

Six U.S. marshals, armed and camouflaged, went onto Weaver's property to conduct undercover surveillance. When Weaver's dog started barking, they shot one of them. When Weaver's son went to check on the dead dog, he fire his gun in the direction of the U.S. marshals. Weaver shouted to his son 'Get back into the house'—his son answer, "I'm coming, Dad" and those were his last word. One of the marshals shot him in the back.

On August 22, 1992, Randy Weaver went to see his son's body in the shack were it lay. He was shot and wounded by FBI sniper Lon Horiuchi. As Weaver struggled to get back to his house, Horiuchi assassinated Vicki Weaver as she stood in the doorway holding their 10-month-old baby. Although the feds later claimed Vicki Weaver's killing was an accident, the New York Times reported in 1993 an internal FBI report justified the killing by saying she put herself in danger.

In July 1993, a jury acquitted Randy Weaver of weapons and murder charges resulting from his set-up and the subsequent siege of his mountain cabin by federal agents. Weaver's friend, Kevin Harris was also found innocent. Harris, witnessing the agents' killing of Weaver's dog and son during the siege, fired at the agents in self-defense. Harris killed one of the agents and the prosecution claimed Harris fired first; the defense produced evidence that the agent had fired seven shots before he was shot himself.

Think about this instance. The Federal Government attacking a family of four (the Weavers) and their friend Kevin Harris because they supposedly were against an oppressive government. The *New York Times* named the Weaver family as an 'armed separatist brigade'. Yet, there are organizations in this country that the government ignores (for what ever reason) and the so called free press gives no coverage. One organization comes to mind— Farrakhan's Islamic Nation.

In an April 13, 1997 interview on NBC's *Meet the Press*, Louis Farrakhan was asked by Tim Russert to explain the Nation of Islam's view on separation:

> Tim Russert: "Once a week, on the back page of your newspaper is The Muslim Program, 'What the Muslims Want' [written in 1965]. The first is in terms of territory, 'Since we cannot get along with them in peace and equality, we believe our contributions to this land and the suffering forced upon us by white America justifies our demand for complete separation in a state or territory of our own.' Is that your view in 1997, a separate state for Black Americans?"

Minister Louis Farrakhan: "First, the program starts with number one. That is number four. The first part of that program is that we want freedom, a full and complete freedom. The second is, we want justice. We want equal justice under the law, and we want justice applied equally to all, regardless of race or class or color. And the third is that we want equality. We want equal membership in society with the best in civilized society. If we can get that within the political, economic, social system of America, there's no need for point number four. But if we cannot get along in peace after giving America 400 years of our service and sweat and labor, then, of course, separation would be the solution to our race problem."

Here is an organization that demands adherence to their program or they will secede from the U.S. and form their own nation. Didn't we fight a civil war over secession? It doesn't matter about the cause for seceding, the idea of seceding and thereby destroying the country—THAT is the issue. Yet, the current government thinks people like the Weavers are more dangerous to the country than followers of Minister Louis Farrakhan. Eliminate the Weavers and ignore the Farrakhans is the rallying cry. (If the government is concern about the religious aspect of the Islamic Nation movement, how can they explain the following Waco massacre?)

Minister Farrakhan wants freedom, justice and social equality for the black people in this country. My question to Mr. Farrakhan is how much more do you want? Since the end of the Civil War:

a America has been the best country on earth for the black people. It was here that over 600,000 black people, brought from Africa in slave ships, grew into a community of 40 million. They were introduced to Christian salvation, and reached the greatest levels of freedom and prosperity blacks have ever known.

b. No people anywhere has done more to lift up blacks than white Americans. Untold trillions of dollars have been spent since the '60s on welfare, food stamps rent supplements, Section 8 housing, Pell grants, student loans, legal services, Medicare, Earned Income Tax Credits and poverty programs designed to bring the African-American community into the mainstream of America.

c. Government, businesses and colleges have engaged in discrimination against the white people with affirmative action, contract set-asides and quotas to advance black applicants over white applicants.

d. Churches, foundations, civic groups, schools and individuals all over America have donated their time and money to support soup kitchens, adult education, day-care, retirement and nursing homes for the blacks.

e. Is white America responsible for the fact that the crime and incarceration rates for African-Americans are seven times those of white America?

f. Is it white America's fault that illegitimacy in the African-American community has hit 70 percent and the black dropout rate from high schools in some cities has reached 50 percent?

g. When something happens in the black community and it is the fault of a white person, does that give the black community the right to riot, loot stores, maim and kill any whites that they come across? Then, when all the stores that are ruin do not reopen, does it give the black community a right to complain about the travel miles to buy clothing, food, drug store items, etc.?

h. Why is it that when any American disagrees with the black leaders, they use the term racist or racism? Racism is ugliest in interracial crime, and especially interracial crimes of violence. Why is it that while white criminals choose black victims 3 percent of the time while black criminals choose white victims 45 percent of the time?

i Why do we always hear black leaders scream loudest about rape cases such as Tawana Brawley, the Duke rape case, and Jena (which all turned out to be hoaxes) but we never hear from them about the epidemic of black assaults on whites that are real? Mr. Farrakhan, read the history of Liberia and why it was established. President Lincoln wanted to free the slaves and send them back to a nation of their own. That was why Liberia was established. Unfortunately, he was assassinated before he could fulfill his plan. Read the history of Liberia, how it got started and what has happen in between. Then you should be thanking God (Allah or Master W. Fard Muhammad) that you are still in 'the land of the free and the home of the brave'!

The Waco Davidian Massacre

Many of you have seen accounts of Waco while the Branch Davidians were under siege and know from the TV news what the conditions were there.

The news media was kept 3 miles from the Mt. Carmel Center by armed guards at all roads into the compound. And the media dutifully aired whatever misinformation the FBI fed them each day at 10:30 AM, calling it "news" as they slandered the Branch Davidians, spreading lies of "child molesting", "planned mass suicide", and "religious whackos in Waco."

No matter, sensationalism sells newspapers; it gets those network ratings up and it wouldn't be a story if they told the truth. The FCC might shut down a network or two or yank a permit. Better that 100 people should die in an inferno than expose the depths of the depravity of the leaders of this country.

The story begins in 1992. Sheri Jewel and her ex-husband were in a custody battle over their daughter, Keri. Sheri was a Branch Davidian and she was killed in the Waco fire. Her ex-husband was a radio announcer. His wife was a TV personality. They had money.

A fellow named Mark Breault, who is reputed to have a felony record, used to be a Branch Davidian. He proclaimed himself to be a prophet. After awhile, he tried to take over the Mt. Carmel compound and was ousted by David Koresh. Breault, an Australian, left, vowing revenge. He often called the compound daily to harass the members.

The Jewel's hired Mark Breault to testify in their custody dispute. In an affidavit, Breault made allegations of child molestation and religious weirdness. This was in Michigan in 1992.

Senators were contacted to investigate these allegations, as was the "Cult Awareness Network." The Cult Awareness Network is a group in Washington, D.C., headed by the wife of late Senator Ryan who was killed at Jonestown. She has a personal vendetta, too. And she wields a lot of power in Washington, apparently, because if someone ends up on her cult hit list, they frequently end up dead.

The allegations of child molestation were investigated in the intervening two years, twice, by Texas welfare department authorities and found to be baseless. The Sheriff's department investigated the allegations of illegal guns and these claims were found to be baseless. The investigations were peaceful. There were no problems.

Mark Breault, however, continued to make his baseless and slanderous allegations against the Branch Davidians. The Cult Awareness Network turned up the pressure.

CFA—the Constitutional Foundational Association, was started by Greg Sali and Bill Griffith, to expose the true story in Waco. They are also now working to establish common law courts throughout the country to put corrupt judicial officials and politicians behind bars, where they belong. Together with Ken Fawcett, they have collected over 300 hours worth of videotapes of the initial onslaught. People who have studied these tapes in slow motion say that they show that the BATF agents who were killed going in through the second story window were killed by friendly fire and their own frag grenade. When they got inside the window, they were in a 10 x 10 room that had a locked steel door. They couldn't get out. They were hit by friendly fire and trapped in the room when the frag grenade went off.

One Branch Davidian, Mike Schroeder, left the Mt. Carmel compound that morning to go to work as usual. He passed by agents who never stopped him. He didn't learn of the initial siege until later that day. When he tried to return home, he was shot in the back as he climbed a fence. His body was left hanging on the fence for days, as his wife and child could see him there, from inside the house. The government finally moved his body, using a grappling hook from a helicopter, at night, to drop it into a nearby field, where it was chewed by wild dogs and buzzards beyond recognition as a human being.

The two old ladies who came out of the compound with the children said that all the children had been in an upstairs room when they were suddenly fired upon by helicopters through the roof the day of the siege. They covered the children with their own bodies to protect them. These old ladies were charged with murder and held in jail. Eventually, they were put under arrest as material witnesses and held in a half-way house out of the city.

For 51 days, the FBI tortured the people inside the Mt. Carmel center. All utilities, including sanitation, were cut off. Loudspeakers were set up all around the house to blare sounds 24-hours a day, including the sounds of rabbits being slaughtered, the sound a phone makes when it is left off the hook, Tibetan monk chants, jet airplanes, babies crying, and songs such as "these boots are made for walking" and Christmas carols.

Stadium lights were set up to keep the place lit up 24 hours a day. Military tanks, including M1 Abrams and Bradley's, were brought in and rapidly circled the house, firing percussion grenades, continuously. The tanks would charge up to the house and then stop within feet of the house repeatedly.

Black helicopters flew overhead. Two Huey gunships also flew over frequently, guns mounted in front.

Around the 40th day of the siege, David Koresh announced that the children and babies were out of milk. Two relief efforts to bring baby food to the Mt. Carmel compound were turned back. Two people, one of them Gary Spaulding from South Bend, Indiana, were arrested for trying to take the food past a roadblock. When ask at the FBI headquarters, "Has it come to this? Does the United States government want babies to starve to death?" The answer was, verbatim, "Yes." An ATF agent, in a pickup truck that said "Wild Bill" on the side, stole the food.

How did the BATF account for what it did when it assaulted the Branch Davidians? Did it offer to show the American public the search warrant they claimed to have? No. In fact, the search warrant and probable cause affidavit, if they existed at all, were "sealed" by court order. A court order from the same judge who apparently signed it in the first place.

The same judge, Walter Smith, Jr., of the Waco Division, Western U.S. District Court in Waco, denied eight petitions for relief filed by various lawyers seeking to order the FBI and BATF to be made to follow the law and the United States Constitution. The government never once filed a single paper in opposition to any of these motions. There was clear, controlling Supreme Court law that required that these petitions be granted. The judge had no legal reason to deny them, yet he did. And he used the same order, nearly a xerox, to deny all of them.

Walter Smith is the same judge who allowed arraignments of people who left the compound to be held in secret. When there was not sufficient probable cause to hold them under arrest, he allowed them to be detained in jails as "material witnesses."

And this same judge is the only judge in that division, where all the remaining Branch Davidians, facing "murder" charges, was put on trial.

After the BATF and FBI learned that the American Justice Federation had released a press release stating that the use of military troops against United States citizens violated federal law, specifically, the Posse Comitatus Act, the BATF released a cover story, claiming that the tanks were "really" not Army, they were National Guard, and had been brought in under the "Drug Interdiction Act" because they had heard there was a "methamphetamine lab"—THREE WEEKS AFTER the FBI had already publicly announced there was never any question whatsoever of drug involvement.

Did any of the news media ever challenge how the BATF might have any jurisdiction at all over "child molesting" allegations? Or their authority to bring in two cattle trailers full of armed men, who threw grenades at the front door and went in shooting at women and children on a Sunday morning? Apparently not.

Calling a religion a "cult" and putting out false information across the media about "child molesting" and "weapons caches" is exactly the same technique that was used by the Nazis to portray the Jews as filthy, disgusting people, so they could be killed. It is the same technique used by every tyrannical government, to kill an unpopular and potentially vocal adversarial group. But in this country, we are supposed to have freedom of religion. It would seem that is a pipe dream.

Paul Fatta, a Branch Davidian, held a Class III dealer's license. That meant that he could legally own, sell, and buy, any type of gun. It is thus highly unlikely that there were any "illegal" guns in the center at all (it was well known in the area that the Branch Davidians went to gun shows to sell and trade guns for income.) And who is responsible for issuing these permits? The BATF. They knew Paul Fatta had a license.

Paul Fatta was not at the Mt. Carmel Center the day the BATF assaulted the Branch Davidians. Nonetheless, he is now listed on the FBI's "10 Most Wanted" list as "armed and dangerous." This gives the government the ability to shoot him on sight and then claim he was a "fleeing felon." It is a license for the government to kill, again. To bury the best evidence against them, again.

In the end, supported by a liberal judge and a sympathetic press, the Waco survivors were subjected to a vicious government prosecution. Some were sentenced to 40 years in prison , even though the jury found them innocent of conspiring to murder. The jurors were aghast! Convicted on minor charges, Judge Walter Smith vastly increased their penalties. Sarah Bain, the jury foreman said afterwards: "the federal government was absolutely out of control here. We spoke in the jury room about the fact the wrong people were on trial, that it should have been the ones who planned the raid and orchestrated it and insisted on carrying out this plan who should have been on trial."

We have seen our leaders, Bill Clinton, Janet Reno, William

Sessions, and Lloyd Bentsen, on the television, lying to us with straight faces, offering justifications for this carnage, as if there could ever be any possible moral explanation or excuse that could be enough. That the people offering these excuses are morally bankrupt and corrupt, should be obvious. A simple, "We're sorry" would at least show a glimmer of common decency and humanity, but those words have never crossed any of their lips.

Here is the Summary at the end of the chapter "Self-Fulfilling Prophecies" by James R. Lewis:

> "The implications of these studies and supporting arguments for the Waco situation should be clear. The Branch Davidians' chances for a fair hearing were severely damaged as soon as the label "cult" was applied. After that, the mass media selectively sought out and presented information about Koresh and his community that conveniently fit the stereotype. It was only a matter of time before law enforcement and the media had completely demonized Koresh and his followers. Anticult organizations provided ample fodder for the ritual and symbolic castigation of this little-known religious sect, simplistically reducing the beliefs and practices of the community to vapid, inane categories of brainwashing rhetoric. After this demonization had been successfully accomplished, the entire community—men, women, and children—could be consigned to their tragic fate with little more than a peep of protest from the American public, a public which overwhelmingly approved of the FBI's tragic final assault on Mt. Carmel."

Or more exactly, a public which would appear to consist mostly of gullible puppets, with no sense of injustice (except when it affects themselves), believing what they were told (with the help of a willing media) by their ill-informed, ill-advised and violence-obsessed (and, as it turned out, murderous) government, a public which overwhelming approved of a shameful instance of government-sanctioned slaughter of people who had broken no law (it is legal to protect oneself against attack), including twenty-one children under the age of 16.

The Case of Martha Stewart

Celebrity homemaker Martha Stewart was sentenced to five months in prison and fined $30,000 for lying to investigators about her sale of ImClone Systems stock in late 2001. U.S. District Court Judge Miriam Cedarbaum also ordered Stewart to two years of supervised probation, including five months of home confinement, after she is released. It was the minimum sentence the judge could impose under federal sentencing guidelines.

This episode was included to show that the Justice Department is NOT to administer Justice, but to be used as a means of punishing American citizens, not for so called crimes that they are supposed to have committed but lying under oath. Yet, the oath that is rendered to the accused is really unconstitutional isn't it? For example, Judges have ruled that it is unconstitutional to pray in schools, display crosses on Federal land, and even the Ten Commandments are unlawful. Also, recently a federal judge ruled that a National Day of Prayer Law passed by Congress and signed by the President was unconstitutional. In effect, Judges have ruled there is no God in Government. Remember, separation of Church and State was meant to mean something else which is discussed later in this book.

Yet the Justice Department and the Courts can put a person in jail for lying under oath. It is perfectly alright for the President, Congress, and Government Employees to lie to the people every day, but the Justice Department says they are not under oath. What is the oath? "Do you swear to tell the truth, the whole truth, and nothing but the truth, so help you GOD?" How can any Judge allow this oath to be given when he and his ilk say that the term 'God' cannot be used because of separation of church and state? Therefore, the oath given is illegal and cannot be used by prosecutors to condemn a person of lying to the Federal Government. Where is the Justice?

Another incident of criminal accusations that were falsely charged so as to bring citizens to Justice follows.

The Valerie Plame Affair

How the Special Prosecutor Office works is a genius invention of the Socialist when they infiltrated into Justice Department. Once Attorney General Reno, under the Clinton Administration , demanded all field Attorney General to submit their resignations, she then fill key slots with socialist who could now control the justice system and cover up for her boss (Bill Clinton). The use of the Grand Jury system and lying under oath came to the surface in the Valerie Plame case.

The expectation of the Democratic socialists that the Valerie Plame affair would blossom into another Watergate, bringing down a second Republican presidency, fizzled. The Social Democrats in Congress and the Socialist Press expected that convictions of one or more persons in the Bush administration for leaking or confirming to columnist Robert Novak that Mrs. Plame, the wife of Bush critic Joseph C. Wilson IV, was an undercover CIA operative. Repeating the claims of Mr. Wilson, prominent socialists, most of them in the press, accused the White House of managing a smear campaign, and sought to drive Karl Rove either out of office or into prison, or both.

Special Prosecutor Patrick J. Fitzgerald, urged on by the social comrades and the mainstream press, searched into the body of reporters and their confidential sources. He issued subpoenas for all types of emails and documents to find out which Bush administration officials were talking to which reporters. He threatened reporters with jail and imprisoned one of them—which may have set a precedent for future prosecutors to compel reporters to disclose their confidential sources. But in the end, the exhaustive investigation produced no criminal charges against any official for leaking Mrs. Plame's name in violation of the 1982 Intelligence Identities Protection Act. Moreover, after three years of destroying peoples lives and their bank accounts paying lawyers it was revealed that the official who revealed Valerie's name in July 2003 to Mr. Novak was not a White House official, but Richard Armitage, who was deputy of Secretary of State Colin Powell.

As the story unraveled, rather than being part of a smear, Mr. Armitage mentioned her name, in response to Columnist Novak's question, as the person who got her husband sent to Niger on a 2002 CIA mission on reports of Saddam Hussein's Iraq trying to acquire uranium. Mr. Novac stated in one of his columns that "After the federal investigation was announced, he (Mr. Armatage) told me through a third party that the disclosure was inadvertent on his part." Yet, it took three years after the assignment of the Special Prosecutor Richardson before the leak by Armatage was revealed to the public. Incidentally, Richardson knew who exposed Mrs. Plame the day he entered his new mandate to find who leaked her name. There should have been no investigation but Richardson was out for blood. He told all who knew not to mention Armatage's name while Richardson went off on a tangent to find other causes to ruin people's lives. He ignored his mandate to find who leaked Mrs. Plame's name. In other words, he assumed powers not granted him by his mandate.

As the story began to unravel further, the so-called leak about Mrs. Plame was not a leak at all. At one time she was an active CIA agent, but on one of her assignments overseas she was discovered by foreign agents and brought home. She was never removed from the active CIA agents list, but assigned an office job within the CIA. Since she was known to be an agent her use in overseas assignments was over. However, the Intelligence Identities Protection Act covers active agents, Mrs. Plame was now only an employee in the CIA, and should have been removed from the active-agent roles. Most people knew this, but the socialist in the press and congress went after the President and his staff with knives drawn and guns blazing. Somebody had to go to jail!

Internet hatchet men crawled out of the woodwork and demand indictments galore. One blogger reported that Carl Rove had been indicted which he had not. Tom Matzzie, Washington Director of the socialist MoveOn.org, wrote in July 2005 "This conspiracy clearly reaches into the highest level of our government. This could be among the worst presidential scandals in our history....Again, we call upon the President to keep his promise, and fire Karl Rove. How long will the cover-up continue?"

Along the same lines, Democrat National Committee Chairman, Howard Dean, likened the scandal to Watergate, which brought down President Nixon. "This is like Watergate," he said. "The deed was done....but the truth is, had the president not misled the American people about the war, this wouldn't have happened. They got into trouble when they tried to discredit people telling the truth, like Joe Wilson." Lies, Lies and more Lies!

The federal trial *United States v. Libby* began on January 16, 2007. On March 6, 2007, Libby was convicted on four counts of perjury, obstruction of justice, and making false statements, and was acquitted of one count of making false statements Libby was sentenced to 30 months in prison, a fine of $250,000, and two years of supervised release after his prison term.

After the verdict, Special Counsel Fitzgerald stated that he did not expect anyone else to be charged in the case: "We're all going back to our day jobs." On July 2, 2007, President Bush commuted Libby's jail sentence, effectively erasing the 30 months he was supposed to spend in jail. The federal felony conviction, probation and fines still remain.

In March 2008, the Government Accountability Office revealed that the investigation had cost $2.58 million. The GAO also reported that "this matter is now concluded for all practical purposes."

This is our government at work today. Lies, character assassinations, misinformation and whatever. No longer does Congress fight our enemies, they just fight each other.

For and accurate complete article on this sordid affair, go to the Internet and Google "Plame Affair" by the Wikipedia encyclopedia. It gives the complete story of the "He said, She said" accusations.

The Sandy Berger Crime.

There has been much literature aired about the stolen secret document that Sandy Berger pilfered from the National Archives.

How he stuffed them down his socks, under his shirt, etc. but the best article that I found was an Editorial in a Colorado newspaper. The Editorial follows:

"Martha Stewart went to jail for lying to federal investigators. But for lying after stealing highly classified documents from the National Archives—in an apparent attempt to alter the historical record on terrorism, no less—Sandy Berger, the former Clinton national security adviser and Kerry campaign adviser, will pay a small fine ($10,000) and get a slap on the wrist (no jail time). His security clearance will be suspended until around the end of the Bush administration—meaningless for a career Democrat like Mr. Berger. It makes us wonder who at the Department of Justice is responsible for letting such a serious offense go all but unpunished.

On April 1 Mr. Berger pleaded guilty to misdemeanor charges for stealing five copies of one of the nation's most highly classified terrorism documents. The document, an "after-action" memo on the millennium 2000 terror plot written by terrorism consultant Richard Clarke, is so highly classified that any person removing it from secure rooms must do so in a case handcuffed to his or her wrist. Mr. Berger stuffed the five copies in his clothing and secreted them out of the archives. He proceeded to cut three of them to pieces with scissors at his downtown offices. Archives officials observed Mr. Berger stealing the documents and reported it to their superiors. .

When confronted, Mr. Berger lied. He told investigators he had mistakenly taken the documents and then disposed of them inadvertently. In public statements he called the thefts "an honest mistake." He declared that his only intent had been to collect materials for testimony about the Clinton administration's counterterrorism policies for the September 11 Commission.

At the time, Bill Clinton dismissed the matter with a chuckle. "The innocent explanation is the most likely one;' Mr. Clinton told reporters in Colorado. "We were all laughing about it on the way over here!'

But it wasn't innocent, and it wasn't a laughing matter. As Mr. Berger admitted later , the account he initially gave federal investigators was a fabrication. The plea agreement he reached with the Department of Justice details that, in fact, he deliberately removed the documents from the National Archives and that far from disposing of them by mistake, he cut them to pieces with scissors. None of this was inadvertent, a Berger associate acknowledged to The Washington Post.

What was Mr. Berger doing with the documents? And why was he destroying only three? The likeliest answer is that he sought to conceal comments he or other Clinton administration officials wrote on them when they were circulating in January 2000. He couldn't have been trying to erase the document itself from the record, since copies exist elsewhere. What's likelier is that jottings in the. margins of the three copies' he destroyed bore telling indications of the Clinton administration's approach to terrorism.

Mr. Clarke's document is said to criticize the Clinton administration's handling of the millennia plots and mostly attributes to luck and an alert airport official the apprehension of a would-be bomber headed for Los Angeles International Airport. If that turns out to be correct, Mr. Berger erased part of the historical record on terrorism.

The Clinton administration's cavalier attitude toward terrorism is well-established; it's likely to be evident in the archival records and will crop up in official communications. An after-action report like Mr. Clarke's, written nearly two years before the September 11 terrorist attacks, is as good a candidate as any for the telling aside in the margin.

Mr. Berger committed an egregious violation of the rules that govern the handling of sensitive national-security documents. His offense would cost most any government employee his job, security clearance and future in government. Quite possibly it would cost him his freedom. In addition, Mr. Berger lied about it to federal investigators. Mr. Berger won't likely suffer any of the consequences. For those who suspect that different rules apply at the top, a case like this invites cynicism.

His associates from the Clinton years are silent, perhaps hoping the scandal will blow over so that Mr. :Berger can remain a don of the

Democratic foreign-policy establishment. One can only speculate as to why the Department of Justice would agree to such lenient terms for the offense. Perhaps career employees or holdovers with ties to Democrats are responsible. Perhaps the Bush administration went soft. Whatever the reason, one can be reasonably sure it wasn't done for reasons of national security, justice or truth."

The above Editorial explains why people are angry at the government. Laws only apply to the average citizen while members of the Government, elected or hired ignore them and even laugh at them. So much for Justice.

'Earmarks: Legalized Congressional Theft.

A lot of billboards Posted at public construction sites read "Your Tax Dollars At Work". They need to be replaced with ones that say "Wasting Your Money." That's the conclusion of one investigative reporter after thumbing through the more than 1,000 plus pages of the $286.4 billion transportation bill that President Bush signed into law.

The bill was loaded with more than. $24 billion in dubious public projects sought by a variety of special-interest groups. The provisions are called "earmarks" because they've been inserted into the bill by lawmakers for a specific client back home or a campaign contribution.. In 1982, the transportation bill contained 10 earmarks costing $386 million. By 1987, they had grown to 152 earmarks, costing $1.4 billion. (These years—1980-1988—are Reagan years that the Democrats who controlled both Houses of Congress claimed that the President was responsible for the huge deficit). In 1991, the number mushroomed to 538, costing $6 billion. In 2004 the bill included 1,850 earmarks that fleeced taxpayers of $9 billion. The bill Bush signed (2007) contained, at last count, more than 6,300 earmark projects that totaled a whopping $24 Billion. The list is nauseating in its fiscal thievery and greed.

Here's a sampling of. some of its worst abuses: $18.75 million to build a bridge that will join Gravina Island, with a population of less than 50 people, to Ketchikan, Alaska, a project that is known on Capitol Hill as the "Bridge to Nowhere." $2.32 million for aesthetic landscaping along the Ronald Reagan Freeway near the Ronald Reagan Presidential library in Simi Valley, something the late president, who built his political career on fighting wasteful spending, would have opposed. $480,000 to restore a historic warehouse along the Erie Canal in Lyons, N.Y. $600,000 for High Knob Horse Trails to install riding paths in the Jefferson National Forest in Virginia. $1.6 million for the Blue Ridge Music Center in Connecticut. $1.2 million for planning, design and engineering of The American Road at the Henry Ford Museum in Dearborn, Mich. $1.28 million for the Cultural and Interpretive Center in Richland, Wash. $1 million for a pedestrian waterfront walkway in Oswego, NY. $400,000 for a jogging, bicycle and trolley trail in Columbus, Ga. $3 million for dust control along rural roads in Arkansas. $850,000 for the Red River National Wildlife Refuge Visitor Center in Louisiana. Who puts projects like these in the transportation bill? Lawmakers who have a virtual free hand in writing the bill (as if it were their own personal, campaign checkbook) are responsible for a lot of the abuse. People like Congressman Don Young, R-Alaska, who chairs the House Transportation Committee. Alaska is the third-least-populated state, but Young made sure it was the fourth-highest in the earmarks—it received $941 million, to be precise—and to promote himself in the process.

One of the bill's earmarks: $231 million for a bridge near Anchorage that will be named "Don Young's Way." Rep. Nick Rahall, D-W.Va., is a top ranking member of the committee; and he got $16 million in the bill for the Nick J. Rahall II Appalachian Transportation Institute at Marshall University. What is especially appalling is the brazen way lawmakers are allowed to stick any kind of spending provision in the bill that is not germane to the legislation. There is, for instance, $2 million for a wood products demonstration at the University of Maine, and $5 million for a study of earthquake hazards at universities in Nevada and Buffalo.

Presidents from both parties have been urged by spending critics to veto bills that are overloaded with pork-barrel projects, but they signed it in the end because the overall bill is usually necessary (boosting construction employment and further strengthening the economy.) But the waste-filled bills that are signed is an abomination that cries out for budget reform— to stop such abuses in the future. Earmarks should be flatly forbidden. Provisions must be germane to the bill. Many say that the president should have the power of a line-item veto, but the Supreme Court, in 1998, has ruled that this move is unconstitutional, and rightly so. If the President were given a line item veto power, he could change the meaning of all laws passed by Congress by removing this paragraph or that paragraph and make a new law (which would be unconstitutional because only Congress has the power to make laws.

The only way that earmarks can be eliminated is by Congress themselves. This is something that will never happen because 'earmarks' are the road to riches for most congressmen/women. They use their congressional seat to push earmarks onto any Bill that goes through Congress for money. They live by the rule: 'This seat is for sale.'

Most people blame the Senator or Representative from a State that the earmark benefits. This is not necessary the truth. Any member of Congress who is in a position of importance (like chairman/chairwoman of a committee) can insert an earmark FOR A PRICE! There is no boundary for Congressman who want to enrich their Campaign Funds. The only way that earmarks will be eliminated is by:

    a. Limiting Representative membership to two terms; The Senate to one term. This law should also state that no member of Congress, once he serves his current term, is eligible for any other government employment or can he/she run again for a seat in Congress.

    b. Earmarks in the future must be stand-alone items that will require two-third of the members of Congress (both Representatives and Senators) before they can become law. The earmarks must list the member of Congress who inserted it.

    c. If the above two items cannot stop these insertion of earmarks into bills of appropriation, than the

President will have the authority to remove them from the appropriation bill by line-item veto. He will declare, in writing, to Congress and the press that the item was an earmark and needed to be removed because it should be a stand-alone item.

Unsolved Mysterious Deaths and Other Strange Activities.

The following deaths, disappearances, cover-up stories and strange happenings can be found on the Internet by using Google Search Engine.

DEATHS—ACCIDENTS

Ron Brown, Plane Crash (Commerce, Pathologists question wound to head on xrays) – see section on Ron Brown Plane Crash

Victor Raisner, Plane Crash (National Finance Co-Chair Clinton for President)

R. Montgomery Raiser, Plane Crash (Clinton campaign)

Herschell Friday, Plane Crash (Presidential Campaign Finance Committee)

Paula Gober, Car Accident (Clinton Speech Interpreter)

Stanley Heard, Plane Crash (Clinton Health Care Advisory Committee)

Steven Dickson, Plane Crash (Clinton Health Care Advisory Committee)

Johnny Franklin Lawhon, Car Accident (Found Whitewater Canceled Check in Car after Tornado)

Theodore Williams, Betty Currie's brother, Beaten before Betty's Senate testimony then Car/Pedestrian Accident during Monica story (Key Witness' brother)

Shelley Kelly, Survived Brown Plane Crash—died hours later

(Stewardess)

Judy Gibbs, Fire (Alleged Clinton Girlfriend, Witness)

Keith Coney, Motorcycle Accident (Ives/Henry Witness)

Dr Donald Chumley, Plane Crash (Physician at the OKC Murrah Federal building)

Jim Wilhite, Ski Accident (Friend of McLarty)

Dr. Ronald Rogers, Plane Crash (Informant)

Paul Olson, Plane Crash (Witness)

Neal Cooper Moody, Car Accident (Step Son of Vince Foster Widow, Lisa)

William Colby, canoe drowning (former Director of the CIA, editor of "Strategic Investment" which hired experts to investigate Vince Foster's suicide note)

Randall Tyson, choked on a cookie (half brother to Don Tyson)

Woody Lemons, wife and mother, private airplane crash (OKC informant)

Mohammed Samir Ferrat, TWA 800 Plane Crash (Brown connections, initial suspect)

Ron Brown Plane Crash section

Jan Kopold, accidental fall in Turkey in 1970

Dan Dutko (Head Injuries, Bike accident) DNC Fund Raiser

David Drye, Plane Crash (friend of Matrisciana – Clinton's Chronicles, etc.)

Lt Colonel Mark Cwick (auto accident, Clinton pilot)

Major Marc Hohle (helicopter crash Okinawa, Clinton pilot)

Eddie Pack (Waco research, microwave exposure)

Reverend Roger Howard (Waco research, automobile)

Manual Howard (Waco research, automobile)

James Ray Dobbins (Waco research, automobile)

Admiral Donald Engen (Accident investigations, glider crash)

Vince Foster (Lawyer, suicide?)

Ralph Baker (Arkansas, automobile)

Lt. Gen. David J. McCloud (air accident)

Robert Deas
(Scientist, Informant, auto accident – see Lanz in suicide section)

The above list is not complete. There were other accidents/ incidents that were not reported. The following are stories (plus their source) about the people and their connection to some crimes and other misdemeanors during the political career of William Clinton.

Lt. Gen. David J. McCloud
Air Force News 8/3/98 "...... Lt. Gen. David J. McCloud, commander of Alaskan Command, and Eleventh Air Force, Elmendorf Air Force Base, Alaska, died when his private aircraft crashed July 26 at Fort Richardson, Alaska. McCloud, 53, of San Fernando, Calif., was piloting his personal YAK-54, a single-engine aerobatic aircraft, when it crashed at 3:20 p.m. EDT. A civilian passenger, Lewis Cathrow of Alexandria, Va., was also killed in the crash. .... Throughout his career, the general flew more than a dozen different fighters, bombers, tankers and experimental aircraft, including the F-117 Nighthawk, the B-1B Lancer and the X-29. He was a command pilot with more than 4,100 flight hours. He commanded three wings during his career: the 24th Composite Wing, Howard AFB, Panama; the 1st Fighter Wing, Langley AFB, Va.; and the 366th Wing, Mountain Home AFB, Idaho. Prior to his assignment to Alaska, he was the director for force structure, resources and assessment for the Joint Staff in the Pentagon. ...". It is hard to conceive that General McCloud with all his experience could have not saved himself and Mr. Cathrow unless some catastrophic failure occurred. The National Aviation Board investigated the crash but no results were published.

Ralph Baker
Michael Whiteley 3/22/98 ARKANSAS DEMOCRAT-GAZETTE "......A pickup truck and a four-wheeler were missing,

but Ralph Baker had more on his mind than stolen vehicles when he set out around 6:15 on the rain-soaked Monday morning of his death. .... He was deeply troubled by state and federal investigations of the Madison County sheriff's office he had run for more than a quarter-century and concerned by newspaper stories that flew against his reputation as a resolute and fearless lawman. He drowned before the sun was up that day, Jan. 5, apparently having misjudged the rising waters of the White River when he drove onto a low-water bridge near St. Paul. ....The death was so contrary to the nature and history of the 59-year-old sheriff that whispers of suicide or foul play colored gossip in the weeks that followed. .... In December, the FBI had subpoenaed Baker's bank records amid questions surrounding nearly $500,000 in land purchases by the sheriff and his family. State auditors had been combing the records of the Madison County Drug Eradication Fund since November. And stories in the Arkansas Democrat-Gazette had detailed allegations of corruption in the sheriff's office and flaws in the investigation of the unsolved 1994 murder of convenience store owner Billie Jean Phillips.......The investigation deals in part with the sheriff's office's handling of drug cases, and, in part, with financial deals that allowed Baker, his wife and two cousins to buy about 2,400 acres of land in Madison, Franklin and Washington counties with payments of $484,250. Nearly all the purchases were made in cash. ......And it eventually touched on Baker's relationship with the top official at an Arkansas financial institution swept up in the Whitewater investigation—Gary W. Bunch, president of Madison Bank & Trust. .... It was the Bank of Kingston when Jim McDougal, Jim Guy Tucker and four others bought it in 1980. One of the renamed bank's early loans was to Hillary Rodham Clinton, who needed $30,000 to build a model home at the Whitewater Development Corp., the project she and Bill Clinton co-owned with Jim and Susan McDougal along the White River in Marion County. Bunch was executive vice president at the time. ......And Bill Clinton, now the nation's chief executive, sent another letter. This one was read aloud for the 2,000 or so people who came for Baker's funeral in St. Paul High School's gymnasium. "Ralph Baker was a wonderful person ... a person who gave so much to his family and community" Clinton wrote. "I'll never forget the support he's given me since the beginning of my career." ....

Eddie Pack

Reverend Roger Howard

Manual Howard

James Ray Dobbins

Fall of 1998 (Glass interviews McNulty) Freeper Ada Coddington 9/29/99 "

http://www.freerepublic.com/forum/a37f23d746afd.htm   (Complete Interview)

A portion of the Interview that covered FLIR (government Forward-Looking Infrared footage, obtained by documentary film producer Mike McNulty under the Freedom of Information Act) were first seen, back in 1996. (Waco Incident.)

".... **GLASS**: Well, what the hell is going on?

McNULTY: ...... But likewise I'm sure that if a reporter from the New York Times asked the current director of the CIA was Colby involved in bringing authoritative information to us in order to expose the FBI – He'd say "I have no idea." And he might be right. But people died. Mr. Colby if indeed he died as a result of his involvement with us and not for some other reason is not the only individual who died during the process of the making of this film.

GLASS: Who else died?

McNULTY: There's a gentleman by the name of Eddie Pack who supplied us with footage in the early stages of my investigation. He died a very mysterious death from exposure to a rather large burst of microwave energy, which dealt him a very serious blow called cancer. Microwave energy can be used to erase videotapes from long distances, which is what happened in this circumstance. It appears that he was in the wrong place at the wrong time. Eddie had a habit of intercepting downlink material off of satellites. He came up with some very unusual videotape that was made originally by television networks regarding the events at Waco. Never saw the light of day on the air.

GLASS: How old was Eddie when he died?

McNULTY: Oh gosh, I'm not sure. I think he was in his mid fifties, early fifties. He wound up receiving very serious radiation burns in his esophagus and his throat as a result of his exposure to this microwave energy. They ulcerated and he couldn't eat. Over a period of time something less than 12 months the ulcers became cancerous. What really got him was the fact that he had been so irradiated that he actually developed cancer of the bone and it spread rapidly throughout his body and in a matter of days he was gone.

There were three others men also killed. Actually four but in two separate instances.

One was an "accident" that involved three of his friends that he was supposed to have been with. He had a musical repair business back in North Carolina. He used to repair musical instruments for all of the school districts in the three-state area. He was a musician – a very accomplished musician and used to play back-up in Nashville for a number of well-known recording artists – country western. He and his friends, his fellow musicians used to go to these recording sessions as back-up studio musicians. On the evening of January 14, 1994, the four of them were supposed to go to a performance. He got a call and went to another gig. These other three gentlemen, one or two of which had been involved in surreptitious activity in support of what we were trying to do in terms of getting videotapes, went to the original performance.

They had been followed and all kinds of strange stuff. The three of them were travelling in a van on U.S. Highway 221, which ran out of gas on a causeway over a lake in North Carolina. They were hit and struck by a car – a plain vanilla sedan with two gentlemen in it. The accident was witnessed by this woman who stopped and hollered at these two men who had exited their vehicle to inspect what had happened to these men now lying on the ground after having been struck by them. She advised them that she would go to the end of the causeway over the lake they were on and call an ambulance. When she came back the plain vanilla car was gone. The two individuals in the car were gone and the three individuals that were laying on the pavement were now in several pieces strung along the highway having been run over multiple times. The local sheriff did not investigate.

GLASS: What are the names of these people?

McNULTY: Reverend Roger Howard, his 17-year-old son, Manual Howard and James Ray Dobbins. ....

The complete interview can be found on the Internet by using the aforementioned address.

This is your Socialist Government at work today. Using the IRS and the FBI as the American Gestapo! Cross us and we will find ways to steal all your money and ruin your life. There is always the threat of elimination of you and your family.

Ronald Rogers

wordarchive.com Dan Jacobson 1/1/99 "......This crash happened near Lawton, Oklahoma on March 3, 1994, two days after the crash near Little Rock, Arkansas that killed Herschel Friday. The pilot and three passengers of the Cessna 310K were all killed when the plane impacted the ground in an inverted position. The cause of this accident was apparently a complete failure (from undetermined causes) of the plane's electrical system, and subsequent disorientation of the pilot. One of the passengers aboard this plane is only possibly tied to Clinton. The then Washington bureau chief for London's Sunday Telegraph was reporting on Clinton's background, and one of his contacts had set up a meeting between him and a dentist from Arkansas. The informant was going to share with the reporter something he claimed to know about Clinton's days in his home state. But the meeting never materialized. The contact called the reporter and told him that his informant had died in a plane crash. Someone else later told the reporter that this informant was Dr. Ronald Rogers, a dentist from Hot Springs, Arkansas who was a passenger on the ill-fated plane. ...."

Vince Foster 7/20/93 Suicide

Chief White House Counsel and personal attorney for Clintons. In 1994, Robert Fiske produced a report stating that the death of Vince Foster was a suicide. Fiske, was appointed by Janet Reno as Whitewater counsel, turned out to be a lawyer for International Paper, Inc., the company that sold Whitewater land to the Clinton / McDougal partnership. Unbeknownst to many because of media distortions, he had reached a conclusion that could not be supported by any of the evidence. In fact, the evidence clearly indicated that Vince Foster was murdered. For example:

- Foster's prints were not on the gun;

- The gun was not Foster's and he had no ammunition for that type of gun;

- The autopsy report showed a rear skull exit wound, but no skull fragments were ever found;

- No bullet was ever found in the park although others dating to the Civil War were found;

- No powder burns were on Foster's mouth, where he allegedly shot himself;

- Powder burns on both forefingers indicate that he tried to push a gun away as he was shot;

- No dirt or grass was on Foster's shoes although his body was found 200 yards into the park;

- Foster's suit, shirt, tie and underwear were covered with carpet fibers (Fort Marcy is definitely not carpeted).

- The suicide note left by Foster was proven to be a fake.

There were so many discrepancies between the conclusion and the FBI lab analysis evidence that the impartiality of Robert Fiske was called publicly into question. Subsequently, a three judge panel decided to appoint Ken Starr as the Whitewater counsel, despite the fact that he had been on Janet Reno's short list when she appointed Fiske. Much investigative work on the death of Vince Foster was submitted by Christopher Ruddy, who had described the discrepancies in many of his news articles for the New York Post and Pittsburgh Tribune Review. Ruddy left the Post for the Tribune Review because the Post stopped printing his stories. The New york Times would not cover the story accurately and completely either. .(see Chapter 11 for the story that the press would not print,)

William Colby

Freeper archy:

27 APR 1996: Former Director of Central Intelligence [CIA director] William Colby, 76 drowned while canoeing in the Wimocico River near Colby's home in Rock Point, Md.

For the previous two years, Colby had been a contributing editor with a monthly financial newsletter, Strategic Investment, co-edited by James Dale Davidson and former Times of London editor Lord William Rees Mogg, and which had been closely covering the unfolding economic and banking aspects of the Whitewater scandal and the contemporaneous shooting death of White House deputy counsel Vincent Foster. In February Colby had begun a weekly column on geo-political matters and their effects on investments in Strategic Weekly Briefings—a facsimile newsletter tailored for high-income investors, and had developed an interest in the Waco events and their connection to the dead White House lawyer.

NewsMax.com 3/25/99 Christopher Ruddy

"…On April 29, 1996, the wires flashed with hot news: Former

CIA Director William Colby had disappeared from his country home on the Wicomico River in Maryland. Authorities suspected he died in a canoeing accident, as his waterlogged canoe was found on the shore near his home. A week later, his body surfaced in the marsh near his home. After a perfunctory autopsy, local police authorities closed the case as an accident. Still, there were many reasons to suspect foul play. These suspicions began as soon as the initial press reports came out. As expected, the Associated Press ran the first wire story. Colby "was missing and presumed drowned" the AP reported. The wire story said he died as the result of "an apparent boating accident." Quoting a source close to Mrs. Colby, who was in Texas at the time her husband disappeared, the AP stated Colby had spoke via phone with his wife on the day he disappeared. He told her he was not feeling well, "but was going canoeing anyway." This would be an important clue pointing to an accidental death, had it been true. But someone fabricated this story out of whole cloth. A week later, Colby's wife rebutted the AP report, telling the Washington Times her husband was well, and made no mention of canoeing. This initial, false report that relieved obvious suspicion was a red flag of a cover-up Interesting, too, were the obituaries being written. All detailed Colby's fabled career in the World War II-era OSS, the James Bond-like spy who parachuted behind Nazi lines and became a stellar CIA agent. After heading up the Company's Phoenix program in Vietnam, Colby was tapped by President Nixon for the position of DCI—Director of Central Intelligence. These obituaries detailed a formidable list of Colby's associations after he left the CIA. Yet, nowhere did any media report Colby's most significant occupation at the time of his death—contributing editor for Davidson's Strategic Investment. Odd that Colby's major affiliation at the same time of his death deserved no notice...."

2/28/94 THE WHITE HOUSE

Office of the Press Secretary

"......The President today announced his intent to nominate

Sally Shelton-Colby as the Assistant Administrator of the Bureau for Global Programs, Field Support and Research. "I am pleased to nominate Sally Shelton-Colby to the position," the President said, adding "Her foreign affairs experience and educational background will be a great asset to the Agency for International Development." Ambassador Shelton-Colby is currently a senior Fellow and Adjunct Professor at Georgetown University's Center for Latin American Studies.

From email

"....... I am aware that your research on the "Body Count" does not offer a motive for anyone to kill William Colby. But look at this material copied from a Freeper post today (entitled What is the life expectancy of a Waco investigator?): Dave Hardy knew Ghigliotti's work and had visited him in his Laurel, Md. office......
"When gunshots on the FLIR (government Forward-Looking Infrared footage, obtained by documentary film producer Mike McNulty under the Freedom of Information Act) were first seen, back in 1996, we took the tape to (CBS television's) '60 Minutes,' " recalls attorney Hardy, who was also using the FOIA at the time to write a book on the militarization of law enforcement. " '60 Minutes' said they wanted a second opinion, so they sent it to a firm called Infraspection, in Vermont, I seem to remember. It came back with a written report that said 'Yeah, those are gunshots, and we can see people moving around.' Then '60 Minutes' killed the story; this is back in 1996. "Afterward, Infraspection refused to publicly confirm its findings, apparently because of potential negative consequences to the firm-I think those were the words they used. At that point, the guy's comment was 'Too many people are in their graves over this already.' I believe he was referring at that point to William Colby, whom Gordon (Novel) said had given him the FLIR gunshot info, and who had been found dead just before this conversation." When Infraspection declined to have anything further to do with analyzing the Waco footage, they referred Hardy to Carlos Ghigliotti, who ran a lab in Laurel, Md....." (See Glass/McNulty interview in this Chapter).

The following information about the Clintons political time-line was extracted from *Just Politics* article 'Arkansas Connections' by Sam Smith:

1998

Jim McDougal tells reporter Chris Ruddy that in all his conversations with the special prosecutors he was never asked about Vince Foster.

Jim McDougal, who once said that the Clintons move through people's lives like a tornado, dies after being placed in solitary confinement again. On 12 medications. There are questions about other drugs given, including Lasix, which is contraindicated for heart patients. In the hours before McDougal died he had complained of dizziness and became ill but was never seen by a doctor. He had also been separated from his heart medication when placed in an isolation cell before his death. An autopsy on McDougal finds "a toxic but non-lethal amount" of Prozac in his body according to the Fort Worth Star-Telegram. The medical examiner declares the death unrelated to the amount of Prozac, which was three times the normal dosage.

Shortly before he dies, McDougal completes a book with Curtis Wilkie, staff writer for the Boston Globe. The NY times writes of the book, "Moments after President Clinton gave videotaped testimony for the criminal trial of James and Susan McDougal, his former Whitewater partners, he privately agreed to give Mrs. McDougal a pardon if she was convicted, a new book by James McDougal says. 'I'm willing to stick with it, but if it doesn't work out, or whatever, can you pardon Susan?" McDougal recalled asking Clinton—shortly after the president had completed his testimony—in the Map Room at the White House two years ago.

' You can depend on that,' Clinton is said to have replied quietly in the private conversation, apparently out of earshot of others. McDougal then asked, 'Like I say with all lawyers, I mean promptly?' The president grinned and nodded, by McDougal's account, and said, 'If you hang with me, I'll do it.'

Curiously, the medical examiner made no mention of having found traces of any of the 12 medications McDougal was taking. There was also a report from an inmate that McDougal had been given Lasix to encourage urination. Lasix must be taken with a potassium supplement—without it serious heart problems can develop. Wesley Phelan of the Washington Weekly, reports that Lasix can cause "excessive diuresis, blood volume reduction, circulatory collapse, and vascular thrombosis." Further, if McDougal was on the heart medication digitalis, the use of Lasix would be even more serious. The ME would not confirm to Phelan whether he had tested for the presence of Lasix.

Not long thereafter, another potential witness in the Clinton scandals investigation dies suddenly. Johnny Franklin Lawhon Jr, 29, was the owner of the auto transmission shop in Mabelville, Arkansas, who discovered a $27,000 cashier's check made out to Bill Clinton in a trunk of a tornado-damaged car. Lawhon strikes a tree in the early hours of March 30 after, according to one witness, "taking off like a shot" from a filling station.

The Lewinksy affair story breaks in the Washington Post. President Clinton appears on television and says that he "never had sexual relations with that woman, Miss Lewinsky," and that he "never told anyone to lie."

Hillary Clinton goes on the Today Show and blames her husband's problems on a "vast right wing conspiracy."

George Stephanopoulos tells ABC This Week that the White House has a "different, long-term strategy, which I think would be far more explosive. White House allies are already starting to whisper about what I'll call the Ellen Rometsch strategy . . . She was a girlfriend of John F. Kennedy, who also happened to be an East German spy. And Robert Kennedy was charged with getting her out of the country and also getting J. Edgar Hoover to go up to the Congress and say, 'Don't you investigate this, because if you do, we're going to open up everybody's closets." . . . . Asks Sam Donaldson, "Are you suggesting for a moment that what they're beginning to say is that if you investigate this too much, we'll put all your dirty linen right on the table? Every member of the Senate? Every member of the press corps?" "Absolutely," says Stephanopoulos. "The president said he would never resign, and I think some around him are willing to take everybody down with him."

Democratic fund-raiser Johnny Chung wins a plea bargain under which he is charged with funneling illegal contributions to the Clinton-Gore campaign.

Linda Tripp is sequestered in an FBI safe house because of threats against her life.

Arkansas Highway Police seize $3.1 million in cash from four suitcases in a tractor-trailer rig's sleeper section. The driver is charged with money laundering among other things. The seizure is the fourth largest in American history and nearly fifty times more than all the illegal money seized by Arkansas highway police in a typical year.

Jorge Cabrera—the drug dealer who gave enough to the Democrats to have his picture take with both Hillary Clinton and Al Gore—is back in the news as a businessman pleads guilty to laundering $3.5 million for Cabrera between 1986 and 1996

Monica Lewinsky tells Linda Tripp that if she would lie under oath, "I would write you a check. " Also: "I mean, telling the truth could get you in trouble. I don't know why you'd want to do that." Also: "I would not cross these—these people—for fear of my life."

Several reports have Lewinsky saying on another occasion that she didn't want to end up like former White House intern Mary Caitrin Mahoney, killed in the Starbucks execution-style murders.

Monica Lewinsky talks with Linda Tripp about filing a false affidavit in the Paula Jones case:

TRIPP: You—you are—are you positive in your heart that you want to do that? I mean—

LEWINSKY: Uh-huh.

TRIPP: I'm only saying—I'm only saying that in case you should change your mind.

LEWINSKY: No. I—I—I—first of all, for fear of my life. I would not—I would not cross these—these people for fear of my life, number one.

The sale of Arkansas prisoners' blood during the 1980s becomes a major scandal in Canada as news of it is published. The story is ignored in the US media.

Prior to her testimony in the Clinton investigation, Kathleen Willey claims that the tires on her car were mysteriously punctured with dozens of nails and the cat she had for many years suddenly disappeared. Reports ABC's Jackie Judd, "Then just days before she testified in the Paula Jones lawsuit in early January, Willey was out jogging near her home when a stranger approached her. . .The man knew what had happened at her home and that he asked her if the tires had been fixed and if the cat had been found." The man then allegedly asked Willey, 'Don't you get the message?' and jogged off."

Department of Justice announcement: "James Tjahaja Riady will pay a record $8.6 million in criminal fines and plead guilty to a felony charge of conspiring to defraud the United States by unlawfully reimbursing campaign donors with foreign corporate funds in violation of federal election law, the Justice Department's Campaign Financing Task Force and the United States Attorney in Los Angeles announced today. In addition, LippoBank California, a California state-chartered bank affiliated with Lippo Group, will plead guilty to 86 misdemeanor counts charging its agents, Riady and John Huang, with making illegal foreign campaign contributions from 1988 through 1994. Riady is one of 26 people and two corporations charged by the Campaign Financing Task Force, which was established four years ago by Attorney General Janet Reno to investigate allegations of campaign financing abuses in the 1996 election cycle. . . The $8.6 million fine represents the largest sanction imposed in a campaign finance matter in the history of the United States . . . During the period of August 1992 through October 1992, shortly after Riady pledged $1 million in support of Arkansas Governor Bill Clinton's campaign for the Presidency of the United States, contributions made by Huang were reimbursed with funds wired from a foreign Lippo Group entity into an account Riady maintained at Lippo Bank and then distributed to Huang in cash. . . The purpose of the contributions was to obtain various benefits from various campaign committees and candidates for Lippo Group and LippoBank, including: access, meetings, and time with politicians, elected officials, and other high-level government officials; contacts and status for Lippo Group and LippoBank with business and government leaders in the United States and abroad; business opportunities for Lippo Group and defendant LippoBank; government policies which would inure to the benefit of Lippo Group and defendant LippoBank, including Most Favored Nation status for China, open trade policies with Indonesia, normalization of relations with Vietnam, Community Reinvestment Act exemptions for LippoBank, a repeal of the Glass-Steagall Act which limited business opportunities for LippoBank, and a relaxation of Taiwanese restrictions on investment by foreign banks; the deposit of funds into LippoBank by political campaign committees and government agencies; and local government support for Lippo Group's California property development projects which would in turn benefit LippoBank's plans for expansion."

Dr. Cyril Wecht, who has done more than 13,000 autopsies, says there is "more than enough" evidence to suggest possible homicide in the Ron Brown death and that an autopsy should have been performed: "It is not even arguable in the field of medical legal investigations whether an autopsy should have been conducted on Brown."

There were numerous other unexplained deaths/muggings and definitely other cover ups that occurred in the recent past, but it would take a single book to cover all of them. A few that comes to mind:

Suzanne Coleman had an affair with Clinton when he was Arkansas attorney general. Died of 'suicide' with a gunshot wound to the back of her head. No autopsy performed. She was pregnant at the time of her death, rumored to be Clinton's.

Others were attacked and badly beaten. Gary Johnson had videotapes of Clinton at Gennifer Flowers apartment. His tapes were stolen.

Jordon Kettleson had information on the Ives/Henry deaths. He was found shot to death in the front seat of his truck in June 1990.

Let it suffice the say that 'there is something wrong in our Government' and it needs correcting before its too late. Who knows? Maybe its too late now!

Chapter 11

Former President Clinton's Impeachment Fiasco and Other Disasters

Government is like a baby. An alimentary canal with a big appetite at one end and no responsibility at the other. President Ronald Reagan

There is much written about the Clinton's Impeachment proceedings, both pro and con, as to being justified or not. Most information given has been self-impressions from correspondents as to their feeling about the procedure. However, each and everyone of us must look at the facts. If perjury is a crime punishable by imprisonment than why does the Senate of these United States think that they have a right to place anyone above the law? The following dissertation by the House Manager during the Impeachment procedure explains the charges, presents the evidence and gives examples of previous impeachments. It is lengthy but should be read by everyone because it is a good example of Constitutional Law:

Mr. Manager SENSENBRENNER. "Mr. Chief Justice, distinguished counsel to the President, and Senators, in his third annual message to Congress on December 7, 1903, President Theodore Roosevelt said:

'No man is above the law and no man is below it; nor do we ask any man's permission when we require him to obey it. Obedience to the law is demanded as a right; not asked as a favor.'

We are here today because President William Jefferson Clinton decided to put himself above the law, not once, not twice, but repeatedly. He put himself above the law when he engaged in a multifaceted scheme to obstruct justice during the Federal civil rights case of Paula Corbin Jones versus William Jefferson Clinton, et. al. He put himself above the law when he made perjurious, false and misleading statements under oath during his grand jury testimony on August 17, 1998. In both instances, he unlawfully attempted to prevent the judicial branch of Government--a coequal branch--from performing its constitutional duty to administer equal justice under law. The United States House of Representatives has determined that the President's false and misleading testimony to the grand jury and his obstruction of justice in the Jones lawsuit are high crimes and misdemeanors within the meaning of the Constitution. Should the Senate conduct a fair and impartial trial which allows each side to present its best case, then the American public can be confident that justice has been served, regardless of the outcome.

We hear much about how important the rule of law is to our Nation and to our system of government. Some have commented this expression is trite. But, whether expressed by these three words, or others, the primacy of law over the rule of individuals is what distinguishes the United States from most other countries and why our Constitution is as alive today as it was 210 years ago.

The Framers of the Constitution devised an elaborate system of checks and balances to ensure our liberties by making sure that no person, institution, or branch of Government became so powerful that a tyranny could ever be established in the United States of America. We are the trustees of that sacred legacy and whether the rule of law and faith in our Nation emerges stronger than ever, or are diminished irreparably, depends upon the collective decision of the message each Senator chooses to send forth in the days ahead.

The evidence you will hear relates solely to the President's misconduct, which is contrary to his constitutional public responsibility to ensure the laws be faithfully executed. It is not about the President's affair with a subordinate employee, an affair that was both inappropriate and immoral. Mr. Clinton has recognized that this relationship was wrong. I give him credit for that. But he has not owned up to the false testimony, the stonewalling and legal hairsplitting, and obstructing the courts from finding the truth. In doing so, he has turned his affair into a public wrong. And for these actions, he must be held accountable through the only constitutional means the country has available--the difficult and painful process of impeachment.

Impeachment is one of the checks the Framers gave to Congress to protect the American people from a corrupt or tyrannical executive or judicial branch of Government. Because the procedure is cumbersome and because a two-thirds vote in the Senate is required to remove an official following an impeachment trial, safeguards are there to stop Congress from increasing its powers at the expense-of the other two branches. The process is long. It is difficult. It is unpleasant. But, above all, it is necessary to maintain the public's trust in the conduct of their elected officials--elected officials, such as myself and yourselves, who through our oaths of office have a duty to follow the law, fulfill our constitutional responsibilities, and protect our Republic from public wrongdoing. The Framers of the Constitution envisioned a separate and distinct process in the House and in the Senate. They did not expect the House and Senate to conduct virtually identical proceedings with the only difference being that conviction in the Senate requires a two-thirds vote. That is why the Constitution reserves the sole power of impeachment to the House of Representatives and the sole power to try all impeachments to the Senate. History demonstrates different processes were adopted to reflect very different roles.

In the case of President Andrew Johnson, no hearings were held or witnesses called by the House on the President's decision to remove Secretary of War Stanton from office. The House first approved a general article of impeachment that simply stated that President Johnson was impeached for high crimes and misdemeanors. Five days later, a special House committee drew up specific articles. Eleven articles were passed by the House, all but two of which were based upon President Johnson's alleged violation of the Tenure of Office Act by his actions in removing Secretary of War Stanton. The trial was then conducted with witnesses in the Senate.

In the case of President Nixon, the House Judiciary Committee passed three articles of impeachment based not upon their own investigation, but upon the evidence gathered by the Ervin

Committee, the Patman Committee, the Joint Tax Committee and material from the special prosecutor and various court proceedings. Nine witnesses were called at the end of the impeachment inquiry, five of them at the request of the White House, and their testimony was not at the center of the impeachment articles.

In the Judge Walter Nixon impeachment in 1989, a trial with live witnesses was held even after the Senate rejected by less than a two-thirds vote a defense motion to dismiss one article of impeachment on the grounds that it did not constitute an impeachable offense.

The House managers submit witnesses are essential to give heightened credence to whatever judgment the Senate chooses to make on each of the articles of impeachment against President Clinton.

The matter of how this proceeding will be conducted remains somewhat unsettled. Senate impeachment precedent has been to hold a trial. And, in every impeachment case, the Senate has heard from live witnesses. Should the President's counsel dispute the facts as laid out by the House of Representatives, the Senate will need to hear from live witnesses in order to reach a proper and fair judgment as to the truthful facts of this case.

The House concluded the President made perjurious, false and misleading statements before the grand jury, which the House believes constitutes a high crime and misdemeanor. Our entire legal system is based upon the courts being able to find the truth. That's why witnesses must raise their right hand and swear to tell the truth, the whole truth, and nothing but the truth. That's why there are criminal penalties for perjury and making false statements under oath. The need for obtaining truthful testimony in court is so important that the Federal sentencing guidelines have the same penalties for perjury as for bribery.

The Constitution specifically names bribery as an impeachable offense. Perjury is the twin brother of bribery. By making the penalty for perjury the same as that for bribery, Congress has acknowledged that both crimes are equally serious. It follows that perjury and making false statements under oath, which is a form of perjury, be considered among the 'high crimes and misdemeanors' the Framers intended to be grounds for impeachment.

The three judicial impeachments of the 1980's were all about lies told by a federal judge. Judge Claiborne was removed from office for lying on his income tax returns. Judge Hastings was removed for lying under oath during a trial, and Judge Nixon was removed for making false statements to a grand jury. In each case, the Senate showed no leniency to judges who lie. Their misconduct was deemed impeachable and more than 2/3rds of the Senate voted to convict.

If the Senate is convinced that President Clinton lied under oath and does not remove him from office, the wrong message is given to our courts, those who have business before them, and to the country as a whole. That terrible message is that we as a nation have set a lower standard for lying under oath for Presidents than for judges. Should not the leader of our country be held to at least as high a standard as the judges he appoints? Should not the President be obliged to tell the truth when under oath, just as every citizen must? Should not our laws be enforced equally? Your decision in this proceeding will answer these questions and set the standard of conduct of public officials in town halls and courtrooms everywhere and the Oval Office for generations.

Justice is never served by the placing of any public official above the law. The framers rejected the British law of, 'The King can do no wrong', when they wrote our basic law in 1787. Any law is only as good as its enforcement, and the enforcement of the law against the President was left to Congress through the impeachment process.

A Senate conviction of the President in this matter will reaffirm the irrefutable fact that even the President of the United States has no license to lie under oath. Deceiving the courts is an offense against the public. It prevents the courts from administering justice and citizens from receiving justice. Every American has the right to go to court for redress of wrongs, as well as the right to a jury trial. The jury finds the facts. The citizens on the jury cannot correctly find the facts absent truthful testimony. That's why it's vital that the

Senate protect the sanctity of the oath to obtain truthful testimony, not just during judicial proceedings but also during legislative proceedings as well.

Witnesses before Congress whether presidential nominees seeking Senate confirmation to high posts in the executive or judicial branches, federal agency heads testifying during investigative hearings, or witnesses at legislative hearings giving their opinions on bills are sworn to tell the truth. Eroding the oath to tell the truth means that Congress loses some of its ability to base its decisions upon truthful testimony. Lowering the standard of the truthfulness of sworn testimony will create a cancer that will keep the legislative branch from discharging its constitutional functions as well.

Mr. Chief Justice, we are here today because William Jefferson Clinton decided to use all means possible--both legal and illegal--to subvert the truth about his conduct relevant to the federal civil rights suit brought against President Clinton by Mrs. Paula Jones. Defendants in civil lawsuits cannot pick and choose which laws and rules of procedure they will follow and which they will not. That's for the trial judge to decide, whether the defendant be President or pauper.

In this case, a citizen claimed her civil rights were violated when she refused then Governor Clinton's advances and was subsequently harassed at work, denied merit pay raises, and finally forced to quit. The court ruled she had the right to obtain evidence showing other women including Miss Lewinsky, got jobs, promotions, and raises after submitting to Mr. Clinton, and whether other women suffered job detriments after refusing similar advances. When someone lies about an affair and tries to hide the fact, they violate the trust their spouse and family put in them. But when they lie about it during a legal proceeding and obstruct the parties from obtaining evidence, they prevent the courts from administering justice. That is an offense against the public, made even worse when a poor or powerless person seeks the protections of our civil rights from the rich or powerful.

When an American citizen claims his or her civil rights have been violated, we must take those claims seriously. Our civil rights laws have remade our society for the better. The law gives the same protections to the child denied entry to a school or college based upon race as to an employee claiming discrimination at work. Once a hole is punched in civil rights protections for some, those protections are not worth as much for all. Many in the Senate have spent their lives advancing individual rights. Their successful efforts have made America a better place. In my opinion, this is no time to abandon that struggle--no matter the public mood or the political consequence.

Some have said that the false testimony given by the President relating to sex should be excused, since as the argument goes, 'Everyone lies about sex.' I would ask the Senate to stop to think about the consequences of adopting that attitude. Our sexual harassment laws would become unenforceable since every sexual harassment lawsuit is about sex, and much of domestic violence litigation is at least partly about sex. If defendants in these types of suits are allowed to lie about sex, justice cannot be done, and many victims, mostly women, will be denied justice.

Mr. Chief Justice, the House has adopted two articles of impeachment against President William Jefferson Clinton. Each meets the standard of 'high crimes and misdemeanors' and each is amply supported by the evidence.

Article 1 impeaches the President for 'perjurious, false and misleading' testimony during his August 17, 1998, appearance before a grand jury of the United States in four areas.

First, the nature and details of his relationship with a subordinate government employee.

Second, prior perjurious, false and misleading testimony he gave in a federal civil rights action brought against him.

Third, prior false and misleading statements he allowed his attorney to make to a federal judge in that federal civil rights lawsuit.

Fourth, his corrupt efforts to influence the testimony of witnesses and to impede the discovery of evidence in that civil rights action.

The evidence will clearly show that President Clinton's false testimony to the grand jury was not a single or isolated instance which could be excused as a mistake, but rather a comprehensive and calculated plan to prevent the grand jury from getting the accurate testimony in order to do its job. Furthermore, it is important to dispel the notion that the President's false testimony before the grand jury simply relates to details of the relationship between President Clinton and Miss Lewinsky. These charges only make up a small part of Article 1. The fact is, the evidence will show that President Clinton made numerous perjurious, false and misleading statements regarding his efforts to obstruct justice.

Before describing what the evidence in support of Article 1 shows, it is also important to clearly demonstrate that the Senate has already decided that making false statements under oath to a federal grand jury is an impeachable offense.

The last impeachment decided by the Senate, that of United States District Judge Walter L. Nixon, Jr., of the United States District Court for the Southern District of Mississippi, involved the Judge's making false statements under oath to a federal grand jury, precisely the same charges contained in Article 1 against President Clinton. Following an unanimous 417 to 0 vote in the House, the Senate conducted a full trial and removed Judge Nixon from office on the two articles charging false statements to a grand jury by votes of 89 to 8 and 78 to 19. The Senate was clear that the specific misconduct, that is, making false statements to a grand jury, which was the basis for the Judge's impeachment, warranted his removal from office and the Senate proceeded to do just that.

These votes, a little more than nine years ago on November 3, 1989, set a clear standard that lying to a grand jury is grounds for removal from office. To set a different standard in this trial is to say that the standard for judicial truthfulness during grand jury testimony is higher than that of presidential truthfulness. That result would be absurd. The truth is the truth and a lie is a lie. There cannot be different levels of the truth for judges than for presidents.

The President's perjurious, false and misleading statements

regarding his relationship with Ms. Lewinsky began early in his grand jury testimony. These statements included parts of the prepared statement the President read at the beginning of his testimony. He referred or reverted to his statement at least 19 times during the course of his testimony. Further, the evidence will show the President made other false statements to the grand jury regarding the nature and details of his relationship with Ms. Lewinsky at times when he did not refer to his prepared statement.

Second, the evidence will show that the President piled perjury upon perjury when he provided perjurious, false and misleading testimony to the grand jury concerning prior perjurious, false and misleading testimony given in Ms. Paula Jones' case. On two occasions, the President testified to the grand jury that his deposition testimony was the truth, the whole truth, and nothing but the truth, and that he was required to give a complete answer to each question asked of him during the deposition. That means he brought to the grand jury his untruthful answers to questions at the deposition.

Third, the evidence will show the President provided perjurious, false and misleading testimony to a Federal grand jury regarding his attorney's use of an affidavit he knew to be false during the deposition in Ms. Paula Jones' case before Federal Judge Susan Webber Wright.

The President denied that he even paid attention to Mr. Bennett's use of the affidavit. The evidence will show he made this denial because his failure to stop his attorney from utilizing a false affidavit at a deposition would constitute obstruction of justice. The evidence will also show the President did not admit that Mr. Bennett's statement was false because to do so would be to admit that he had perjured himself earlier that day during the grand jury testimony, as well as at the deposition.

Fourth, the evidence will show that the President provided perjurious, false and misleading testimony to the grand jury concerning his corrupt efforts to influence the testimony of witnesses and to impede the discovery of evidence in Ms. Paula Jones' civil rights action. The evidence will show that these statements related to at least four areas:

First, his false statements relating to gifts exchanged between the President and Ms. Lewinsky. The subpoena served on Ms. Lewinsky in the Jones case required her to produce each and every gift she had received from the President. These gifts were not turned over as required by the subpoena, but ended up under Ms. Betty Currie's bed in a sealed container. The President denied under oath that he directed Ms. Currie to get the gifts, but the evidence will show that Ms. Currie did call Ms. Lewinsky about them and that there was no reason for her doing so unless directed by the President.

Second, the President made perjurious, false and misleading statements to the grand jury regarding his knowledge that the Lewinsky affidavit submitted at the deposition was untrue. The evidence will show that the President testified falsely on this issue on at least three separate occasions during his grand jury testimony. He also provided false testimony on whether he encouraged Ms. Lewinsky to file a false affidavit.

Third, the President made false and misleading statements to the grand jury by reciting a false account of the facts regarding his interactions with Ms. Lewinsky and Ms. Currie, who was a potential witness against him in Ms. Jones' case. The record reflects the President tried to coach Ms. Currie to recite inaccurate answers to possible questions should she be called as a witness. The evidence will show the President testified to the grand jury that he was trying to figure out what the facts were, but in reality the conversation with Ms. Currie consisted of a number of very false and misleading statements.

Finally, the President made perjurious, false and misleading statements to aides regarding his relationship with Ms. Lewinsky. In his grand jury testimony, the President tried to have it both ways on this issue. He testified that his statements to aides were both true and misleading--true and misleading. The evidence will show that he met with four aides who would later be called to testify before the grand jury. They included Mr. Sidney Blumenthal, Mr. John Podesta, Mr. Erskine Bowles, and Mr. Harold Ickes. Each of them related to the grand jury the untruths they had been told by the President. I have recited this long catalogue of false statements to show that the President's false statements to the grand jury were neither few in number nor isolated, but rather pervaded his entire testimony.

There can be no question that the President's false statements to the grand jury were material to the subject of the inquiry. Grand juries are utilized to obtain sworn testimony from witnesses to determine whether a crime has been committed. The Attorney General and the Special Division of the United States Court of Appeals for the District of Columbia Circuit appointed an independent counsel pursuant to law and added areas of inquiry because they believed there was evidence that the President may have committed crimes. Grand jury testimony relevant to the criminal probe is always material to the issue of whether someone has committed a crime.

Based upon the precedent in the Judge Nixon impeachment, the law, the facts, and the evidence, if you find the President made perjurious, false and misleading statements under oath to the grand jury, I respectfully submit that your duty will be to find William Jefferson Clinton guilty with respect to article I and to remove him from office.

Article II impeaches William Jefferson Clinton for preventing, obstructing and impeding the administration of justice in the Jones case by either directly or through subordinates and agents engaging in a scheme to delay, impede, cover up, and conceal the existence of evidence and testimony relating to Ms. Jones' Federal civil rights action. As in the case of article I, the President's direct and indirect actions were not isolated mistakes, but were multifaceted actions specifically designed to prevent Ms. Paula Jones from having her day in court.

While the Senate determined in the Judge Nixon trial that the making of false statements to a Federal grand jury warranted conviction and removal from office, no impeachment on an obstruction of justice charge has ever reached the Senate. Therefore, this article is a matter of first impression. However, the impeachment inquiry of the House Judiciary Committee into the conduct of President Richard Nixon, as well as the relevant Federal criminal statutes, clearly show President Clinton's actions to be within the definition of 'high crimes and misdemeanors' contained in the Constitution.

The first article of impeachment against President Nixon approved by the Judiciary Committee charged Mr. Nixon with 'engaging personally and through his subordinates and agents in a course of conduct or plan designed to delay, impede and obstruct the investigation of such unlawful entry; to cover up, conceal and protect those responsible and to conceal the existence and scope of other unlawful activities.' The article charged that the implementation of the plan included nine separate areas of misconduct. Included among these were, one, making or causing to be made false and misleading statements to investigative officers and employees of the United States; two, withholding relevant and material evidence from such persons; three, approving, condoning, acquiescing in and counseling witnesses with respect to the giving of false and misleading statements to such persons as well as in judicial and congressional proceedings. History shows us that President Nixon's resignation was the only act that prevented the Senate from voting on this article, and that the President's conviction and removal from office were all but certain.

There are two sections of the Federal Criminal Code placing penalties on those who obstruct justice. Title 18, United States Code, section 1503, punishes '(whoever * * * corruptly, or by threats or force * * * obstructs, or impedes or endeavors to influence, obstruct or impede the due administration of justice.'

The courts have held that this section relates to pending judicial process, which can be a civil action. Ms. Jones' case fits that definition at the time of the President's actions as alleged in article II, as does the Office of Independent Counsel's investigation.

Title 18, United States Code, section 1512, punishes, 'Whoever * * * corruptly persuades another person, or attempts to do so, or engages in misleading conduct toward another person, with intent to * * * influence, delay or prevent the testimony of any person in an official proceeding * * * (or) cause or induce any person to * * * withhold testimony, or withhold a record, document, or other object from an official proceeding * * *.'

The evidence will show that President Clinton's actions constituted obstruction of justice in seven specific instances as alleged in Article II. Paragraph one alleges that on or about December 17, 1997, the President encouraged Miss Lewinsky, who would be subpoenaed as a witness in Mrs. Jones' case two days later, to execute a sworn affidavit that he knew would be perjurious, false, and misleading.

The evidence will show the President's actions violated both federal criminal obstruction statutes.

Second, Article II alleges that on or about that same day, the President corruptly encouraged Miss Lewinsky to give perjurious, false, and misleading testimony if and when called to testify personally in that proceeding. Miss Lewinsky, on the witness list at that time, could have been expected to be required to give live testimony in the Jones case and in fact she was subsequently subpoenaed for a deposition in that case. The evidence will show the President's actions violated both federal criminal obstruction statutes.

Third, Article II alleges on or about December 28, 1997, the President corruptly engaged in, encouraged, or supported a scheme to conceal evidence which had been subpoenaed in Mrs. Jones' civil rights case. He did so by asking Ms. Betty Currie to retrieve evidence from Miss Lewinsky that had been subpoenaed in the case of Jones v. Clinton. The evidence will show the President's actions violated the second federal criminal obstruction statute.

Fourth, Article II alleges that beginning on or about December 7, 1997, and continuing through and including January 14, 1998, the President intensified and succeeded in an effort to secure job assistance to Miss Lewinsky in order to corruptly prevent her truthful testimony in the Jones case at a time when her truthful testimony would have been harmful to him.

While Miss Lewinsky had sought employment in New York City long before the dates in question, helping her find a suitable job was clearly a low priority for the President and his associates until it became obvious she would become a witness in the Jones case. The evidence will clearly show an intensification of that effort after her name appeared on the witness list. This effort was ultimately successful and the evidence will show that the President's actions violated both federal obstruction statutes.

Fifth, Article II alleges on January 17, 1998, the President corruptly allowed his attorney to make false and misleading statements to Judge Wright characterizing the Lewinsky affidavit in order to prevent questioning deemed relevant by the judge. The President's attorney, Robert Bennett, subsequently acknowledged such false and misleading statements in a communication to Judge Wright. The evidence will show the President's actions clearly violate the second federal criminal obstruction statute.

Sixth, Article II alleges that on or about January 18, 20, and 21, 1998, the President related a false and misleading account of events relevant to Mrs. Jones' civil rights suit to Ms. Betty Currie, a potential witness in the proceeding, in order to corruptly influence her testimony. The evidence will show that President Clinton attempted to influence the testimony of Ms. Betty Currie, his personal secretary, by coaching her to recite inaccurate answers to possible questions that might be asked of her if called to testify in Mrs. Paula Jones' case. The President did this shortly after he had been deposed in the civil action. During the deposition, he frequently referred to Ms. Currie and it was logical that based upon his testimony, Ms. Currie would be called as a witness. The evidence will show that two hours after the completion of the deposition, the President called Ms. Currie to ask her to come to the office the next day, which was a Sunday. When Ms. Currie testified to the grand jury, she acknowledged the President made a series of leading statements or questions and concluded that the President wanted her to agree with him. The evidence will show the President's actions violated both statutes, but most particularly section 1512.

In *United States* v. *Rodolitz* 786 F2d 77 at 82 (2nd Cir 1986) cert. Den. 479 US 826 (1986), the United States Court of Appeals for the 2nd Circuit said,

'The most obvious example of a sec. 1512 violation may be the situation where a defendant tells a potential witness a false story as if the story were true, intending that the witness believes the story and testify to it before the grand jury.' If the President's actions do not fit this example, I'm at a loss to know what actions do.

Seventh, and last, Article II alleges on or about January 21, 23, and 26, 1998, the President made false and misleading statements to potential witnesses in a federal grand jury proceeding in order to corruptly influence this testimony of those witnesses. The articles further alleges these false and misleading statements were repeated by the witnesses to the grand jury, causing the grand jury to receive false and misleading information. The evidence will show that these statements were made to presidential aides Mr. Sidney Blumenthal, Mr. Erskine Bowles, Mr. John Podesta and Mr. Harold Ickes. They all testified to the grand jury. By his own admission seven months later, on August 17, 1998, during his sworn grand jury testimony, the President said that he told a number of aides that he did not have an affair with Ms. Lewinsky and did not have sex with her. He told one aide, Mr. Sidney Blumenthal, that Miss Monica Lewinsky came on to him and he rebuffed her. President Clinton also admitted that he knew these aides might be called before the grand jury as witnesses. The evidence will show they were called; they related the President's false statements to the grand jury; and that by the time the President made his admission to the grand jury, the damage had already been done.

This is a classic violation of 18 U.S.C. Section 1512.

The seven specific, allegations of obstruction of justice contained in Article II were designed to prevent the judicial branch of government, a separate and coequal branch, from doing its work in Ms. Paula Jones' lawsuit. Based upon the allegation of Article 1 against President Nixon in 1974, as well as repeated and calculated violations of two key criminal obstruction statutes, William Jefferson Clinton committed an impeachable offense.

In Article II, the evidence is conclusive that President Clinton put himself above the law in obstructing justice, not once, not just a few times, but as a part of a extensive scheme to prevent Ms. Jones from obtaining the evidence she thought she needed to prove her civil rights claims.

Complying with the law is the duty of all parties to lawsuits and those who are required to give truthful testimony. A defendant in a federal civil rights action does not have the luxury to choose what evidence the court may consider. He must abide by the law and the rules of procedure. William Jefferson Clinton tried to say that the law did not apply to him during his term of office in civil cases were concerned. He properly lost that argument in the Supreme Court in a unanimous decision.

Even though the Supreme Court decided that the President wasn't above the law and that Ms. Jones' case could proceed, William Jefferson Clinton decided--and decided alone--to act as if the Supreme Court had never acted and that Judge Wright's orders didn't apply to him. What he did was criminal time and time again. These criminal acts were in direct conflict with the President's obligation to take care the laws be faithfully executed.

Based upon the repeated violations of federal criminal law, its effect upon the courts to find the truth, and the President's duty to take care that the laws be faithfully executed, if you find that the President did indeed obstruct the administration of justice through his acts, I respectfully submit your duty will be to find William Jefferson Clinton guilty with respect to Article II and to remove him from office.

It is truly sad when the leader of the greatest nation in the world gets caught up in a series of events where one inappropriate and criminal act leads to another, and another and another.

Even sadder is that the President himself could have stopped this process simply by telling the truth and accepting the consequences of his prior mistakes. At least six times since December 17, 1997, William Jefferson Clinton could have told the truth and suffered the consequences. Instead he chose lies, perjury, and deception. He could have told the truth when he first learned that Ms. Lewinsky would be a witness in the Ms. Jones' case. He could have told the truth at his civil deposition. He could have told the truth to Betty

Currie. He could have told the truth when the news media first broke the story of his affair. He could have told the truth to his aides and cabinet. He could have told the truth to the American people. Instead, he shook his finger at each and every American and said, 'I want you to listen to me,' and proceeded to tell a straight-faced lie to the American people. Finally, he had one more opportunity to tell the truth. He could have told the truth to the grand jury. Had he told the truth last January, there would have been no independent counsel investigation of this matter, no grand jury appearance, no impeachment inquiry and no House approval of articles of impeachment. And, we would not be here today fulfilling a painful but essential constitutional duty. Instead, he chose lies and deception, despite warnings from friends, aides, and members of the House and Senate that failure to tell the truth would have grave consequences.

When the case against him was being heard by the House Judiciary Committee, he sent his lawyers, who did not present any new evidence to rebut the facts and evidence sent to the House by the Independent Counsel. Rather, they disputed the Committee's interpretation of the evidence by relying on tortured, convoluted, and unreasonable interpretations of the President's words and actions.

During his presentation to the House Judiciary Committee, the President's very able lawyer, Charles Ruff, was asked directly, 'Did the President lie?' during his sworn grand jury testimony.

Mr. Ruff could have answered that question directly. He did not, and his failure to do so speaks a thousand words.

Is there not something sacred when a witness in a judicial proceeding raises his or her right hand and swears before God and the public to tell the truth, the whole truth, and nothing but the truth? Do we want to tell the country that its leader gets a pass when he is required to give testimony under oath? Should we not be concerned about the effect of allowing perjurious, false, and misleading statements by the President to go unpunished on the truthfulness of anyone's testimony in future judicial or legislative proceedings? What do we tell the approximately 115 people now in federal prison for the crime of perjury?

The answers to all these questions ought to be obvious.

As elected officials, our opinions are frequently shaped by constituents telling us their own stories. Let me tell you one related to me about the poisonous results of allowing false statements under oath to go unpunished.

Last October while the Starr report was being hotly debated, one circuit court judge for Dodge County, Wisconsin approached me on the street in Mayville, Wisconsin. He said that some citizens had business in his court and suggested that one of them take the witness stand and be put under oath to tell the truth. The citizen then asked if he could tell the truth, 'just like the President.'

How many people who have to come to court to testify under oath about matters they would like to keep to themselves think about what that citizen asked Judge John Storck? And, how will the courts be able to administer the, 'equal justice under law' we all hold so dear if we do not enforce the sanctity of that oath even against the President of the United States?

When each of us is elected or chosen to serve in public office, we make a compact with the people of the United States of America to conduct ourselves in an honorable manner, hopefully setting a higher standard for ourselves than we expect of others. That should mean we are careful to obey all the laws we make, execute and interpret. There is more than truth in the words, 'A public office is a public trust.'

When someone breaks that trust, he or she must be held accountable and suffer the consequences for the breach. If there is no accountability, that means that a President can set himself above the law for four years, a Senator for six, a Representative for two, and a judge for life. That, Mr. Chief Justice, poses a far greater threat to the liberties guaranteed to the American people by the Constitution that anything imaginable.

For the past 11 months, the toughest questions I've had to answer have come from parents who want to know what to tell their children about what President Clinton did. Every parent tries to teach their children to know the difference between right and wrong, to always tell the truth, and when they make mistakes, to take responsibility for them and to face the consequences of their actions. President Clinton's actions at every step since he knew Ms. Lewinsky would be a witness in Mrs. Jones' case have been completely opposite to the values parents hope to teach their children.

But being a poor example isn't grounds for impeachment. Undermining the rule of law is. Frustrating the courts' ability to administer justice turns private misconduct into an attack upon the ability of one of the three branches of our government to impartially administer justice. This is a direct attack upon the rule of law in our country and a very public wrong that goes to the constitutional workings of our government and its ability to protect the civil rights of even the weakest American.

What is on trial here is the truth and the rule of law. Failure to bring President Clinton to account for his serial lying under oath and preventing the courts from administering equal justice under law will cause a cancer to be present in our society for generations.

Those parents who have asked the questions should be able to tell their children that even if you are the President of the United States, if you lie when sworn to tell the truth, the whole truth and nothing but the truth, you will face the consequences of that action even when you won't accept the responsibility for it.

How those parents will answer those questions is up to the United States Senate.

While how today's parents answer those questions is important, equally important is what parents tell their children in the generations to come about the history of our country and what has set our government in the United States of America apart from the rest of the world.

Above the President's dais in this Senate chamber appears our national motto. 'E pluribus unum'--'out of many, one.' When that motto was adopted more than two hundred years ago, the First Congress referred to how thirteen separate colonies turned themselves into one, united nation.

As the decades have gone by, that motto has taken an additional meaning. People of all nationalities, faiths, creeds, and values have come to our shores, shed their allegiances to their old countries and achieved their dreams to become Americans. They came here to flee religious persecution, to escape corrupt, tyrannical and oppressive governments, and to leave behind the economic stagnation and endless wars of their homelands. They came here to be able to practice their faiths as they saw fit--free of government dictates and to be able to provide better lives for themselves and their families by the sweat of their own brows and the use of their own intellect. But they also came here because they knew America has a system of government where the Constitution and laws protect individual liberties and human rights. Everyone--yes, everyone--can argue that this country has been a beacon for individual citizen's ability to be what he or she can be.

They fled countries where the rulers ruled at the expense of the people, to America, where the leaders are expected to govern for the benefit of the people. And, throughout the years, America's leaders have tried to earn the trust of the American people, not by their words, but by their actions.

America is a place where government exists by the consent of the governed. And, that means our Nation's leaders must earn and re-earn the trust of the people with every thing they do. Whenever an elected official stumbles, that trust is eroded and public cynicism goes up. The more cynicism that exists about government, its institutions, and those chosen to serve in them, the more difficult the job is for those who are serving.

That's why it is important, yes vital, that when a cancer exists in the body politic, our job--our duty--is to excise it. If we fail in our duty, I fear the difficult and dedicated work done by thousands of honorable men and women elected to serve not just here in Washington, but in our State capitals, city halls, courthouses and school board rooms will be swept away in a sea of public cynicism. We must not allow the beacon of America to grow dim, or the American dream to disappear with each waking morning.

In 1974, the Congress did its painful public duty when the President of the United States broke the public trust.

During the last decade, both Houses impeached and removed three Federal judges who broke their trust with the people.

During the last 10 years, the House of Representatives disciplined two Speakers for breaking the rules and their trust with the public.

And, less than 6 years ago, this honorable Senate did the same to a senior Senator whose accomplishments were widely praised.

In each case, Congress did the right thing to help restore the vital trust upon which our Government depends. It wasn't easy, nor was it always popular, but Congress did the right thing. Now, this honorable Senate must do the right thing. It must listen to the evidence; it must determine whether William Jefferson Clinton repeatedly broke our criminal laws and thus broke his trust with the people--a trust contained in the Presidential oath put into the Constitution by the Framers--an oath that no other Federal official must take--an oath to insure that the laws be faithfully executed.

How the Senate decides the issues to be presented in this trial will determine the legacy we pass to future generations of Americans.

The Senate can follow the legacy of those who have made America what it is.

The Senate can follow the legacy of those who put their 'lives, fortunes and Sacred Honor' on the line when they signed the Declaration of Independence.

The Senate can follow the legacy of the Framers of the Constitution whose preamble states that one of its purposes is, 'to establish justice.'

The Senate can follow the legacy of James Madison and the Members of the First Congress who wrote and passed a Bill of Rights to protect and preserve the liberties of the American people.

The Senate can follow the legacy of those who achieved equal rights for all Americans during the 1960s in Congress, in the courts, and on the streets and in the buses and at the lunch counters.

The Senate can follow the legacy of those who brought President Nixon to justice during Watergate in the belief that no President can place himself above the law.

The Senate can follow the legacy of Theodore Roosevelt who lived and governed by the principle that no man is above the law.

Within the walls of the Capitol and throughout this great country there rages an impassioned and divisive debate over the future of this presidency. This Senate now finds itself in the midst of the tempest. An already immense and agonizing duty is made even more so because the whims of public opinion polls, the popularity and unpopularity of individuals, even questions over the strength of our economy, risk subsuming the true nature of this grave and unwelcome task.

We have all anguished over the sequence of events that have led us to this, the conclusive stage in the process. We have all identified in our own minds where it could have, and should have stopped. But we have ended up here, before the Senate of the United States, where you, the Senators, will have to render judgment based upon the facts.

A scientist in search of the basic nature of a substance begins by boiling away what is not of the essence. Similarly, the Senate will sift through the layers of debris that shroud the truth. The residue of this painful and divisive process is bitter, even poisonous at times. But beneath it lies the answer. The evidence will show that at its core, the question over the President's guilt and the need for his conviction will be clear. Because at its core, the issues involved are basic questions of right versus wrong--deceptive, criminal behavior versus honesty, integrity and respect for the law.

The President engaged in a conspiracy of crimes to prevent justice from being served. These are impeachable offenses for which the President should be convicted. Over the course of the days and weeks to come, we, the House managers, will endeavor to make this case. May these proceedings be fair and thorough. May they embody our highest capacity for truth and mutual respect. With these principles as our guides, we can begin with the full knowledge our democracy will prevail and that our Nation will emerge a stronger, better place.

Our legacy now must be not to lose the trust the people should have in our Nation's leaders.

Our legacy now must be not to cheapen the legacies left by our forebearers.

Our legacy must be to do the right thing based upon the evidence.

For the sake of our country, the Senate must not fail. Thank you.

After the above condemnation of William Clinton's actions, the so called patriotic Senators voted as follows:

[SUBJECT: ARTICLE I--ARTICLES OF IMPEACHMENT AGAINST PRESIDENT WILLIAM JEFFERSON CLINTON] GUILTY--45 NOT GUILTY—55
[Subject: Article II--Articles of Impeachment against
President William Jefferson Clinton]
Guilty--50
Not guilty--50

Since it required two-thirds of the Senate to find former president Clinton guilty, it was a forgone conclusion that he was not going to be judged guilty by the current Democratic members of the Senate. The Social Democrats in Congress and other departments of government have a philosophy that states that they are above the law, they can do no wrong. The law applies only to other fools. In essence what they said by their decision that Democrats can commit perjury but others like Martha Stewart, Scooter Libby, etc., must go to jail. That is their message loud and clear. A list of the Senators that believe *they* are above the law and voted Bill Clinton not Guilty are as follows:

ARTICLE II VOTES:

Arkansas: Blanche Lambert Lincoln (D): Not guilty
California:Sen. Barbara Boxer (D): Not guilty
Sen. Dianne Feinstein (D): Not guilty
Connecticut:Sen. Christopher Dodd (D): Not guilty
Sen. Joseph Lieberman (D): Not guilty
Delaware:Sen. Joseph Biden (D): Not guilty
Florida:Sen. Bob Graham (D): Not guilty
Georgia:Sen. Max Cleland (D): Not guilty
Hawaii:Sen. Daniel Akaka (D): Not guilty
Sen. Daniel Inouye (D): Not guilty
Illinois:Sen. Richard Durbin (D): Not guilty
Indiana:Sen. Evan Bayh (D): Not guilty
Iowa: Sen. Tom Harkin (D): Not guilty
Louisiana:Sen. John Breaux (D): Not guilty
Sen. Mary Landrieu (D): Not guilty
Maine:Sen. Susan Collins (R): Not guilty (RINO –Republican In Name Only)
Sen. Olympia Snowe (R): Not guilty (RINO)
Maryland:Sen. Barbara Mikulski (D): Not guilty
Sen. Paul Sarbanes (D): Not guilty
Massachusetts: Sen. Edward Kennedy (D): Not guilty
Sen. John Kerry (D): Not guilty
Michigan:Sen. Carl Levin (D): Not guilty
Minnesota:Sen. Paul Wellstone (D): Not guilty
Montana:Sen. Max Baucus (D): Not guilty
Nebraska:Sen. Bob Kerrey (D): Not guilty
Nevada:Sen. Richard Bryan (D): Not guilty
Sen. Harry Reid (D): Not guilty
New Jersey:Sen. Frank Lautenberg (D): Not guilty
Sen. Robert Torricelli (D): Not guilty
New Mexico:Sen. Jeff Bingaman (D): Not guilty
New York;Sen. Daniel Patrick Moynihan (D): Not guilty
Sen. Charles Schumer (D): Not guilty
North Carolina: Sen. John Edwards (D): Not guilty
North Dakota:Sen. Kent Conrad (D): Not guilty
Sen. Byron Dorgan (D): Not guilty

Oregon:Sen. Ron Wyden (D): Not guilty
Pennsylvania:Sen. Arlen Specter (R): Not guilty (RINO)
Rhode Island:Sen. John Chafee (R): Not guilty (RINO)
Sen. Jack Reed (D): Not guilty
South Carolina: Sen. Ernest "Fritz" Hollings (D): Not guilty
South Dakota:Sen. Thomas Daschle (D): Not guilty
Sen. Tim Johnson (D): Not guilty
Vermont:Sen. James Jeffords (R): Not guilty (RINO)
Sen. Patrick Leahy (D): Not guilty
Virginia:Sen. Charles Robb (D): Not guilty
WashingtonSen. Patty Murray (D): Not guilty
West Virginia:Sen. Robert Byrd (D): Not guilty
Sen. Jay Rockefeller (D): Not guilty
Wisconsin:Sen. Russell Feingold (D): Not guilty
Sen. Herb Kohl (D): Not guilty

ARTICLE I VOTES
Include all the above Not Guilty votes plus five additional Republicans:
Alaska:Sen. Ted Stevens, (R): Not guilty (Half RINO?)
Alabama:Sen. Richard Shelby, (R): Not guilty (Half RINO?)
Tennessee:Sen. Fred Thompson, (R): Not guilty (Half RINO?)
Virginia:Sen. John Warner, (R), Not guilty (Half RINO?)
Washington: Sen. Slade Gorton, (R): Not guilty (Half RINO?)

The ill-advised findings of the Senate was more than approved by the findings of Judge Susan Weber Wright, who oversaw the proceedings in the case of *Jones vs Clinton* in Arkansas on 12 April 1999. Although the Jones vs Clinton case was over, Judge Wright said she would not release her verdict until after the impeachment trial was over. She stated that she didn't want to influence the outcome. One might doubt her reasoning because isn't withholding evidence in a court trail a crime? I presume not if it involves a high-level government official.

When Judge Wright did release her findings, many judicial scholars could only scratch their heads. Some of her statements in the finding are as follows:

"In his deposition on 17 January 1998, Bill Clinton gave testimony that was later recognized as false..."

"Bill Clinton subsequently admitted what he euphemistically characterized as an 'inappropriate relationship' with Monica Lewinsky. The Starr report shows that Clinton clearly testified falsely in his January 1998 deposition..."

'At his August 17th [1998] appearance before the grand jury, the President directly contradicted his deposition testimony by acknowledging that he had indeed been alone with Ms Lewinsky on numerous occasions during which they engaged in inappropriate intimate contact..."

"It is difficult to construe President's sworn statement in this civil lawsuit concerning his relationship with Ms Lewinsky as anything other than the willful refusal to obey this Court's discovery Orders.

Given the President's admission that he was misleading with regard to questions being posed to him and the clarity with which his falsehoods are revealed by the record, there is no need to engage in an extended analysis of the President's sworn statements in the lawsuit...."

"The President never challenged the legitimacy of plaintiff's lawsuit by filing a motion pursuant to Rule 11, however, and it is simply not acceptable to employ deceptions and falsehoods in an attempt to obstruct the judicial process..." "In sum, the record leaves no doubt that the President violated this Court's discovery Orders regarding disclosure of information deemed by this Court to be relevant to plaintiff's lawsuit...."

"....the President contumacious conduct in this case, coming as it did from a member of the bar and chief law enforcement of the Nation, was without justification and undermines the integrity of the judicial system."

From the above, many law abiding citizen are asking where is the Justice. Why are some people in jail for perjury while other's go free? Unless the law books define the following words differently than the standard dictionary than *Noblesse Oblige* only applies to the Socialist in government. The words:

> deposition: n, :1. An act of removing from a position of authority. 2. a testifying esp. before a court. b. *DECLARATION, specif: testimony taken down in writing under oath.* 3. An act or process of depositing. 4. Something deposited; DEPOSIT
>
> perjury: n, the voluntary violation of an oath or vow either by swearing to what is untrue or by omission to do what has been promised under oath; false swearing.

From the court case of Judge Wright her decision not to mention the word perjury is a mystery that only she can answer. Her charges were that President Clinton disobey a Court Order (to disclose all the fact in the case) and therefore the case was closed and needed no further investigation into things such as perjury!

To close this portion of the Impeachment section of this book one must remember that our current members of Government are politicians that will do anything to keep their jobs. The way it works is that 'I do what I want, you do what I say.' Why did so many senators vote against impeachment of President Clinton? One can only go back to Sam Donaldson's interview with Stephanopoulos (see Chapter 10). It is repeated here for emphasis on how our current government works (bribes, blackmail, etc.): Asks Sam Donaldson, "Are you suggesting for a moment that what they're beginning to say is that if you investigate this too much, we'll put all your dirty linen right on the table? Every member of the Senate? Every member of the press corps?" "Absolutely," says Stephanopoulos. "The president said he would never resign, and I think some around him are willing to take everybody down with him."

There are many stories about government cover-ups that it would take another tome to cover them all. The one cover-up that explains the current government operations and why the average citizen doesn't have a chance in court when the government charges you is the apparent cover-up of Vincent Foster's death. There was an article on the Internet titled "The Death of Vincent Foster— Evidence of a Cover-up" It shows how the Press would not touch the story because it was too hot for them.

One thing high profile scandals such as Nixon's Watergate demonstrate is that a scandal itself rarely brings down a president. Rather, it is the concerted effort by government officials to cover up the scandal that does. Why? Because a *cover-up always involves a conspiracy* of various persons in government violating, in one way or another, their sworn duty to uphold the law and prosecute illegal activity.

In like manner, government officials who engage in dark side operations are constantly having to cover up for their crimes. Successful cover-ups of these operations always point to a broad conspiracy at work because higher officials must join in to cover for what lower echelon henchmen did – a fact that must be kept even more secret than the crime itself. The extension of such collusion across government agency boundaries is proof of *systematic corruption in government*, which is a whole different ballgame in terms of criminal evil than the actions of mere rogue agents. To cover up a crime that is part of systematic government corruption, the perpetrators must consistently stop or sabotage investigations in a wide range of jurisdictions around the country. This means many years of cultivating, subverting and corrupting other key law enforcement personnel, judges and prosecutors, all from different agencies.. All of this constitutes high crimes and treason as the very nature of constitutional government is subverted in the process.

The murder of White House counsel Vince Foster was a classic dark-side operation. Vince Foster was the man who knew too much. The following are excerpts from the article: "The Death of Vince Foster—Evidence of A Cover-up":

"Allan Favish's Freedom Of Information Act lawsuit achieved a breakthrough recently when a Federal District Judge ordered 5 of the 10 crime scene Polaroid photographs released. One of these is no doubt the photo of the dark blued steel revolver and Foster's hand previously leaked by the White House to Reuter's News Service. But the other four are photos not publicly seen before.

Prologue:

"Vincent Foster had been struggling with the Presidential Blind trust. Normally a trivial matter, the trust had been delayed for almost 6 months and the U.S. trustee's office was beginning to make noises about it. Foster was also the keeper of the files of the Clinton's Arkansas dealings and had indicated in a written memo that "Whitewater is a can of worms that you should NOT open!"

"But Vincent's position at the White House did not sit well with him. Only days before, following a public speech stressing the value of personal integrity, he had confided in friends and family that he was thinking of resigning his position. Foster had even written an outline for his letter of resignation, thought by this writer to have been used as the center portion of the fake "suicide note". Foster had scheduled a private meeting with Bill Clinton for the very next day, July 21, 1993 at which it appeared Foster intended to resign. "

Vincent Foster had spent the morning making "busy work" in his office and had been in attendance at the White House announcement of Louis Freeh as the new head of the FBI earlier in the day (passing by the checkpoint manned by White House uniformed guard.

This is a key point. The White House is the most secure private residence in the world, equipped with a sophisticated entry control system and video surveillance system installed by the Mitre Corporation. **Yet no record exists that Vincent Foster left the White House under his own power on July 20th, 1993. No video of him exiting the building exists. No logbook entry shows he checked out of the White House.**

Several hours after he was last seen inside the White House, Vincent Foster was found dead in Fort Marcy Park, in a Virginia suburb just outside Washington D.C.

The death was ruled a suicide (the first major Washington suicide since Secretary of Defense James Forrestal in 1949), but almost immediately rumors began to circulate that the story of a suicide was just a cover-up for something much worse.

The first witness to find the body insisted that there had been no gun near the body. The memory in Foster's pager had been erased. Critical evidence began to vanish. Many witnesses were harassed. Others were simply ignored. There were even suggestions that the body had been moved, and a Secret Service memo surfaced which reported that Foster's body had been found in his car! The official reports were self-contradictory.

Evidence of a Cover-up

"While the U.S. Park Police (a unit not equipped for a proper homicide investigation) studied the body, **Foster's office at the White House was being looted. Secret Service agent Henry O' Neill watched as Hillary Clinton's chief of staff, Margaret Williams, carried boxes of papers out of Vincent Foster's office before the Park Police showed up to seal it.** Amazing when you consider that the official identification of Vincent Foster's body by Craig Livingstone did not take place until 10PM! Speaking of Craig Livingstone, another Secret Serviceman saw him remove items from Vincent Foster's office in violation of the official seal. Witnesses also saw Bernard Nussbaum in Foster's office as well. Three witnesses noted that Patsy Thomason, director of the White House's Office of Administration, was desperate to find the combination to Vincent Foster's safe. **Ms. Thomason finally opened the safe, apparently with the help of a special "MIG" technical team signed into the White House in the late hours. Two envelopes reported to be in the safe by Foster's secretary Deborah Gorham, addressed to Janet Reno and to William Kennedy III, were never seen again.** When asked the next day regarding rumors of the safe opening, Mack McLarty told reporters Foster's office did not even have a safe, a claim immediately shot down by former occupants of that office."

"The next day, when the Park Police arrived for the official search of Vincent Foster's office, they were shocked to learn that Nussbaum, Thomason and Williams had entered the office. Conflicts channeled through Janet Reno's Department of Justice resulted in the Park Police merely sitting outside Foster's office while Bernard Nussbaum continued his own search of Foster's office. During this search, he opened and upended Vincent Foster's briefcase, showing it to be empty. Three days later, it would be claimed that this same briefcase was where the torn up suicide note was discovered."

"The boxes of documents removed from Foster's office by Hillary Clinton's chief of staff, Margaret Williams, were taken to the private residence area of the White House! Eventually, only 54 pages emerged. "

"One set of billing records, under subpoena for two years, and thought to have originated in Foster's office, turned up unexpectedly in the private quarters of the White House, with Hillary's fingerprints on them! "

"So, who ordered the office looting?"

"Bill Clinton was unavailable, being on camera with Larry King. But Hillary Clinton, who had only the day before diverted her planned return to Washington D.C. to Little Rock, was on the phone from Little Rock to someone at the White House in the moments before the looting took place. "

The Initial Reactions

"Back in Little Rock, Foster's friends weren't buying it. Doug Buford, friend and attorney, stated, "...something was badly askew." Foster's brother-in-law, a former congressman, also did not accept that depression was what had been behind the "suicide": "That's a bunch of crap." And Webster Hubbell, former Clinton deputy attorney general, phoned a mutual friend to say, "Don't believe a word you hear. It was not suicide. It couldn't have been."

"Outside experts not connected the official investigation also had their doubts.

Vincent J. Scalise, a former NYC detective, Fred Santucci, a former forensic photographer for NYC, and Richard Saferstein, former head of the New Jersey State Crime Lab formed a team and did an investigation of the VWF case for the Western Journalism Center of Fair Oaks, Calif. They arrived at several conclusions:

(1) Homicide cannot and should not be ruled out.

(2) The position of the arms and legs of the corpse were drastically

inconsistent with suicide.

(3) Neither of VWF's hand was on the handgrip when it was fired. This is also inconsistent with suicide. The investigators noted that in their 50 years of combined experience they had "never seen a weapon or gun positioned in a suicide's hand in such an orderly fashion."

(4) VWF's body was probably in contact with one or more carpets prior to his death. The team was amazed that the carpet in the trunk of VF's car had not been studied to see whether he had been carried to the park in the trunk of his own car.

5) The force of the gun's discharge probably knocked VF's glasses flying; however, it is "inconceivable" that they could have traveled 13 feet through foliage to the site where they were found; ergo, the scene probably was tampered with.

(6) The lack of blood and brain tissue at the site suggests VF was carried to the scene. The peculiar tracking pattern of the blood on his right cheek also suggests that he was moved.

Despite numerous official assurances that Vincent Foster really did commit suicide, more and more Americans, over 70% at the last count, no longer believe the official story. TV specials, most notably the one put out by A&E's "Inside Investigations" with Bill Kurtis, have failed to answer the lingering questions, indeed have engaged in deliberate fraud to try to dismiss the evidence that points to a cover-up.

This website

"**This** web site is built primarily from official records, newspaper reports, and other hard data. Careful analysis of those records reveals a pattern of deliberate obfuscation surrounding Vincent Foster's death. This pattern of obfuscation, this cover-up, is a matter that should concern all Americans, not because of what it means for Vincent Foster, but because of what it means for the rest of us. "

"One thing is for certain. As we approach the fifth anniversary of this crime, it is clear from the amount of resources being brought to bear by the government that there is something about this particular crime that has made those in power very afraid. With the latest Zogby Poll revealing that the majority of Americans no longer believe the official claim of suicide, the perpetuation of the cover-up must be to prevent an examination of the motive, why *was Vincent Foster murdered* and his body dumped in Fort Marcy Park? "

NEW! Photo of Vince Foster's shirt after he was removed from Fort Marcy Park proves Foster had to have been shot where he was found.

"One of the many false trails put out by government disinformation operatives was the claim that Vince Foster really did kill himself but did so someplace embarrassing and his body was moved to Fort Marcy Park post-mortem, explaining away the many inconsistencies in the evidence of a suicide at Fort Marcy Park itself. Contradicting that claim was the observation that, while the body was rather bloodless as found (suggesting that Foster was already dead by other means when a gun was fired into his mouth to simulate a suicide) once paramedics moved the body, blood poured from the wounds, staining Foster's shirt"

"On Friday, March 11, 1994, in response to rumors which were even then beginning to circulate regarding Foster's death, ABC News broadcast the following photograph, which had been leaked by the White House to Reuter's news agency. The intent was to reinforce the claim that Foster's death had indeed been a suicide. I was not a political activist at the time, nor did I ever intend to become one. My career is in feature film and TV visual effects, which I have been doing for almost thirty years. I know about film fakery. And the instant I saw the above photo on TV I turned to my wife and said to her half jokingly, "This is staged! If I did work this sloppy I wouldn't be working." But the more I thought about it, the less funny it all seemed. "

"There are several troubling aspects in this photograph, which reveal it to be a staged shot. First and foremost among them the total lack of blood anywhere in the scene."

"This lack of blood is the single, strongest proof that Vincent

Foster did NOT put the gun into his own mouth and pulls the trigger. Had he done so, the blowback from the gunshot would have coated the gun, hand, and white sleeve of Foster's shirt with a spray of blood and organic matter. None appears in the photo anywhere. "

"The FBI lab report reveals that even with the most sensitive chemical test available, no blood was found on the gun that Foster (we are told) inserted into his mouth and fired. Not only that, Foster's fingerprints were not on the gun. "

"This is the crux of the suicide theory put forward by the government, that Vincent Foster, under stress, on a hot July day, put the barrel of a .38 revolver into his mouth and pulled the trigger, and did not leave blood OR FINGERPRINTS on that gun. "

The Lack of Blood.

"Was Foster already dead when the headshot was fired?"

"One of the key pieces of information that argued against suicide was the lack of blood at the scene. "

"When the brain is destroyed, the heart will continue to beat on its own, for as long as it has oxygenated blood to feed it. This is why head trauma victims provide most donor hearts. The heart remains alive as long as blood is still in the body. "

"In the case of a gunshot into the mouth, the bullet has to pass through the sinus cavities. Any child who has been in a schoolyard fight knows how easy it is for the nose to start bleeding and how hard it can be to stop. "

"Had Foster really shot himself in the mouth, his heart would have continued to beat, pumping most of his blood out through the shattered sinus cavities and the entrance wound in his mouth, as well as out through the supposed exit wound. "

"But this did not happen. Witnesses at the scene reported a "trickle" of blood from the mouth and nose (one of the tracks appeared to have flowed up hill). "

The Fiske Report.

"Note that Fiske's report was only preliminary. His final report on Vincent Foster remains sealed. When the Wall Street Journal filed a Freedom Of Information Act request to force the release of Fiske's final report, the court, in an unprecedented prior restraint, ordered the Wall Street Journal not to report on the case, or to even mention what the final ruling actually was. "

"This illegal prior restraint is one of the indicators, which reveals how terrified the government is of the facts behind the death of Vincent Foster. "

THE COVER-UP UNRAVELS

"No sooner had the preliminary Fiske report been issued than it met with immediate criticism, even from the U.S. House of Representatives. "

"Careful analysis of the report by private citizens, typified by Hugh Sprunt's "Citizen's Investigative Report" revealed dozens and dozens of obvious and clumsy contradictions. "

"Yet another outstanding series of articles was written by Dave Martin called, "America's Dreyfus Affair".

THE SILVER BLACK GUN

"Among the most damning pieces of evidence to emerge from the official records was the deliberate and fraudulent manufacturing of the testimony of Lisa Foster in regards to the gun found with Vincent Foster's body. "

"Vincent Foster was found with a .38 revolver made by Colt Arms. It was built from parts taken from two other guns, and as a result had two serial numbers. The Frame number was 355055, and according to the records of the Colt Arms Company , the gun was manufactured with a standard dark blue, almost black, finish. "

"In the Park Police record, the gun is described as black. The accompanying photographs in the Park police report show a black gun. "

"The photograph leaked by the White House to ABC-TV also shows a dark gun. Compare the reflectivity of the gun to Foster's gold ring on his finger, just an inch away.

In all the statements by the Fort Marcy Park witnesses, in

the Park Police reports, in the reports by experts at the FBI and ballistics lab, the gun is never described as anything but dark blue or (more often) black. The photographs recently obtained in Allan Favish's FOIA lawsuit clearly show a dark surface to the gun. "

"No connection exists between that gun and Vincent Foster. Foster's fingerprints were not on the gun. Neither was any of his blood . The DNA traces on the gun, while "not inconsistent" with Foster, were more likely to have originated with a black or a Hispanic than with a Caucasian. No gunpowder or bullet fragments were found in Foster's wounds that could be matched to the gun! "

"Despite this, Robert Fiske inserted a comment on page 38 of his report on Foster; a statement that Lisa Foster thought the gun found with her husband was one she had brought up from Little Rock, Arkansas. "

"This statement came from an interview of Lisa Foster conducted by the FBI on May 9th, 1994, more than nine months after Vincent Foster's death. In the handwritten notes and final FD-302a report of the interview, the interviewing FBI agents describe the gun being shown to Lisa Foster as "silver colored", not just once, but many times. The gun is never described as dark blue or black. "

"The FBI agents are not quoting Lisa Foster, they write down THEIR impressions of what is being said and done. In their own words, on the bottom of page 16 and the top of page 17 of the FD-302a form, "LISA FOSTER believes that the gun found at Fort Marcy Park may be the silver gun which she brought up with her other belongings when she permanently moved to Washington."

"In order for Lisa Foster to believe that the gun presented to her as the Fort Marcy Park gun might be the family silver gun, the gun presented as the Fort Marcy Park gun must also be silver. Lisa Foster doesn't have to be a gun expert to know that silver is not black. From the official record, its clear that Lisa Foster was shown a gun she recognized as the gun she brought up from Little Rock, but its equally clear that this is not the same gun as that found with Vincent Foster. Black is not silver."

Patrick Knowlton

"The credibility of the suicide claim took another hit when one of the witnesses at Fort Marcy Park, Patrick Knowlton, came forward to claim that the FBI had altered his testimony. Patrick was then harassed and threatened, which prompted the filing of a lawsuit for witness tampering. "

Perry/Patterson

"The White House had come forward to claim that they were not notified of the discovery of Vincent Foster's body until quite late in the evening. This was a critical item relating to when Vincent Foster's office was officially sealed for the investigation and (as it later came out) when it was being looted of records. "

'But two Arkansas State Troopers put the White House's official time of notification in doubt. Roger Perry and Larry Patterson had both come forward to report a phone call made from the White House to the Arkansas Governor's mansion approximately two hours earlier than the White House claimed it had learned of Foster's death. The Clinton's nanny, Helen Dicky, made the call. "

"During the Whitewater hearings, Helen placed the call much later, and to bring the issue to an end the committee members announced to all that the "former" troopers had changed their minds and would not testify to receiving the call any earlier than Helen stated. This, of course, was yet another lie. Perry and Patterson were not "former" anything; they were still Arkansas State troopers who had wanted to testify but were kept out. Angered and with no other venue, Perry and Patterson swore out affidavits stating the facts as they knew them. "

Linda Tripp

"Recently, at the end of her appearance before the Monica Lewinsky Grand Jury, Linda Tripp issued a public statement that hinted at the deceptions behind the death of Vincent Foster.

THE "SUICIDE" NOTE

AT LEAST PARTLY A FORGERY.

"No single item connected to the Foster death has aroused as much controversy as the so-called "suicide" note. "

"This was a note, allegedly written by Vincent Foster and discovered in his briefcase some days after his death. The problem was that Bernard Nussbaum, in controlling the Park Police search of Foster's office, had shown them that same briefcase empty just two days before. Coupled with that was the fact that the White House did not report the existence of the note for almost 36 hours after it was allegedly discovered. "

"Adding another odd aspect to the note was the great pains taken to conceal it from the public. Even though the text itself had been published, Jim Hamilton made a point, during Lisa Foster's FBI interview to remind everyone that photos of the note were not to be allowed out, even in response to a Freedom of Information Act Request. "

"Hamilton went to far as to request, in a letter (page 1—page 2) to Janet Reno, the return of the actual "suicide" note as soon as possible, and thanks her again for refusing to allow photographs of the note to be allowed in public "

"The availability of the note prompted James Davidson at Strategic Investment to commission three of the world's top document examiners to examine the note. In their report, all three experts judged the note to be a forgery! "

"This hardly came as a surprise. An even cursory examination reveals that at last two different hands worked on that note, suggesting that Foster's outline for a letter of resignation (for that is what Lisa Foster thought the note had been) was modified. A botched attempt at a signature may have required the strange tearing of the note with the loss of one-piece right where the signature would go."

"The note had fingerprints on it. Officially, the origin of the prints remains undetermined, but while testifying before the Whitewater committee, the FBI expert reported that one palm print was identified as belonging to Bernard Nussbaum. "

THE AUTOPSY

FOSTER'S "MAGIC" BULLET HOLE.

"Virtually the entire case for supposed suicide rests firmly on the autopsy done by Dr. James C. Beyer, a pathologist for Fairfax County, Virginia with strong ties to the FBI.

Dr. Bayer's autopsy report at first reading seems unremarkable. It's conclusion is that Vincent Foster died of a single gunshot wound entering the roof of the mouth and exiting the back of the skull. "

"But on closer examination, problems become apparent. "

"Dr. Beyer's co-worker at the Fairfax County, Virginia, medical examiner's office is Dr. Donald Haut. It was Dr. Haut, not Dr. Beyer, who actually examined Vincent Foster's body while it was still at Fort Marcy Park, assisted by John Rolla. On page two of Dr. Haut's signed report, the wound track is described as a "gunshot wound mouth to neck".

"This corroborates the eyewitness testimony of EMS Technician Richard Arthur, who described the gunshot wound in some detail, placing it under the right ear. This is consistent with the news story reported by Ambrose Evens-Pritchard, who described a photograph of that wound. "

"Was there really an exit wound out the back of Foster's head?

Prior to the body's delivery to Beyer, nobody reported a gunshot wound out the back of the head. EMS Sergeant Gonzalas stated he did NOT see a gunshot wound out the back of the head. John Rolla did not report a gunshot wound out the back of the head. Another EMS Technician, Cory Ashford, testified is a tape recorded interview with reporter Chris Ruddy that he was certain there was NO exit wound at the back of the head while Vincent Foster was at Fort Marcy Park! "

"Outside of the obviously altered page one of Dr. Haut's report, there isn't a single official record of a gunshot wound exiting the back of Foster's head while he's still at Fort Marcy Park. "

"It is not until the body arrives at Dr. Beyer's morgue that the neck wound seen by Arthur and Haut seems to go away and the wound out the back of the head appears.

On the wound description page in the Beyer autopsy, the box

for neck wounds has been left blank. "

"But the wound that Beyer DOES describe is rather odd. Supposedly, the wound is the result of a soft nosed unjacketed lead bullet being fired through two dense bones, first at the base of the skull and then at the rear. There should be metal fragments all over the wound track. For a comparison, take a look at the X-ray taken of John F. Kennedy's skull following his assassination. Metal fragments are seen throughout the interior of the skull, and this is from a full metal jacket round, the type that LIMITS fragmentation! "

"Yet in describing the wound track in Vincent Foster's head, Beyer notes on page 2 of his report that no metallic fragments were recovered during the examination! There should have been lead scrapings all over the bone perforations, had a soft-nosed lead bullet really made them! "

"More recently, a FBI telex was uncovered which reported that the autopsy conducted by the Fairfax County Medical Examiner had found a bullet entry but NO EXIT WOUND! "

The Missing X-rays

"Beyer himself checked and signed the boxes on his report indicating that X-rays had been taken. Dr. Beyer told Park Police Detective James G. Morrissette that the X-rays showed no bullet fragments at all. Again, with the type of ammunition on the gun wound with Foster's body, this is impossible. "

"Of course, the X-rays were not to be found.

Beyer later claimed that they hadn't been taken, and that his X-ray machine was broken, although the service records on that machine do not bear out this claim. "

The Missing Crime Scene photos

"With the exception of a few Polaroid photos that are currently the subject of Allan Favish's FOIA lawsuit, no photographs of the crime scene exist. "

"The 35mm photographs taken by the Park Police were supposedly underexposed in the laboratory (although Starr investigator Miquel Rodriguez reportedly used an outside lab to successfully recover images from the film, just prior to his conflict with Mark Touhey and subsequent resignation from the OIC). "

"In addition to the 35mm photos, many more of the Polaroids of the crime scene simply vanished. "

"It turns out that Beyer was the last person known to be in possession of the now-vanished crime scene Polaroids. Rolla was unable to attend the autopsy of Vincent Foster because the autopsy was moved up 24 hours unexpectedly. As Rolla stated in his testimony, "Normally you like to have at least one of the scene investigators at the autopsy to answer questions for the medical examiner [Dr. James C. Beyer], but he had the photographs and copies of the reports."

"Of course, the X-rays were not to be found. Beyer later claimed that they hadn't been taken, and that his X-ray machine was broken, although the service records on that machine do not bear out this claim.

"Rolla testified that the photos were inside the case jacket when the jacket went to Beyer. After it had come back, the photos were gone. Note also that whereas it is normal to have investigators present for the autopsy, the last minute schedule change, moving the Foster up a day, meant that Beyer performed a significant part of the autopsy unobserved. By the time Park Police observers saw the body, Beyer had removed Foster's entire tongue and upper palette, obliterating the "mouth to neck" gunshot wound Dr. Haut had seen. "

"Clearly, something is very wrong with the autopsy and the preponderance of evidence points to Beyer as author of the deception. Certainly, he was well positioned to tamper with Dr. Haut's original report, altering the page 1 description. "

"Beyer's past history isn't the most reassuring. Indeed he seems to be the Virginia version of the infamous Dr. Fahmy Malek, the Arkansas M.E. who ignored clear evidence of homicide in the deaths of Don Henry and Kevin Ives and in one case ruled that a man who had been beheaded was dead of natural causes. "

"Beyer himself, in the case of Tommy Burkett, ignored a broken jaw in order to rule that Burkett had killed himself with a gun. Despite having shown the autopsy photos to Burkett's father, Beyer later claimed (as he did with the Foster X-rays) that they had never really existed. After a second autopsy, the case was reopened as a homicide. "

"Likewise, in 1989 there was an autopsy on establishing the death of a man named Tim Easley. Mr. Beyer, the coroner, ruled that Easley killed himself by stabbing himself in the chest. He failed to notice a defensive wound on the man's hand. The case was reopened, and, after an outside expert reviewed the case, Easley's girlfriend confessed to murdering him. "

"In short, Dr. Beyer's consistent performance (indeed his "specialty") appears to be the cover-up of murder by declaration of suicide! "

"In the case of Vincent Foster, the question must be asked if Dr. Beyer, given his past history, changed a non-fatal neck wound seen by witnesses at Fort Marcy Park into a fatal head shot needed for the suicide cover up.

The Starr Report.

Long before the actual release of Kenneth Starr's report on Vincent Foster, and despite an appearance of a sincere effort at investigation, there were indications of an impending continuance of the cover-up started by Starr's predecessor, Robert Fiske (the BCCI lawyer).

"The first indication came with Starr's handling of investigator Miquel Rodriquez' conflicts with fellow investigator Mark Touhey. Rodriquez had uncovered what he thought was clear evidence of a cover-up in the death of Vincent Foster; in hindsight it would be almost impossible not to. "

"By way of example, Rodriguez had taken the 35mm negatives taken at the Fort Marcy Park location, which had been declared unusable, and taken them to an outside image enhancement lab which succeeded in recovering images from the negatives. "

"Under normal circumstances, one would assume such a success at recovering data would meet with approval, but such was not to be. Rodriguez came under severe criticism and opposition from fellow investigator Mark Touhey. When Rodriguez took the conflict to Kenneth Starr, Starr backed Touhey and Rodriguez was forced to resign, his enhanced photographs of the crime scene have never been released. "

"Further confirmation of Starr's intentions came when the FBI records regarding the showing of a silver gun to Lisa Foster first surfaced. Hugh Sprunt, in one of his many meetings with investigators from Kenneth Starr's office, informed them of this discovery. Starr's investigators, echoing the claims being put out on the internet at the time, assured Hugh Sprunt that the photo leaked by the White House to Reuter's was quite misleading with regard to the gun's color, and that it was reasonable to consider the gun to be of "silver color". As can be seen by the high quality photographs of the gun released as part of Allan Favish's Freedom Of Information Act lawsuit, the gun is quite dark, and not to be confused with a shiny silver gun."

"With such an obvious pander to the official story coming from the lips of Starr's own investigators, it therefore came as no surprise that Kenneth Starr's report on Vincent Foster continued the claim of suicide. But unlike the Fiske Report, Starr's Report had something new. It had an addendum."

"This addendum had been submitted by the attorney for Patrick Knowlton, John Clarke, and had been added to Starr's Report by the three-judge panel supervising his work over Starr's strenuous objections! "

"The addendum so undermined the conclusions of Starr's report that Starr had it published in a second, separate volume from his own report. Copies of the Starr report were then distributed to the media without the second volume. Most Americans to this day are not aware of the existence of the court ordered addendum to the Starr Report. "

Kenneth Starr Caught In A Lie.

"In his report on Vincent Foster, Kenneth Starr attempted to resolve some of the lingering questions regarding the claim of suicide. "

"One such question involved the dark blued steel gun found with Foster's body (the gun that the FBI had fraudulently tried to link to Vincent Foster) which did not have any of his fingerprints on it. "

"Kenneth Starr included in his report the comment that glove box of Vincent Foster's car contained an oven mitt. Dr. Henry Lee had concluded that Vincent Foster had carried the dark blued steel revolver to Fort Marcy Park inside the oven mitt and that this explained the lack of fingerprints. "

"Of course, there is a huge logic flaw in the claim. Star reports that the oven mitt was left in the car, photographed inside the glove box by the Park Police the very next day. Foster would therefore have to have carried the dark blued steel revolver with him from the car, without the protection of the oven mitt, then placed it inside his mouth and pulled the trigger. The presence of the oven mitt in the glove box therefore does not explain the lack of fingerprints on the dark blued steel revolver found next to Foster's body.

"While there may be legitimate reasons for an oven mitt to be in the glove box there is some question as to whether the oven mitt was really in Foster's car as represented by Kenneth Starr. "

"Starr states that the oven mitt was photographed by the Park Police in their impound lot the day after Foster's body was found, July 21st, 1993. And, in the photographs from Allan Favish's FOIA lawsuit, there are photographs showing an oven mitt quite prominently on display inside the glove box. "

"But there is a problem. A photograph taken at Fort Marcy Park the night of July 20th 1993 clearly shows debris on the passenger side floor. "

"In the Park Police records, Detective Braun emptied the glove box of all items PRIOR to detective Smith removing and cataloguing the debris from the passenger seat floor. Records show Braun emptying the glove box prior to leaving the Park Police impound lot as 6:35 AM July 21st. Detective Smith's paperwork has him cleaning off the passenger side floor after noon on July 21st. "

"Clearly, a photograph showing the glove box with items in it over a clean passenger side floor is in direct contradiction to the Park Police record of the search of Foster's car.

"The photographs of the oven mitt appear to be after-the-fact stagings at best, complete frauds at worst. When Detective Braun emptied the glove box from Vincent Foster's car, her inventory did not record the presence of an oven mitt. "

Lisa Foster

"It's easy to simply dismiss Lisa Foster as the hapless victim of a tragedy, and to (as so many supporters of the suicide theory have argued) declare her off-limits in any analysis of the events surrounding the death of her first husband. "

"However, there are indications that Lisa Foster has had her own suspicions regarding just how her husband died. "

"When John Rolla first arrived at the Foster's D.C. home to inform Lisa Foster of the discovery of her husband's body at Fort Marcy Park, Rolla noted an unusual event in his report. "

"What Rolla saw fit to comment on was the strange reaction of Lisa Foster to Rolla's describing the gun found with her husband's body, in which at the mention of the gun's color Lisa simply exits the room in a highly emotional state. "

"In Lisa Foster's FBI interview it was established that the only gun that was in the Foster's Washington D.C. Residence was a chrome plated revolver. It is apparent that Lisa would have had to know that the black gun being described to her by Rolla was not her husband's. "

"But rather than say anything about the discrepancy, Lisa Foster simply terminated the discussion. "

"Yet another indication of acquiescence if not complicity was found in Lisa Foster's New Yorker interview, basically a spin piece in which Lisa Foster talked about the stresses of the preceding two years but said nothing to challenge the suicide theory of her husband's death. "

"Now, at the time Lisa Foster did this interview, she had to know deception existed in the case. John Rolla had told her that the gun found with her husband's body was black. Lisa knew that the black gun could not be the Foster family's silver gun. When shown a photograph of the dark blued steel gun she did not identify it. But by the time this interview took place, she had been through the FBI interview in which a silver gun was presented to her as the gun found with her husband's body! Lisa Foster did not comment on the magically changed gun during the interview, nor did she take the opportunity to mention the issue during her interview with the New Yorker. "

"It's important not to ascribe a sinister motive to Lisa Foster's actions. A mother who has seen her children lose one parent and is reasonably concerned that they not lose another easily explains them."

Shortly after the New Yorker interview, Lisa Foster married Judge Moody in Arkansas. Shortly after that, Moody's son Neil was killed in a high-speed traffic accident. Witnesses reported he was being pursued at the time of the crash. "

The Endless Spin

"No sooner had questions surfaced regarding the circumstances of Vincent Foster's death than a crowd of people surged forth to assure America that Vincent Foster had indeed been depressed even though he had clearly concealed it from everyone around him. "

"Leading the attack was CBS "60 Minutes", which had openly admitted biasing its handling of the Gennifer Flower's segment in 1992 to help Bill Clinton win the nomination. Quit a far cry from the media handling of Gary Hart's infidelities! "

"So, when reporter Chris Ruddy started writing a series of article for the New York Post regarding the inconsistencies in the Vincent Foster case, "60 Minutes" again stepped to Bill Clinton's defense with a hit piece on Ruddy. The misreporting was so outrageous and error filled that Accuracy in Media issued some highly critical reports, as did Congressman Dan Burton. "

"Next came a segment of the A&E program "Inside Investigations" with Bill Kurtis, which attempted to explain the absence of fingerprints on the gun found with Foster's body by showing how the deep grooves of a modern automatic pistol simply do not provide the surfaces needed to capture fingerprints. That Foster's body was not found with a modern automatic pistol with deep grooves and heavy texturing, but with a smooth metal revolver, was not mentioned. "

End of Article.

"Don't believe a word you hear. It was not suicide. It couldn't have been." -Assistant Attorney General Webster Hubbell, 7/20/93, cited in Esquire, 11/93.

Never did our forefathers ever dream of the so called "Free Press" be part of the conspiracy to destroy this country. They always presumed that the Press would be fair, factual and objective. But today that is not the case. The current Media only prints or televises the propaganda of the one-world leaders. It matters not if its lies, misinformation or omissions. Just don't tell the people what is happening—keep them in the dark.

\#

Chapter 12

Inept Congress—Illegal Immigration

"In this present crisis, government is not the solution, government is the problem."   President Ronald Reagan

"Reconquista" is the name given to the "Aztlán Plan", the retaking by Mexico of the seven Southwestern states, the "Aztlán or Northern Territory". Many look upon this statement as crazy but it is not. It is happening now and has been going on for quite some time.

A brief summary of what the plot is all about follows:

Illegal immigration into the United States is a highly profitable proposition for both employers and the U.S. government, and it also benefits Mexico, which is the largest source country of undocumented immigrants into the US. The US and Mexican governments actively entice illegal immigrants to enter this country and to work illegally for profit-hungry U.S. employers. Poverty-stricken immigrants , who are often desperate to house and feed their families, respond to the financial enticements... and then are blamed by U.S. citizenry for illegally being in the US.

The United States borders are porous to say the least. The illegal immigrant population of the United States in 2008 was estimated by the Center for Immigration Studies to be about 11 million people, down from 12.5 million people in 2007.

About 75% of undocumented immigrants arrive across the United States southern border with Mexico, and hail from Mexico, El Salvador, Guatemala, Colombia and other Central and South American countries. The bulk...about 50% of all 'illegals'.... are Mexican-born people.

Time magazine stated that illegal immigration accelerated

under the Bush Administration, with the United States gaining 3 million additional illegal immigrant residents in 2004. A third of all illegal immigrants in the United States live in California. Other states with large illegal populations are, in descending order, Texas, New York, Illinois, Florida and Arizona.

After more than 100 years in existence, President Bush dissolved the United States Immigration and Naturalization Service (INS) in March 2003 and absorbed it into the new Homeland Security Department, along with FEMA and dozens of other federal agencies created to protect and help citizens and residents.

Until its dissolution, the INS had been part of the Justice Department since 1940, and before that, part of the US Labor Department. After the September 11, 2001 tragedy, the Bush Administration complained that the INS was insufficiently *focused on deporting and expelling* illegal immigrants, and thus asked that it be transferred to Homeland Security.

The US Border Patrol is charged with the responsibility of enforcing illegal immigration across US borders. Until 2003, the Border Patrol was part of the INS, but was also folded into Homeland Security (as a separate agency from INS).

The massive United States intelligence agencies overhaul passed by Congress and signed by President Bush in January 2005 required Homeland Security to hire 10,000 more Border Patrol agents, 2,000 per year starting immediately. The Border Patrol currently employs over 20,200 agents who patrol 8,000 miles of border. Its Agents are primarily responsible for immigration and border law enforcement as codified in the Immigration and Nationality Act. Their duty is to prevent terrorists and terrorist weapons from entering the United States and to deter, detect, and apprehend illegal aliens and individuals involved in the illegal drug trade who enter the United States other than through designated ports of entry.

But the Bush Administration (at that time the Border Patrol had about 20,000 Agents) ignored the law mandating the hiring of new agents. Said Congressman John Culberson (R-TX) to CNN's Lou Dobbs, "Unfortunately, the White House ignored the law, and only asked us for 200 more agents. That's unacceptable." Culberson was referring to the federal budget for 2006 in which President Bush provided funds for only 210 new agents, not 2,000 additional agents.

Both houses of Congress worked together twice in 2005 to bypass the White House, and hired 1,500 new Border Patrol agents -500 shy of that required by law, but far surpassing the mere 210 planned by President Bush.

The US-Mexico border remains significantly under-patrolled. On October 7, 2005, 80 members of the House of Representatives sent a letter to the President, calling on him to enforce immigration laws, and deferring consideration of the White House's proposed guest-worker immigration program. "History has shown that enforcement provisions are ignored and underfunded..." said the Congressional letter.

Meanwhile, Congressman Culberson told CNN's Lou Dobbs on October 7, 2005, "We've got a full-scale war going on our southern border. You don't need to go to Iraq to see a war. We've got widespread lawlessness... We need boots on the ground... ASAP." Today, the latest information from the Border Patrol confirms the lack of personnel to patrol all the known immigration routes over federal lands. One private organization, planted hidden cameras to monitor one of the routes. The route selected showed illegal aliens pouring through the route at the rate of over 500 a month. The cameras also showed that many were carrying back-packs loaded with what appeared to be drugs, guns, etc. Since this was one of many routes not being patrolled, one can extrapolate to give a fairly accurate count of how many illegals are crossing our borders annually.

There has always been widespread poverty and hunger in Mexico. According to the World Bank, 53% of Mexico' population of 104 million residents live in poverty, which is defined as living on less than $2 a day. Close to 24% of Mexico's population live in extreme poverty, which means they live on less than $1 a day.

The bottom 40% of Mexican households share less than 11% of the country's wealth. Millions live in extreme poverty and children are compelled to work on the streets in order to help provide food for their families.

Unemployment in Mexico is realistically estimated near 40%, and there are no government unemployment benefits. There are also virtually no welfare benefits to provide the basics for poverty-stricken, often-starving women, children and families.

Illegal immigrants continue to outpace the number of legal immigrants—a trend that's held steady since the 1990s. While the majority of illegal immigrants continue to concentrate in places with existing large communities of Hispanics, increasingly illegal immigrants are settling throughout the rest of the country.

An estimated 13.9 million people live in families in which the head of household or the spouse is an unauthorized immigrant. Illegal immigrants arriving in recent years tend to be better educated than those who have been in the country a decade or more. A quarter of all immigrants who have arrived in recent years have at least some college education. Nonetheless, illegal immigrants as a group tend to be less educated than other sections of the U.S. population: 49 percent haven't completed high school, compared with 9 percent of native-born Americans and 25 percent of legal immigrants.

In 2003, then-President of Mexico, Vicente Fox stated that remittances "are our biggest source of foreign income, bigger than oil, tourism or foreign investment" and that "the money transfers grew after Mexican consulates started giving identity cards to their citizens in the United States." He stated that money sent from Mexican workers in the United States to their families back home reached a record $12 billion. Two years later, in 2005, the World Bank stated that Mexico was receiving $18.1 billion in remittances and that it ranked third (behind only India and China) among the countries receiving the greatest amount of remittances.

The Rockridge Institute argues that globalization and trade agreement affected international migration, as laborers moved to where they could find jobs. Raising the standard of living around the world, a promise the North American Free Trade Agreement (NAFTA), Central American Free Trade Agreement (CAFTA), the

World Trade Organization (WTO), the International Monetary Fund (IMF), and the World Bank, would reduce the economic incentive for illegal immigration. However, governments have not followed through on all of these programs.

This transit migrations cause economic, social, and human rights problems in Mexico. The illegal immigrants also cause several problems in their final destinations. Therefore, according to the United Nations, the current waves of illegal migration are considered as a *threat* to democracy.

In 1997 Foreign investors have announced major new investments in Mexico. Ford announced plans to invest $2 billion in an auto assembly plant in Chihuahua that will put together 400,000 cars a year with 1,000 workers. Sharp Electronics Corp. of Japan plans a $27 million assembly facility in Rosarito Beach, Mexico, 20 miles south of the U.S.-Mexico border, that will employ 1,000 workers to assemble one million television sets and 1.5 million vacuum cleaners each year.

In Tijuana, an independent union, STIMAHCS, a member of the independent union federation Frente Autentico de Trabajo (FAT), won recognition as the representative of workers in the Korean-owned Han Young factory after state government officials in Baja California reversed course and approved the certification of an independent union at the Han Young plant.

The Mexican government failed to make promised investments of billions of dollars in roads, schooling, sanitation, housing, and other infrastructure to accommodate the new maquiladoras (border factories) envisioned under NAFTA. As a result few were built, and China surpassed Mexico in goods produced for the United States market. Instead of the anticipated increase, the number of manufacturing jobs in Mexico dropped from 4.1 million in 2000 to 3.5 million in 2004. The 1994 economic crisis in Mexico, which occurred the year NAFTA went into effect, resulted in a devaluation of the Mexican peso, decreasing the wages of Mexican workers relative to those in the United States. Meanwhile, more efficient agricultural operations in the United States and the elimination of tariffs under NAFTA caused the price of corn to fall 70% in Mexico between 1994 and 2001, and the number of farm jobs to decrease from 8.1 million in 1993 to 6.8 million in 2002.

Corruption hurts the economy of Mexico, which in turn leads to migration to the United States. Mexico was perceived as the 72nd least corrupt state out of 179 according to Transparency International's 2006 Corruption Perceptions Index, a survey of international business (for comparison, the United States ranked as the 20th least corrupt). Global Integrity estimates that in 2006, corruption cost the Mexican economy $60 billion per year. A survey by the Mexican research firm, Centro de Estudios Económicos del Sector Privado, found that 79 percent of companies in Mexico believe that "illegal transactions" are a serious obstacle to business development.

Although corruption is rampant throughout the Mexican government, President Calderon blames all Mexican troubles on the United States. He stated that if it wasn't for the desire of U. S. Americans for drugs, the Drug Cartel's would disappear and Mexico would have no problems. Although it is a well know fact that drugs enter Mexico through its southern border by bribing the border authorities. President Calderon doesn't say anything about this because it is a way of life in Mexico. Money talks.

The US Department of Homeland Security and some advocacy groups have criticized a program of the government of the state of Yucatan and that of a federal Mexican agency directed to Mexicans migrating to and residing in the United States. They claim that the assistance includes advice on how to get across the U.S. border illegally, where to find healthcare, enroll their children in public schools, and send money to Mexico. The Mexican federal government also issues identity cards to Mexicans living outside of Mexico.

• In 2005 the government of Yucatan produced a handbook and DVD about the risks and implications of crossing the U.S.-

Mexico border. The guide told immigrants where to find health care, how to get their children into U.S. schools, and how to send money home. Officials in Yucatan said the guide is a necessity to save lives but some American groups accused the government of encouraging illegal immigration.

• Also, in 2005, the Mexican government was criticized for distributing a comic book which offers tips to illegal aliens emigrating to the United States. That comic book recommends to illegal immigrants, once they have safely crossed the border, "Don't call attention to yourself. ... Avoid loud parties. ... Don't become involved in fights." The Mexican government defends the guide as an attempt to save lives. "It's kind of like illegal immigration for dummies," said the executive director of the Center for Immigration Studies in Washington, Mark Krikorian. "Promoting safe illegal immigration is not the same as arguing against it." The comic book does state on its last page that the Mexican Government does not promote illegal crossing at all and only encourages visits to the U.S. with all required documentation.

Groups in favor of strict immigration enforcement oppose Matrícula Consular ("Consular Registration"), an identification card issued by the Government of Mexico through its consulate offices. The purpose of the card is to demonstrate that the bearer is a Mexican national living outside of Mexico. Similar consular identification cards are the Guatemalan CID card and the Argentinian CID card as well as a number of other CID cards issued to citizens of Colombia, El Salvador, and Honduras. The document is accepted at financial institutions in many states and, in conjunction with an IRS Taxpayer Identification Number, allows illegal immigrants to open checking and saving accounts. California Governor Arnold Schwarzenegger and former President Bill Clinton promote the use of foreign government CID cards in U.S. financial institutions. In December 2008, Governor Schwarzenegger launched 'Bank on California' which calls on California mayors to specifically encourage the use of the Mexican CID and Guatemalan CID card by banks and credit unions as a primary identification when opening an account.

As of 2005, Operation Community Shield had detained nearly fourteen hundred illegal immigrant gang members. Members from the Salvadoran gang are believed by authorities to establish a smuggling ring in Matamoros, Mexico. The smuggling involved transporting illegal aliens from foreign countries into the United States. The Salvadoran gang has shown extreme violence against Border Patrol security to "teach them a lesson." "Mexican alien smugglers plan to pay violent gang members and smuggle them into the United States to murder Border Patrol agents, according to a confidential Department of Homeland Security memo obtained by the Daily Bulletin."

Waves of illegal immigrants are taking a heavy toll on U.S. public lands along the Mexican border, federal officials say. Mike Coffeen, a biologist with the Fish and Wildlife Service in Tucson, Arizona found the level of impact to be shocking. "Environmental degradation has become among the migration trend's most visible consequences, a few years ago, there were 45 abandoned cars on the Buenos Aires refuge near Sasabe, Arizona and enough trash that a volunteer couple filled 723 large bags with 18,000 pounds of garbage over two months in 2002." "It has been estimated that the average desert-walking immigrant leaves behind 8 pounds of trash during a journey that lasts one to three days if no major incidents occur. Assuming half a million people cross the border illegally into Arizona annually, that translates to 2,000 tons of trash that migrants dump each year."

There are Judges who are out to destroy the sovereignty of this country whenever they can. The following story was in the New York Post dd 9 May 2010: 'An illegal immigrant with a long rap sheet got a $145,000 parting gift from New York City taxpayers before he was deported, after a federal judge ruled his civil rights had been violated when he was held too long on Rikers Island.'

Federal rules allow local law enforcement to detain suspected illegal immigrants for 48 hours after their criminal cases are resolved, to give Immigration and Customs Enforcement a chance to pick them up and move them to federal facilities.

Former Brooklyn resident Cecil Harvey, 55 -- backed by an

immigration-rights advocacy group -- argued that his rights were violated when he spent more than a month in a Rikers holding pen before being transferred to ICE. Harvey was shipped to his native Barbados in October 2007; the city settled his civil suit late last year.

The landmark settlement has prompted the Correction Department to dump scores of illegal immigrants on the streets, since federal officials often fail to pick them up within the required two-day window.

Federal immigration agents have office space on Rikers Island, and the city allows them to interview roughly 4,000 inmates each year. They put a hold, or "detainer," on 3,200 of those inmates who they discover are illegals.

Illegal immigrants trying to get to the United States via the Mexican border with southern Arizona are suspected of having caused eight major wildfires in 2002. The fires destroyed 68,413 acres (276.86 km²) and cost taxpayers $5.1 million to fight.

Illegal immigrants have also used many parks inside the United States to grow and then distribute illegal drugs, turning previously protected nature areas into "heavily armed drug compounds". Yet the Obama administration just shrugs their shoulders and say, "So What!"

The highly publicized murder of Arizona rancher Rob Krentz in March 2010, suspected to have been committed by an illegal immigrant, provided a strong rallying cry for immigration opponents and called public attention to other crimes— notably property crimes— committed by foreign nationals during their border crossings into the U.S. Krentz had previously reported that illegal immigrants had done over $8 million dollars in damage to his ranching operations during a five-year period, and in the wake of his murder, interviews with his family and friends focused on similar crimes and break-ins committed by immigrates.

The influence of anti-immigrant public sentiments generated by the murder was demonstrated only a few weeks later, when Arizona responded by passing Arizona SB1070, the nation's toughest state immigration law. While the law's writers have defended Arizona's new illegal immigration law by pointing to the lawless acts shown above that it is necessary to fight violent crime. Phoenix police Chief Jack Harris stated his disagreement, arguing that this new law will distort police priorities.

Following the passage of Arizona's Support Our Law Enforcement and Safe Neighborhoods Act in April, 2010, which authorizes police officials to question persons on their immigration status if there is reasonable suspicion that they are illegally in the country or committing other violations not related to their immigration status, numerous polls showed widespread support for the law. A Rasmussen poll found that 60% of the electorate support such a law while 31% are opposed to such a law. A New York Times poll showed similar results: 51% of Americans felt the law was "about right" in its dealings with illegal immigration, 9% felt that its measures did not go far enough to address the problem while only 36% have negative opinions regarding such a law.

A recently retired agent from ICE pointed to these facts facing Americans; "We are in a de facto state of war with Mexico. Mexican nationals illegally invade this country, commit murders and other crimes, killing and kidnapping U.S. citizens, run back to Mexico to seek the protection of the Mexican government and somehow this is 'normal?' And the Mexican government, through El Presidente Calderon, told us 'it's reality and we need to get used to it,' suggesting it's somehow our fault. The 'reality' that El Presidente Calderon speaks of is that we are in a state of war with his country, but we're still asleep at the switch. It's time to stop hitting the snooze button."

This country is being mocked by illegal immigrants, opportunistic Democratic politicians, and even the President of the United States, intentionally lumping legal immigration with illegal immigration to make conservatives appear to be racists who are against legal immigration (which is patently false). Democrats don't seem to believe in rule of law when there are votes to be had if amnesty is granted to illegals. What Democrats argue is that Hispanics are the fastest growing minority in the US, and will be the largest minority group within the next 20 years. But racial politics is no reason to usurp the rule of law, and censure Arizona for protecting its borders when President Obama refuses to execute the Immigration Law and protect the lives and properties of the citizens of Arizona.

Another eye-witness report concerning the invasion of our counrty is as follows: Olga Robles and her husband Frank live just eight blocks from the international boundary that separates Douglas, Arizona, from the Mexican city of Agua Prieta. For years men have illegally crossed the border on their way north looking for work. Mrs. Robles said she frequently saw them pass through town in pairs or in small groups. Then about two years ago the trickle swelled to a flood with groups of thirty to well over a hundred people at a time pouring across the border, hurrying through alleys, through people's yards and between their houses, climbing over roofs and clambering over graves in the cemetery. They knocked down fences, trampled flowers and shrubs, and cluttered neighborhoods with litter. They came in groups all day long and in a steady stream throughout the night while dogs in town barked till dawn. In frustration Mrs. Robles finally told the authorities, "If you can't do anything about the trespassers, then at least shoot the dogs so I can get some sleep."

The mob scene through Douglas finally ceased once a strengthened and illuminated fence was erected, and once the border patrol had beefed up its presence in town. The stream of migrants, however, did not stop but simply flowed around Douglas, mainly to the west where ranch lands with water tanks and a network of roads facilitate this kind of mass smuggling operation. Ranchers and other rural property owners then began to experience what the rural population of eastern San Diego County experienced a few years earlier. The ranchers complained about fences broken daily by crowds of migrants, about gates left open leaving cattle free to stray, about cattle that were killed, watchdogs poisoned, water tanks drained, buildings broken into, and property stolen. One rancher estimates that the cost of constant repairs has run into tens of thousands of dollars. And everywhere there is the trash: piles of empty plastic water bottles, food wrappers, dirty diapers, clothing, feces, toilet paper, anything left by masses of people on the move. Indeed if you saw nothing but the litter you could well believe that a mass migration is underway.

Mexican President Felipe Calderon, an out and out Socialist, took his opposition to a new Arizona immigration law to Congress Thursday May 20, 2010, saying it "ignores a reality that cannot be erased by decree." Calderon's comments on the Arizona law and his request that Congress do something about the availability of high-powered weapons along the border drew criticism from several lawmakers saying he was interfering in U.S. internal matters.

Calderon, the first foreign national leader to address Congress this year, said he strongly disagrees with the Arizona law that requires police to question people about their immigration status if there's reason to suspect they are in the country illegally. President Barack Obama, agreed with Calderon saying that the law was a "misdirected expression of frustration."

The Mexican leader said his country was doing its best, by promoting more jobs and opportunities at home, to reduce the flow of immigrants to the United States. But he stressed the "need to fix a broken and inefficient system ... the time has come to reduce the causes of migration and to turn this phenomenon into a legal, ordered and secure flow of workers and visitors." Throughout Calderon's speech condemning Arizona, the gun laws, and the U.S. treatment of illegal aliens from Mexico, the entire Democratic Congress rose as one body to applaud his tirade. Watching the Democrats on TV, one has to wonder what country they are serving?

One only has to compare the Arizona law (SB 1070) with Mexico's own law concerning immigrants to know that Calderon and apparently our own President and the Democrats in Congress are hypocrites. The comparison is as follows:

The **Arizona law** bans sanctuary cities that refuse to enforce immigration laws, stiffens penalties against illegal alien day laborers and their employers, makes it a misdemeanor for immigrants to fail to complete and carry an alien registration document, and allows the police to arrest immigrants unable to show documents proving they are in the U.S. legally.

Using the Federal Immigration Law as authority, the provisions of SB 1070 are:

1. Requires a reasonable attempt to be made to determine the immigration status of a person during any legitimate contact made by an official or agency of the state or a county, city, town or political subdivision (political subdivision) if reasonable suspicion exists that the person is an alien who is unlawfully present in the U.S.

2. Requires the person's immigration status to be verified with the federal government pursuant to federal law.

3. Requires an alien unlawfully present in the U.S. who is convicted of a violation of state or local law to be transferred immediately to the custody of ICE or Customs and Border Protection, on discharge from imprisonment or assessment of any fine that is imposed.

4. Allows a law enforcement agency to securely transport an alien who is unlawfully present in the U.S. and who is in the agency's custody to:

   a) a federal facility in this state or

   b) any other point of transfer into federal custody that is outside the jurisdiction of the law enforcement agency.

5. Allows a law enforcement officer, without a warrant, to arrest a person if the officer has probable cause to believe that the person has committed any public offense that makes the person removable from the U.S.

6. Prohibits officials or agencies of the state and political subdivisions from being prevented or restricted from sending, receiving or maintaining an individual's immigration status information or exchanging that information with any other governmental entity for the following official purposes:

   a) determining eligibility for any public benefit, service or license provided by any federal, state, local or other political subdivision of this state;

b) verifying any claim of residence or domicile if that verification is required under state law or a judicial order issued pursuant to a civil or criminal proceeding in the state;

c) confirming a detainee's identity; and

d) if the person is an alien, determining whether the person is in compliance with federal alien registration laws.

7. Disallows officials or agencies of the state or political subdivisions from adopting or implementing policies that limit immigration enforcement to less than the full extent permitted by federal law, and allows a person to bring an action in superior court to challenge an official or agency that does so.

8. Requires the court, if there is a judicial finding that an entity has committed a violation, to order any of the following:

a) That the plaintiff recover court costs and attorney fees;

b) That the defendant pay a civil penalty of not less than $1,000 and not more than $5,000 for each day that the policy has remained in effect after the filing of the action.

9. Requires the court to collect and remit the civil penalty to the Department of Public Safety (DPS), which must establish a special subaccount for the monies in the account established for the Gang and Immigration Intelligence Team Enforcement Mission (GIITEM) appropriation.

10. Specifies that law enforcement officers are indemnified by their agencies against reasonable costs and expenses, including attorney fees, incurred by the officer in connection with any action, suit or proceeding brought pursuant to this statute to which the officer may be a party by reason of the officer being or having been a member of the law enforcement agency,

except in relation to matters in which the officer is adjudged to have acted in bad faith.

All these provisions listed below are enshrined in Mexico's *Ley General de Población* (General Law of the Population) and were spotlighted in a 2006 research paper published by the Washington, D.C.-based Center for Security Policy:

- The Mexican government will bar foreigners if they upset "the equilibrium of the national demographics." (How's that for racial and ethnic profiling?)

- If outsiders do not enhance the country's "economic or national interests" or are "not found to be physically or mentally healthy," they are not welcome. Neither are those who show "contempt against national sovereignty or security." They must not be economic burdens on society and must have clean criminal histories. Those seeking to obtain Mexican citizenship must show a birth certificate, provide a bank statement proving economic independence, pass an exam and prove they can provide their own health care.

- Illegal entry into the country is equivalent to a felony punishable by two years' imprisonment. Document fraud is subject to fine and imprisonment; so is alien marriage fraud. Evading deportation is a serious crime; illegal re-entry after deportation is punishable by ten years' imprisonment. Foreigners may be kicked out of the country without due process and the endless bites at the litigation apple that illegal aliens are afforded in our country (for example, President Obama's illegal alien aunt — a fugitive from deportation for eight years who is awaiting a second decision on her previously rejected asylum claim).

- Law enforcement officials at all levels — by national mandate— must cooperate to enforce immigration laws, including illegal alien arrests and deportations. The Mexican military is also required to assist in immigration enforcement operations. Native-born Mexicans are empowered to make citizens' arrests of illegal aliens and turn them in to authorities.

- Ready to show your papers? Mexico's National Catalog of Foreigners tracks all outside tourists and foreign nationals. A National Population Registry tracks and verifies the identity of every member of the population, who must carry a citizens' identity card. Visitors who do not possess proper documents and identification are subject to arrest as illegal aliens.

In addition, Comrade Calderon demanded that the U.S. ignored the second Amendment to our Constitution by banning assault rifles and similar arms to the citizens of the U.S. He stated these arms are getting into the hands of the drug cartels and the Mexican government is having a hard time fighting the cartel members when they are armed with AK-47 assault weapons. He further stated that these guns can be traced to the United States and therefore it is the fault of the Americans for killing all his citizens.

No one can say that Mr. Calderon is a fool, because he isn't. He is a good socialist that uses the smoke and mirror act to cover up the real truth. The sad tale of guns and drugs can be traced back to Mexico but the President of Mexico would rather place the blame for his problems on others — and the President of the United States and the Democrats in Congress applaud him, loud and long. The true story that has been published but not in the liberal press in this country is as follows:

The Drug Trail from the southern border of Mexico is hard and costly, but drug members have been usually unmolested because they are well armed and brutal when necessary. Rather than engage in crude violence, unscrupulous Mexican officials typically exact bribes or mordides. The payments may be a few dollars to allow a single person to transit the border or thousands of dollars to permit the passage of drugs, weapons, stolen cars, prostitutes, exotic animals or archeological artifacts.

How anyone can have the audacity to stand in front of another group of foreign officials and condemn them or one of their States for being racist, intolerant, etc. is beyond one's comprehension. Yet this same group of foreign officials (all Democrats and the President of the United States) applaud his condemnation is sickening, to say the least.

First the AK-47s: Calderon says that these guns are coming from over 5000 gun shops in the states bordering Mexico. However he neglected to mention an incident that was reported in August 2007. The headlines: "Did Over 100,000 Missing U.S.A. AK-47s End Up In Venezuela?"

This article dd 7 August 2007, stated that the Daily Mirror of Northern Ireland reported that a 99-ton cache of AK-47s that was secretly flown out from a base in Bosnia to Iraq had vanished. The deal was put together by the U.S. Department of Defense and was contracted out to a complex web of private arms traders. Allegedly the planes used to fly out the AK-47s were registered to Aerocom, a company controlled by the fugitive Russian arms dealer Victor Blunt. At about the same time, U. S. Defense Secretary Donald Rumsfeld condemned Hugo Chavez of Venezuela for purchasing 100,000 AK-47s.

Amnesty International chief spokesman Mike Blakemore said: "It's unbelievable that no one can account for 200,000 assault rifles. If these weapons have gone missing it's a terrifying prospect." American defense chiefs hired an American firm to take the guns from the Bosnia war to Iraq, however, flights, which supposedly took off between July 2004 and July 2005 were not recorded by air traffic controllers in Baghdad. A spokesperson for the coalition forces confirmed they had not received 'any weapons from Bosnia" and added they were 'not aware of any purchases for Iraq from Bosnia".

A NATO spokesman said: "There's no tracking mechanism to ensure they don't fall into the wrong hands. There are concerns that some may have been siphoned off."

Since private arms traders were the carrier, these AK-47s appear to have been hi-jacked and sold to the drug Cartels—especially in South America. Since Venezuela appears to have bought 100,000 AK-47s that leaves 100,000 AK-47s that apparently were gobbled up by the drug Cartels. If this is the case, it is an easy matter for the Columbian Cartel to arm their people in Mexico. How? Just follow the cocaine pipe line from Columbia to the northern border of Mexico.

How did the Drug Cartels get so great a foothold in Mexico that they cannot be eliminated? As a matter in fact, how did the Drug Cartels get a foothold into the United States and our Government, past and present, can't eliminate them? The answer is simple—MONEY! Politicians since time began cannot refuse a fast dollar when it comes their way. An article in La Voz de Aztlán, Los Angeles, Alta California - May 30, 2008:

'Mexican President Felipe Calderon dropped a bombshell at a meeting with the governors of U.S./Mexico bordering states. At the official presidential residence of Los Pinos, President Calderon told the governors that Mexico is paying with the lives of a large number of law enforcement and military officials because of the immense drug addiction problem north of the border. The president said that the USA has the largest number of drug consumers in the world.'

Those present at the meeting were the governors of California, New Mexico, Texas, Nuevo León, Coahuila, Chihuahua, Sonora, and Baja California. Absent were the governors of Arizona and Tamaulipas. Three Mexican bordering states have experienced extraordinary violence and deaths as police and the Mexican army battle extremely well armed and bold drug cartels. These states are Baja California, Chihuahua and Tamaulipas. Some of the bloodiest battles have occurred in the border towns of Tijuana in Baja California, Cd. Juarez in Chihuahua and in Nuevo Laredo in Tamaulipas.

The battles have now spread to the interior of Mexico. Recently two top level federal law enforcement officials were killed in their homes in Mexico City. Also, the police chief and the entire police department of the town of Villa Ahumada in the state of Chihuahua had to flee to escape certain death at the hands of "narco-commandos" who invaded and took over the town. The bold take-over of Villa Ahumada was accomplished with military precision and the utilization of military grade weapons including assault rifles, grenades and bazookas. The well organized cartel cadres are now recruiting and receiving political support among Mexico's destitute populations.

President Felipe Calderon is correct when he blames the USA for the drug problem and its negative effects on Mexico. The American people are in denial about its huge addiction problem. Marijuana, Heroin, Cocaine and Meth use is now rampant in all levels of American society. Many so called Hollywood "Stars" use them on a regular basis and there have been countless entertainers who have died of overdoses. Also, drug use at USA universities is now quite common. Recently authorities arrested 75 students at San Diego State University for using or dealing in drugs. Most of the dealing was being done through campus fraternities. San Diego State University officials started an investigation when a sorority member, a nice Jewish freshman student, died of a Cocaine overdose after partying all night.

The American people are also quite ignorant about the nature of the multi-billion dollar drug trade and who in the USA is actually behind it. The use of drugs and the drug trade have now corrupted entire police departments in major cities in the USA and this corruption has reached the highest levels of the US government. Two US presidents have now admitted to using illicit drugs, they are Bill Clinton and George Bush. Bill Clinton admitted to using Cannabis commonly known as Marijuana and in a recent book, by former White House Press Secretary Scott McClellan, President George Bush admits to having used Cocaine.

There are certain individuals, government officials, banks, and corporations in the USA that profit immensely from the drug trade. The Los Angeles Police Department has been involved in a "drug trade protection racket" better known as the "Rampart Corruption Scandal" in which dirty cops provided immunity to drug dealers in return for some of the drug profits. All Americans, who are half awake, should be aware of the Central Intelligence Agency's (CIA) complicity in the international drug trade. This complicity is summarized in an editorial "Plan Mexico and the CIA". Also, some of the largest banks in the USA are making incredible profits through the "laundering" of drug money. In addition there are two major US corporations in the chemical industry that have accumulated vast fortunes by exporting to Colombia the chemicals necessary to convert the coca leaves to cocaine.

There is a simple solution to this major problem. The American voting public must first become enlightened about the nature of drugs. Then as a united block they must take out the profit out of the trade in drugs. They must treat the use of drugs not as a criminal act but as a medical problem and eliminate their use through education. Instead of wasting billions of dollars yearly in the so called "War on Drugs" and in imprisonment, this money could be funded to a national level medical institution empowered to treat addicts or those who choose to use drugs and for research and education. The major problem is not in the use of drugs. It exists because of the countless entities, both on the drug enforcement bureaucracy side and in the supply side, which have become "addicted" to the immense profits that the drug trade generates.

(An added suggestion to the above solution should be that all drug pushers, be they high in society or street walkers should be tried in special courts. If convicted they would have no appeal but be put to death and all of their possessions confiscated. Why? That is what they are doing to their customers—killing them in one fashion or another but they are killing them and destroying their lives completely.)

Another article in La Voz De Aztlán dd May 17 2010, concerning the Drug Wars follows:

"There are many questions that lead one to believe that the war on drugs is a complete sham. Here in the USA, the principal consumer of drugs, the multi-billion effort to combat the sale and use of drugs has made not difference over the years. School children in every major city in the country will tell you that it is easier to buy a joint of marijuana or a rock of crack cocaine than it is to buy a can of beer. In addition, there have been numerous prison interviews of inmates which indicate that drugs are available to them in any quantity they want inside the prisons. So what is going on?"

There are clear indications that there is a brutal struggle along the US/Mexico border between the CIA and Mexican cartels for control of drug trafficking routes. The present problems along the US/Mexico border has more to do with this battle than with migrant Mexican workers. Unfortunately undocumented Mexican immigrants are being utilized as scapegoats and it appears that President Felipe Calderon is unwittingly cooperating in return for a few drug gringo dollars. One example of this is the savage home invasion and murder of little Brisenia Flores and her father Raul in Arivaca, Arizona by the Minutemen vigilantes.

Shawna Forde and the serial killer Jason Bush of the Minutemen American Defense organization invaded the home of the Flores family looking for drugs and money in 2009. It has now been confirmed that Shawna Forde had various meetings and was connected with the notorious CIA covert operative Joseph Adams of "Nicaraguan Contra/Crack Cocaine Scandal" fame prior to the operation. Many independent journalists now believe that the Minutemen are actually CIA funded operatives who's mission is to obtain intelligence information along the border in order to better protect their CIA drug operations.

One can judge for him/herself of the validity of the above. It is difficult to find any answers, especially where the CIA is concerned because they are so secretive in all their operations. However, some ex-CIA operators, have expressed their opinion about some of the things that are occurring in the CIA.

On September 24, 2007 a Grumman Gulfstream II jet airplane crashed near Cancun, Mexico with 4 tons of cocaine. The jet plane had been circling around the town of Tixkokob when it apparently ran out of fuel. Citizens of Tixkokob called authorities and Mexican army helicopters arrived to find the jet plane in three pieces and with 4 tons of high grade cocaine.

Mexican authorities have determined that the shipment of cocaine was to be delivered to Mexican drug cartels and have now focused on who owned the jet plane. Their preliminary findings of who owned the Gulfstream II jet plane with, tail number N987SA, now threatens to open up another Iran/Contra - CIA Crack Cocaine type scandal.

Apparently the same jet plane N987SA was used by the CIA

to transport Muslim prisoners to Guantanamo Bay, Cuba in 2003, 2004 and 2005. The CIA is known to use a number of front corporate entities to hide their operations. Also, when registering their planes, they utilize a complex series of "change of ownership" filings with the Federal Aviation Administration (FAA) in order to make it very difficult to trace the true owner of the planes they use in their operations.

The Gulfstream II jet plane with tail number N987SA was initially traced to William Achenbaum, a wealthy New York real estate tycoon. Mr. Achenbaum says that the jet plane was being managed by Air Rutter International that according to the New York Post is owned by Arik Kislin of Long Island in New York (See New York Post 'CRASH JET HAD AIR OF MYSTERY'). Kislin and Achenbaum are principals of the Hotel Gansevoort in New York. (See New York Post 'SHADY 'INN' CROWD') Arik Kislin is the nephew of Semyon Kislin that the Center for Public Integrity alleges is a powerful Russian Mafia member. (See http://publicintegrity.org/report.aspx?aid=323) The Kislin family have made very large contributions to the political campaigns of Rudy Giuliani.

William Achenbaum says that he sold the plane in August to a Florida company called Donna Blue Aircraft run by Brazilians Joao Luiz Malago and Eduardo Dias Guimaraes. The two Brazilians in turn say that they sold the jet plane on September 16 to Clyde O'Connor and Greg Smith of Fort Lauderdale, Florida. The Federal Aviation Administration initially said that it was never informed of the sales and that they never issued any certificates. Later, the FAA posted a temporary registration certificate to Donna Blue Aircraft dated 08/31/2007 that was to expire on 09/30/2007 but still no certificate for Clyde O'Connor or Greg Smith)

Two days after the alleged purchase, the Gulfstream II left Fort Lauderdale to Cancun, Mexico and then to Río Negro, Colombia. The jet plane loaded with the 4 tons of cocaine than left to Cancun where it crashed on September 24, 2007.

The problem of illegal Immigration runs deeper than people invading our Country from Mexico. Whether they are here legally or illegally, there are those who will take advantage of the situation for their own gain. They do not assimilate into the melting pot as envisioned by our forefathers. They gather in communities of their own nationality and when the community becomes large enough, it becomes a political entity. This is what has happened to the Mexican influx of personnel. Most of them have been brought up in a socialistic background and rely upon the Federal Government for their sustenance. The Democrats have used this tool to garner most of the Mexican votes. Is it any wonder why the Federal Government under President Obama does not want to seal the borders. Every illegal immigrant that crosses the border is a potential Democratic vote. Bill Clinton recognized this during the 1996 Presidential election and by Presidential decree allowed most of the illegal and legal immigrants to vote in California, thus stealing the state of California's Electorial vote for the Democratic Party.

Today, we have States being torn apart by the Illegal movement. The city of Los Angeles, for example, has boycotted Arizona for their crack down on illegal aliens. But then again the city of Los Angeles is no longer a part of the United States according to some of its mayors.

This is not a pipe dream. On November 5, 2001, Los Angeles Mayor Hahn stated that the city of Los Angeles was a Mexican city. He said, " *"Our city is a Mexican city, and Mexican Americans have greatly shaped our cultural, political and commercial landscape."* On November 6, 2001 the following article appeared in a Mexico City newspaper:

> "MEXICO CITY - November 6, 2001 - (ACN) Los Angeles Mayor James K. Hahn met with Mexican President Vicente Fox on Monday at the presidential home at Los Pinos. The two leaders met for the first time to begin forging a closer and more practical working relationship. This is Mayor Hahn's first foreign trade mission and the first official visit of a Los Angeles mayor to Mexico in almost a decade. The meeting highlighted the growing ties between California and Mexico. Mayor Hahn reaffirmed Mexico's interwoven history with that of Los Angeles, which was once governed by Mexico."

"Mexican-Americans have been warming up to Kenneth Hahn ever since he defeated the corrupt Chicano candidate Tony Villar (aka Antonio Villargairoza) who was implicated in the "prison pardon scandal" of the notorious crack cocaine dealer Carlos Vignali. Tony Villar was a lackey of the westside L.A. Jewish community who failed to convinced many in the Mexican-American community that he was the right man for the job. The small Afro-American community overwhelmingly rejected Villar but he managed to receive over 80% of the gay and lesbian vote of the West Hollywood community."

Mayor Hahn also told Mexican officials that he wants to be a strong advocate for immigrant rights in California. Mayor Hahn informed Fox that he called Governor Davis several times in recent months to urge him to support two bills that would assist Mexicans living in the state. One will allow children of immigrants to pay state tuition to attend California colleges, and another would permit immigrants applying for legal status to receive driver's licenses.

Los Angles continues to support illegal immigrants. An article in the newspaper declared:

"April 10, 2008 : '**L.A. Mayor warns ICE to back off immigration raids**'

"Los Angeles Mayor Antonio Villaraigosa warned federal authorities to stop work-site raids because of the potential of collapsing the area's economy. The mayor said in a letter to Homeland Security Secretary Michael Chertoff that work-site raids by Immigration and Customs Enforcement (ICE) could have "severe and long-lasting effects" on the local economy, the Los Angeles Times reported today."

"Los Angeles is the city most populated with residents of Mexican descent in the USA and has become a favorite target of bigots like Lou Dobbs of CNN News. There is now a campaign by the anti-Mexican racists to pit Blacks against Latinos. One entity in this campaign is the Walt Disney radio station KABC. "

The infiltration of our higher education facilities by those who want a separate homeland which they refer to as Aztlán can be seen in an article by the Associated Press . The article is as follows:

"ALBUQUERQUE, N.M. — A University of New Mexico Chicano Studies professor predicts a new, sovereign Hispanic nation within the century, taking in the Southwest and several northern states of Mexico. Charles Truxillo suggests the "Republica del Norte," the Republic of the North, is "an inevitability."

He envisions it encompassing all of California, Arizona, New Mexico, Texas and southern Colorado, plus the northern tier of Mexican states: Baja California, Sonora, Chihuahua, Coahuila, Nuevo León and Tamaulipas.

Along both sides of the U.S.-Mexico border "there is a growing fusion, a reviving of connections," Truxillo said. "Southwest Chicanos and Norteño Mexicanos are becoming one people again."

Truxillo, 47, has said the new country should be brought into being "by any means necessary," but recently said it was unlikely to be formed by civil war. Instead, its creation will be accomplished by the electoral pressure of the future majority Hispanic population in the region, he said.

The organizers of Aztlán movement are serious and determined to unite certain U.S. border states and Northern Mexico into a separate unit. They are working cross-borders and agitating every chance that they get. For example, the following article appeared in La Voz de Aztlán newspaper, dd Mar. 8, 2001:

"History of great significance to Aztlán was made on Sunday as Dr. Armando Navarro led a U.S. National Delegation of Chicanos and Mexicanos into the "Heart of Mexico." The immense emotional feeling of re-connecting, along with hundreds of thousands of our brothers and sisters, with the ancient ancestral center of our world, "El Templo Mayor", was simply overwhelming......."

"Over the years, and since the bloody conquest of the Aztecs (or Mexicas) of Tenochtitlan by Hernan Cortez and the Spaniards, Mexico's indigenous people have been victimized by centuries of oppression and exploitation. The various indigenous groups, which are comprised of over 60 different ethnic groups, have been increasingly marginalized and losing ground in relation to language, culture and ownership of precious land. In the resource rich state of Chiapas, the onslaught against native peoples has been particularly decimating. The "Caciques" in the region have over the course of years been able to expropriate the land through questionable policies that have included the "Alcoholization" of indigenous men....."

As one can see, these people are serious about a separate nation. Following in the steps of Farrakhan's 'Nation of Islam', the Aztlán's want to destroy the U.S.A. by dividing and conquering. Revolution or by piecemeal they will continue their journey.

The Mexican revolution in the United States is alive and active. The leaders continue to tear down this country at every opportunity. The newspaper La Voz de Aztlán constantly carry articles such as *Twilight's last gleaming: The disintegration of the USA* by Ernesto Cienfuegos. This article and others can be found on the internet at LaVoz.com.

There are truths, half-truths, and spins in the articles but overall, they are a tear-down of the American Republic. This is the approach being used to feed the minds of legal and illegal aliens alike. The Los Vox de Aztlán is only one Mexican newspaper in this country— there are many others in many communities throughout the U.S. All of them are of the same Communist bent.

There are many other articles that could be cited, but the articles cited above give you an idea of what is going on. President Obama and the Democrats who are in control of the Government are planning to give away a part of this country to Mexico for a few measly votes. California is already controlled by a socialist government and one can only look at its condition (economically) to realize that socialism is an accident going somewhere to happen.. California is billions of dollars in debt, and have no way out except by borrowing from the Federal Government. This is what President Obama wants: complete control of all the states. Once this occurs plus the millions of Democratic voters which he will receive from the illegal aliens, dictatorship follows.

President Obama is using every device and shortcut he can to push through a Socialist Democratic Congress an amnesty law that will grant automatic citizenship to all illegal aliens that are in the country today. He demands that illegal immigrants be granted citizenship before he will try to secure the borders. As I stated previously, his object is to pad the Democratic voters base with such numbers that no other party will ever get elected to the Federal Government again.

When thinking of President Obama's action, one must recall the actions of President Hoover, President Truman and President Eisenhower.

    a. Back during the great depression (1929—1932), Herbert Hoover ordered the deportation of ALL illegal aliens in order to make jobs available to American citizens that desperately needed work.

    b, Harry Truman ordered over two-million illegal aliens to be deported after WW II to create jobs for returning veterans.

    c. In 1954, Dwight Eisenhower deported 13 million Mexicans. The program was called Operation Wetback. It was done so WW II and Korean veterans would have a better chance at jobs. It took two years but they deported them.

If they could deport the illegal aliens back then, they could do it today. If you have doubts about the above information, get on the internet and have your search engine look up Operation Wetback and confirm it yourself.

Why can't they do this today? Actually, the answer is simple. Hoover, Truman and Eisenhower were men of honor not untrustworthy politicians looking for votes!

Today we have the specter of how the socialist have infiltrated the Government and making rules of individual Departments more conducive to a Democratic Dictatorship. We know how the Justice Department permits voter intimidation by the Black Panthers but recently there appeared articles in the press about how the Census Bureau , in taking it's 2010 census, changed the forms to permit illegal aliens to be counted so as to pad the population in favor of the Democrats.

The CONSTITUTIONAL justification for taking a census every ten years is the head count for apportioning taxes or to determine the number of representatives in the House of Representatives. And that's it. Should we really have to inform the US Census Bureau that the US Census ONLY applies to US citizens? Or do we now allow foreign nationals "residing" within the United States, affect the determination of US tax dollar apportionment and the number of representatives in the US House of Representatives?

In 1790, the first Census Act provided that the enumeration of that year would count "inhabitants" and "distinguish" various subgroups by age, sex, status as free persons, etc. Inhabitant was a term with a well-defined meaning that encompassed, as the Oxford English Dictionary expressed it, one who "is a bona fide member of a State, subject to all the requisitions of its laws, and entitled to all the privileges which they confer."

Thus early census questionnaires generally asked a question that got at the issue of citizenship or permanent resident status, e.g., "what state or foreign country were you born in?" or whether an individual who said he was foreign-born was naturalized. Over the years, however, Congress and the Census Bureau have added inquiries that have little or nothing to do with census's constitutional purpose.

By 1980 there were two census forms. The shorter form went to every person physically present in the country and was used to establish congressional apportionment. It had no question pertaining to an individual's citizenship or legal status as a resident. The longer form gathered various kinds of socioeconomic information including citizenship status, but it went only to a sample of U.S. households. That pattern was repeated for the 1990 and 2000 censuses.

The 2010 census used only the short form. The long form has been replaced by the Census Bureau's ongoing American Community Survey. Dr. Elizabeth Grieco, chief of the Census Bureau's Immigration Statistics Staff, told the press in a recent interview that the 2010 census short form does not ask about citizenship because "Congress has not asked us to do that."

Dr. Elizabeth Grieco knew that her decision to count illegal aliens would skew future elections, but that didn't seem to bother her. The following future elections will be skewed as follows:

According to the Census Bureau's latest American Community Survey data (2007), states with a significant net gain in population by inclusion of non-citizens include Arizona, California, Florida, Illinois, Nevada, New Jersey, New York and Texas. (There are tiny net gains for Hawaii and Massachusetts.) This makes a real difference. Here's why:

According to the latest American Community Survey, California has 5,622,422 non\citizens in its population of 36,264,467. Based on round-number projection of a decade-end population in that state of 37,000,000 (including 5,750,000 non-citizens), California would have 57 members in the newly reapportioned U.S. House of Representatives.

However, with non-citizens not included for purposes of reapportionment, California would have 48 House seats (based on an estimated 30 million total population in 2010 with 28 million citizens, or 650,000 citizens per House seat). Using a similar projection, Texas would have 38 House members with non-citizens included. With only citizens counted, it would be entitled to 34 members.

Of course, other states lose out when non-citizens are counted for reapportionment. According to projections of the 2010 Census by Election Data Services, states certain to lose one seat in the 2010 reapportionment are Iowa, Louisiana, Massachusetts, Michigan, New Jersey, New York, Ohio and Pennsylvania; states likely (though not certain) to lose a seat are Illinois, Minnesota, Missouri, and Ohio could lose a second seat. But under a proper census enumeration that excluded illegal residents, some of the states projected to lose a representative would not do so.

The census has drifted far from its constitutional roots, and the 2010 enumeration will result in a malapportionment of Congress. In the 1964 case of *Wesberry v. Sanders*, the Supreme Court said, "The House of Representatives, the [Constitutional] Convention agreed, was to represent the people as individuals and on a basis of complete equality for each voter." It ruled that Georgia had violated the equal-vote principle because House districts within the state did not contain roughly the same number of voting citizens. Justice Hugo Black wrote in his majority opinion that "one man's vote in a congressional election is to be worth as much as another's." The same principle is being violated now on a national basis because of our faulty census.

The Census Bureau can collect whatever data Congress authorizes. But Congress must not permit the bureau to unconstitutionally redefine who are "We the People of the United States." That is just what Dr. Elizabeth Grieco and her liberal cohorts did to the voters of these United States –Disenfranchise Them! Damn the Constitution—full speed ahead!

Chapter 13

U.S.A.—AN AMORAL SOCIETY

Alexis de Tocqueville stated in 1837:

"I sought for the greatness and genius of America in fertile fields and boundless forests; it was not there. I sought for it in her free schools and her institutions of learning; it was not there. I sought for it in her matchless Constitution and democratic Congress; it was not there. Not until I went to the churches and temples of America and found them aflame with righteousness did I understand the greatness and genius of America. America is great because America is good. When America ceases to be good, America will cease to be great."

Today America is not great!

The United States is, by heritage, a Christian nation in which the founders of the American constitution were men of God who believed in the inspiration of the scriptures. References are largely given to some of the notables of American history who were involved in the early forming of American destiny and the Constitution by which Americans would be governed.

History is replete with facts that our Declaration of Independence and Constitution are based on Judeo-Christian teachings. The base of their teachings being the Holy Bible, or "The Book of Instructions" for our nation. This does not mean that all the people were or are Christian. It merely means that there was a Christian consensus and all our founding documents, laws, moral codes and institutions are based on Christian principles taken from the Bible.

"It is impossible to rightly govern the world without God and the Bible" President George Washington, September 17th, 1796.

The Declaration of Independence (1776) says:

"We hold these truths to be self evident, that all men are

created equal, that they are endowed by their Creator with certain unalienable rights, that among these are life, liberty and the pursuit of happiness—That to secure these rights, governments are instituted among men ... "

Abraham Lincoln stated (1861):

"It is the duty of all nations, as well as of men, to own their dependence upon the overruling power of God and to recognize the sublime truth announced in the Holy Scriptures and proven by all history, that those nations only are blessed whose God is the Lord."

President Theodore Roosevelt stated (1901):

"After a week on perplexing problems ... it does so rest my soul to come into the house of The Lord and to sing and mean it, 'Holy, Holy, Holy, Lord God Almighty' ... (my) great joy and glory that in occupying an exalted position in the nation, I am enabled, to preach the practical moralities of the Bible to my fellow-countrymen and to hold up Christ as the hope and Savior of the world."

President Woodrow Wilson (1913) stated:

"America was born to exemplify the devotion to the elements of righteousness which are derived from the Holy Scriptures."

President Ronald Reagan (1980) stated:

"The time has come to turn to God and reassert our trust in Him for the Healing of America ... our country is in need of and ready for a spiritual renewal."

President George Bush (1990) proclaims a National Day of Prayer:

"The great faith that led our Nation's Founding Fathers to pursue this bold experience in self-government has sustained us in uncertain and perilous times; it has given us strength to this very day. Like them, we do very well to recall our 'firm reliance on the protection of Divine Providence,' to give thanks for the freedom and prosperity this nation enjoys, and to pray for continued help and guidance from our wise and loving Creator."

(But we have Judges who will deny the people the right to have a National Day of Prayer. On the other hand we must submit ourselves to the Gay Pride days and parades!)

DID YOU KNOW?

As you walk up the steps to the building which houses the U.S. Supreme Court you can see near the top of the building a row of the world's law givers and each one is facing one in the middle who is facing forward with a full frontal view—it is

Moses and he is holding the Ten Commandments!

DID YOU KNOW?

As you enter the Supreme Court courtroom, the two huge oak doors have the Ten Commandments engraved on each lower portion of each door.

DID YOU KNOW?

As you sit inside the courtroom, you can see the wall, right above where the Supreme Court judges sit, a display of the Ten Commandments!

DID YOU KNOW?

There are Bible verses etched in stone all over the Federal Buildings and Monuments in Washington, D.C.

DID YOU KNOW?

James Madison, the fourth president, known as "The Father of Our Constitution" made the following statement: "We have staked the whole of all our political institutions upon the capacity of mankind for self-government,upon the capacity of each and all of us to govern ourselves, to control ourselves, to sustain ourselves accordingto the Ten Commandments of God."

DID YOU KNOW?

Patrick Henry, that patriot and Founding Father of our country said, "It cannot be emphasized too stronglyor too often that this great nation was founded not by religionists but by Christians, not on religions but on the Gospel of Jesus Christ".

DID YOU KNOW?

Every session of Congress begins with a prayer by a paid preacher, whose salary has been paid by the taxpayer since 1777.

DID YOU KNOW?

Fifty-two of the 55 founders of the Constitution were members of the established orthodox churches in the colonies.

DID YOU KNOW?

Thomas Jefferson worried that the Courts would overstep their authority and instead of interpreting the law would begin making law...an oligarchy...the rule of few over many.

DID YOU KNOW?

The very first Supreme Court Justice, John Jay, said, "Americans should select and prefer Christians as their rulers."

DID YOU KNOW?

The Laws of Hamarabi are written on the walls of the Supreme Court, right along with the Ten Commandments?

Although our forefathers were God-fearing men, they had a greater fear of a government sponsored state religion. England, as an example, bounced back and forth between Catholics and Protestant religions depending upon who was king or queen. This was a continuous cause of trouble. The same applies to Ireland today—between Northern Ireland and Southern Ireland.

The Founding Fathers rarely practiced Christian orthodoxy. Although they supported the free exercise of any religion, they understood the dangers of religion. Most of them believed in deism and attended Freemasonry lodges. According to John J. Robinson, "Freemasonry had been a powerful force for religious freedom." Freemasons took seriously the principle that men should worship according to their own conscious. Masonry welcomed anyone from any religion or non-religion, as long as they believed in a Supreme Being. Washington, Franklin, Hancock, Hamilton,

Lafayette, and many others accepted Freemasonry. That was why the 1st Amendment to the Constitution was established. The 1st Amendment clearly states: "Congress shall make no law respecting an **establishment** of religion, or **prohibiting** the free exercise thereof; nor abridging the freedom of speech, ..."

How, then, have we gotten to the point that everything we have done for 220 years in this country is now suddenly wrong and unconstitutional? It has gone awry because the Judicial System no longer serves the people. It is being used by activists (progressive) Judges to destroy the original meaning of the Constitution. Jefferson was correct in his concern about Judges overstepping their authority, thus establishing an oligarchy. The case in point being one concerning Judge Roy Moore.

Judge Roy Moore had installed a monument that contained the Ten Commandments in the Alabama state Supreme Court House. The A.C.L.U. went to court to have it removed.

Their first attempt fail, but they finally found a Federal Judge who agreed with them and order Judge Moore to remove the monument forthwith. Judge Moore refused. At that point, on November 13, 2003, Alabama's Court of the Judiciary unanimously removed Moore from his post as Chief Justice.

The trial, titled *Glassroth v. Moore*, began on October 15, 2002. Evidence for the plaintiffs included testimony that lawyers of different religious beliefs had changed their work practices, including routinely avoiding visiting the court building to avoid passing by the monument, and testimony that the monument created a religious atmosphere, with many people using the area for prayer.

Moore argued that he would not remove the monument, as doing so would violate his oath of office:

> "The monument serves to remind the Appellate Courts and judges of the Circuit and District Court of this State and members of the bar who appear before them, as well as the people of Alabama who visit the Alabama Judicial Building, of the truth stated in the Preamble to the Alabama Constitution that in order to establish justice we must invoke 'the favor and

guidance of almighty God.'"

On this note, Moore claimed that the Ten Commandments are the "moral foundation" of U.S. law, stating that in order to restore this foundation, "we must first recognize the source from which all morality springs...by recognizing the sovereignty of God." He added that the addition of the monument to the state judiciary building marked "the beginning of the restoration of the moral foundation of law to our people" and "a return to the knowledge of God in our land."

Moore contends that federal judges who ruled against his actions consider "obedience of a court order superior to all other concerns, even the suppression of belief in the sovereignty of God."

Judge Moore was correct. Philosophers of centuries past have written about the freedom of man. Once he receives this freedom let no Court tear it asunder. Yet some current Judges believe that religion, especially Christianity, is false and like Karl Marx believe that religion is "the opiate of the people." To these Judges, there is only one religion and that is socialism. In their decisions, they imply that atheists can suppress the Christian religion because it offends their God Satan.

The same goes for other religions that testified against the Ten Commandments. The ten Commandments were supposedly written by God according to the Bible. These Commandments are moral guides for man to live by. How does this establish a religion any more than the Laws of Hamarabi? Is there any wonder why the people of the United States believe that our Justice System is a failure?

Most Americans grew up anchored in place by certain ideas and values. They organized their lives around them. There was a consensus about right and wrong, and good and bad. They knew what the rules were, and moral guideposts clearly pointed in the direction they should go. But somewhere along the way, somehow, somebody changed the rules and tore down the guideposts. Those institutions—marriage, family, religion, schools—which historically have preserved our social learning curves, and served as bulwarks against moral degeneration, are under broad attack and crumbling. Alas the American family is in tatters, the church is in denial, our schools have been infiltrated, and our nation has had leaders with the political principles of Marx and ethics of Nero.

This movement that has taken over the country is called Secular Humanism. **Secular Humanism** is a secular philosophy that espouses reason, ethics, and justice, and specifically rejects supernatural and religious dogma as the basis of morality and decision-making. Secular Humanism is a life stance that focuses on the way human beings can lead good, happy and functional lives.

Secular Humanism is distinguished from various other humanisms. Though Secular Humanism posits that human beings are capable of being ethical and moral without religion, or God, that is not to say it assumes humans to be *inherently* or *innately* good. Nor does it present humans as "above nature" or superior to it; by contrast, the Humanist life stance emphasizes the unique responsibility facing humanity and the consequences of our ethical decisions.

The term "Secular Humanism" was coined in the 20th century, and was adopted by non-religious humanists in order to make a clear distinction from "religious humanism". Secular Humanism is also called "scientific humanism". Biologist E. O. Wilson claimed it to be "the only worldview compatible with science's growing knowledge of the real world and the laws of nature".

We have judges who cannot read or understand the Constitution and rewrite it according to their desires not the desires of the majority. We have judges who, under the guise of social justice, are trying destroy the marriage rite. We have judges who believe that the criminal has more rights than the victim. It's relatively easy to maintain values and inculcate them in one's children if these values are supported and buttressed by popular heroes, media icons, political leaders and educators. It is another matter to keep the faith when there are fears that the moral center is not holding, when others around you are retreating and sounding the alarm that merciless heathens have won the day and are advancing.

Many social conservatives worry that their religious "walk" is out of step with the prevailing culture. They are no longer admired for their faith; they are castigated for it. When in the middle of the noise and clutter of current events and caught up in the passion of them, it is difficult to know what they mean. Are we experiencing a middle-age national crisis that will soon play itself out, or is this a momentous and enduring shift in the American character?

We are infested with hypocritical Judges who set themselves up as demigods and try to destroy the one instrument that they swore under oath to uphold: The Constitution.

In 1787, thirty-nine men signed the document that became the longest-lasting national government on paper: the Constitution of the United States. While some countries regularly change governments (Italy has had over 50 governments since 1946), the United States has had the good fortune of living under the same government given it by those 39 men at Independence Hall over 220 years ago.

In the twentieth century, enter: former Chief Justice Charles Evans Hughes who, in a speech in 1907, said "we are under a Constitution, but the Constitution is what the judges say it is..." Today, though Hughes is dead, he leads the chorus of jurists and activists that seek societal change and are rewriting the Constitution to do it.

Is the Constitution whatever the judges say it is? Does the Constitution have no meaning independent of the jurists who interpret it? If so, get ready because if the judges are the voice of the Constitution, then we no longer live under the rule of law—we have government by tribunal. Such a document under the boot of the current justices is not a law to be obeyed; it's a device to be manipulated. If the Constitution is whatever the judges say it is, then they can make it say whatever they want. "Up" becomes "down" under Hughes' constitution.

How did we get to where the Constitution, that document Prime Minister Gladstone called the "the most wonderful work ever struck off at a given time by the brain and purpose of man," is the subordinate to judges and lawyers rather than the law of the land?

Then for some unfathomable reason the good Lord gave us President Obama who stated:

"We're no longer a Christian nation."—June 2007

" America has been arrogant."—

"After 9/11, America didn't always live up to her ideals."-

"You might say that America is a Muslim nation."- Egypt 2009

The beliefs and attitudes that this president has can be found everywhere—in the governments of the left the world over—and, above all, in the academic establishment, here in the United States, packed with tenured radicals and their political ideology . The places where it is taught that the United States is now, and has been throughout its history, the chief cause of injustice and oppression in the world.

These are the beliefs to be found everywhere, but never before in a president of the United States. Mr. Obama may not hold all of these views, but there can be no doubt by now of the influences that have shaped him. They account for his grand apology tour through the capitals of Europe and to the Muslim world, during which he maligned America's moral failures—her arrogance, insensitivity. They were the words of a man to whom reasons for American guilt came naturally. Americans were shocked by this behavior in their newly elected president. But he was telling them something from those visits to foreign lands—something about his distant relation to the country he was about to lead. The truth about that distance is now being realized by many, which is all to the good. A country governed by leaders too principled to speak the name of its mortal enemy needs every infusion of reality it can get.

Since President Obama has enter the White House, strange things are occurring that makes one wonder about his loyalty to this country. For example:

a. A great part of America now understands that this president's sense of identification lies elsewhere, and is in profound ways unlike theirs. He is hard put to sound convincingly like the leader of the nation, because he is, at heart and by instinct, the voice mainly of his ideological class. He is the alien in the White House, a matter having nothing to do with his birthright. He was educated by communist sympathizers and naturally hates all things of a Capitalistic nature.

b. One of his first reforms was to remove from the White House the bust of Winston Churchill—a gift from former PM Tony Blair—by sending it back to 10 Downing Street. A mystery has surrounded the subject ever since, but the central fact remains clear. The new administration had apparently found no place in our national Capitol for the British leader who still exists in the American mind.

c. Since President Obama has entered the scene, socialist doctrines have flowed steadily from Washington. The president's appointees, makers of social policy, have a hard time delivering the change of policies. Their work is not easy finding ways to avoid any public mention of the indisputable Islamist identity of the enemy at war with us. For example: Eric Holder, America's attorney general, confronting the question put to him by Rep. Lamar Smith (R., Texas) of the House Judiciary Committee: 'Did Mr. Holder think that in the last three terrorist attempts on this soil, one of them successful (Maj. Nidal Hasan's murder of 13 soldiers at Fort Hood, preceded by his shout of "Allahu Akbar!"), that radical Islam might have played any role at all?' Mr. Holder seemed addled by the question. "People have different reasons" he finally answered—a response he repeated three times. He didn't want "to say anything negative about any religion."

d. Today we are letting the fox guard the henhouse; the wolves will be herding the sheep! President Obama along with Home Land Security Secretary Janet Napolitano appointed two devout Muslims to Homeland Security posts. They appointed Arif Alikhan, a devout Muslim as Assistant Secretary for Policy Department and Kareem Shora, a devout Muslim, who was born in Damascus, Syria, as ADC National Executive Director as a member of the Homeland Security Advisory Council. Everyone should read Dr. Peter Hammond's book: "Slavery, Terrorism and

Islam: The Historical Roots and Contemporary Threat." The book will explain the statement: 'fox guarding the henhouse, and the wolves herding the sheep.'

e. Another Obama member had his opinion on Muslims. For example: The lectures on jihad by John Brennan, Mr. Obama's chief adviser on counterterrorism. Mr. Brennan has in the past charged that Americans lack sensitivity to the Muslim world, and that we have particularly failed to credit its peace-loving disposition. In a speech at the Center for Strategic and International Studies, Mr. Brennan stated angrily on who was not our enemy. "Our enemy is not terrorism because terrorism is just a tactic. Our enemy is not terror because terror is a state of mind, and as Americans we refuse to live in fear." He went on to announce that we do not refer to our enemies as Islamists or jihadists because jihad is a holy struggle, a legitimate tenet of Islam. How then might one be permitted to describe our enemies? One hint comes from another of Mr. Brennan's pronouncements in that speech: "That "violent extremists are *victims* of political, economic and social forces." Of course he was implying that the cause of terrorism in the world was the fault of Americans.

What Mr. Brennan ignored was history. In case he missed it, WW III began in November 1979 under another Democratic President named Jimmy Carter. It started in a country going through a religious/political revolt when a group of Islamic fanatics attacked and seized the American Embassy in Tehran. This seizure was an act of war! This attack on the U.S. set the stage for events that followed in the next twenty-five years.

All the world watch and waited to see what the U.S. would do. Politically, President Carter had to do something but his one-world orientation left him dangling in thin air. He did not want to do anything that would offend any other country in the world. Since the U. N. just set back and waited, President Carter chose to conduct a clandestine raid in the desert of Iran. This ill-fated mission ended in ruin, but stood as a symbol of America's inability to deal with Islamic terrorist thugs.

Shortly after the failed desert mission, Americans began to be kidnapped and killed throughout the Middle East. Under President Carter nothing could be done to protect American citizens living and working abroad. The state was set for Islamic jihadists to set up training camps and staging areas throughout the Middle East for clandestine operations against Americans, world-wide. The sovereignty of the countries could not be violated by U.S. attacking them without the local governments permission. The terrorist were home free to do what they wanted, thus, the following events occurred:

a. In April of 1983, a large truck packed with high explosives was driven into the U.S. Embassy in Beirut, killing 63 people.

b. Six months later in 1983, a large truck heavily laden with over 2500 lbs of TNT, smashed through the main gate of the U.S. Marine Corps headquarters in Beirut and killed 241 U.S. servicemen.

c. Two months later in December 1983, another truck loaded with explosives was driven into the U.S. Embassy in Kuwait.

d. Soon the terrorism spread to Europe. In April 1985 a bomb exploded in a restaurant frequented by U. S. soldiers in Madrid.

e. Then in August 1985, a Volkswagon car loaded with explosives was driven into the main gate of the U.S. Air Force Base at Rheine-Main, Germany killing 22 people.

f. Fifty-nine days later in 1985 a cruise ship, the Achille Lauro was hijacked and the whole world watched the Islamic terrorists select a wheel-bound American and executed him.

g. The Islamic terrorist than began bombing civilian airliners. They bombed TWA Flight 840 in April 1986 that killed 4 (one a nine month infant) and wounded five.

h. The most tragic civilian airline bombing was Pan Am Flight 103 over Lockerbie, Scotland in 1988, killing 259.

i. The Islamic terrorist brought their act to America. In January 1993, two CIA agents were shot and killed as they entered CIA headquarters in Langley, Virginia.

j. The following month, February 1993, a group of Islamic terrorists are arrested after a rented van packed with explosives was driven into the underground parking garage of the World Trade Center in New York City and exploded. Six people were killed and over 1000 were injured.

k. A few month later, June 1996, another truck bomb explodes only 35 yards from the U.S. military compound in Dhahran, Saudi Arabia. It destroys the Khobar Towers, a U. S. barracks, killing 19 and injuring over 500.

l. Islamic terrorists, in coordinated attacks, hit the U. S. Embassies in Kenya and Tanzania, killing 224.

m. The U. S. Cole was docked in the port of Aden, Yemen for refueling on 12 October 2000. A small craft pulled along side the ship and exploded killing 17 U. S. Navy sailors. (Attacking a U.S. War Ship is an act of war, but all we did was send the FBI to investigate the crime.)

n. Then we have the big event of 11 September 2001. Killing over 3000 people injuring thousands of others.

Revue the above list and then reread what our counterintelligence advisor (Mr. Brennen) to the President of the United States says:

a. 'Americans lack sensitivity to the Muslim world, and that we have particularly failed to credit its peace-loving disposition'.

b. 'Our enemy is not terrorism because terrorism is just a tactic. Our enemy is not terror because terror is a state of mind, and as Americans we refuse to live in fear.'

c. 'we do not refer to our enemies as Islamists or jihadists because jihad is a holy struggle, a legitimate tenet of Islam.

So much for our current President's opinion and his selected advisers. With people like Mr. Brennen and President Obama in charge do you think the Islamic terrorist are worried?

Most Americans do not want another committee. There are too many already. What they want is a man of significant stature to hold the allegiance of the people, and to lift them out of economic morass into which we are sinking. They want a man who is a true American who loves this country. Send them such a man and be it god or devil, they will receive him. This was what the American people wanted. Then they got President Obama —God help them!

The need and call for a strong man has been a major premise of one world globalists. The beginning to a one-world government is one in which powerful and secretive societies are plotting to eventually rule the world via an autonomous world government, which would replace sovereign states and other checks and balances in world power struggles. Historical and current events are seen as steps in an on-going plot to rule the world primarily through a combination of politics, finance, social engineering, mind control, and fear-based propaganda. The creation of the European Union and the emergence of the North American Union are seen as strategic directives towards a one-world, global government.

A viewpoint shared by some researchers is that the American government is controlled by global conspirators and various power groups such as the Council on Foreign Relations and Trilateral Commission who are run by men from the financial cabal with an intent for ushering in a global government in accordance with the aims of the Illuminati. According to this view, most Christians hear the word Zionism and think of Jerusalem, but this is a clever ploy of those who worship Satan to confuse the terminology of their political agendas to lull the people to sleep and get them to agree to their policies because they sound good. Zionism is a political agenda, but when Christians hear it they think of Biblical Zion and Jerusalem.

Some of the world's most respected researchers on the history of the Illuminati and their secret plan for global government believe that Zionism became a political agenda of the Bolshevik Illuminati to capture the area of Israel for their world leader. In fact, their agenda is to rule the world from Jerusalem. According to scripture when the Battle of Armageddon takes place the Antichrist gathers all the world's armies to Israel through a series of power conflicts to eventually unite in a fight against the Second Coming of Jesus Christ. At that time, the Antichrist is ruling from Jerusalem. General Pike followed this idea in his plan to produce a one-world government.

This part of Pike's plan started back when the Edomite Bolshevik Jews financed Hitler's rise to power in Germany to set up the conditions to establish their own Nation of Israel for Illuminati rule and that is exactly what happened with the Nazi Holocaust. Who was behind the holocaust? The Edomite Jews? Is this because they wanted to exterminate the Torah believing Jews and establish a Babylonian Talmudic Jewish nation in Israel. Evidence suggest this is what we have today. Talmudic apostate Jews ruling, pushing the agenda of the New World Order and Illuminati (See Chapter 5) to set the nation up for the rule of the Antichrist.

The Washington Post has published the results of a two year investigation into the world of Top Secret programs in the U.S. Titled: *Top Secret America,* the investigation aims to expose the waste, redundancy and lack of oversight of many of the Top Secret programs created in response to the 9/11 attacks. It states: "The top-secret world the government created in response to the terrorist attacks of Sept. 11, 2001, has become so large, so unwieldy and so secretive that no one knows how much money it costs, how many people it employs, how many programs exist within it or exactly how many agencies do the same work." One of the findings of the report is that the military chain of command is routinely undermined as personnel are ordered not to reveal their activities to their commanding officers. This supports the claims of whistleblowers who have come forward to reveal cases of military personnel being ordered not to tell commanders about Top Secret programs to which they had been recruited. The programs in question concerned UFO technology and extraterrestrial life, and commanding officers denied access included senior admirals and generals,

A world gone mad! Secrets within secrets. Secret societies embedded with other secret societies. Is it all for real or just more smoke and mirrors? Did you know that there are those who claim that the Messiah (Jesus) has already made his second coming a reality and is living in an apartment in London? Far fetched? No according to one group of pundits. Their story is as follows:

The 20th century has seen the decline of traditional Christian beliefs and the rise of the seemingly all inclusive, multi-dimensional belief system known loosely as "New Age" spirituality. Helena Blavatsky and Alice Bailey were two of the most well known organizers of this movement. Blavatsky founded the Theosophical Society and Bailey, later a president of the Theosophical Society founded the organization known as the Lucis Trust, which has counted as members men of great influence such as David Rockefeller, Henry Kissinger, Paul Volker and George Schultz.

Blavatsky and Bailey were avid trance-channelers who claimed to receive messages from spirit entities and both recorded many predictions that were made to them regarding the inevitable appearance of "The Lord Maitreya" or "The Christ" on the earth immediately prior to earth's initiation into the utopian "New Age." Because these women engaged in the biblically-forbidden practice of spiritism and because the messages they received were deeply anti-Christian, mocking and ridiculing traditional Christianity, bible-believing Christians have understood that the appearance of the man whom Bailey and Blavatsky predicted was not a reference to the second coming of Jesus Christ, but was in fact a prediction of the future Antichrist.

Benjamin Creme, a self-described disciple of both Blavatsky and Bailey, appears to have taken over where they left off. Through his early studies of their works he became convinced in the reality of the "Ascended Masters," (the supposed inter-dimensional beings who direct humanity's evolution), and claims that in 1959 he was first contacted by them. According to Creme's biography, "He was told, among other things, that Maitreya, the World Teacher—the Master of all the Masters—would return in about 20 years and that he (Creme) would have a role to play in the event if he chose to accept it." Creme claims that he has been in constant telepathic contact with "Maitreya the Christ" since the early 70s and that Maitreya finally entered civilized society privately in 1977 when he materialized in human form and took up residence in a suburb of London. Since then Creme has travelled the world, giving lectures and appearing on talk shows, to prepare the world for the public emergence of Maitreya. He also claims that a major American television network has agreed to interview Maitreya at a time of Maitreya's choosing.

Many now expect the return of their awaited Teacher, whether they call him the Christ, Messiah, the fifth Buddha, Krishna, or the Imam Mahdi. Millions now know that the Messiah, who fulfills all these expectations, is already living among us.

One major aspect of Creme's mission was the formation of Share International Foundation and the publication of it's monthly self-titled magazine. Each issue contains a brief synopsis of the emergence of Maitreya on the first two pages and then a brief message that has been trance-channeled through Benjamin Creme from an Ascended Master known simply as "The Master" on page three. The spiritual thrust of Share International is clearly obvious in each issue that is published. Despite this fact Share International has a long list of prominent, well respected patrons. They include articles written by former UN leader Boutros Boutros-Ghali; present leader Kofi Annan; former President of Ireland Mary Robinson; Gro Harlem Brundtland who is director-general of the World Health Organization and former Prime Minister of Norway; the Dalai Lama; and recently even Britain's Prince Charles of Wales.

Even though the average man/woman on the street would most likely laugh at being presented with the beliefs of Creme and Share International, it is easily shown that this magazine is well-respected and taken seriously by many influential members of the Global

Elite. In fact, Share International Foundation is accredited as an official non-governmental organization (NGO) by the United Nations, and the magazine, as stated on the inside cover of each issue, is published by Share International" in association with the Department of Public Information at the United Nations."

Another significant cornerstone of world peace through religion is being promoted through the World Parliament of Religion. There have been several meetings referred to as a Parliament of the World's Religions, most notably the World's Parliament of Religions of 1893, the first attempt to create a global dialogue of faiths. The event was celebrated by another conference on its centenary in 1993. This led to a new series of conferences under the official title "Parliament of the World's Religions".

In 1993 the Parliament of World Religions convened in Chicago with 8000 people worldwide coming together to celebrate diversity and religious harmony and to explore how religion could address some of the world major social problems. During this event a major document was constructed called "Towards a Global Ethic: An initial Declaration" which would lay the basis of an ethical common understand amongst the world religions and spiritual traditions.

As one can see from above the one-world organizers are out to combine all religions under one roof where they can be controlled by the U.N. Most of the members named in this group are members of the Bildenberg Group in Europe (Rockefeller, Kissinger, etc.). This is just another organization that is trying to destroy religion in any form and have the religious leaders bow to the new Master— the Antichrist who will appointed by the U.N. to lead the world.

As the evangelical movement becomes the fastest growing sector within the American Christian churches, estimates of the number of evangelicals range from 100—130 million, Yet with the evangelical movement and the other orthodox churches we still end up being a country without morals. How did these Christian people install a corrupt Congress and a number of corrupt Presidents?

Over the last 110 years we have put rogues in the President's chair and filled the halls of Congress with greedy members who cared less about this country or its people. What was once a clarion call of 'We The People' has become 'How much money can I steal today!' All politicians today are career men—they care less about what happens to the country, only 'how can I get reelected.' Most of them are corrupt as history will prove.

Americans expect all levels of government to competently guard the nation from enemies outside and inside our country. The majority of the citizens want our borders secured. They want our streets safe to walk in again at any time of the day or night, NOT some politicians screaming for gun controls while doing nothing to eliminate the gangs and hoodlums that have taken over our cities. Taking guns out of the hands of citizens so they cannot protect themselves (because the police cannot) is insanity at its peak. This is not a rap at the police efforts in this country but the results of decisions handed down by the Warren Court (Miranda Decision, etc.) which removed the ability of police to be a 'crime prevention' organization to the status of investigating crimes *after* they happen. Just take a close look at European countries that have removed the rights of people to protected themselves and their families. In those countries, crimes are rampant. The crime rates that are reported show a decline but that is because the only crimes that are reported are those that are solved. If a crime is not solved it is not reported because (in their reasoning), it is being investigated and until finished it may not end up a crime. Some noted results of Social justice as dispensed by the socialistic philosophy that a man has no rights when it comes to protecting himself, his family, or his property can be found in numerous European cases that are on the books in Europe—especially, in England.

Americans expect all levels of government to be organized and handle disaster efficiently when they occur. The political patronage system has produced incompetent but lifetime employees and allowed partisan abuse of public resources, including distribution of sensitive information in a partisan fashion, running political errands on public time (such as picking up campaign contributions), and using congressional equipment for political campaign mailings. Implicit in promises of reform was the idea that the opportunities for massive patronage and corruption that this army of aides represented would vanish under nonpartisan administration.

The enormous subsidies for congressional mail, which increase the federal budget and tilt federal elections in favor of incumbents, also remained essentially unchanged. Lawmakers should answer constituent queries, but over nine-tenths of franking costs derive from mass mailings initiated by Congressmen, not from responses to constituents. Although previous Congresses have cut franking accounts and required disclosure of Members' total expenditures, such reforms as limiting the mention of the sender's name to eight per page and capping his pictures at two per page only raise questions about what prior abuses had occurred. Republicans have pressed repeatedly for further reform of franking, but most committees have refused to hold any meetings on the subject. The political uses of the frank were illustrated during the tumultuous 1992 elections, when three of the four heaviest House users of the frank lost their reelection bids. On average, the four sent out over a million mass-mailed letters apiece. Although these mailings failed to save them, they demonstrate that those in greatest political peril often use the frank the most. Remember, this franking privilege is free to the Congressman, however the Postal Service is going broke and must go to Congress every year for additional funds which are paid by the taxpayers. THAT is what Congressional members think of the taxpayers.

Why didn't Congress over the years amend the 1970 National Environment Policy Act? They knew it was flawed but to appease the Environmental Bloc which donates much funds to members of Congress, they did nothing. They cannot plead ignorance because story after story was printed on how the NEPA was being used by environmentalists to block construction of much needed services to prevent disaster. It became apparent early after the enactment of NEPA that it was unworkable. NEPA requires the U.S. government to evaluate the environmental impact of any significant project undertaken by a federal agency, financed with federal money, or requiring a federal permit. It further mandates that the results of the government assessment be made public and that the public decide whether its benefits outweigh its costs. The task force said NEPA lawsuits, at least twice, had prevented system improvements to protect New Orleans from a hurricane. It said the Sierra Club and other environmental groups in 1996 sued the U.S. Army Corps of Engineers and blocked a project to raise and fortify levees around New Orleans.

The task force also cited a Los Angeles Times story that said a Save the Wetlands lawsuit filed in 1977 killed plans approved by Congress to create a "massive hurricane barrier to protect New Orleans." The plan was created after Hurricane Betsy in 1965. A federal judge stopped plans for the hurricane barrier after finding that an environmental impact statement drafted by the Army Corps of Engineers was flawed. The corps abandoned the project by the mid-1980s. A member of the congressional NEPA task force, says it is clear that NEPA "plays' a role in hampering our ability as a nation to develop efficient supply chains capable of providing Americans with affordable energy! "For years, construction projects that could have mitigated adverse impacts to our supply have been needlessly blocked due to endless red tape and a sluggish federal bureaucracy," the congresswoman added.

Yet after all these stories over the intervening years from 1970, an inept Congress and other Social Democrats refused to take action to prevent these disastrous natural events from doing so much damages. Greed and incompetent are the only descriptions that can describe Congress.

The 5th Amendment to the Constitution has been completely destroyed. By the decision of five dictators in black robes, property is no longer private and can now be taken from us and sold to others when it suits government's "public purpose." Religion and religious practices, especially those of the Christians faith, are increasingly regulated by government. It is almost impossible to do anything without permission from one or more departments of government and complying with their often-conflicting dictates. Thoughts, speeches and even opinions are not tolerated in this atmosphere of judicial tyranny and penalties abound for those who try to resist the system. As Saint-Simon said, "They will do as we tell them or we will treat them like chattel".

Corruption is the land grabs, the power grabs, the gun grabs, the bribery, the shady deals, the high crimes and treason. Corruption is the theft of campaign dollars through forced labor union deductions. Corruption is the systematic indoctrination of several generations of our youth with socialist dogma via government school systems. Corruption is the removal of God from public life and substituting in the evil homosexual/feminist agenda and the destruction of moral society. Corruption is lying to the public about global warming and the selling of the Kyoto treaty. Corruption is giving up our national sovereignty to the United Nations. Corruption is the abuses of office, obstruction of justice, lying, perjury and subornation of perjury.

Mark Twain once said that America is a nation without a distinct criminal class "with the possible exception of Congress" and the Congress of today is even worse than it was in Twain's time more than a century and a half ago. Currently, a Congressman has to think continually throughout his term of office about raising money for the next campaign. He has to raise at least $5000 every day he's in office. Current limitations on donations (passed in the early 1970s) strictly limit the size of the donations. This forces the Congressman to follow the money on every vote he makes, every day in office! A number of years ago, the National Taxpayers Union did a study of Congressmen's voting records and campaign contributions. They found linkage showing that 95% of all the votes made in Congress are bought and paid for by someone!

Unfortunately, the United States Congress has 535 members, most of whom think themselves as fully qualified cabinet members, or great policy makers, or brilliant military tacticians, or highly qualified on a number of subjects which need and deserve his or her own review and modification. And many have presidential ambitions. It is interesting that reportedly within this same august group there are: 29 who have been accused of spousal abuse; 7 have been arrested for fraud; 19 have been accused of writing bad checks; 117 have bankrupted at least two businesses; 3 have been arrested for assault; 71 cannot get a credit card due to bad credit; 14 have been arrested for shoplifting/drug-related charges; 21 are currently defendants in lawsuits; 84 have been arrested for drunk driving. Add to these figures, at least one was caught plagiarizing in college (Sen. Biden who is now our vice-President); one was caught cheating on a Spanish exam (former Sen. Ted Kennedy) and forced to leave school for a semester; one was involved in a negligent driving accident that resulted in the female passenger drowning (former Sen. Ted Kennedy); two were rebuked separately on the House floor for their highly questionable involvement in homosexual related activities (Reps. Studds and Frank); one served prison time for his involvement in a House stamp fraud activity (Rep. Rostenkowski); and one was forced to resign from an intelligence oversight committee for leaking classified information relative to the Iran-Contra hearings (Sen. Frank Leahy). And that's just what has surfaced publicly. (It is of interest to note that two of the above listed characters, Senator Biden and Senator Kennedy, were two of the Democratic Senators that trashed the character of Judge Bork, and laughed while doing it!).

In February 1990, the GAO made public its report on the House Bank. This time, instead of referring in footnotes to sums "due from members", the GAO made it clear that members were kiting checks. A number of news stories followed. In September 1991, another GAO audit said members had written 8,331 bad checks in the fiscal year ended June 30, 1990.

The subsequent investigation by the ethics committee found that 269 current and 56 former members of the house had been allowed to routinely overdraw their accounts without paying interest or penalties. Among the then current members the biggest abusers were Stephen J. Solarz, a New York Democrat, who had written $594,646 in bad or overdraft checks and was overdrawn for thirty months; Carl C. Perkins, a Kentucky Democrat, who had written $565,651 in bad checks and overdrawn for fourteen months; Harold E. Ford, a Tennessee Democrat, who had overdrawn, his account by a total of $552, 447 and was overdrawn for thirty-one months, and Robert J. Mrazek, a New York Democrat, who had written $351,609 in bad checks and was overdrawn for twenty-three months. Charles Hatcher, a Georgia Democrat, had written 819 bad checks and had been overdrawn a total of thirty-five months. Ronald D. Coleman, a Texas Democrat, had written 673 bad checks and had been overdrawn a total of twenty-three months. Among the abusers from the Republican side was Newt Gingrich, the minority whip, who had written twenty-two bad checks with a face value totaling $26,891." "The scandal and its initial cover-up was but another example of how members of Congress expect everyone but themselves to play by the rules.

For more than one hundred years, the House Bank had quietly cashed the members' pay checks out of a little first floor Capitol office. The bank neither paid nor charged interest. It made no loans. Other than members salaries, it took no deposits. Yet to House members, it was another way to steal money from the federal government.

Needless to say, Congress was forced to close the House Bank.

Once elected to Congress, fellow Congressmen will protect and keep you no matter what. The following cases illustrate this corrupt organization.

In March of 1998, Congressman Jay Kim admitted to committing the largest amount of campaign violations ever by a member of Congress. More than one-third of the contributions to his 1992 primary campaign, which he won by only 889 votes, were illegal. After pleading guilty to accepting more than $250,000 in illegal corporate and foreign campaign contributions, Kim was sentenced to two months of "house arrest," restricted to his suburban Virginia home and the halls of Congress. But he kept his job, and all the perks that went with it. The following month, House Speaker Newt Gingrich (R-Ga.) appointed Kim to the House-Senate group negotiating the budget-busting highway bill. "He's a very active member," said House Transportation Committee Chairman Bud Shuster.

"His plight has not diminished his effectiveness here in Congress," said fellow California Republican David Drier. Kim's estranged wife, June, was less charitable. "It's really frustrating that our law is not tough enough to get him out right away," she said. "He's humiliated us enough." Despite her wishes, and the demands of others, the law did not require Kim to quit and Congressional leaders, as a rule, usually find a way to accommodate, not punish, fellow members who break the law.

At the time Gingrich showed such leniency to Kim, he was himself making payments on a $300,000 fine by the ethics committee, the worst ever levied against a member of Congress. The fine grew out of charges filed by Michigan Democrat David Bonior, who openly admitted he was getting even with Gingrich for the Georgia Republican's role in bringing down former Democratic Speaker Jim Wright of Texas. "It's called payback," Bonior told reporters. "Our political system doesn't act out of a sense of justice," says a former Southern Illinois University political scientist. "What you have is political expediency, driven by revenge and gain. So the reaction of those in power is to protect their own. Members of Congress operate on a different plane where right and wrong don't exist—only winning and losing."

Another example of Congressional leaders protecting their members or others of their ilk who have committed crimes but being good Liberals (Socialists) we will just pat them on the back of their hand and say 'naughty, naughty'. How did the Socialist accomplish this protection for themselves? The concept of taking over the Justice Department with socialist in position of all the field Attorney Generals. This was done under President Clinton's administration by Janet Reno being appointed Attorney General of the Justice Department. One of her first directives was to demand that all field Attorney Generals submit their resignation immediately or be fired! She then accepted the resignations of those Attorney Generals that were not Liberals and replaced them with Socialists who would destroy anyone not following the Socialists path. Today active special prosecutors from the Justice Department and other State Attorneys are out to destroy Republicans who oppose their views. Most of the time they cannot prove anything, but they convene Grand Juries filled with selected members that will do their bidding and then bring charges against the victim not because of the original investigation but some other trumped up charge like perjury. Now if you're a good Socialist, perjury is not that bad (remember President Clinton) but if you're a Republican or Conservative it's a hideous crime and you should go to jail forever! Double standards has been the hallmark of Socialists all over the world.

Other House members have kept their seats even while serving in prison: Rep. Thomas Lane (D-Mass.) went to jail from May 7 to Sept. 7, 1956, for tax evasion and Rep. Matthew Lyon (R-Vt.) was imprisoned for violating the Sedition Act in 1798 but returned to Congress after a mob broke him out of jail.

Wake up America! Politicians are glib talkers but once in Congress it is all for the party and oneself. There can never be any give and take between the current parties in Congress today. That is why we have grid-lock most of the time and bills that should be passed are usually weak and useless or they do not pass. Moreover. they are bill that leave the definitions of the bill to a bunch of bureaucrats that write rules that they decide should be in the law. Every member of Congress should be voted out of office and let us start over with liberty-loving Americans and not politicians. Put into Congress members who love America more then those special interest groups that want to destroy the Constitution. Eliminate many of the Departments that have been formed to carry out and destroy the true meaning of the Constitution.

Another area that has been subverted and destroying this country is our Educational System. It has been going on for some time, but has gotten little or no attention from the so called free press. Secular Humanism (mentioned previously) is a secular philosophy that espouses reason, ethics, and justice, and specifically rejects supernatural and religious dogma as the basis of morality and decision-making. Secular Humanism is a life stance that focuses on the way human beings can lead good, happy and functional lives.

The term secularism was created in 1851 by George Jacob Holyoake in order to describe "a form of opinion which concerns itself only with questions, the issues of which can be tested by the experience of this life." Once a staunch Owenite, Holyoake was strongly influenced by Auguste Comte, the founder of positivism and of modern sociology. Comte believed human history would progress in a 'law of three stages' from a 'theological' phase, to the 'metaphysical', toward a fully-rational 'positivist' society. In later life, Comte had attempted to introduce a 'religion of humanity' in light of growing anti-religious sentiment and social malaise in revolutionary France. This 'religion' would necessarily fulfill the functional, cohesive role that supernatural religion once served. Whilst Comte's religious movement was unsuccessful, the positivist philosophy of science itself played a major role in the proliferation of secular organizations in the 19th century. Thus, from the 19th century until the present day we have religious movements such as the New Age, 'Born-again Christians', etc.

From these secular movements have sprung a group of individuals that decided to change Educational Systems in the World and to use this movement to establish a one-world church under the supervision of a one-world government. In order to do this in the United States, they had to change the educational concept. Thus the Progressive method of education came into being.

Progressive educators thought that traditional education should be reformed. Famous progressive educators of the 1800's included Francis Parker and G. Stanley Hall. In the early 1900's, John Dewey became a well-known spokesman for progressive education. The traditional school stressed specific subjects—reading, writing, arithmetic, geography, history, and grammar. The teacher lectured or dictated a lesson, and the students copied it in their notebooks. The students then learned by heart what was in their notebooks and recited what they learned from their textbooks. The teacher enforced order and quiet except for recitation periods. Students sat at rows of desks fastened to the floor, and they could not move or talk without permission.

Progressive educators tried to reform elementary school methods in several ways. They thought teachers should pay more attention to the individual child and not treat all children alike. Progressive educators believed that children learn best when they are genuinely interested in the material, and not when they are forced to memorize facts that seem useless to them. Children should learn by direct contact with things, places, and people, as well as by reading and hearing about them. Thus, elementary schools should include science laboratories, workshops, art studios, kitchens, gymnasiums, and gardens. Progressive educators believed this procedure would develop the child's physical, social, and emotional nature as well as its mind. They believed that children learn better when they can move about and work at their own pace. They thought children should gather materials from many sources rather than from just one textbook, and should work in groups with other students. Discussion, dramatics, music, and art activities became a larger part of classroom procedures. Progressive education spread more widely through elementary schools than it did in high schools or colleges. Teachers planned individual instruction and centered it around projects, units, or activities rather than the usual courses or subjects. They taught students of different abilities in separate groups.

Many writers and some educators began increasingly to criticize progressive education during the 1940's and 1950's. They charged students did not learn fundamental subjects well enough. Other educators said that students learned as well under progressive education as under traditional methods. But by the early 1960's, many schools had begun to experiment with different teaching methods. Many experiments used "progressive" principles but did not use the term.

The philosophy of John Dewey (the leader of the Progressive movement in U. S. education) is firmly embedded in the educational system and it should be removed. It is nothing but one man's philosophy and it has proven to be wrong more times than not. Dewey's philosophy (in his own words):

"I believe that the only true education comes through the stimulation of the child's powers by the demands of the social situations in which he finds himself. Through these demands he is stimulated to act as a member of a unity, to emerge from his original narrowness of action and feeling, and to conceive of himself from the standpoint of the welfare of the group to which he belongs. Through the responses which others make to his own activities he comes to know what these mean in social terms. The value which they have is reflected back into them. For instance, through the response which is made to the child's instinctive babblings the child comes to know what those babblings mean; they are transformed into articulate language and thus the child is introduced into the consolidated wealth of ideas and emotions which are now summed up in language."

"I believe that this educational process has two sides-one psychological and one sociological; and that neither can be subordinated to the other or neglected without evil results following. Of these two sides, the psychological is the basis. The child's own instincts and powers furnish the material and give the starting point for all education. Save as the efforts of the educator connect with some activity which the child is carrying on of his own initiative independent of the educator, education becomes reduced to a pressure from without. It may, indeed, give certain external results, but cannot truly be called educative. Without insight into the psychological structure and activities of the individual, the educative process will, therefore, be haphazard and arbitrary. If it chances to coincide with the child's activity it will get a leverage; if it does not, it will result in friction, or disintegration, or arrest of the child nature. I believe that knowledge of social conditions, of the present state of civilization, is necessary in order properly to interpret the child's powers. The child has his own instincts and tendencies, but we do not know what these mean until we can translate them into their social equivalents. We must be able to carry them back into a social past and see them as the inheritance of previous race activities. We must also be able to project them into the future to see what their outcome and end will be. In the illustration just used, it is the ability to see in the child's babblings the promise and potency of a future social intercourse and conversation which enables one to deal in the proper way with that instinct. "

John Dewey also included in his treatise in 1897 the following

Socialist propaganda: " I believe that the individual who is to be educated is a social individual and that society is an organic union of individuals. If we eliminate the social factor from the child we are left only with an abstraction; if we eliminate the individual factor from society, we are left only with an inert and lifeless mass. Education, therefore, must begin with a psychological insight into the child's capacities, interests, and habits. It must be controlled at every point by reference to these same considerations. These powers, interests, and habits must be continually interpreted--we must know what they mean. They must be translated into terms of their social equivalents--into terms of what they are capable of in the way of social service."

This metaphysical tirade is the current guidepost to educational disaster.

Are Democratic socialists embarrassed of this overwhelming evidence of the failure of their educational ideas and experiments? Of course not. Virtually every national attempt to raise standards has been hijacked by the socialists. One must remember that an educated, intelligent community is the socialists bane. People who can think for themselves are anti-social. They must be like cattle so that the Central Committee can use them like slaves.

Has the system failed? Yes it has. There are high school students that cannot make proper change from a sale, when a customer pays for it with a larger bill that the cost of the sale. A recent poll showed that approximately 30% of high school students cannot locate the capitol of the U. S. Some think it is in Washington State. Others think it is located in the State of D.C. (wherever that is).

Chapter 14

Surrendering U.S. Sovereignty To The United Nations

During President's Reagan's first Inaugural Address he stated: "I am told that tens of thousands of prayer meetings are being held on this day, and for that I am deeply grateful. We are a nation under God, and I believe God intended for us to be free. It would be fitting and good, I think, if on each Inauguration Day in future years it should be declared a day of prayer.

This is the first time in history that this ceremony has been held, as you have been told, on this West Front of the Capitol. Standing here, one faces a magnificent vista, opening up on this city's special beauty and history. At the end of this open mall are those shrines to the giants on whose shoulders we stand.

Directly in front of me, the monument to a monumental man: George Washington, Father of our country. A man of humility who came to greatness reluctantly. He led America out of revolutionary victory into infant nationhood. Off to one side, the stately memorial to Thomas Jefferson. The Declaration of Independence flames with his eloquence.

And then beyond the Reflecting Pool the dignified columns of the Lincoln Memorial. Whoever would understand in his heart the meaning of America will find it in the life of Abraham Lincoln.

Beyond those monuments to heroism is the Potomac River, and on the far shore the sloping hills of Arlington National Cemetery with its row on row of simple white markers bearing crosses or Stars of David. They add up to only a tiny fraction of the price that has been paid for our freedom.

Each one of those markers is a monument to the kinds of hero I spoke of earlier. Their lives ended in places called Belleau Wood, The Argonne, Omaha Beach, Salerno and halfway around the world on Guadalcanal, Tarawa, Pork Chop Hill, the Chosin Reservoir, and in a hundred rice paddies and jungles of a place called Vietnam.

Under one such marker lies a young man—Martin Treptow—who left his job in a small town barber shop in 1917 to go to France with the famed Rainbow Division. There, on the western front, he was killed trying to carry a message between battalions under heavy artillery fire.

We are told that on his body was found a diary. On the flyleaf under the heading, "My Pledge," he had written these words: 'America must win this war. Therefore, I will work, I will save, I will sacrifice, I will endure, I will fight cheerfully and do my utmost, as if the issue of the whole struggle depended on me alone.'

The crisis we are facing today does not require of us the kind of sacrifice that Martin Treptow and so many thousands of others were called upon to make. It does require, however, our best effort, and our willingness to believe in ourselves and to believe in our capacity to perform great deeds; to believe that together, with God's help, we can and will resolve the problems which now confront us."

Millions of men have given their lives so that this country could stay free. Freedom meant an awful lot to them. However today our government is infested with traitors who wish to take these freedoms from us and subject us to a one-world dictatorship. Some of these traitors have been elected while others have infiltrated our government and placed in high positions to accomplish their nefarious work.

As mentioned before, there can be few sights more humiliating for the American people than a US president kowtowing to a foreign leader or to supranational institutions. Continental Europeans are used to that sort of thing after decades of dominance by unelected bureaucrats in Brussels, and have grudgingly accepted, over time, the gradual and undemocratic erosion of their freedoms. But most

Americans fiercely defend their national sovereignty, and find the idea of giving international organizations a say over their laws and lives completely unacceptable.

President Obama gave a speech in Cairo, Egypt which assures the world that we are ready to give up our Sovereignty to a one world government whenever they ask for it. His speech was nothing more than traitorous. Excerpts are as follows:

> "More recently, tension has been fed by colonialism that denied rights and opportunities to many Muslims and a Cold War in which Muslim majority countries were too often treated as proxies without regard to their own aspirations. Moreover, the sweeping change brought by modernity and globalization led many Muslims to view the West as hostile to the traditions of Islam"

> "Violent extremists have exploited these tensions in a small but potent minority of Muslims. The attacks of September 11, 2001, and the continued efforts of these extremists to engage in violence against civilians has led some in my country to view Islam as inevitably hostile not only to America and western countries but also to human rights..."

> "I've come here to Cairo to seek a new beginning between the United States and Muslims around the world, one based on mutual interest and mutual respect, and one based upon the truth that America and Islam are not exclusive and need not be in competition. Instead, they overlap and share common principles, principles of justice and progress, tolerance and the dignity of all human beings."

The above statements indicate that the President is either naïve or a one-world member who wants to destroy this nation. He is saying 'let us talk' while the Muslim terrorists are saying 'let us kill'. The only way you can talk to these terrorists is by meeting force with force.

President Reagan did that with Libya. For those who are not familiar with the Libyan episode a brief history follows:

In March 1986, the United States, asserting the 12-nautical-mile (22 km; 14 mi) limit to territorial waters recognized by the international community, sent a carrier task force to the region. Libya responded with aggressive counter-maneuvers on March 24 that led to the Gulf of Sidra incident. Less than two weeks later on April 5, a bomb exploded in a West Berlin disco, La Belle, killing two American servicemen and a Turkish woman and wounding 200 others. The United States claimed to have obtained cable transcripts from Libyan agents in East Germany involved in the attack.

On April 14, Eighteen F-111F strike aircraft of the 48th Tactical Fighter Wing, flying from RAF Lakenheath supported by four EF-111A Ravens of the 20th Tactical Fighter Wing, from RAF Upper Heyford in England, in conjunction with fifteen A-6, A-7, F/A-18 attack aircraft and EA-6B Prowler Electronic Warfare Aircraft from the aircraft carriers USS *Saratoga*, USS *America* and USS *Coral Sea* on station in the Gulf of Sidra, struck five targets at 02:00 on April 15, with the stated objective that their destruction would send a message and reduce Libya's ability to support and train terrorists. Reagan warned that "if necessary, they shall do it again."

For the Libyan raid, the United States was denied overflight rights by France, Spain and Italy as well as the use of European continental bases, forcing the Air Force portion of the operation to be flown around France, Spain and through the Straits of Gibraltar, adding 1,300 miles (2,100 km) each way and requiring multiple aerial refueling. (This is the thanks that the U.S. gets for saving the countries in Europe and refinancing their recovery after WW I and WW II.)

In October 2008 Libya paid $1.5 billion into a fund which was used to compen-sate relatives of the
- *Lockerbie bombing* victims with the remaining 20%;
- American victims of the *1986 Berlin discotheque bombing*;
- American victims of the 1989 *UTA Flight 772* bombing; and,
- Libyan victims of the 1986 US bombing of Tripoli and Benghazi.

You CANNOT negotiate with Muslim terrorists as President Carter will attest.

More excerpts from President Obama's Cairo speech:

"So I have known Islam on three continents before coming to the region where it was first revealed. That experience guides my conviction that partnership between America and Islam must be based on what Islam is, not what it isn't. And I consider it part of my responsibility as president of the United States to fight against negative stereotypes of Islam wherever they appear."

(Apparently, our President has never heard about the Separation of Church and State. It is NOT the responsibility of the president of the United States to fight to further ANY religion!)

"Moreover, freedom in America is indivisible from the freedom to practice one's religion. That is why there is a mosque in every state in our union and over 1,200 mosques within our borders. That's why the United States government has gone to court to protect the right of women and girls to wear the 'hijab', and to punish those who would deny it."

'We can't disguise hostility towards any religion behind the pretense of liberalism. In fact, faith should bring us together. And that's why we're forging service projects in America to bring together Christians, Muslims, and Jews. That's why we welcome efforts like Saudi Arabian King Abdullah's interfaith dialogue and Turkey's leadership in the Alliance of Civilizations. Around the world, we can turn dialogue into interfaith service so bridges between peoples lead to action, whether it is combating malaria in Africa or providing relief after a natural disaster."

(President Obama is pledging our resources (paid for by American taxpayers) to all countries in the world. This is his one-world ambition. To subjugate the U.S. citizens to a one-world government leadership. He is also pledging to promote a one-world Religion. All must join this one world religion or they will be left out in the cold!)

When President Obama speaks about Human Rights, he is speaking about World Human Rights. In the U.S., according to President Obama, the United States is the worst country in the

World when it comes to upholding Human Rights.

To prove a point, the Obama administration has submitted a report to the UN Commissioner on Human Rights, South African judge Navanethem Pillay, which makes direct reference to a popular Arizona immigration law aimed at tackling illegal immigration, which is fiercely opposed by the White House, and is the subject of legal action by the Justice Department.

The Report references the recent Arizona law, S.B. 1070, which has generated significant attention and debate at home and around the world. The issue is being addressed in a court action that argues that the federal government has the authority to set and enforce immigration law. That action is ongoing; parts of the law are currently enjoined.

The highly controversial reference to the Arizona law serves only one purpose – to gain UN and international support for the Obama administration's position in the face of mounting opposition from Arizona legislators and a majority of the American people. A recent Rasmussen poll showed 61 percent of Americans backing Arizona-style laws for their own states, and just 28 percent supporting a Justice Department challenge .

By doing so, Obama officials hope to stir up international condemnation of the Arizona policy in advance of the UN General Assembly meetings in the fall of 2010, which they believe will increase pressure on Arizona to back down. It is a highly cynical move that speaks volumes about the Obama team's willingness to undercut American sovereignty and popular will on the world stage.

This approach has been strongly condemned by Arizona Governor Jan Brewer, who described the Arizona reference in the government report as "downright offensive", and called on it to be removed. The State Department announced that it will stand by its decision to include Arizona in its UN submission, with Secretary of State Hillary Clinton strongly in favor of it.

It is important to note that the Obama administration's report to the United Nations will go before the UN Human Rights Council, which includes in its current membership some of the world's worst human rights abusers. The likes of China, Cuba, Libya, Russia, and Saudi Arabia, will have a right to pass judgment over the Arizona immigration law, a humiliation for a great superpower before some of the most brutal regimes on the face of the earth.

Over the course of the last 19 months, Barack Obama has bowed before Emperors and Kings, and apologized for his country on numerous occasions, from Cairo to Strasbourg. By deliberately placing the immigration policy of a US state before the Human Rights Council, he is now bowing before the United Nations, and undercutting the sovereignty of his own nation. This is not leadership but a surrender of US interests before a declining world body that is a hotbed of anti-Americanism, and a bully pulpit for many of the world's most repugnant tyrants. It is another example of an imperial-style presidency that is increasingly out of touch with the American people and public opinion.

The president's first-ever report on U.S. human rights to the UN Human Rights Council contains a rich source of offensive material. Throughout the report, which sounds like an Obama campaign speech, the president discusses "the original flaw" of the U.S. Constitution, America's tolerance for slavery, and his version of our long and despicable history of discriminating against and oppressing minorities, women, homosexuals, and the handicapped.

The national report is but the first step of the international government's review process. On November 5, the United States will be examined by a troika of UN bureaucrats from France, Japan, and Cameroon (an oppressive nation which is a member of the Organization of Islamic Conference). This trio will consider three items: Obama's self-flagellating report, reports written about America by UN tribunals or international governing bodies, and testimony from NGOs with a pronounced anti-American bias. It will also consider "voluntary pledges and commitments made by the State," such as suspending an Arizona state law. Then the French, Japanese, and Cameroon diplomats will draw up a plan of action for the United States to implement.

Nations are re-examined every four years. The Human Rights

Council looks for voluntary compliance. However, its website asserts, "The Human Rights Council will decide on the measures it would need to take in case of persistent non-cooperation by a State with the World Body.

The Geneva-based Human Rights Council was established in March 2006 to replace the 60-year-old Human Rights Commission. However, the decision to seek a seat on the council is in keeping with what President Obama has called a "new era of engagement" with other nations to advance U.S. security interests and meet the global challenges of the 21st century. The council is scheduled to undergo a formal review of its structure and procedures in 2011, offering an opportunity for reform.

The members of the General Assembly elect the members who occupy the UNHRC's forty-seven seats. The term of each seat is three years, and no member may occupy a seat for more than two consecutive terms. The seats are distributed among the UN's regional groups as follows: 13 for Africa, 13 for Asia, six for Eastern Europe, eight for Latin America and the Caribbean, and seven for the Western European and Others Group.

In regard to the United Nations Human Rights Council, the position of the United States is: "human rights have been a cornerstone of American values since the country's birth and the United States is committed to support the work of the UN Commission in promoting the principles embodied in the Universal Declaration of Human Rights. U.S. President George W. Bush declared that the United States would not seek a seat on the Council, saying it would be more effective from the outside. He did pledge, however, to support the Council financially. State Department spokesman Sean McCormack said, "We will work closely with partners in the international community to encourage the council to address serious cases of human rights abuse in countries such as Iran, Cuba, Zimbabwe, Burma, Sudan, and North Korea."

The U.S. State Department said on 5 March 2007 that, for the second year in a row, the United States has decided not to seek a seat on the Human Rights Council, asserting the body had lost its credibility with repeated attacks on Israel and a failure to confront other rights abusers. Spokesman Sean McCormack said the council has had a "singular focus" on Israel, while countries such as Cuba, Myanmar and North Korea have been spared scrutiny. He said that though the United States will have only an observer role, it will continue to shine a spotlight on human rights issues. The most senior Republican member of the Foreign Affairs Committee of the U.S. House of Representatives, Ileana Ros-Lehtinen, supported the administration decision. "Rather than standing as a strong defender of fundamental human rights, the Human Rights Council has faltered as a weak voice subject to gross political manipulation," she said.

Upon passage of UNHRC's June 2007 institution building package, the U.S. restated its condemnation of bias in the institution's agenda. Spokesman Sean McCormack again criticized the Commission for focusing on Israel in light of many more pressing human rights issues around the world, such as Sudan or Myanmar, and went on to criticize the termination of Special Rapporteurs to Cuba and Belarus, as well as procedural irregularities that prevented member-states from voting on the issues; a similar critique was issued by the Canadian representative. On September 2007, The US Senate voted to cut off funding to the council.

The distrust and critique of the UN's Human Rights activities occur because of their selection of countries to sit in control of its agenda. For example: U.N. Appoints Iran to Women's Rights Commission. Iran already punishes women with public lashings with bullwhips for violating "modesty laws"

In one of the more bizarre episodes of Iranian law concerning women, Tehran police chief Brig. Gen. Hossien Sajedinia has issued a stern warning that all women with a sun tan will be arrested and imprisoned due to them violating the "spirit of Islamic law." Thus, any woman that looked like a "walking mannequin" will be punished.

Iran also recently executed by public hanging 16-year-old

Atefah Sahaaleh for "violating chastity" due to her being sexually assaulted by a 51-year-old former Revolutionary Guard, Ali Darabi. Sahaaleh was hung by the neck until dead on a crane for being raped. Darabi received a whipping for raping her.

The United Nations General Assembly voted to appoint Libya to the Human Rights Council. In 2003, Libya was elected to the chairmanship of the very same council. In 2004, Libya accepted responsibility for the terrorist attack on Pan Am flight—103 over Lockerbie, Scotland, killing 270 men, women and children.

As stated previously, Libya was implicated in the 1986 terrorist bombing of the *Le Belle* nightclub in Berlin, Germany. The Libyan government has agreed to pay a total of $1.5 billion to non-US nationals who were injured. The Libyan-sponsored terrorist attack on the club, which was frequented by US servicemen, killed two American soldiers and a Turkish woman and wounded more than 200 people.

Mauritania is also a member of the U.N. Human Rights Council. It was not until 1981 that slavery was officially banned, but never criminalized. Hereditary/generational slavery continues to this day. Children of slaves are openly passed on to the children of masters.

A group of United Nations appointed human rights experts expressed their "serious concern" over the new immigration law enacted by the state of Arizona. The alleged experts claim that Arizona is guilty of "a disturbing pattern of legislative activity hostile to ethnic minorities and immigrants."

Jim Anaya, a Law Professor at the University of Arizona was an expert in International Human Rights and Indigenous peoples law, Professor Anaya is the author of the acclaimed book, *Indigenous Peoples in International Law* (Oxford Univ. Press, 1996, 2d. ed. 2004), and currently serves as the United Nations Special Rapporteur on the situation of human rights and fundamental freedoms of indigenous peoples.

Human Rights Council resolution 15/14 authorizes and requests the Special Rapporteur to "examine ways and means of overcoming existing obstacles to the full and effective protection of the human rights and fundamental freedoms of indigenous people, in conformity with his/her mandate, and to identify, exchange and promote best practices".

Additionally, the Special Rapporteur is to "gather, request, receive and exchange information and communications from all relevant sources, including Governments, indigenous people and their communities and organizations, on alleged violations of their human rights and fundamental freedoms" and to "formulate recommendations and proposals on appropriate measures and activities to prevent and remedy violations."

Professor Anaya has lectured in many countries in all continents of the globe. He has advised numerous indigenous and other organizations from several countries on matters of human rights and indigenous peoples, and he has represented indigenous groups from many parts of North and Central America in landmark cases before courts and international organizations.

Among his noteworthy activities, he participated in the drafting of the United Nations Declaration on the Rights of Indigenous Peoples and was the lead counsel for the indigenous parties in the case of *Awas Tingni v. Nicaragua*, in which the Inter-American Court of Human Rights for the first time upheld indigenous land rights as a matter of international law. He is anti-sovereign when it comes to Human Rights and is a firm believer that the U.N. should control all countries when Human Rights are an issue.

He has cast his lot with the Obama Administration in giving a jaundiced look to Arizona for enforcing federal immigration law, something that the government on the federal level has been sadly inadequate on for decades. According to Anaya, "I've joined a number of human rights experts speaking in our capacity as United Nations human rights experts raising concerns about the possible application of the law and the underlying sentiments that it seems to represent." These same experts have no comment on Iran, Libya,

Mexico or Mauritania.

In 2008, the U.N. General Assembly instructed the U.N. Human Rights Council to launch a new program called the Universal Periodic Review (UPR) on the human rights obligations and responsibilities of all U.N. Member States. Each State has a date assigned to them between 2008 and 2011 to review their progress before the U.N. Human Rights Council in Geneva, Switzerland.

The United States Universal Periodic Review will be held in December 2010.

Preparation of the United States National Report for the Universal Periodic Review in 2010 is an opportunity for the Obama administration to report on the link between local delivery of Social Services by churches and religious organizations; national issues on Separation of Church and State; and obligations to international Human Rights Standards on Freedom of Religion or Belief.

President Obama in his inaugural address said; "We know that our patchwork heritage is strength, not a weakness. We are a nation of Christians and Muslims, Jews and Hindus, and nonbelievers. In his first interview with an Arab-Muslim television station, Al Arabiya from Dubai, he cited the variety of religious beliefs and nonbelievers in the United States. President Obama said members of his family are Muslim and he has lived in the largest Muslim country in the world. In the first 100 days of his administration he will deliver a major address in a Muslim capital. President Obama's use the word "nonbelievers" to a Muslim television audience indicates the inclusive approach of his administration.

During the primaries President Obama proclaimed his intention to be "an instrument of God" and create "a kingdom right here on earth." Candidate Obama, as a Christian, said the use of churches and religious organizations for delivery of services to the poor would be the "moral center" of his administration. The challenge is to reconcile international human rights standards on freedom of religion or belief as a "moral center" with all religious and non-religious beliefs.

The programs of the White House Council of Faith-Based and Neighborhood Partnerships should include ways to implement

Article 18 of the ICCPR and the 1998 mandate of the 1981 U.N. Declaration. Preparation of the United States National Report for the Universal Periodic Review in 2010 is an opportunity for the Obama administration to propose ways of doing this by linking local, national and international human rights standards on freedom of religion or belief.

As a Senator running for the Presidency, Barack Obama said that if elected president he would expand the delivery of social services through churches and other religious organizations, vowing to achieve a goal he said President Bush had fallen short on during his two terms. "The challenges we face today – from saving our planet to ending poverty – are simply too big to solve alone, we need an all-hands-on-deck approach."

But Mr. Obama's plan pointedly departed from the Bush administration's stance on one fundamental issue: whether religious organizations that get federal money for social services can take faith into account in their hiring. Mr. Bush has said 'yes' and Mr. Obama 'no'. "If you get a federal grant, you can't use that grant money to proselytize to the people you help and you can't discriminate against them – or against the people you hire – on the basis of their religion," Mr. Obama said. "Federal dollars that go directly to churches, temples, and mosques can only be used on secular programs. (This eliminates many regular churches from participating in the redistribution process—especially, Catholic Charities, Jewish Charities, etc.)

Mr. Obama's plan – his campaign said it would be the "moral center" of his administration – was unfurled against a backdrop freighted with electoral ramifications...If elected, Mr. Obama said, he would call for a pre-inauguration review of all executive orders pertaining to the religion-based program, particularly those dealing with hiring. In one example of how he would use the approach to carry out a policy goal, Mr. Obama proposed $500 million per year to provide summer education for one million poor children, with a goal of closing the achievement gaps between wealthy students and poorer ones. (The $500 million is taxpayers money and it is call 'redistributing the wealth.' Let the poor working man take food off the table of his children so the President Obama can put food on his poor friends table.)

But the Rev. Barry Lynn, executive director of Americans United for Separation of Church and State, criticized Mr. Obama's support of a program that Mr. Lynn said had undermined civil liberties and civil rights. "I am disappointed that any presidential candidate would want to continue a failed policy of the Bush administration," Mr. Lynn said. "It ought to be shut down, not continued."

The Tandem Project: a non-governmental organization founded in 1986 to build understanding, tolerance and respect for diversity, and to prevent discrimination in matters relating to freedom of religion or belief. The Tandem Project, a non-profit Non-Government Organizations (NGO), has sponsored multiple conferences, curricula, reference materials and programs on Article 18 of the International Covenant on Civil and Political Rights – Everyone shall have the right to freedom of thought, conscience and religion—and 1981 United Nations Declaration on the Elimination of All Forms of Intolerance and Discrimination Based on Religion or Belief.

The Tandem Project initiative is the result of a co-founder representing the World Federation of United Nations Associations at the United Nations Geneva Seminar, Encouragement of Understanding, Tolerance and Respect in Matters Relating to Freedom of Religion or Belief, called by the UN Secretariat in 1984 on ways to implement the 1981 UN Declaration. In 1986, The Tandem Project organized the first NGO International Conference on the 1981 UN Declaration.

The Tandem Project Executive Director is: Michael M. Roan, roan@tandemproject.com.

United Nations Secretary General Ban Ki Moon, at the Alliance of Civilizations Madrid Forum said; 'never in our lifetime has there been a more desperate need for constructive and committed dialogue, among individuals, among communities, among cultures, among and between nations'. Another writer in different setting said; 'the warning signs are clear, unless we establish genuine dialogue within and among all kinds of belief, ranging from religious fundamentalism to secular dogmatism, the conflicts of the future will probably be even more deadly'.

Did God create us or did we create God? This question calls for inclusive and genuine dialogue, discussion of taboos and clarity by persons of diverse beliefs. Inclusive and genuine is dialogue between people of theistic, non-theistic and atheistic beliefs, as well as the right not to profess any religion or belief. These UN categories are embodied in international law to promote tolerance and prevent discrimination based on religion or belief.

Inclusive and genuine dialogue is essential as a first step in recognition of the inherent dignity, equal and inalienable rights of all members of the human family, and a foundation for freedom, justice and peace in the world. Leaders of religious and non-religious beliefs sanction the truth claims of their own traditions. They are a key to raising awareness and acceptance of the value of holding truth claims in tandem with human rights standards on freedom of religion or belief.

To build understanding and support for Article 18, International Covenant on Civil and Political Rights –Everyone shall have the right to freedom of thought, conscience and religion—and the 1981 UN Declaration on the Elimination of All Forms of Intolerance and Discrimination Based on Religion or Belief. Encourage the United Nations, Governments, Religions or Beliefs, Academia, NGOs, Media and Civil Society to use International Human Rights Standards on Freedom of Religion or Belief as essential for long-term solutions to conflicts in all matters relating to religion or belief.

On August 24. 2010, the following report was submitted to the press by the Office of the Spokesman:

"On August 20, the United States submitted to the Office of the UN High Commissioner for Human Rights a report on the U.S. human rights record, in accordance with the UN Human Rights Council's Universal Periodic Review (UPR) process.

The report's submission is one step in the UPR process. The next step will be a formal presentation by the U.S. government to the UN Human Rights Council in Geneva in November. The report stands as just one element of the U.S. effort to engage broadly and constructively with the UN and other international organizations.

The review, which has featured an unprecedented level of consultation and engagement with civil society across the country, provides an opportunity to reflect on our human rights record and we hope will serve as an example for other countries on how to conduct a thorough, transparent, and credible UPR presentation. It involved support and assistance from the Department of Justice as well as over ten other federal departments and other offices, and the White House."

The above report by the Office of the Spokesman tell the whole story about how the President and his administration is surrendering the sovereignty of these United States to the rule of the United Nations. As stated 'the report stands as just one element of the U.S. effort to engage broadly and constructively with the UN and other international organizations. Also, it lies when it states 'The review, which has featured an unprecedented level of consultation and engagement with civil society across the country...' Who were these civil organizations? The NAACP, ACLU, Farrakhan's Islamic Nation, The Black Panthers, etc?

Our great country is being sold down the river because a number of people in government today HATE it! Wake up, America it is not too late to do something about it!

Chapter 15

Restoring Our Constitution

Ex Prime Minister of England , Margaret Thatcher, said: "The trouble with Socialism is, sooner or later you run out of other people's money."

The story behind President Obama's plan is ingenious. Once one strips away the smoke and mirrors that the liberal press presents, the story becomes frightening. We, the people of this great country, are about to return to a slave society.

Presicent Obama is no fool. He is not incompetent. To the contrary, he is Machiavellian. He knows exactly what he's doing. He is purposely overwhelming the U.S. economy to create systemic failure, economic crisis and social chaos—thereby destroying capitalism and our country from within.

As Glenn Beck correctly predicted from day one, Obama is following the plan of Cloward & Piven, two professors at Columbia University .They outlined a plan to socialize America by overwhelming the system with government spending and entitlement demands. Add up the clues below. Taken individually they're alarming. Taken as a whole, it is a nothing more than following Marx Communist Manifesto.

The plan to turn the United States into a socialist/Marxist state with a permanent majority that desperately needs government for survival, and can be counted on to always vote for bigger government. Why not? They have no responsibility to pay for it

Universal health care.

The health care bill had very little to do with health care. It had everything to do with unionizing millions of hospital and health care workers, as well as adding 15,000 to 20,000 new IRS agents (who will join government employee unions). Obama doesn't care that giving free health care to 30 million Americans will add trillions to the national debt. What he does care about is that it cements the dependence of those 30 million voters to Democrats and big government. Who but a socialist revolutionary would pass this reckless spending bill in the middle of a depression?

Cap and Trade.

Like health care legislation having nothing to do with health care, cap and trade has nothing to do with global warming. It has everything to do with redistribution of income, government control of the economy and a criminal payoff to Obama's biggest contributors. Those powerful and wealthy unions and contributors (like GE, which owns NBC, MSNBC and CNBC) can then be counted on to support everything Obama wants. They will kick-back hundreds of millions of dollars in contributions to Obama and the Democratic Party to keep them in power. The bonus is that all the new taxes on Americans with bigger cars, bigger homes and businesses helps Obama "spread the wealth around."

Make Puerto Rico a state.

Why? Who's asking for a 51st state? Who's asking for millions of new welfare recipients and government entitlement addicts in the middle of a depression?, Certainly not American taxpayers. But this has been Obama's plan all along. His goal is to add two new Democrat senators, five Democrat congressman and a million loyal Democratic voters who are dependent on big government.

Legalize 12 million illegal immigrants.

Just giving these 12 million potential new citizens free health care alone could overwhelm the system and bankrupt America . But it adds 12 million reliable new Democrat voters who can be counted on to support big government. Add another few trillion dollars in welfare, aid to dependent children, food stamps, free medical, education, tax credits for the poor, and eventually Social Security.

Stimulus and bailouts.

Where did all that money go? It went to Democrat contributors, organizations (ACORN), and unions—including billions of dollars to save or create jobs of government employees across the country. It went to save GM and Chrysler so that their employees could keep paying union dues. It went to AIG so that Goldman Sachs could be bailed out (after giving Obama almost $1 million in contributions). A staggering $125 billion went to teachers (thereby protecting their union dues). All those public employees will vote loyally Democrat to protect their bloated salaries and pensions that are bankrupting America The country goes broke, future generations face a bleak future, but Obama, the Democrat Party, government, and the unions grow more powerful. The ends justify the means.

Raise taxes on small business owners, high-income earners, and job creators.

Put the entire burden on only the top 20 percent of taxpayers, redistribute the income, punish success, and reward those who did nothing to deserve it (except vote for Obama). Reagan wanted to dramatically cut taxes in order to starve the government. Obama wants to dramatically raise taxes to starve his political opposition.

With the acts outlined above, Obama and his regime have created a vast and rapidly expanding constituency of voters dependent on big government; a vast privileged class of public employees who work for big government and a government dedicated to destroy capitalism and installing themselves as socialist rulers by overwhelming the system. Add it up and you have got the perfect Marxist scheme—all devised by Columbia University professors Cloward and Piven plan.

What President Obama and his followers do not tell the public is what will eventually happen to this country. History is staring us in the face, yet we cannot see. Take a look at what is happening in Europe today. With all the socialization and big government the problem has come home to roost. The Greek government has taxed and spent all the wealth that was once Greek. The people have no more money for the government to steal and Greece can no longer pay its entitlement payments to the public nor its debt to other countries. They decided to cut salaries and make the government workers retire later and now they have the union members going on strike blocking roads and railroads and people are rioting in the streets. The end result will be chaotic anarchy. If it happen in Greece, it will certainly happen here. (It has already happened in Ireland! Spain and Italy are already feeling the pinch and they could go down with the Greeks.)

Things required to give this country back to the people:

1. Revoke the Law establishing the Federal Reserve. Return the power of printing money to Congress. As stated previously, the Federal Reserve is responsible for the huge National Debt and the cause of up coming high inflation. Recently, the Treasury has requested $600 billion from the Federal Reserve to buy back expiring Treasury Bills that are due. The Federal Reserve has requested that the U.S. Mint print the $600 billion. The Feds will lend the money to the Treasury at 7% interest (or higher) which will increase the National Debt. Since this $600 billion has no gold backing but is just paper promissory notes the value of the dollar will decrease.

   a. The dollar bill has decreased in value to a point where the Chinese and other foreign investors are not longer willing to invest in the weekly Treasury Bill sale. This means that the Federal Reserve will require that U.S. Federal Banks must pick up the new Treasury Bills, removing loan-money from the economy. This will cause higher interest rates and businesses will be unable to borrow money to operate at full production. Business will began to feel the pinch and begin laying off workers, causing higher unemployment.

   b. If one takes two charts (one Chart shows the monthly value of the U.S. dollar and the other Chart shows the monthly price of Commodities) and look at them side by side, you will find as the value of the dollar declines the cost of Commodities goes up. This picture will give you the Inflation Index. At the grocery stores the tax payers will find that the cost of meat, eggs, cereal, vegetables, etc increases. Everything else will also increase –Utilities, dry goods, etc.

c. The Obama administration will blame the greedy Corporations for gouging the people, but DON'T you believe them. The cause of inflation is a greedy government that is spending this country into bankruptcy!

2. Amend the Constitution to make Congress balance the budget every year. Congress should establish a realistic budget without raising taxes or other funds by any other means. If Congress does not control the budget and a deficit occurs, all members of Congress (both the House of Representatives and the Senate must resign or be removed by the Justice Department and charged with the crime of dereliction of duty with the penalty being a minimum of two years in a federal prison. In either case the culprits will never be allowed to work in any capacity for the government again. Congress will be required to reduce the size of government by ten percent each year for five years following the enact of the afore- mentioned Amendment.

a. The Governors of the States will appoint replacement to the House of Representatives and the Senate for the duration of their ousted terms. New elections will be held at the normal election time to replace these temporary replacements.

b. Congress must *revoke* the Budget Act of 1974. This law has been the destruction of our financial system. It is an abomination that was put into place by the communist led Democratic Party to ensure that the government would increase in size every year at the expense of the tax payers. For example the Budget Act requires:

(1) All entitlement programs will be increased every year according to the cost of living increase.

(2) The budget of all Departments will increase each year accord-

410

ing to the cost of living increase.

(3) All Departments must spend ALL of their Budget before the end of the fiscal year or have their budgets reduced by the amount NOT spent next year. Before the Budget Act of 1974, Presidents could freeze the budgets of Departments toward the end of the fiscal year to save useless spending, but the Budget Act of 1974 removed that privilege from the President.

(4) The Office of Budget Management was made into a Department and placed under the control of the Executive Branch of government. That way Congress could blame the President for all budget deficits. The Constitution clearly gives the responsibility of enacting Bills of Appropriation to Congress, putting the OBM under Executive jurisdiction was only a ploy to blame others for Congress's failures. This Budget Act also tells the OBM how it must operate. Therefore, the President has little or no control over the Budget. But he makes a good whipping boy for the Democrats in Congress, especially if he is a Republican.

(5) Amend the Constitution to require all Federal Voting districts in States to be reviewed every five years to contain the following registered voters:

a. One third Democrats

b. One third Republicans

c. One third Unaffiliated voters

d. Each District must contain the same number of voters with approximately (percentage wise) of black, Mexican/South American and other. Percentages will be according to national survey. For example: Blacks—17 percent; Spanish —17 percent; other —6 percent; Caucasian—60 percent. This will prevent minority groups from loading the voting scales in their favor and it will ensure equality in voting.

4. Amend the XVI Amendment to establish a flat tax rate of 1% on income for all. This tax rate will apply to all gross income. It will be the same for the rich and the poor; for all business, Corporations, Trust Funds, Foundations, Institutions,

Charities, Memorials, Churches, etc. (The 'etc' includes all organizations, such as Unions and their offshoots, and all other organizations not currently taxed.)

a. This tax will be submitted to the Treasury of the United States who will monitor all income. Those not paying their taxes will be turned over to the Justice Department for prosecution. This will eliminate the I.R.S. which has become political in its execution of tax collecting.

b. All other taxes will be repealed. If a new tax is needed in the future it will require two-thirds votes of both Houses of Congress to pass.

5. Term limits will be established as follows: All members of the House of Representatives will be limited to no more than two terms (four years). All members of the Senate will be limited to no more than one term (six years). Terms to be staggered so that one-third of the Senate will be up of election every two years. Once a person has served his/her full term (listed above), they will not be eligible to hold or work in any capacity for the Fed- eral Government. in the future. Nor will they be allowed to lobby any mem- ber of Government that is not from their home district after leaving Congress.

a. This term limitation is vitally needed to prevent any one from making politics a career. Tort lawyers will always find a way to make a fast dollar but this term limitation should eliminate many of the bribery channels.

b. The Constitution should be amended to indicate the number of weeks that Congress will sit in session. Currently, the Constitution states that Congress will meet at least once a year. It should be amended to state that Congress will meet for two weeks every four months to take care of business. The salaries of Congressmen/Congresswomen will be $80,000 a year plus $15,000 a year for travel and lodging while in session. If they want offices in Washington D.C. or their home State or District they must pay for these out of their Campaign funds. In case of an emergency, the President can call Congress into session to cover the emergency. While in session members in Congress will be paid $800 a day for travel and lodging. This allowance will only cover a two week period. If the emergency has not been handled, than the pay will be $400 a day for up to $100, 000. If the emergency is deemed to be a fraud (called to appease Party members) the money will come out of the President and his Staff's pay. Always remember, you cannot trust career politicians.

c. All 'earmark appropriations' will be outlawed.

6. The Criminal Law should be revised to define treason to include all misrepresentations of the Constitution or other laws. All Federal Judges that deviate from the Constitution and its original intent will be removed from office and charged with the crime of treason. All laws that have been passed because of Judicial Fiat shall be declared unconstitutional and removed from the books. This law should also cover all Amendments, especially the IV, V, X and XIV Amendments. For those Judges that are not familiar with the true intent of the Constitution , they had better go back to school.

7. All Presidential Proclamations must be approved by 2/3rd of the members of both houses of Congress before they are legal proclamations. This will eliminate all dictatorial ambitions of some Presidents.

8. Currently the list of taxes are: Social Security Tax (and it is a tax according to the Supreme Court), we have the:

- Income Tax
- Accounts Receivable Tax
- Building Permit Tax
- Tobacco Tax
- Corporate Income Tax
- Dog License Tax
- Unemployment Tax (FUTA)
- Fishing License Tax
- Food License Tax
- Fuel Permit Tax
- Gasoline Tax
- Hunting License Tax
- Inheritance Tax

- Inventory Tax
- IRS Interest Charges (tax on top of taxes)
- IRS Penalties (Tax on top of tax)
- Liquor Tax
- Marriage License Tax
- Medicare Tax
- Property Tax
- Real Estate Tax
- Road Usage Taxes (truckers)
- Sales Tax
- State Income Tax
- State Unemployment Tax
- Telephone Federal Excise Tax
- Telephone Federal Universal Service Fee Tax
- Telephone Federal, State and Local Surcharge Tax
- Telephone Minimum Usage Surcharge Tax
- Telephone Recurring and Non-recurring Charges Tax
- Telephone State and Local Tax
- Telephone Usage Charge Tax
- Utility Tax
- Vehicle License Registration Tax
- Vehicle Sales Tax
- Watercraft Registration Tax
- Well Permit Tax
- Luxury Item Tax

Many hidden taxes that never shows up on the sales slip, but are figured into the cost of the product. And the Democrats say that the common worker does not pay enough taxes! This is a Congress that is completely out of control.

a. There must be a Constitutional Amendment that requires the Treasury Department to establish a trust fund for each tax and that all moneys collected from the public for that tax can only be use for the reason established by the tax law. That way the greedy politicians will not be able to spend taxes willy-nilly to pay off bribes received.

9. The Senate must revoke our membership in the United Nations Organization. This Organization is corrupt and is using the United States as a whipping boy and yet they want us to prop up all the Socialist country around the World that have failed miserably.

a. The UN is now telling us that this country has failed in supporting Human Rights in this country and President Obama is cheering them on. This is unacceptable to any sovereign State. We should get out of all world orders and World Banks. We should no longer give foreign aid to anyone in the world. If any country wants foreign aid have them request it through the State Department for review by the Executive Branch of the government. If the country that is requesting the aid has supported us in the past when we were in the U.N. then their request will be reviewed and recommend to Congress by the President.

Congress will review the appropriations and approve it if they deem it appropriate. Congress will also ensure that the money goes for the purpose requested. This can be done by monitoring the cash flow.

b. The Senate should also cancel our membership in NATO. Ever since the turn of the 20th century (1900) we have been involved in Wars that have saved most countries in Europe from destruction. Millions of American soldiers have died and trillions of dollars have been spent saving these people who now hate us. When we needed their help they turned us down (France, Spain and Italy refused us fly-over when we went after Libya). Now, Europe is a united Continent and should be able to stand on their own feet. We have poured trillions of dollars into rebuilding Europe after two WW and have got nothing back. We should pull all of our troops and equipment out of Europe and bring them back home. Jefferson, Washington, Franklin, etc. warn this country about getting involved in foreign affairs. We have not listened! Why? Because the one- world government agents that are running this country today will not let us. They say that leaving international affairs alone would be Isolationism. I say, 'So What?' We can use the cost of internationalism better here at home than abroad.

The election scheduled for November 2010 is going to be one of identification. By that I mean, will the Tea Party come into existence as a force to be reckoned with or will it peter-out into oblivion? Only time will tell.

It is hope by many that it will flourish and become a power in the political arena. It is badly needed. The Democratic Party, under Obama, has shown its true nature—a dictatorial communist State that rules all aspects of everybody's life. The Republican Party is a group of politicians that think only of themselves. This is easily verified by reviewing the years 1994-2004. During these years, the Republicans had the majority of both houses of Congress and nothing changed. The earmarks increased and their wallets got fatter but the debt kept growing with little or no complaint from their party. They did reduce taxes in certain areas but not permanently. So what good were they?

Today the Republicans who are running for office in 2010 are claiming that they are now conservatives and want to reduce taxes, reduce spending, reduce the debt, etc. But I am warning the Tea Party members—those candidates that you are backing during the up-coming election should be watch carefully. Remember the election in 1994 when the Republicans in the House made a contract with the public on what they planned on doing if elected. Immediately after the election, Senator Chaffee, Republican, stood on the Capitol steps and said: 'The House may have made a contract with the American people, but the Senate didn't.' With the RINOs in the Senate and the Democrats, they still controlled the socialistic state agenda.

Recommendation to the incoming House members in November 2010:

a, If the Republicans take over the House of Representatives than your fight has just begun. However you have got your foot in the door.

b. Your first priority is to reinstate the Bush's Tax cuts and make them permanent. The Department of Education , Labor, Energy and Human Rights Commission should be eliminated. They are a good place to start to reduce the size of government.

c. Your second priority is to set up a budget program for each Department in government. DO NOT PASS A BUDGET APPROPRIATIONS BILL AS A SINGLE UNIT!

The Senate may submit to the House their Budget as one Unit, but ignore it. The Constitution is quite clear and says that all appropriations Bills will be made by Congress. Submitting Department Budgets individually will force the President and the Senate to either pass the budget or shut down the Department involved. If no Budget is submitted for the Department of Education, Labor and Human Rights Commission they will effectively go out of business. Be careful because the order of submitting the different budget items are important. Recommended order is as follows:

Executive Departments
- *Department of Defense (DOD)*
- *Department of the Treasury*
- *Department of State (DOS)*
- *Department of Justice (DOJ)*
- *Department of Agriculture (USDA)*
- *Department of Veterans Affairs (VA)*
- *Department of the Interior (DOI)*
- *Department of Transportation (DOT)*
- *Department of Homeland Security (DHS)*
- *Department of Commerce (DOC)*
- *Department of Health and Human Services (HHS)*
- *Department of Housing and Urban Development (HUD)*

- *Department of Education (ED)* (No Budget)
- *Department of Energy (DOE)* (No Budget)
- *Department of Labor (DOL)* (No Budget)

If the order is not followed, the Democrats will hold hostage the country's Defense, Agricultural programs, etc until they get what they want. If shutting down vital Departments is necessary they will do it and blame it on the Republicans.

It is going to be a long, hard haul but if you have the courage and will, do not buckle in to these career Socialists. As Admiral David Glasgow Farragut said: 'Damn the torpedoes—Full speed ahead!' You have to fight fire with fire. When they turn nasty, you do the same.

Remember Watergate? Congress went all out trying to impeach Nixon over what was a relatively small crime. Obama's crimes are huge. He hates Capitalism and is actively trying to destroy the economic freedom that is the foundation of the American economy and in the process he is wrecking our economy. He stole GM from its owners and gave it to the auto workers' union. He openly practices theft, sedition, sabotage, and subversion. An angry House should pursue impeachment against Obama for his major crimes. Many of the upcoming new members of the House are only going to Washington for one term. They don't care about surviving politically for a second term. They just want to fix problems that are happening now, and then leave. They won't have any problems going out on a limb and pushing aggressively for real reform. They don't care about getting reelected.

A special House panel should be established to set up the impeachment charges. The panel should hire a number of Constitutional lawyers headed by someone like retired Judge Bork and have them investigate the following events for impeachment:

1. Accepting a bribe from a foreign agency. The bribe referred to is Barack Obama's acceptance of the $1.4 million of Nobel Peace Prize money. The Nobel Peace Prize recipient was chosen by members of the government of Norway and it was specifically and clearly given to Obama not for what he had done, but for what they wanted him to do. Geir Lundestad, secretary of the Prize committee said they gave him the prize

because he "put the accent on international cooperation, the United Nations, dialogue, negotiation, the struggle against climate change and disarmament." In other words, these are the kinds of things they wanted him to do more of. Struggle against climate change, lay down his arms, and chat with the United Nations. President Obama distributed most of the money to Charitable Orgainzations such as:

$200,000 to the Clinton-Bush Haiti Fund
$125,000 to the Posse Foundation
$125,000 to the United Negro College Fund
$125,000 to the Hispanic Scholarship Fund
$125,000 to the Appalachian Leadership and Education Foundation
$125,000 to the American Indian College Fund
$100,000 to AfriCare
$100,000 to the Central Asia Institute

One can see from the above, nothing for the white U.S. poor.

2. He has violated his oath to defend the US Constitution by exercising powers forbidden by the Constitution.

3. He has used public money to purchase private companies.

4. He has illegally tried to use public money to create publicly owned companies.

5. He has embezzled public money allocated by Congress for rescuing distressed private financial institutions, and used it to purchase automobile manufacturing companies.

6. He has given our public money to finance foreign automobile companies.

7. He has given our public money to a foreign state to finance their state-run oil company while refusing to allow us to develop our own oil resources. By Executive Order, he has given $2 billion of tax payers dollars to Brazilian Oil Exploration Company (which is the eighth largest company in the entire world) to drill for oil off the coast of Brazil. The oil that comes from this operation is for the sole purpose and use of China and not for the USA. China has already purchased all the oil that will be produced. Financier Soros who owns one-third of the Brazilian Oil Exploration Company has donated large

sums of money to the Democratic National Committee during Obama's run for the presidency in 2008.

8. He has violated the principle of balance of powers by usurping Congress' role of law maker.

9. He has ignored the laws protecting us from the insolvency of financial institutions.

10. He has demanded and implemented Tax-and-Spend laws that inevitably lead to economic collapse.

11. He has obstructed the Administration of Justice by appointing a judge to the Supreme Court based not on ability to interpret the Constitution, but on radical ideology and color of skin.

12. He has erected a multitude of New Offices, and sent hither swarms of Czars to harass our people and eat out their substance.

13. He has violated the balance of powers by appointing Czars with far reaching powers who are accountable to no one but himself.

14. He has as a matter of patronage stolen private industries from shareholders and given them to workers' unions.

15. He has attempted to create a public industry, a health insurance company, that would compete with existing and similar private industries in open defiance of the consent of the people, and the letter and intent of the Constitution.

16. He has attempted to annul freedom of speech by setting up an illegal reporting system for recording the names of dissenters and by publicly attacking private citizens who oppose him.

17. He has counted illegal aliens as citizens to skew his standing with Congress.

18. He has taken the Student Loan program away from the banks and has set up an Agency in the Government to use taxpayers money to supply loans to certain students for their College education. A Czar has been appointed to oversee who gets the loans and where they can be spent. Repayment has been given a time line. The loan must be repaid within twenty years AFTER the student graduates from collage. The bottom line is white students whose parents are working need not apply..

19. He has attempted to force all citizens into mandatory servitude to the government.

20. He has refused to release his Birth Certificate to prove that he is eligible to hold the Office of Presidency.

A President whose character is thus marked by every act which may define a tyrant is unfit to be the Chief Executive of a free people. Congress should act accordingly!

In addition, Congress must reduce the size of government by fifty percent over a five-year period. All departments should be reviewed and eliminated where possible by distributing their work load to the remaining departments. Jobs from the eliminated departments will not be transferred to the new department—only the work load.

Congress should pass a law that only open-shop organizations are eligible to bid on government contracts. That means the Taft-Hartley Labor Law should be repealed.

There are many other things that has to be done, but the above lists and others noted throughout this book are a good starting points.

APPENDIX A

BILDERBERG MEMBERS

Bilderberg membership and Organizational Structure (2002) is as follows:

Members Advisory Group

Or 'inner circle':
Italy—Giovanni Agnelli
Great Britain—Eric Roll of Ipsden
USA—David Rockefeller
Germany (D)- Otto Wolff von Amerongen

Steering Committee

The 31 national BB 'outer circle' Steering Group Representatives:

HONORARY SECRETARY GENERAL

Great Britain—J. Martin Taylor

Chairman, WH Smith Group PLC;

International Advisor, Goldman Sachs International

HONORARY CHAIRMAN

Belguim—Etienne Davignon

Vice Chairman, Societe Generale de Belgique

EXECUTIVE SECRETARY

Maja Banck-Polderman

USA Allaire, Paul A.—Former Chairman and C.E.O., Xerox Corporation

P Balsemao, Francisco Pinto—Chairman, IMPRESA, S.G.P.S.; former Prime Minister

I Bernabe, Franco—Chairman, Franco Bernabe & C. S.p.A.

CDN Black, Conrad M.—Chairman, Telegraph Group Limited

GB Clarke, Kenneth—Member of Parliament, former Chancellor of the Exchequer

F Collomb, Bertrand—Chairman and C.E.O., Lafarge

GR David, George A.—Chairman, Coca-Cola H.B.C. S.A.

NL Halberstadt, Victor—Professor of Public Economics, Leiden University

USA Johnson, James A.—Vice Chairman, Perseus LLC

USA Jordan, Jr., Vernon E.—Managing Director, Lazard Freres & Co. LLC

TR Kiraq, Suna—Vice-Chairman of the Board of Directors, Koq Holding A.S.

USA Kissinger, Henry A.—Chairman, Kissinger Associates, Inc.

D Kopper, Hilmar—Chairman of the Supervisory Board, Deutsche Bank A.G.

USA Kravis, Marie-Josee—Senior Fellow, Hudson Institute, Inc

F Levy-Lang, Andre—Former Chairman, Paribas

USA Mathews, Jessica T.—President, Carnegie Endowment for International Peace

N Myklebust, Egil—Chairman of the Board, Norsk Hydro ASA

D Nass, Matthias—Deputy Editor, Die Zeit

FIN Ollila, Jorma—Chairman of the Board and C.E.O., Nokia Corporation

INT Padoa-Schioppa, Tommaso—Member of the Executive Board, European Central Bank

E Rodriguez Inciarte, Matias—Executive Vice Chairman, BSCH

D Schrempp, Jiirgen E.—Chairman of the Board of Management, DaimlerChrysler AG

INT Schwab, Klaus—President, World Economic Forum

DK Seidenfaden, Toger—Editor-in-Chief, Politiken

IRL Sutherland, Peter D.—Chairman and Managing Director,

Goldman Sachs International

CH Vasella, Daniel L.—Chairman and C.E.O., Novartis AG

A Vranitzky, Franz—Former Federal Chanoellor

S Wallenberg, Jacob—Chairman of the Board, Skandinaviska Enskilda Banken

USA Wolfensohn, James D.—President, The World Bank

Bilderberg Members
I—Agnelli, Giovanni
I—Agnelli, Umberto
GB—Airey, Terence
DK—Andersen, Tage
A—Androsch, Hannes
GR—Arliotis, Charles C.
USA—Ball, George W.
S—Barnevik, Percy
F—Baumgartner, Wilfrid S.
GB—Bennett, Frederic M.
USA—Bennett, Jack F.
INT—Bertram, Christoph
D—Bertram, Christoph
TR—Beyazit, Selahattin
TR—Birgi, Nuri
CH—Boveri, Walter E.
USA—Brady, Nicholas F.
GR—Carras, Costa
E—Carvajal Urquijo, Jaime
USA—Cary, Frank T.
GB—Cavendish-Bentinck, Victor F.W.
DK—Christiansen, Hakon
I—Cittadini Cesi, Gian G.
USA—Collado, Emilio
USA—Corzine, Jon S.
USA—Dam, Kenneth W.
USA—Dean, Arthur H.

DK—Deleuran, Aage
NL—Duisenberg, Willem F.
CDN—Duncan, James S.
USA—Finley, Murray H.
GB—Frame, Alistair
GB—Franks, Oliver
CDN—Frum, David
GB—Gaitskell, Hugh T.N.
USA—Gerstner, Louis V.
USA—Getchell, Charles
CDN—Griffin, Anthony G.S.
GB—Gubbins, Colin
S—Gustafsson, Sten
ICE—Hallgrimsson, Geir
USA—Hauge, Gabriel
N—Hauge, Jens
GB—Healey, Denis W.
USA—Heinz, Henry J.
D—Herrhausen, Alfred
N—Hoegh, Leif
N—Hoegh, Westye
USA—Holbrooke, Richard C.
A—Igler, Hans
FIN—Iloniemi, Jaakko
A—Jankowitsch, Peter
B—Janssen, Daniel E.
NL—Karsten, C. Frits
GB—Knight, Andrew
I NT—Kohnstamm, Max
A—Kothbauer, Max
NL—Korteweg, Pieter
CH—Krauer, Alex
F—Ladreit de Lacharriere, Marc
B—Lambert, Leon J.G.
USA—Lord, Winston
S—Lundvall, Bjorn

CH—Lutolf, Franz J.
CDN—Macdonald, Donald S.
USA—MacLaury, Bruce K.
USA—Mathias, Charles McC.
GB—Maudling, Reginald
NL—Meynen, Johannes
USA—Mitchell, George J.
F—Montbrial, Thierry de
I—Monti, Mario
USA—Moyers, Bill D.
USA—Murphy, Robert D.
DK—Norlund, Nils
NL—Oort, Conrad J.
USA—Perkins, James A
GR—Pesmazoglu, John S.
I—Prodi, Romano
CH—Pury, David de
USA—Ridgway, Rozanne L.
USA—Rockefeller, David
USA—Rockefeller, Sharon Percy
GB—Roll of Ipsden, Eric
F—Rothschild, Edmond de
INT—Ruggiero, Renato
NL—Rijkens, Paul
GB—Sainsbury, John
I—Saraceno, Pasquale
F—Seilliere, Ernest-Antoine
USA—Sheinkman, Jack
I—Silvestri, Stefano
GB—Smith, John
B—Snoy et d'Oppuers, Jean C.
D—Sommer, Theo
USA—Stone, Shepard
GB—Taverne, Dick
USA—Taylor, Arthur R.
DK—Terkelsen, Terkel M.

N—Tidemand, Otto Grieg
I—Valetta, Vittorio
CH—Umbricht, Victor H.
S—Wallenberg, Marcus
N—Werring, Niels
USA—Whitehead, John C.
USA—Whitman, Marina von Neumann
USA—Williams, Joseph H.
USA—Williams, Lynn R.
D—Wischnewski, Hans-Jurgen
D—Wolff von Amerongen, Otto
USA—Wolfowitz, Paul
I—Zannoni, Paolo

APPENDIX B

PROGRESSIVE CAUCUS

House members

All Progressive Caucus members are members of the Democratic Party or caucus with the Democratic Party. There are currently 82 total declared Progressives including 79 voting Representatives, 2 non-voting Delegates, and 1 Senator.

Arizona

- *Ed Pastor* (AZ-4, Phoenix)
- *Raúl Grijalva* (AZ-7, Tucson)—**Co-Chair**

California

- *Lynn Woolsey* (CA-6, Santa Rosa)—**Co-Chair**
- *George Miller* (CA-7, Richmond)—Chairman, *House Education and Labor Committee*
- *Barbara Lee* (CA-9, Oakland)—Chairwoman, *Congressional Black Caucus*
- *Pete Stark* (CA-13, Fremont)
- *Michael Honda* (CA-15, San Jose)
- *Sam Farr* (CA-17, Monterey)
- *Henry Waxman* (CA-30, Los Angeles)—Chairman, *House Energy and Commerce Committee*
- *Xavier Becerra* (CA-31, Los Angeles)
- *Judy Chu* (CA-32, El Monte)
- *Diane Watson* (CA-33, Los Angeles)
- *Lucille Roybal-Allard* (CA-34, Los Angeles)
- *Maxine Waters* (CA-35, Inglewood)
- *Laura Richardson* (CA-37, Long Beach)
- *Linda Sanchez* (CA-39, Lakewood)

- *Bob Filner* (CA-51, San Diego)—Chairman, *House Veterans Affairs Committee*

Colorado

- *Jared Polis* (CO-02, Boulder)

Connecticut

- *Rosa DeLauro* (CT-3, New Haven)

Florida

- *Corrine Brown (FL-3, Jacksonville)*
- *Alan Grayson (FL-8, Orlando)*
- *Alcee Hastings* (FL-23, Fort Lauderdale, **Georgia**
- *Hank Johnson* (GA-4, Lithonia)
- *John Lewis* (GA-5, Atlanta)

Hawaii

- *Neil Abercrombie* (HI-1, Honolulu)
- *Mazie Hirono* (HI-2, Honolulu)

Illinois

- *Bobby Rush* (IL-1, Chicago)
- *Jesse Jackson, Jr.* (IL-2, Chicago Heights)
- *Luis Gutierrez* (IL-4, Chicago)
- *Danny Davis* (IL-7, Chicago)
- *Jan Schakowsky* (IL-9, Chicago)
- *Phil Hare* (IL-17, Rock Island)

Indiana

- *André Carson* (IN-7, Indianapolis)

Iowa

- *Dave Loebsack* (IA-2, Cedar Rapids)
- *Chellie Pingree* (ME-1, North Haven)

Maryland

- *Donna Edwards* (MD-4, Fort Washington)

- *Elijah Cummings* (MD-7, Baltimore)

Massachusetts

- *John Olver* (MA-1, Amherst)
- *Jim McGovern* (MA-3, Worcester)
- *Barney Frank* **(MA-4, Newton)—Chairman, House Financial Services**
- *John Tierney* (MA-6, Salem)
- *Ed Markey* (MA-7, Malden)

Michigan

- *Carolyn Cheeks Kilpatrick* (MI-13, Detroit)
- *John Conyers* (MI-14, Detroit)—Chairman, *House Judiciary Committee*

Minnesota

- *Keith Ellison* (MN-5, Minneapolis)
- *Bennie Thompson* (MS-2, Bolton)—Chairman, *House Homeland Security Committee*

Missouri

- *William Lacy Clay, Jr.* (MO-1, St. Louis)
- *Emanuel Cleaver* (MO-5, Kansas City)

New Jersey

- *Frank Pallone* (NJ-06)
- *Donald Payne* **(NJ-10, Newark)**

New Mexico

- *Ben R. Luján* (NM-3, Santa Fe)

New York

- *Jerry Nadler* (NY-8, Manhattan)
- *Yvette Clarke* (NY-11, Brooklyn)
- *Nydia Velazquez* (NY-12, Brooklyn)—Chairwoman, *House Small Business Committee*
- *Carolyn Maloney* (NY-14, Manhattan)

- *Charles Rangel* (NY-15, Harlem)—Chairman, *House Ways and Means Committee*
- *Jose Serrano* (NY-16, Bronx)
- *John Hall* (NY-19, Dover Plains)
- *Maurice Hinchey* (NY-22, Saugerties)
- *Louise Slaughter* (NY-28, Rochester)— Chairwoman, *House Rules Committee*
- *Eric Massa* (NY-29, Corning)

North Carolina

- *Mel Watt* (NC-12, Charlotte)
- Ohio*Marcy Kaptur* (OH-9, Toledo)
- *Dennis Kucinich* (OH-10, Cleveland)
- *Marcia Fudge* (OH-11, Warrensville Heights

Oregon

- *Earl Blumenauer* (OR-3, Portland)
- *Peter DeFazio* (OR-4, Eugene)

Pennsylvania

- *Bob Brady* (PA-1, Philadelphia)—Chairman, *House Administration Committee*
- *Chaka Fattah* (PA-2, Philadelphia)

Tennessee

- *Steve Cohen* (TN-9, Memphis)

Texas

- *Sheila Jackson-Lee* (TX-18, Houston)
- *Eddie Bernice Johnson* (TX-30, Dallas)

Virginia

- *Jim Moran***(VA-8, Alexandria)**

Vermont

- *Peter Welch* (VT-At Large)

Washington

- *Jim McDermott* (WA-7, Seattle)

Wisconsin

- *Tammy Baldwin* (WI-2, Madison)
- *Gwen Moore* (WI-4, Milwaukee)
- Non-voting*Donna M. Christensen* (Virgin Islands)
- *Eleanor Holmes Norton* (District of Columbia)

Senate member

- *Bernie Sanders* (Vermont)

Former members

- *Sherrod Brown* (OH-13)—Elected to Senate
- *Julia Carson* (IN-07)—Died in December 2007
- *Lane Evans* (IL-17)—Retired from Congress
- *Cynthia McKinney* (GA-4)—Lost Congressional seat to current caucus member Hank Johnson
- *Major Owens* (NY-11)—Retired from Congress
- *Nancy Pelosi* (CA-8)—Left Caucus when Elected House Minority Leader
- *Hilda Solis* (CA-32)—Became *Secretary of Labor* in 2009
- *Stephanie Tubbs Jones* (OH-11)—Died in 2008
- *Tom Udall* (NM-3)—Elected to Senate
- *Paul Wellstone* (MN Senate)—Died in plane crash in 2002
- *Robert Wexler* (FL-19)—Resigned in January 2010 to become President of the Center for Middle East Peace and Economic Cooperation

The current government in Washington D.C. is controlled by the above people who's one desire is to push this government into bankruptcy and result into a revolution which will install a Socialist Dictatorship in the White House. This Socialist Dictator that will be selected will declare a national Emergency and confiscate all banks, businesses, and property. Everything will be nationalized and the enslavement of the citizenship completed.

They will rewrite the Constitution and take complete control while the citizens sit around and wondered how did this happen. At that time, IT WILL BE TOO LATE!

APPENDIX C

CFR MEMBERS IN GOVERNMENT

The Council on Foreign Relations (established in 1921) *is part of an international group of co-conspirators*, that have been carrying out successful covert operations since the mid-1800's. The American Branch is the 'Council on Foreign Relations' and it sister The British Branch is the 'Royal Institute of International Affairs'. They have a web site at http://www.riia.org/.

Council on Foreign Relations (CFR)
Special Group & Secret Team Members in Government

PRESIDENTIAL CANDIDATES
Bill Clinton ('96,'92)
Reuben Askew ('84)
Alan Cranston '84)
John Glenn ('84)
Walter Mondale ('84)
John Anderson ('80)
Howard Baker ('80)
George Bush ('80)
Jimmy Carter ('80)
Dwight Eisenhower ('80)
Adlai Stevenson ('80)

DEPT OF STATE MEMBERS(1995)
Secretary Warren Christopher
Dep Secretary Cliff R. Wharton Jr.
Under Sec.Pol. Afr Pete Tarnoff
Under Secretary Maj. Gen. t Dick Moose
Under Secretary Global Afrs Tim Wirth

Ass Secretary E. Asian Pacific
Affairs Winston Lord (Pres. and a Rep),
AssSecretary Europ Canadian Affairs Stephen Oxman

AssSecretary Intel Res Tobi Gati
AssSecretary Intr-American Affairs Alex F. Watson

CIA DIRECTORS—MEMBER
Richard Helms (66-73 Johnson),
James R. Schlesinger (73 Nixon),
William E. Colby (73-76 Nixon),
George Bush (76-77 Ford),
Adm Stansfield Turner (77-81 Carter),
William J. Casey (81-87 Reagan)
William H. Webster (87-91 Reagan),
Robert M. Gates (91-93 Bush)
R. James Woolsey (93- Clinton).
John Deutch, chosen to replace Woolsey as CIA Director

DEPARTMENT OF THE TREASURY
(Past and Present Partial Listing)
Donald Regan
John Helmann
CD. Lord
William Simon
Michael Blumenthal
C. Fred Bergsten
Anthony M. Solomon
Arnold Nachmanoff Helen B. Junz
Richard Fisher
Roger Altman
George Pratt Shultz

UNION PRESIDENTS
I.W. Abel (United Steelworkers)
Sol Chick Chaikin (Pres. Ladies Garment Workers)
Tom R. Donahue (Sec/Tres AFL/CIO)
Murray H. Finley (Pres. Amal. Clothing Textile Workers)Victor

Gautbaum (Amer Fed. State County Muni Employees)
Lane Kirkland (Pres. AFL/CIO)
H. D. Samuel (Pres Ind. Union Dept. AFL/CIO)
M. J. Ward (Pres. U. Ass. Plumbing Pipe)
Glenn E. Watts (Pres Comm. Workers of Amer)
Len Woodcock (Pres UAW)
Jerry Wurf (Pres. Amer F. County. and Muni. Emp.)

PRESIDENTS COMMISSION EXECUTIVE EXCHANGE

David Rockefeller Willard Butcher (Pres. Chase Manhattan Bank)
Thorton Bradshaw (Pres. Atlantic Richfield)
John McKinley, (Pres. Texico)
Ruben Mettler (Pres. TRW)
John Whitehead (Goldman Sachs)
Marina N. Whitman (GM Corp)

CFR Secret Team Members in the Military (Partial List)

ALLIED SUPREME COMMAND

49-52 Eisenhower
52-53 Ridgeway
53-56 Gruenther
56-63 Norstad
63-69 Lemnitzer
69-74 Goodpaster
80-Rogers

SECRETARIES OF DEFENSE

57-59 McElroy
59-61 Gates
61-68 McNamara
69-73 Laird
73-Richardson
77-77 Rumsfield
77-Brown
80 Weinberger
87-89 Frank C. Carlucci
93-95 Les Aspin

DEPUTY SECRETARY OF DEFENSE
Frank Carlucci
John Deutch
UNDER SECRETARY OF DEFENSE
Fred Ikel
Gen. Stillwell
Frank Wisner
ASSISTANT SECRETARY OF DEFENSE
Lawrence Korb
MILITARY FELLOWS

Army Maj. Gen. T. Ayers
Air Force Col. K Baker
Army Lt. Gen. S. Berry, Jr.
Army Capt. Dewienter
Army Col. A. Dewey
Navy Capt. H Fiske
Air Force Col. E. Foote
Army Lt. Gen. R. Gard
Air Force Maj. Gen. R. Ginsburgh
Army Brig. Gen. M. Green
Air Force Col. R. Head
Air Force Brig. Gen. T. Julian
Navy Capt. W. Kerr
Air Force Col. I. Klette
Navy Capt. R. Kurth
Air Force LT. Col. J. Levy
Army Col. G. Loeftke
Air Force Lt. Gen. G. Loving
Air Force Col. M. McPeak
Navy Capt. R. Miale
Air Force Lt. Gen. J. Pfautz
Air Force Col. L. Pfeiffer
Navy Capt. S. Ring
Air Force Col. M. Sanders
Army Col. J. Sewall

Navy Rear Adm. C. Tesh
Air Force Col. F. Thayer
Army Maj. Gen. J. Thompson
Air Force Maj. Gen. W. Usher
Army Gen. S.Walker
Navy Rad. R. Welander
Air Force Col. J. Wolcott
Navy Capt. Gentry
Air Force Col. T. Eggers

SUPERINTENDENTS US MIL
WEST POINT

60-63 Westmoreland
63-66 Lampert
66-68 Bennett
70-74 Knowlton
74-77 Berry, Jr.
77-Goodpaster

PRESIDENT, NATIONAL DEFENSE UNIY

Lt. Gen. Robert Gard, Jr.
SECRETARY OF NAVY
John Lehman, Jr.
CHIEF OF STAFF ARMY
Gen. J. Wickham

JOINT STAFF

Gen. David Jones
Vice Adm. Thor Hanson
Lt. Gen. Paul Gorman
Maj. Gen. R.C. Bowman
Brig. Gen. F, Brown
LT. Col. W. Clark
Capt. Raplh Crosby
Adm. Wm. Crowe
Col. P. Dawkins
Vice Adm. Thor Hanson
Col. W. Hauser
Col. B. Hosmer

Maj. R.Kimmitt
Capt. F. Klotz
Gen. W. Knowlton
Vice Adm. J. Lee
Capt. T. Lupter
Col. D. Mead
Maj. Gen. Jack Merritt
Gen. E. Meyer
Col. Wm E. Odom
Col. L. Olvey
Col. Geo. K. Osborn
Maj. Gen. . J. Pustuay
Capt. P.A. Putignano
Lt. Gen. E. L. Rowny
Capt. Gary Sick
Maj. Gen. J. Siegal
Maj. Gen. Dewitt Smith
Brig. Gen. Perry Smith
Col. W. Taylor
Maj. Gen. J. N. Thompson
Rear Adm. C.A.H. Trost
Adm. S. Turner
Maj. Gen. J. Welch

CFR Secret Team Members in the Media (Partial List—Past & Present)

CBS

C.C. Collingwood
Lawrence LeSuer
Dan Rather
Harry Reasoner
Richard Hottelet
Frank Stanton
Bill Moyers

NBC/RCA

Jane Pfeiffer
Lester Crystal
R. W. Sonnenfeldt
T.F. Bradshaw
John Petty
David Brinkley
John Chancellor
Marvin Kalb
Irvine Levine
P.G. Peterson John Sawhill

ABC

Ray Adam
Frank Cary
T.M. Macioce
Ted Koppel
John Scali
Barbara Walters

CABLE NEWS NETWORK

Daniel Schorr

PUBLIC BROADCAST SERVICE

Hartford Gunn
Robert McNeil
Jim Lehrer
C. Hunter-Gault
Hodding Carter III

ASSOCIATED PRESS

Keith Fuller
Stanley Swinton
Louis Boccardi
Harold Anderson

U.P.I.

H.L. Stevenson

REUTERS

Michael Posner

BOSTON GLOBE

David Rogers

L.A. TIMES SDICATE

Tom Johnson
Joseph Kraft

L.A. TIMES MIRROR

Richard W. Murphy
Charles A. Kupchan
Michael Clough Zygmunt Nagorski
Nancy Bodurtha
Richard T. Childress
Carl W. Ford Jr.. Nomsa Daniels
Alton Frye
Gregory F. Treverton

NEWSDAY

Jessica Mathew
Michael Mandelbaum
Richard N. Haass
Richard W. Murphy
John L. Hirsch
Alexander J. Motyl
Nicholas X. Rizopoulos.
Alan D. Romberg
C.V. Starr
Gidion Gottlieb
Charles A. Kupchan

BALTIMORE SUN

Henry Trewhitt

CHICAGO SUN TIMES

James Hoge
MINNEAPOLIS STARR/TRIBUNE
John Cowles Jr.
HOUSTON POST
William P. Hobby
NY TIMES CO.
Richard Gelb
James Reston
William Scranton
A.M. Rosenthal
Seymour Topping
James Greenfield
Max Frankel
Jack Rosenthal
Harding Bancroft
Amory Bradford
Orvil Dryfoos
David Halberstram
Walter Lippmann
L.E. Markel
H.L. Matthews
John Oakes
Harrison Salisbury
A. Hays Sulzberger
A. Ochs Sulzberger
C.L. Sulzberger
H.L. Smith
Steven Rattner
Richard Burt
TIME INC.
Ralph Davidson
Donald M. Wilson
Louis Banks
Henry Grunwald
Alexander Herard
Sol Lionwitz

Rawleigh Warner Jr.
Thomas Watson Jr.
NEWSWEEK/WASH POST
Katherine Graham
Philip Graham
Arjay Miller TC
N. deB. Katzenbach
Frederick Beebe
Robert Christopher
A. De Borchgrave
Osborne Elliot
Phillipo Geyelin
Kermit Lausner
Murry Marder
Eugene Meyer
Malcolm Muir
Maynard Parker
George Will
Robert Kaiser
Meg Greenfield
Walter Pincus
Murray Gart
Peter Osnos
Don Oberdorfer
DOW JONES CO. (**Wall Street Journal**)
William Agee
J. Paul Austin
TC Charles Meyer
Robert Potter
Richard Wood
Robert Bartley
Karen House
NATIONAL REVIEW
Wm. F. Buckley Jr.
Richard Brookhiser

REFERENCES

BOOKS:

"An Album for Americans" Editor David Appel, Triangle Publications Inc., 1983

"America" by Alistair Cooke, 1973

"American Hegemony And The Trilateral Commission" by Stephen Gill, 1990

"(The) Architecture of History" by Eric Rainbolt & essays by Dr. Henry Makow

"Architects of Deception" by Jüri Lina

"Armageddon In Waco" by Stuart A. Waight, University of Chicago Press, 1995

"Bilderberg Group, The Global Manipulators" by Robert Gringer. 1980

"The Century" by Peter Jennings and Todd Brewster, Doubleday Publisher, 1998

"Conspiracies, Cover-ups and Crimes" by Jonathan Vankin, 1992

"The Drug Story" by Morris A. Bealle, 1975; Publisher 'The Hornet's Nest"

"Fabian Freeway: High Road to Socialism in the U.S.A." by Ross I. Martin, 1966

"The Federal Reserve Hoax Exposed" by Wickliffe B. Vennard, 1973

"Foundations: Their Power and Influence" by Rene Wormser, 1958

"Gentleman Spy, 'Life of Allen Foster Dulles'" by Peter Grose, 1994

"The House of Morgan" by Ron Chernow, 1990

"Inside the Company: CIA Diary" by Philip Agee, 1975

"Kissinger ON THE COUCH" by Admiral Chester Ward, 1975

"Memoirs" by Nelson Rockefeller, 2002

"Murder By Injection" by Eustace Mullins

"The New Unhappy Lords: An Exposure of Power Politics" by A. K. Chesterton, 1972

"New World Order" by William T. Still, 1990

"None Dare Call It Conspiracy" by Gary Allen/Terry Abraham, "Concord Press," 1971

"Our Nation Betrayed" by Garland Favorito, 2002

"Our Republic In Peril" by Robert E. McCarthy, Red Anvil Press, 2004

"The Powers That Be" by G. William Domhoff, 1978

"The Rich and The Super Rich" by Ferdinand Lundberg, Bantam Press, 1969

"The Road to Serfdom" by Friedrich A Hayek, 1944

"The Robber Barons" by Matthew Josephron, 1934

"The Rockefeller File" by Gary Allen, Seal Beach, CA; 76 Press, 1976

"Ronald Reagan & the Holy Spirit" by Norm Wymbs, Elderberry Press Inc., 2005

"The Satori And New Mandarins" by A. H. Krieg, 1998 (Note: This book lists all Known Bilderberg members. http//www.Sover.net)

"Secret Societies" by Nesta H. Webster, 1924

"Secret Societies And Their Power In The 29th Century" by S. L. Ewertverlag, 1995

"The Shadows of Power" by James Perloff, 1988

"Slavery, Terrorism And Islam: The Historical Roots And Contemporary Threat" by Dr. Peter Hammond

"State Autonomy Or Class Dominance" by G. William Domhoff, 1996

"The Strange Death Of Vincent Foster" by Christopher Ruddy, Free Press of Simon & Schuster

"Treason In America" by Anton Chailkin, 1985

"Treason: Liberal Treachery From The Cold War To The War On Terrorism" by Ann Coulter, 2003

"Who Rules America" by G. William Domhoff

ARTICLES

"Annual Report" by The Council On Foreign Relations, 1993

"The Art And Science Of Psychological Operations: Case Studies" by Daniel Pollock,

Project Director, 'Military Application' Vol. One, dd April 1976

"At The Hand Of Man—The White Man's Game" by David Bonner

"Bilderberg: List of Trustees" by U.S. Department of Defense, 1996

"Bill Clinton's Foundational Philosophy For The Socialist State" by www .jerimiahproject. com/Trashingamerica/Clintonsocialism.html

"The CIA Report The President Doesn't Want You To Read" by Arron Latham, 'Special Supplement' Village Voice, 1976

"Clinton's Rogues Gallery" by Google Search Engine, article dd 1/8/01

"Cover-up: Vince Foster" from Google Search Engine 'Worldaffairsbrief.com

"Freemasonry is the Common Denominator" by Henry Makow @www.savethemales.ca

"Globalization Changing Societal Rules" by Jim Hoagland, (Washpost.com)

"The Historical Progress Of The Anti-Christ" by ReaMarketing. com

"The Hotel de Bilderberg" by Alden Hatch, 1962

"Jan. 14: Sensenbrenner's Overview" from the Congressional Record, Jan 14, 1999

"Massacre At Ruby Ridge" by Stormfront.org/ruby.html

"The New Right & Secular Humanism Conspiracy Theory" by Chip Berlet, 1994 (publiceye.org)

"Oboma– communist mentor" from aim.org, 5/25/2010

"Our Man at Bilderberg: In Pursuit Of The Worlds Most Powerful Cabal" in Guardian.com, 13 May 2009

"Right Woos Left: John Birch Society" by Chip Berlet, 1994 (publiceye.org)

"The Root Problem: Illuminati or Jew?" by Henry Makow, PhD, 2007

"The Ruby Ridge Massacre" by Mstarzone.com/RIDGE.html

"A Short History Of The Round Table" by Nexus Magazine., Vol. 12, Dec 2004-Jan 2005

"Sociology" Internet by Wikipedia Encycolpedia

"State Department Document #7277" dd Sept 1961

"Trading With The Enemy, The Nazi-American Money Plot" by Charles Highem, 1983

"True Conspiracies: The Illuminati And One World Government" by Richard Hole

"Wall Street And The Rise Of Hitler" by Anthony Sutton, 1976

"Weak Dollars, Weak Presidents" by Stephen Moore & John Tamny, 2008-2009

"What Happened At Waco" by Linda Thompson, Internet 'Serendipity' Home page

"Untangling Whitewater" by Dan Fromkin, Washington Post

Lightning Source UK Ltd.
Milton Keynes UK
UKHW03f2331090318
319213UK00001B/157/P